UNIX Unbounded
A Beginning Approach

Amir Afzal
Strayer College

Prentice Hall

Englewood Cliffs, New Jersey   Columbus, Ohio

Library of Congress Cataloging-in-Publication Data
Afzal, Amir
    UNIX unbounded : a beginning approach / Amir Afzal.
        p.   cm.
    Includes index.
    ISBN 0–13–328246–5
    1. UNIX (Computer file). 2. Operating systems (Computer)
I. Title.
QA76.76.063A366   1995
055.4'3--dc20   94–29725
                                                                                    CIP

Editor: Charles E. Stewart, Jr.
Production Editor: Stephen C. Robb
Text Designer: MS Editorial Service
Cover Designer: Brian Deep
Production Buyer: Deidra M. Schwartz
Production Supervision: MS Editorial Service
This book was set in Times New Roman by MS Editorial Service and was printed and bound
    by Courier Corporation/Westford. The cover was printed by Phoenix Color Corp.

 © 1995 by Prentice-Hall, Inc.
A Simon & Schuster Company
Englewood Cliffs, New Jersey 07632

UNIX is a registered trademark of AT&T.

BSD is a trademark of the University of California, Berkeley.

DEC and PDP are trademarks of Digital Equipment Corporation.

Printed in the United States of America

10 9 8 7 6 5 4 3 2 1

ISBN: 0-13-328246-5

Prentice-Hall International (UK) Limited, *London*
Prentice-Hall of Australia Pty. Limited, *Sydney*
Prentice-Hall of Canada, Inc., *Toronto*
Prentice-Hall Hispanoamericana, S. A., *Mexico*
Prentice-Hall of India Private Limited, *New Delhi*
Prentice-Hall of Japan, Inc., *Tokyo*
Simon & Schuster Asia Pte. Ltd., *Singapore*
Editora Prentice-Hall do Brasil, Ltda., *Rio de Janeiro*

To my wife, Emma

Contents

1

2

3

Getting Started 31

4

The vi Editor: First Look 53

12

Shell Scripts: Writing Applications 325

Preface

At Strayer College, where I am teaching, we offer two operating system courses. One covers UNIX specifically and the other covers operating systems in general, discussing UNIX briefly. I have had the opportunity to review and choose UNIX textbooks for both of these courses. Plenty of excellent books are available, covering every aspect of the UNIX operating system. However, most of the books that I have reviewed are either too detailed, cluttered with information that is not appropriate for an introductory UNIX course, too technical, or more like reference books than textbooks.

The price break for the UNIX operating system on microcomputers and recent hardware advances have boosted the acceptance and popularity of UNIX for icros. Consequently, there are students and novice UNIX users with computer skills but no experience with any operating system.

This book is for this group of users and students. It is neither an operating system book per se nor a UNIX reference book. It is a textbook written in a tutorial manner, intended as a teaching/learning tool in a classroom/lab environment. It is an introductory book for introductory operating system courses. It discusses operating systems concepts in general, leading into a presentation of UNIX and the UNIX environment. It covers the necessary topics for the UNIX user to function independently and do most of the everyday, routine jobs. It also gives readers a good base of knowledge so they can move on to more advanced courses or books.

I wrote this book relying mostly on my experience as a UNIX teacher. The organization of the chapters is what I follow, and the examples are what I usually use in my UNIX classes. This book is an introductory book but not a simple book. I did not try to change the technical aspect of the material to some sort of storytelling way of explanation, nor did I use irrelevant stories to make the material lighter or more interesting. And, as I have promised my students, I have not used the word *obviously* in the context of meaning the material is so simple or obvious that it does not need any explanation.

Chapters are short, and in cases where the extent of coverage of a topic requires more pages, the material is presented in two chapters. As much as possible, the format of the chapters is kept the same. However, consistency is sacrificed when the format does not serve as an appropriate vehicle for presenting material.

Each chapter starts with a general explanation of concepts and topics. Simple commands and examples clarify the explanations or show the commands usage, followed by more detailed and complex commands and examples as the chapter progresses. Each chapter ends with questions and a review section, and, when appropriate or necessary, practical exercises for using a terminal are added.

Chapter 1 briefly describes the fundamentals of computer hardware and software and explains basic computer terms and concepts. It discusses the types of software and moves the emphasize to the system software. It explains the importance of the operating system and explores its primary functions.

Chapter 2 presents a brief history of the UNIX operating system. It explores the UNIX development over the years, discusses the major UNIX versions, and explains some of the system's important features.

Chapter 3 explains how to start and end a UNIX session. Simple UNIX commands are introduced and their applications are explained. The process of establishing contact with UNIX is explored, and some internal UNIX operations are discussed.

Chapter 4 is the first of the two chapters that cover the UNIX operating system vi editor. After a brief discussion of the editors that are supported by UNIX, the vi editor is introduced, and the rest of the chapter presents the basic commands necessary to do a simple editing job.

Chapter 5 is the first of two chapters that discuss the file structure of the UNIX system. It covers the basic concepts of files and directories, and their arrangement in a hierarchical tree structure. It presents commands that facilitate the manipulation of the file system.

Chapter 6 is the second chapter about the vi editor. It shows more of the vi editing power and flexibility by covering the more advanced vi commands, and explains various ways the vi editor can be customized.

Chapter 7 is the second chapter about the UNIX file system and its associated commands. It presents more file manipulation commands, explains the shell input/output redirection operators, and files substitution metacharacters.

Chapter 8 covers the shell and its role in the UNIX system. It explains the shell features and capabilities, the shell variables, and the shell metacharacters. Startup files and process management under UNIX are also covered.

Chapter 9 concentrates on the UNIX communication utilities. It explains the UNIX e-mail facilities and shows the commands and options available. It discusses the shell and other variables that effect the e-mail environment. It shows how to make a startup file that customizes use of the e-mail utilities.

Chapter 10 discusses the essentials of program development. It explains the steps in the process of creating a program. It makes an example of a simple C program and walks through the process of writing the source code to making it an executable program.

Chapter 11 concentrates on shell programming. It explains the capabilities of the shell as an interpretive high-level language. It covers shell programming constructs and particulars. It shows the creation, debugging, and running of shell programs.

Chapter 12 builds on the commands and concepts of the previous chapter and covers more of the shell programming commands and techniques. It also presents a simple application program and shows the process of developing programs using the shell language.

Chapter 13 presents a few additional important UNIX commands. Disk commands, file manipulation commands, and security are the major topics of this chapter.

Appendix A is a quick index to the commands covered in this book. The commands are listed in alphabetical order.

Appendix B is an index to the commands, categorized according to their functions.

Appendix C is a summary of the commands and their options presented in tables similar to the command summary at the end of the chapters.

Appendix D is a summary of the vi editor commands.

Appendix E is a table of the ASCII codes.

Appendix F is a list of some of the books I've evaluated.

Acknowledgments

This book would not have been possible without the help and support of many of my colleagues and the staff at Strayer College, and my friends in the industry. I am grateful to all of them. The following is only a short list of them.

Thanks to Ron Bailey, Strayer College president, for his continuous support of this and my other projects.

Thanks to professor Susan Bahcall for proofreading many drafts of this book for grammar, style, and criticism.

Thanks to my colleagues and staff at Strayer College for their support, encouragements, and services.

Thanks to the students in my C and UNIX classes; they are the main reason for writing this book.

Thanks to Frank Erwin, RBH president, and his staff for providing computer time and other services.

Thanks to the Prentice Hall professional staff, in particular Alice Barr, who started it all. Thanks to Holly Hodder, who after having seen only the outline and one chapter of my book, decided to go ahead with it. Thanks to Charles Stewart, who took over at the middle of the project and saw the book through to completion.

Thanks to the reviewers who critiqued several drafts.

Finally, thanks to my wife for her patience and my three sons who were deprived playing computer games while I was using the computer.

How to Read This Book

If this is the first time you are learning about the UNIX operating system, I suggest that you start from the first chapter and continue the chapters in the same sequence in which they are presented.

If you already know some aspects of the UNIX operating system, I suggest that you browse through the chapters about things you know and read the main points as a review and to help you understand the other chapters. Most of the chapters are related to one another in the sense that your skills from the previous chapter help you—and sometimes are necessary for you—to go to the next one.

A number of concrete examples clarify concepts or show different ways you can use a command. I encourage you to try them on your system.

UNIX comes in many dialects and is also easily modifiable. This means you may find discrepancies between the manual and the reality, and some of the screen displays or command sequences in this book may not exactly match those on your system.

Typographical Notes

Throughout the text of this book, certain words are emphasized by using different typefaces. In the running text, **bold** words are UNIX commands or specific characters that you type on the keyboard as part of an example; sans serif words are directory names, pathnames, or filenames; and *italic* words are keywords or terms being introduced for the first time.

The following shows an example of a terminal screen. This is what you expect to see on your system when you practice the commands.

```
UNIX System V release 4.0
login: david
password:
```

The following is an example of the command sequences. Characters you type on the keyboard are indicated in bold type. The information at the right is commentary on the action being performed at the left. This format is used when a line-by-line explanation of the commands or outputs is necessary.

$ **pwd [Return]**. . . . . Check your current directory.

/usr/david . . . . You are in david.

$ **cd source [Return]** . . . . Change to source directory.

Icons

Icons are used throughout the text to draw your attention, list some features, or present action to be taken. There are four icons used throughout the text.

Note

- Lists the important points
- Draws your attention to a particular aspect of a command or a screen display

Flag

- Draws your attention (flags you) to notice the common users' mistakes
- Warns you of the consequences of your action

Computer

- Shows how the commands work on the system
- Lets you try the commands on your system

□ **Box**

- Shows a sequence of the keys that you must press to perform a specified task

Keyboard Conventions

[ ]: The keys on the keyboard are represented by placing the specified character between brackets. For example [A] means press the uppercase A on the keyboard.

[Return]: This is the Return key, sometimes called CR (for carriage return) or Enter key. You usually press this key at the end of your command or input line.

[Ctrl-d]: This means simultaneously holding down the key labeled Ctrl (for control) and pressing letter [d]. Other control characters that consist of the Ctrl key and a letter are shown similarly.

CHAPTER 1

First Things First

This chapter briefly describes the fundamentals of computer hardware and software and explains basic computer terms and concepts. It discusses the types of software, explains the importance of the operating system, and explores its primary functions.

In This Chapter

1.1   INTRODUCTION

Most people acquire fundamental knowledge about computers by taking introductory computer courses or using computers in a work or home environment. In case you have not had any computer courses (or you have forgotten what you have learned), this chapter starts with a brief introduction to computers in general and explains some common hardware and software terms. The chapter goes on to discuss operating system software.

1.2   COMPUTERS: AN OVERVIEW

What is a computer? *Merriam Webster's Collegiate Dictionary* defines *computer* as "a programmable electronic device that can store, retrieve and process data." This chapter expands on that definition and explores each component of a computer system.

Computers can be grouped according to their sizes, capabilities, and speed into four classifications as follows:

- Supercomputers
- Mainframe computers
- Minicomputers
- Microcomputers

 These are rather arbitrary classifications; the low-end systems of one category can overlap the high-end systems of the other.

Supercomputers *Supercomputers* are the fastest and the most expensive computers and are 1000 times faster than mainframe computers. Supercomputers are designed for the most demanding of computational applications, such as weather forecasting, three-dimensional modeling, and computer animation. All these tasks require an extremely large number of complex calculations and need supercomputer performance. Supercomputers usually have hundreds of processors and they are used with the very latest and most expensive devices.

 Supercomputers are used for numerous other applications. Even Hollywood uses the advanced graphics capabilities of supercomputers, to create special effects for movies.

Mainframe Computers *Mainframe computers* are large, fast systems designed to meet the information processing needs of the large organizations. Mainframes can support several hundred users and execute hundreds of programs simultaneously. They have extensive *input/output* (I/O) capabilities

---

See page xxii for an explanation of icons used to highlight information in this chapter.

Table 1–1
Computer classifications.

Class	Typical Specifications	Approximate Speed
Microcomputer	8 million main memory cells 240 million disk storage cells single user	5 million instructions per second
Minicomputer	16 million main memory cells 1 billion disk storage cells 1 tape drive 64 interactive users	25 million instructions per second
Mainframe	256 million main memory cells 10 billion disk storage cells multiple tape drives 512 interactive users 4 central processing units	50 million instructions per second
Supercomputers	1 billion main memory cells 10 billion disk storage cells 64 central processing units	2 billion floating-point operations per second

and support a large amount of primary and secondary storage. Mainframes
are mostly used in large business environments, such as banks and hospitals,
and in other large institutions, such as universities. They are costly and usually require a trained support staffontrol U for operation and maintenance.

*I/O devices are the means by which a computer communicates with the
external world (humans or other computers). They vary in speed and
communication medium.*

Minicomputers   Until the late 1960s, all computers were mainframes, and
only large organizations could afford them. Then *minicomputers* were developed. Their original function involved performing specialized tasks, and they
were used primarily in universities and scientific environments. Minicomputers quickly became popular among small and medium-sized organizations
with data processing needs. Some of today's "minis" rival mainframes in
power and capability, and most are general-purpose computers. Like mainframes, minicomputers are capable of providing information processing services for multiple users and can execute many application programs
concurrently. However, they are cheaper than mainframes and are easier to
install and maintain.

Microcomputers   Also called *personal computers* or *PCs, microcomputers*
are the least costly and most popular computers on the market. They are
small enough to fit on top of a desk or in a briefcase. *Microcomputers* vary
widely in cost and power, with some models rivaling the minicomputers and
older mainframes. They are capable of running many business applications
and can function as stand-alone units or be hooked up with the other computers to extend their capabilities.

Table 1–1 shows each class of computers, their typical specifications (memory size, number of users, etc.), and their approximate speeds.

1.3   COMPUTER HARDWARE

Regardless of how complex or simple a computer system is, it has four fundamental functions: *input*, *processing*, *output,* and *storage.* Also, computers consist of two distinct parts: *hardware* and *software.* These two parts complement each other, and the integration of hardware and software enables computers to perform their fundamental functions.

Figure 1–1 shows the four functions of a computer system and the typical hardware devices associated with each function.

Most computer systems have five basic hardware components that work together to accomplish the computer's required tasks. The number, implementation, complexity, and power of these components varies among computer systems. However, the functions performed by each component are generally quite similar. These components are as follows:

- Input devices
- Processor unit
- Internal memory
- External storage unit
- Output devices

The way these components are put together and arranged is called the *system hardware configuration.* For example, in one system the processor unit and the external storage unit may be housed in a single component; in another system, they may be separate components.

Figure 1–1
Four functional parts of a computer system.

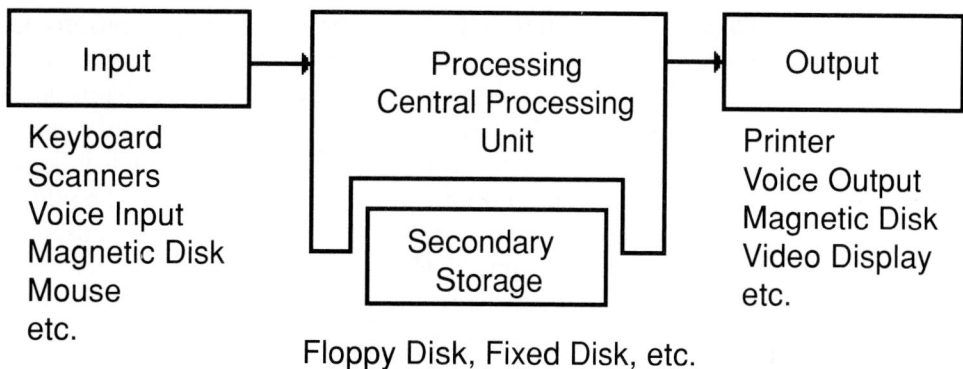

1.3.1   Input Devices

Input devices are used to enter instruction or data into the computer. Numerous input devices are available, and their number is growing. The keyboard, light pen, scanner, and mouse are the most popular input devices, with the keyboard being used almost universally.

Certain devices can be used for either input or output—magnetic disks and touch screen terminals, for example.

1.3.2   Processor Unit

The *processor unit* is the intelligent part of the computer system. It is called the *central processing unit*, or *CPU*, and it directs computer activities. The CPU controls the performance of tasks such as sending keyboard data to the main memory, manipulating stored data, or sending the results of an operation to the printer. The CPU consists of three basic sections:

- Arithmetic and Logic Unit (ALU)
- Registers
- Control Unit (CU)

The CPU is also called the brain, heart, or thinking part of the computer.

Arithmetic and Logic Unit   The *arithmetic and logic unit*, or *ALU*, is a section of the CPU's electronic circuitry that controls all arithmetic and logic operations. *Arithmetic operations* include addition, subtraction, multiplication, and division. More advanced computational functions such as exponentiation and logarithms can also be implemented. The *logic operations* include comparisons of letters, numbers, or special characters to recognize whether they are equal to, greater than, or less than one another.

To summarize, the ALU is responsible for the following:

- Performing arithmetic operations
- Performing logical operations

Registers   A small set of temporary storage locations is generally located within the **CPU**. These storage cells are called *registers*. A register can typically hold a single instruction or data item. Registers are used to store data and instructions that are needed immediately, quickly, and frequently. For example, if two numbers are about to be added, each is kept in a register. The ALU reads these numbers and stores the result of the addition in another register. Because registers are located within the CPU, their contents can be accessed quickly by other CPU components.

To summarize, registers are used for the following:

- Storing instructions and data within the CPU

Control Unit   The *control unit* is a section of the CPU's electronic circuitry that directs and coordinates the other parts of the system to carry out program instructions. It does not execute the directions itself; instead it sends electronic signals along the appropriate circuitry to activate other parts. It is primarily responsible for the movement of data and instructions from the main memory and for controlling the ALU. As program instructions and data are needed by the the CPU, they are moved from primary storage to registers by the control unit.

To summarize, the control unit is responsible for the following:

- Activating the other components
- Transferring instructions and data from the main memory to the registers

1.3.3   Internal Memory

A computer is a two-states machine. These two states can be interpreted as 0 or 1, yes or no, up or down, and so on. Almost any device that can store either of two states can serve as storage. However, most computers use integrated circuit memory, which holds binary digits or bits. Each *bit* can be either 0 or 1, therefore representing one state or the other. A small computer might have enough memory to store millions of bits; a larger one might store billions. The difference is one of degree, not of memory functionality.

The internal memory (also called main or primary memory) is storage for the following:

- Holding current program instructions
- Holding data to be processed by program
- Holding intermediate results created by executing program instructions

 Main memory is short-term and retains data only for the period that a program is running.

The main memory storage consists of storage cells that hold programs and their associated data that are currently being executed. The execution of programs requires a great deal of data movement between the main memory and the CPU.

The CPU is a fast device; thus it is desirable to implement main memory using devices capable of fast access. In the current computer hardware, main memory is implemented with silicon-based semiconductor devices called *memory chips*. Computers usually have two types of main memory:

- Random access memory (RAM)
- Read only memory (ROM)

Random Access Memory   *Random access memory* (RAM) is the working memory of the computer. It provides the access speed the CPU requires and allows the CPU to read and write a specific memory location by referring to its address. While the computer is on, programs and data are stored temporarily in RAM. Data stored in RAM can be changed, modified, and erased.

RAM is a volatile memory and does not provide permanent storage. When you turn off the computer (or power to RAM is turned off by any other means), its contents are lost.

Read Only Memory   The second type of the memory, *read only memory* (ROM), contains the permanently stored programs and data that manufacturers place in the system. The CPU can only read instructions from ROM; it can not alter, erase, or write over them. When you turn the computer off, none of the information stored in ROM is lost. Programs in ROM are sometimes called *firmware*, something between hardware and software.

Data Representation

We are accustomed to using the decimal numbering system. The decimal system (base 10) consists of ten digits that range from 0 to 9. On the other hand, computers work with a binary system (base 2) that consists of 2 digits, 0 and 1.

Bit (Binary Digit)   Each *bit* can hold either a 0 or a 1. A *bit* is the smallest unit of information a computer can understand.

Byte   Computer memory must be able to store letters, numbers, and symbols, and a single bit by itself cannot be of much use. Bits are combined to represent some meaningful data. A group of eight bits is called a *byte* (pronounced *bite*) and it can represent a character. A character could be uppercase and lowercase letters, numbers, punctuation marks, and special symbols.

ASCII   When you input data to a computer, the system must change it from what you recognize (letters, numbers, and symbols) into some format that the computer understands. The American Standard Code for Information Interchange (ASCII, pronounced *ask-ee*) is one of the coding schemes used to represent characters in an eight-bit byte.

The ASCII code can represent a maximum of 256 characters, including all uppercase and lowercase letters, numbers, punctuation marks, and special symbols.

Word   Bytes are fine for storing characters but are too small to hold a large number. In fact, 256 is the largest number that can be stored in one byte. Certainly, to be of any use, computers need space for larger numbers. Most computers are able to manipulate a group of bytes called *word*. The *word* size is system dependent and could vary from 16-bit (2 bytes) to 32-bit (4 bytes) or even 64-bit (8 bytes).

The Memory Hierarchy

The basic unit of storage is a *bit*. *Bits* are grouped together to form a *byte*; in turn, bytes are grouped together to form a *word*. Figure 1–2 depicts the memory hierarchy and the numerical value that each storage size can store.

Figure 1–2
The memory hierarchy.

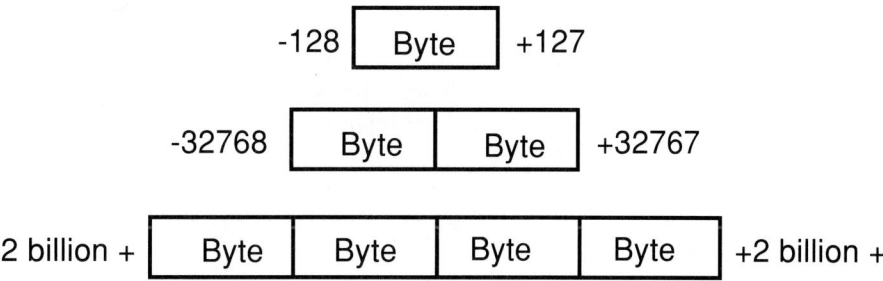

Memory Size   Letter *K* is used to express the size of the main memory, or disk space. K stands for kilo, which means *thousand* in the metric system. However, when measuring computer memory, K stands for *kilobytes*, which represent 1,024 bytes of storage (2 to the power of 10). For example, 32K of memory means 32,768 bytes (32 times 1024). There are other measurements referring to the size of the computer memory:

- *megabyte* (MB) is approximately one million bytes
- *gigabyte* (GB) is approximately one billion bytes

Addressing Memory

You can think of *main memory* (primary storage) as a sequence of continuous or adjacent memory cells. Each physical storage unit (cell) is assigned a unique address corresponding to its location in the sequence. In byte-addressable computers, each byte in the memory has its own *electronic address*, a code name identifying its exact location in the memory.

On most computers, the bytes or word addresses are assigned sequentially, 0, 1, and so on. The CPU uses these addresses to specify which instructions or data are to be loaded (read) into the CPU and which data are to be written. For example, if you input the letter *H* from the keyboard, the character is read into main memory and stored in a specific address, say address 1000. Address 1000 references a single byte of memory, and at any time the system can reference and process the data stored at this address.

The CPU requires instructions and data from many part of the main memory; thus it is necessary for the main memory to be what is referred to as *direct access*, or a *random access device*. It must have the ability to specify a specific location to be read from or written to.

1.3.4   External Storage

External or secondary storage is a *nonvolatile* extension of the main memory. Main memory is expensive, and on most computers it is a scarce resource. Main memory is *volatile*; it loses its contents when the power is cut. Hence it makes sense to save your programs and data on another media. Secondary storage media could be a floppy disk (diskette), hard disk, and/or magnetic tape.

Table 1–2
Summary of the different storage types.

Storage Type	Location	Usage
Registers	Within the CPU Very high speed devices	Currently executing instructions; part of the related data
Primary Storage	Outside of the CPU High speed devices (RAM)	Entire or part of the programs currently being executed; part of the associated data
Secondary Storage	Low speed devices electromagnetic or optical	Programs not currently being executed; large amount of data

1. *Secondary storage is an extension of main memory, not a replacement for it. A computer cannot execute a program or manipulate data stored on disk unless the data are first copied into main memory.*

2. *Main memory holds the current programs and data while the secondary storage are for long-term storage.*

Table 1–2 summarizes the computer's various types of storage devices and their usual contents.

1.3.5   Output Devices

A basic output device is the *display terminal*. The terms *CRT* (cathode ray tube), *VDT* (video display terminal), and *monitor* refer to the TV-style device that displays character images. The image displayed on a screen is temporary and is called *soft copy*. By routing the output to a printer, a permanent copy called *hard copy* is obtained. Of course, other output devices are available, including voice response or a plotter to generate hard copy graphic outputs.

1.4   PROCESS OPERATION

A complex chain of events occurs when a computer executes a program. To begin, the program and its associated data are loaded into the main memory. The *control unit* (CU) reads the first instruction and its data inputs from the main memory into the CPU. If the instruction is a computational (or comparison) instruction, the control unit signals the ALU what function to perform, where the input data are located, and where to store the output data. Some instructions, such as input and output to secondary storage or I/O devices, are executed by the control unit itself. After the first instruction is executed, the next instruction is read and executed. This process continues until the last instruction of your program is read from the main memory into the registers in CPU and is executed.

Figure 1–3
Sequence of the processor operation.

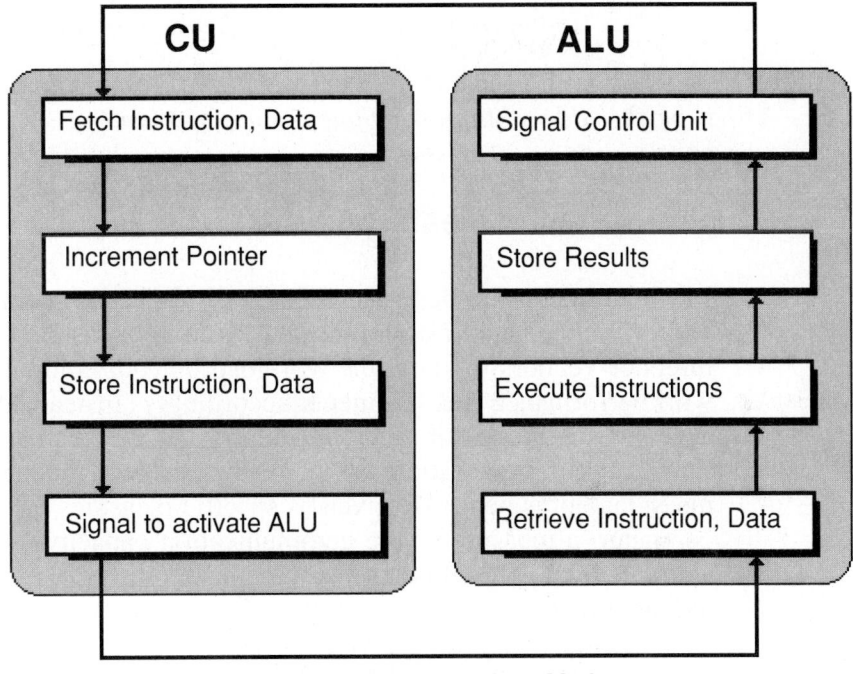

Central Processing Unit

 Each instruction is known to the ALU by a unique number called the instruction code or the operation code or the op code.

The steps required to process each instruction can be grouped into two phases: the *instruction cycle* and the *execution cycle*. The operation of the instruction and the execution cycles is depicted in figure 1–3, followed by the explanation for sequence of events.

Instruction Cycle   The sequence of events during the *instruction cycle*, also referred to as the *fetch cycle*, are as follows:

Step 1:   The control unit reads an instruction from main memory into a CPU register called *instruction register*.

Step 2:   The control unit increments the *instruction pointer register* to show the location of the next instruction in the main memory.

Step 3:   The control unit generates a signal to the ALU to execute the instruction.

Execution Cycle   The sequence of events during the execution cycle are as follows:

Step 1:   The ALU accesses the operation code of the instruction in the instruction register to determine what function to perform and to obtain the input data for the instruction.

Step 2:   The ALU executes the instruction.

Step 3:   The results of the instruction are stored in registers or are returned to the control unit to be written to memory.

The instruction cycle *is performed within the control unit; the* execution cycle *is performed within the arithmetic and logic unit.*

1.4.1   Performance Measurement

Most computers are designed to be general-purpose computers; they support a wide variety of application programs. It is not possible for computer manufacturers or vendors to know the workload of your computer and to provide you with performance measurements accordingly. Instead, they provide performance measurements for various machine actions, such as executing an instruction, accessing main memory, or reading from a magnetic disk. Performance measurement is generally given as specific measures of each component of the computer, a measure of the communication capacity among the components, and a general measurement that attempts to summarize all of the performance measurements.

CPU Speed   Within the CPU, the primary performance consideration is the speed at which an instruction can be executed. This is usually specified in terms of *millions of instruction per second* (MIPS). Unfortunately not all instructions take the same amount of time to execute. Certain instructions, such as addition of whole numbers, execute quickly; others, such as division of fractional (floating point) numbers, might execute more slowly. The measurement that is specially oriented to computation of fractional numbers is *millions of floating-point operations per second* (MFLOPS).

The MFLOPS performance measure is commonly given for workstations and supercomputers. It is expected that the applications running on these machines perform mostly floating-point computations.

Access Time   The speed at which the CPU can retrieve data from storage or input/output (I/O) devices depends on the *access time*. Access time is normally measured in milliseconds (millionths of a second) or nanoseconds (billionths of a second).

Channel Capacity   When *access time* is stated for a specific device, there is no guarantee that the communication channel between the device and the CPU is capable of supporting that speed. The ability of the communication channel to support data movement between CPU and a device, or vice versa, is normally specified as a *data transfer rate*. This rate specifies the amount of data that can be moved over the channel in a specified interval of time—for example, one million data items per second.

Overall Performance   The overall performance of a computer system is a combination of the CPU speed, the access time of the storage and I/O devices, and the capacity of the communication channels connecting them to the CPU. Different applications create different demands on the various computer components. Thus, overall performance measurement is valid only for a particular instance or class of applications.

1.5   WHAT IS SOFTWARE?

A computer off the assembly line with no software is just a machine (hardware) and is not capable of doing much. It is the software that gives a computer its diverse capabilities. Through software, a computer can take on any one of many personalities. With the right software, a computer can become a word processor, a calculator, a database manager, or a sophisticated communication device—or even all of them at the same time.

 In general, computer programs are called software. You run numerous programs on the same machine (hardware) to perform different tasks.

Program   A *program* is a set of instructions that directs the activities of a computer system. It consists of instructions that are logically sequenced to perform a specific operation. Programs are written in one of the available computer programming languages. Computer programming languages are necessary to facilitate the creation of the application programs. A wide range of program development tools are available to aid the programmers in developing application and system programs.

Software Categories   The computer software can be categorized into two types: *system software* and *application software*. The operating system is the most important system software and the only software that is absolutely necessary for the computer to function. However, it is the application software that makes computers useful in different environments and for so many jobs. Figure 1–4 shows the general categories of the software and examples of their associated software programs.

Figure 1–4
Types of software.

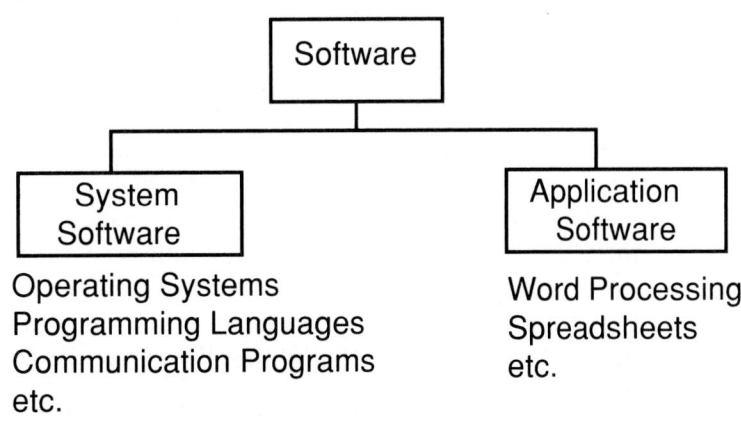

Figure 1–5
User interaction with software layers.

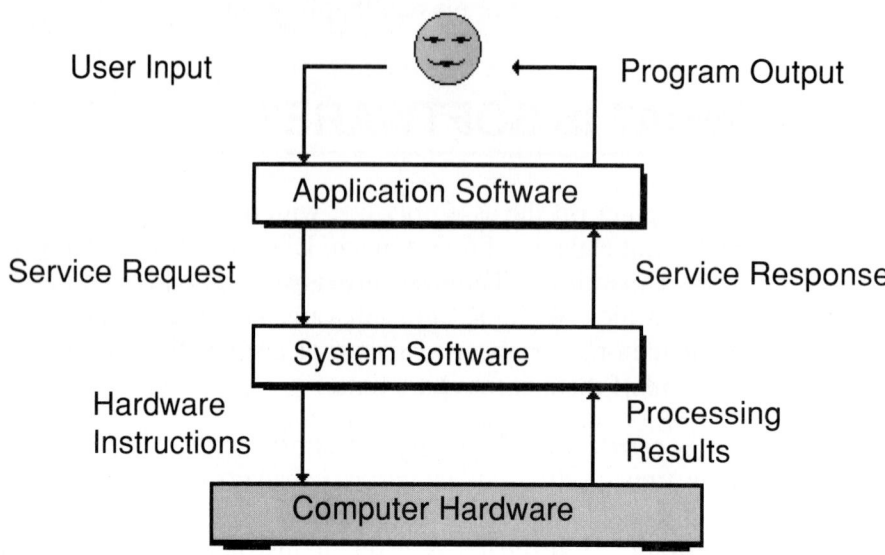

Users generally interact with application software and part of the system software. Figure 1–5 shows a layered approach to software. The advantage of this approach is that the user and application programmers do not need to comprehend and deal with the technical details of physical processing. With the layered approach, the machine's physical details and many basic processing tasks are embedded within the system software and hidden from the user.

1.5.1   System Software

The *system software* is a set of programs that mostly control the internal performance of a computer. The most important software in this category is the *operating system*, which controls the basic functions of the computer and provides a platform for application programs. Other system software includes database management system (DBMS), communication software, etc.

Who Is the Boss?

The operating system is the boss and is the most important system software component of a computer. It is a collection of programs that controls all hardware and software in a computer. The necessary parts of the operating system are loaded into the main memory when you turn the computer on and remain there until you turn it off. The operating system plays different roles as *service provider*, *hardware manager*, and facilitator of the *user interface*. Instead of looking for a universally accepted definition of the operating system, let's explore its roles and responsibilities. These are the primary purpose and functions of an operating system:

- To provide an interface for users and application programs to low-level hardware functions
- To allocate hardware resources to users and their application programs
- To load and accept the application programs on behalf of the users
- To manage secondary storage

The necessary parts of the operating system are always resident in the main memory.

Operating System as Resource Manager

The operating system is in control of computer resources: main memory, CPU time, and peripheral devices. In a typical computer system, several jobs are executing concurrently. All are competing for the available resources, and the operating system allocates resources to programs according to the availability of the resources and priority of the running programs. It allocates the CPU time. After all, there is only one CPU and many users, and only one user can have the CPU attention at a time.

The operating system monitors and allocates the main memory between programs, which have different sizes and memory requirements, preventing your program from being be mixed with someone else's program that happens to be in the main memory. It coordinates use of the peripheral devices, including things such as whose turn it is to read from the disk or write to it, and what job goes to the printer first.

The operating system continually responds to the program's resource requirements, resolves resource conflicts, and optimizes the allocation of resources.

Operating System as User Interface

The operating system provides the means for users to communicate with the computer. Every operating system provides a set of commands for directing the operation of the computer, a *command-driven user interface*. Command syntax is difficult to learn, remember, and use. One alternative is the *menu-driven user interface*, which provides a set of menus and lets users choose desired functions from the menus. Another popular alternative is the icon-driven, graphically based user interface, called *graphic user interface* (GUI). You can execute most of the operating system commands by manipulating graphical images on the video screen. For example, the graphical image (*icon*) of a file folder may represent files, or a picture of a typewriter may represents a word processing program. This visual metaphor for commands and functions provides an easy-to-learn interface. With a GUI, users can choose an icon, usually with a pointing device such as mouse, to activate programs.

Operating System Model

Using the software layers approach, you can view the operating system as a layered set of software. Figure 1–6 shows a model of an operating system and its program layers. Input from a user or an application program travels through the layers to reach the hardware, and results from the hardware travel back to the

Figure 1–6
Operating system layers.

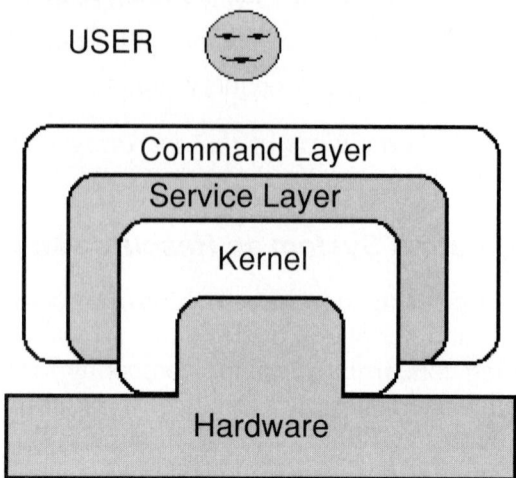

user through the same layers. Let's explore the general responsibilities of each layer.

Kernel Layer   The *kernel* is the innermost layer of the operating system software. It is the only layer that interacts directly with the hardware. This provides a measure of machine independence within the operating system. At least in theory, an operating system can be altered to interact with a different set of computer hardware by making changes to the kernel only. It provides the most basic functions of an operating system, including loading and executing programs and allocating hardware resources (CPU time, access to disk drives, and so on) to individual programs. Localizing the interaction between hardware and software in this layer insulates the users of the application level from direct knowledge of hardware specifics.

Service Layer   The *service layer* accepts service requests from the *command layer*, or the application programs, and translates them into detailed instructions to the kernel. Processing results, if any, are passed back to the program that requested the service. The service layer consists of a set of programs that provide the following type of services:

- Access to I/O devices—for example, the movement of data from an application to a printer, or terminal
- Access to storage devices—for example, the movement of data from a tape drive or a magnetic disk to an application program
- File manipulation—for example, opening and closing files, reading from a file, and writing into a file
- Other services such as window management, access to communication network, basic database services

Command Layer   The *command layer*, also called the *shell* (because it is the outermost layer), provides the user interface and is the only part of the operating system with which users can interact directly. The command layer responds to a set of specific commands supported by each operating system. The set of the commands and their syntax requirements is referred to as a *command language*. There are other alternatives to the command language.

Operating Systems Environment

Operating system functions can be fulfilled in many ways. In single-user environments, like most microcomputers, all available resources are allocated to a single program. That program is the only program in the computer. On larger computers (and on microcomputer networks), where more than one user is sharing the computer resources, the operating system must resolve conflicts arising from the request for the same resource by different programs. Let's explore some basic concepts and terminology describing the different operating systems and their environments.

Although several programs can be in the memory of a microcomputer, only one program is active at a time.

Single-tasking   A *single-tasking* (*single-programming*) operating system is designed to execute only one process at a time. This is the usual arrangement with the *single-user* environment and is generally restricted to microcomputers and certain specialized applications.

Multitasking   A *multitasking* (*multiprogramming*) operating system is capable of executing more than one program at a time for a user. It can run several programs in the background while you are working on another task in the foreground. For example, you can direct the operating system to sort a large file in the background while you are typing memos using a word processor in the foreground. The operating systems inform you when a background task is finished. Multitasking is the capability that allows one user (terminal) to execute more than one program concurrently.

Multiuser   In a multiuser environment, more than one user (terminal) can use the same host computer. The multiuser operating system is complex software that provides services for all users concurrently. The users' programs are in the main memory and it appears that they are executed simultaneously; however, there is only one CPU, and the processor can execute only one program at a time. The multiuser operating system takes advantage of the speed disparity between the computer and its peripheral devices (disks, printers, and so on). In comparison with the processor speed, input/output devices are very slow. Thus, when one program is waiting for its I/O request, the processor has plenty of time and can turn its attention to another program in the memory. The process of switching programs is concealed from the user and can give the illusion that the user is the only one using the system.

Figure 1–7 shows an example of a *multiuser* system. There are four users, one printer, and some other I/O devices. The users share the same host computer and its resources.

Figure 1–7
A multiuser computer system.

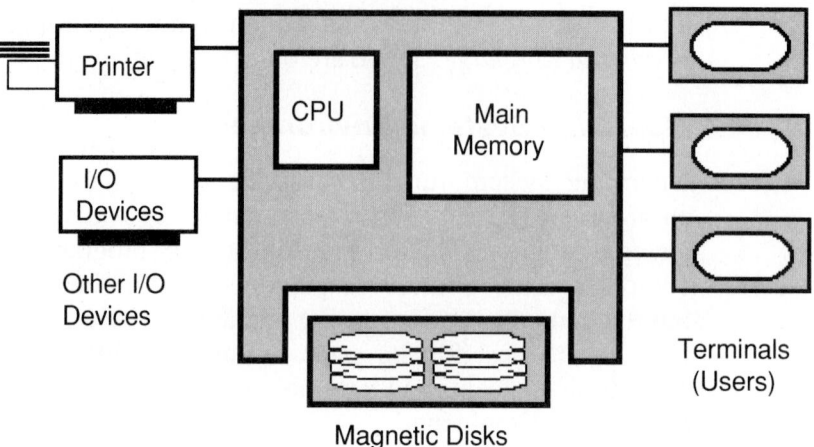

 The multiuser operating system is capable of providing services for many users (terminals), using the same host computer.

Another way to set up a *multiuser* system is to connect two or more computers together and create a network. Figure 1–8 shows a network computer system

Figure 1–8
The multiuser in network environment.

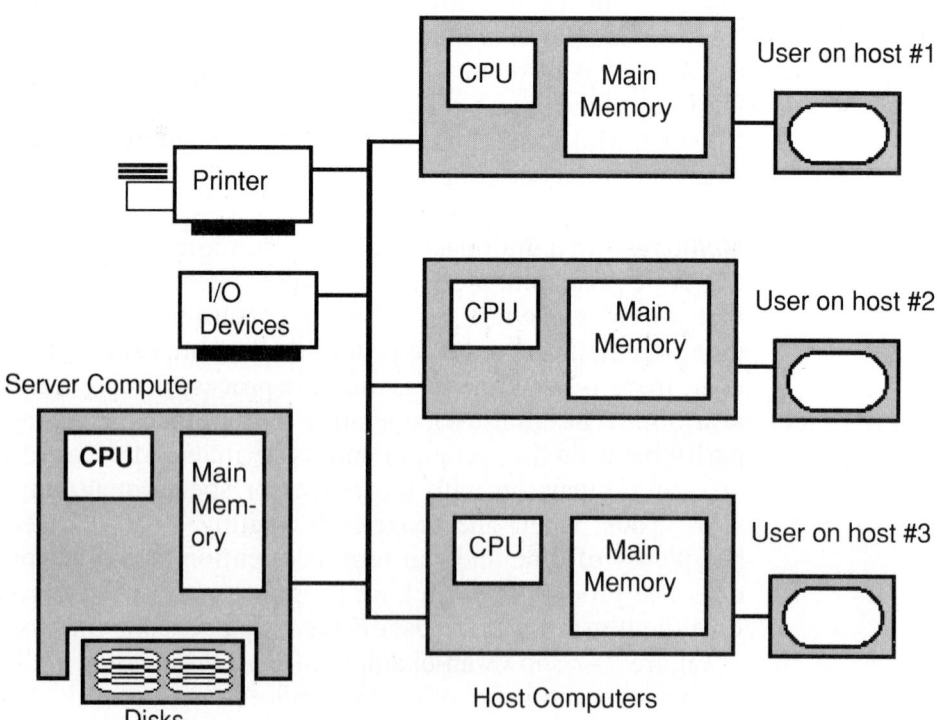

consisting of four computers. Three of the computers stand alone as single-user hosts, and one is functioning as a server, providing disk space for others.

Time-sharing   A *time-sharing* operating system is designed for online processing environments where active user involvement is required. It refers to multiple users sharing time on a single host computer. A time-sharing operating system allocates a slice of a time to each user task. It rapidly switches among tasks and each time executes a small portion of each user task.

Batch   The *batch* operating system is designed to execute programs (*batch process*) that do not require active user intervention. A *batch process* normally uses noninteractive I/O devices such as disks or document scanners for input and returns results to those same devices. The batch processing is used only in especially large transaction processing environment, for example, nightly processing of checks in a bank.

Memory Capacity Limitation

How large can a computer program be? Remember, the entire program and its associated data must be in the memory throughout its execution. Thus the capacity of the computer's main memory becomes the limitation on the size of an application program. However, that is not as limiting as it might seem at first. The computer is a sequential machine; it executes one instruction at a time in each processing cycle, so it is not necessary for the entire application to be in the main memory continually.

Virtual Memory   Under *virtual memory*, programs are subdivided into smaller portions called *pages*. Under the control of the operating system only the necessary pages of a program are swapped into the main memory to support the ongoing process. This approach permits you to use a relatively large program with minimal demands for the main memory space.

 Within a virtual memory system, secondary storage devices can be regarded as an extension of the main memory.

1.5.2   Application Software

Application software is designed and written to solve problems or provide automation and efficiency in personal, business, and scientific environments. Application programs are available for most data processing needs. You can buy off-the-shelf programs such as payroll systems, inventory systems, word processing, electronic spreadsheets, and so on. All you need to do is to select the right application program for the job. If you are not happy with off-the-shelf application programs, you can write your own program, using one of the available computer programming languages.

Review Exercises

1. What is a CPU? What are its primary components?

2. What are registers? What are their functions?

3. What is main memory?

4. Explain the steps of the instruction cycle. Explain the steps of the execution cycle.

5. What is the instruction set of a computer system?

6. Explain single-tasking and multitasking. How do they differ?

7. Explain single-user and multiuser. How do they differ?

8. What is system software?

9. What is application software?

10. What are the primary components (functions) of an operating system?

11. Explain the operating system software layers.

12. What is a kernel layer? What function does it perform?

13. What is a service layer? What function does it perform?

14. What are the differences between primary storage and secondary storage?

15. Explain virtual memory. Why is it used?

CHAPTER 2

The UNIX Operating System

This chapter briefly describes the history of the UNIX operating system. It explores UNIX development over the years, discusses the major UNIX versions, and explains some of the system's important features.

In This Chapter

2.1   THE UNIX OPERATING SYSTEM: A BRIEF HISTORY

During the early 1960s, many computers were working in *batch mode*, running single jobs. Programmers had to use punch cards to input their programs and then wait for the output on the line printer. The UNIX operating system was born in 1969 as a response to the frustration of the programmers and the need for new computing tools to help them with their projects.

The UNIX operating system is the brainchild of Ken Thompson and Dennis Ritchie, two Bell Laboratories researchers. At the time, Ken Thompson was working on a program called Space Travel, a program simulating the motion of the planets in the solar system. The program was under an operating system called *Multics*, one of the first operating systems that provided a multiuser environment, and ran on a General Electric 6000 Series computer. But Multics was large, slow, and required substantial computer resources. Thompson found a smaller computer and transferred the Space Travel program to run on it. The smaller computer was a little-used PDP-7, one of a series of machines made by Digital Equipment Corporation (DEC). On that computer, Thompson created a new operating system that he called UNIX, and to that operating system he adapted some of the advanced Multics concepts. Operating systems other than Multics existed that had more or less the same capabilities, and UNIX took advantage of the work that had gone into those operating systems by combining some of the most desirable aspects of each of them.

UNIX was transferred to the PDP-11/20 in 1970, and then to PDP-11/40, PDP-11/45, and eventually to PDP-11/70. Each of these machines had features that gradually added to the complexity of the hardware that UNIX could support. Dennis Ritchie and others at Bell Labs continued the development process of UNIX, adding utilities (such as a text processor).

Like most of the operating systems, UNIX was originally written in assembly language. *Assembly language* is a primitive set of instructions that depend on the computer architecture. Programs written in assembly language are machine-dependent and work on only one computer (or one family of computers). Therefore, moving the UNIX from one computer to another involved significant rewriting of the programs.

Thompson and Ritchie were experienced users of Multics, which was written in high-level language called PL/1, and they were aware of the advantages of using a high-level language to write operating systems. (A high-level language is much easier to use than the assembly language.) They decided to rewrite the UNIX operating system in a high-level language. The language of their choice was C. The C programming language is a general-purpose language featuring the commands and structures of modern, high-level computer languages. In 1973, Ken and Dennis successfully rewrote the UNIX in C.

See page xxii for an explanation of icons used to highlight information in this chapter.

About 95 percent of the UNIX operating system is written in C. A very small part of the UNIX is still written in assembly language; that part is mostly concentrated in the kernel, the part that interacts directly with the hardware.

Universities and colleges have played an important role in popularity of the UNIX operating system. In 1975, Bell Labs offered the UNIX operating system to educational institutions at minimal cost. UNIX courses were incorporated into the computer science curriculum, and in turn, students became familiar with UNIX and its sophisticated programming environment. As those students graduated and joined the work force, they carried their UNIX skill to the commercial world and UNIX was introduced to industry.

There are two major versions of the UNIX operating system:

- AT&T UNIX version V
- Berkeley UNIX

Other UNIX varieties are based on one or the other of these two versions.

2.1.1   UNIX System V

In 1983, AT&T released the standard UNIX system V, which was based on the UNIX that AT&T was using internally. The UNIX development effort continued, and other features were added or some existing features were improved. Over the years, UNIX grew larger in size as well as in its number of tools and utilities. The improvements and new features were incorporated into the UNIX operating system's later releases. AT&T introduced UNIX System V Release 3.0 in 1986 and UNIX System V Release 4.0 in 1988.

UNIX System V Release 4.0 was an effort to merge most of the popular features of the Berkeley UNIX and other UNIX systems. This unification helped simplify the UNIX product and reduced the need for manufactures to create new UNIX variants.

This book describes the commands applicable to the UNIX System V Release 4.

2.1.2   Berkeley UNIX

The Computer Systems Research Group at the University of California at Berkeley added new features and made significant changes to the UNIX operating system. This version of the UNIX is called the Berkeley Standard Distribution (BSD) of UNIX system and has been distributed to other colleges and universities.

2.1.3   UNIX Standards

The UNIX operating system is available on all types of computers (micros, minis, mainframes, and supercomputers) and is an important operating system in computer industry. As more UNIX-based systems were introduced into the market, and more application programs became available, an effort toward UNIX standardization started. AT&T's UNIX System V Release 4.0 was an effort to standardize the UNIX system and in turn to facilitate the writing of the applications that run on all versions. The written UNIX standard from AT&T is called *System V Interface Definition* (SVID). Other companies that market UNIX operating systems or related UNIX products have joined together and developed a standard called *Portable Operating System Interface for Computer Environments* (POSIX). POSIX is largely based on the System V Interface Definition.

2.1.4   Overview of the UNIX Operating System

A typical computer system consists of the hardware, the system software, and application software. The *operating system* is system software that controls and coordinates the activities of the computer. Like other operating systems, the UNIX operating system is a collection of programs that includes text editors, language compilers, and other system utility programs.

Figure 2–1 shows the UNIX operating system architecture. The UNIX operating system is implemented in a layered-style software model.

Kernal   The UNIX *kernel*, also called the *base operating system*, is the layer that manages all the hardware-dependent functions. These functions are spread over a number of modules within the UNIX *kernel*. The *kernel* layer consists of modules closest to the hardware that are for the most part protected from the application programs; users have no direct access to it.

1.   The utility programs and UNIX commands are not part of the kernel.

2.   A user's application programs are protected from inadvertent writes by other users.

Figure 2–1
The UNIX system components.

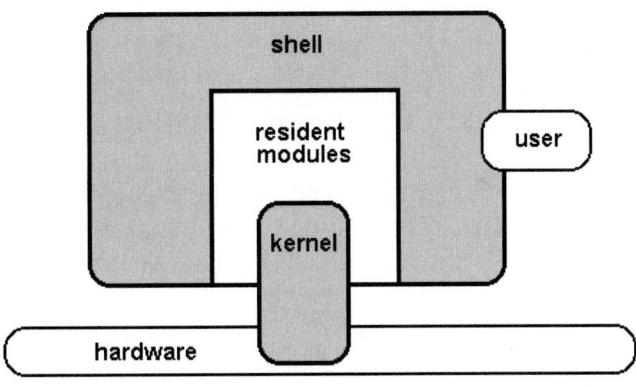

Resident Modules Layer The *resident modules layer* provides service routines that perform user-requested services. These services include input/output control services, file/disk access services (called *file system*), and process creation and termination. A system call is used by application programs to access this layer.

Utility Layer The *utility layer* is the UNIX user interface, commonly referred to as *shell*. The shell and each of the UNIX other commands and utilities are separate programs. They are part of the UNIX distribution software but are not considered as part of the kernel. There are more than 100 commands and utilities in UNIX that provide various types of services to users and application programs.

Vitrual Computer The UNIX operating system allocates an execution environment to each user in the system. This environment, or *virtual computer*, consists of a terminal for user interface and shared access to the other computer resources such as memory, disk drives, and most importantly, the CPU. UNIX, a multiuser operating system, is implemented as a collection of virtual computers. To the users, it appears that they each have their own private psuedocomputer. The virtual computers are slower than the base computer due to sharing the CPU and other hardware resources with other virtual computers.

Processes The UNIX operating system allocates resources to users and programs by way of processes. Each process has a process identification number, and a set of resources is associated with that number. Each is executed in a virtual computer environment. What this really means is that a process runs in a virtual computer much as if it had a dedicated single-user CPU.

2.2   UNIX FEATURES

This section briefly discusses some features of the UNIX operating system. UNIX has some features that are common to most operating systems; it also has some unique features.

2.2.1   Portability

The use of the C programming language made UNIX a portable operating system. Today, The UNIX operating system works on variety of machines ranging from microcomputers to supercomputers. The portability feature helps to decrease the user's learning time when moving from one system to another. It also provides more choices among hardware vendors.

2.2.2   Multiuser Capability

Under UNIX, a number of users can share computer resources simultaneously. Depending on the machine being used, UNIX may be able to support more than one hundred users, each running different programs. UNIX provides security measures that permit users to access only the data and programs for which they have permission.

2.2.3   Multitasking Capability

UNIX allows the user to initiate a task and then proceed to perform other tasks while the original task is being run in the background. UNIX also allows users to switch back and forth between the jobs.

2.2.4   Hierarchical File System

UNIX provides users with the ability to group data and programs in a manner that provides easy management. Users can find data, and programs can be located with little difficulty.

2.2.5   Device-Independent Input and Output Operations

Input and output operations are device-independent because UNIX treats all devices (such as printers, terminals, and disks) as files. With UNIX, you can redirect the output of your commands to any device or file. This redirection process is also possible with input data. You can redirect the input that comes from your terminal to come from a disk instead.

2.2.6   User Interface: Shell

The UNIX user interface was designed primarily for users with programming backgrounds. Experienced programmers find UNIX simple, concise, and elegant. Beginners, on the other hand, find it terse, not very friendly, and sometimes difficult to learn; it provides no feedback, warning, or hand-holding. For example, the command **rm *** deletes all the files, silently and with no warning.

The user's interaction with UNIX is controlled by a program called *shell*, which is a powerful command interpreter. The shell is the face of UNIX and the part with which most of the users interact. However, shell is only one part of the operating system and one way of interacting with UNIX. The shell is not really part of the operating system, so it can be changed. A user might choose a technical shell (*command-driven user interface*), or prefer selecting commands from a menu (*menu-driven user interface*) or by pointing at pictures (icons), in what is called *graphical user interface* (GUI). You can even write your own user interface.

The UNIX shell, a complex and sophisticated user interface, provides plenty of innovative and exciting features. You can create new functions by combining the existing commands. For example, the command **date | lp** combines the two commands **date** and **lp** to print the current date on the line printer.

Shell Script Many data processing applications are run frequently—at daily, weekly, or other regular intervals. In other situations, a set of commands must be entered many times. Typing the same set of commands again and again is annoying and prone to error. A way to remove this difficulty is to write a shell script. A *shell script* is a file that consists of a series of commands.

The UNIX shell is a highly sophisticated programming language. Chapters 11 and 12 discuss UNIX shell script capabilities and programming methods.

2.2.7   Utilities

The UNIX system includes more than one hundred utility programs, also called *commands*. Utilities are part of the standard UNIX system and are designed to perform a variety of functions required by the users. These utilities include the following:

- Text editing and text formatting utilities (see chapters 4 and 6)
- File manipulation utilities (see chapters 5 and 7)
- Electronic mail (e-mail) utilities (see chapter 9)
- Programmers' tools (see chapter 10)

2.2.8   System Services

The UNIX system provides a number of services that facilitate administration and maintenance of the system. A description of these services is beyond the scope of this text. However, the following are some of these services:

- System administration service
- System reconfiguration service
- File system maintenance service
- File transfer service (called UUCP for *UNIX to UNIX file copy*)

Review Exercises

1. What are the two major UNIX system versions?

2. What is the kernel?

3. What is the shell?

4. Briefly explain the virtual computer concept.

5. What is a process?

6. Why was UNIX rewritten? What computer language was used?

7. Is UNIX a multiuser, multitasking operating system?

8. Is UNIX portable?

9. What is the shell script?

CHAPTER 3

Getting Started

This chapter explains how to start and end (log in and log out) a UNIX session. Following that, it explains the function of passwords and how to change your password. After showing the command line format, the chapter introduces a few simple UNIX commands and explains their applications. It also describes how you can correct typing mistakes. Finally, the process of establishing contact with UNIX is explored in more detail, and some internal UNIX operations are discussed.

In This Chapter

3.1   ESTABLISHING CONTACT WITH UNIX

The process of establishing contact with the UNIX operating system consists of
a number of prompts and user's inputs that start and end a session. A *session* is
the period of time that you use the computer.

3.1.1   Logging In

UNIX is a multiuser operating system, and you are not likely to be the only person using the system. The process of identifying yourself and letting UNIX
know that you want to use the system is called the *logging in process*. The first
thing you must do to use a UNIX system is log in.

To get the attention of the UNIX operating system, you need a means of
communicating with UNIX. In most cases, a keyboard (input) and a screen
display (output) provide the means of communication. Starting from having
the screen display on your computer turned on, you begin the logging in
process by pressing [Return]. When UNIX is ready for you to log in, it displays some messages (that vary from system to system) and then the **login:**
prompt (see figure 3–1).

Figure 3–1
The login prompt.

```
UNIX System V release 4.0
login:
```

Login Name   Most UNIX systems require that you set up an account before
you can use the computer. When your account is created, your *login name*
(also called *User Id* or *User Name*) and password are also established. User
Id (user identification) is usually issued by the system administrator (or your
professor if you a working on a college or university computer system). Your
User Id is unique and identifies you to the system.

Respond to **login:** prompt by typing your User Id and then pressing [Re-
turn]. After you type your User Id (for this example, we'll use **david**), the
UNIX system displays the **password:** prompt (see figure 3–2).

Figure 3–2
The password prompt.

```
UNIX System V release 4.0
login: david
password:
```

See page xxii for an explanation of icons used to highlight information in this chapter.

Figure 3–3
The logging in process.

```
UNIX System V release 4.0
login: david
password:

Welcome to super duper UNIX system
Sat Nov 29 15:40:30 EDT 2001
* This system will be down from 11:00 to 13:00
* This message is from your friendly system manager!


$ _
```

If no password has been assigned to your account, UNIX does not display the **password:** prompt, and the logging in process ends.

Password   Like the User Id, a password is supplied by the system administrator. A password is a sequence of letters and digits used by UNIX to verify that the user is allowed to use this User Id.

Type your password, and press [Return]. In order to protect your password from others, UNIX does not echo the letters you type; you do not see them on the screen. UNIX verifies your User Id and password; if they are correct, a pause occurs while the system sets things up for you.

After verifying the User Id and password, the UNIX system displays some messages. Often the date is displayed, along with a "message of the day" (which contains messages from the system administrator). The UNIX system indicates that it is ready to accept your commands by displaying the system prompt. The *standard prompt* is usually a dollar sign ($) or a percent sign (%). Let's assume the prompt is a dollar sign ($), and it will be displayed as the first character on the line (see figure 3–3).

3.1.2   Changing Your Password: The *passwd* Command

The **passwd** command changes your current password, and if you do not have a password, it creates one.

Type **passwd** and press [Return]. UNIX displays the **Old password:** prompt (see figure 3–4).

Figure 3–4
Old password: prompt.

```
$ passwd
Changing password for david
Old password:
```

Figure 3–5
New password: prompt.

```
$ passwd
Changing password for david
Old password:
New password:
```

For security reasons, UNIX never displays your password on the screen.

UNIX verifies your password, to ensure that an unauthorized user is not changing your password. (UNIX does not display the **Old password:** prompt if you do not have a password yet.) Enter your current password and press [Return]. Next UNIX displays the **New password:** prompt (see figure 3–5).

After you enter your new password, UNIX shows the **Re-enter new password:** prompt. Retype the new password again. UNIX is verifying that you did not make a mistake the first time you entered the new password (see figure 3–6).

If you typed the new password the same both times, UNIX has changed your password.

Figure 3–6
Re-enter new password: prompt.

```
$ passwd
Changing password for david
Old password:
New password:
Re-enter new password:
```

Make sure you remember your new password; you will need it the next time you want to log in.

Password Format The **passwd** command does not accept just any sequence of alphanumeric characters as a password. Your password must comply with the following criteria:

- The new password must differ from the old one by at least three characters.
- The password must be at least six characters long and must contain at least two characters and one number.
- The password must differ from your User Id.

If UNIX detects anything wrong with your password, it displays an error message and shows **New password:** prompt again (see figure 3–7).

Figure 3–7
Password error message.

> Password is too short - must be at least 6 digits.
> New password:
>
> Password must differ by at least 3 positions
> New password:

3.1.3   Logging Off

The process of signing off when you have finished with the system is called *logging off* or *logging out*. When you want to log off, the prompt sign must be displayed on the screen; you cannot log off in the middle of a process. To log off, at prompt sign press [Ctrl-d]. (This means simultaneously holding down the key labeled Ctrl (for control) and pressing letter *d*.) When this key sequence is pressed, nothing is displayed on the screen; however, the command is recognized by the system. The UNIX system responds first by displaying logging off messages that your system administrator has set up. Then the screen shows your system's standard welcome message and **login:** prompt. This lets you know that you have logged off properly and that the terminal is ready for the next user.

The terminal session shown in figure 3–8 shows the logging in and logging out processes.

Turning off the terminal without logging off does not terminate your session with UNIX.

Figure 3–8
The logging in and logging out process.

> UNIX System V release 4.0
> login: **david**
> password:
> Welcome to super duper UNIX system
> Sat Nov 29 15:40:30 EDT 2001
> * This system will be down from 11:00 to 13:00
> * This message is from your friendly system manager!
>
> $ **[Ctrl-d]**
>
> UNIX system V release 4.0
> login:

3.2   USING SOME SIMPLE COMMANDS

When you are using a UNIX system, you have hundreds of UNIX commands and utilities at your disposal. Some basic commands you will use frequently, some you will use occasionally, and some you may never use! The difficult part of systems that have a rich set of commands is learning to master the details of each command. Fortunately, most UNIX commands share the same basic structure, and on-line help is available on most of the UNIX systems to assist your memory.

3.2.1   The Command Line

Every operating system has commands that facilitate use of the system. By typing the commands, you tell the UNIX system to do something. For example, the command **date** tells the system to display the date and time; to see this, type **date** and press [Return]. This line of instruction is known as the *command line*. UNIX interprets the press of [Return] as end of the command line and responds by showing date and time on the screen:

    Sat Nov 29 14:00:52 EDT 2001
    $ _

Each time you give UNIX a command, it carries out the command and then displays a new prompt, indicating that it is ready for the next command.

3.2.2   Basic Command Line Structure

Each command line consists of three fields:

- Command name
- Options
- Arguments

Figure 3–9 shows the general form of a UNIX command.

Figure 3–9
The command line format.

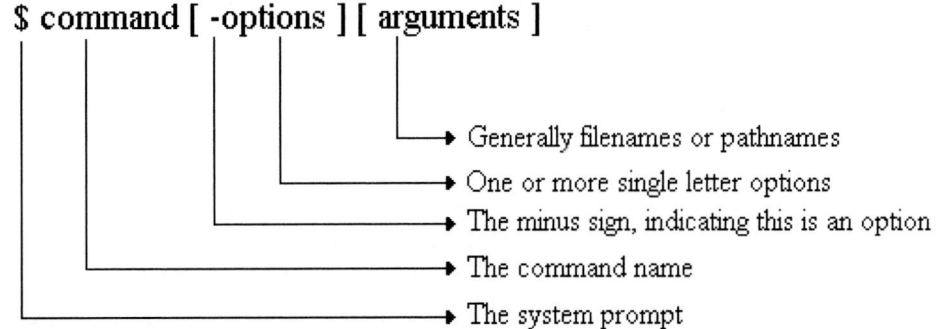

1. *Fields are separated by one or more spaces.*

2. *Fields enclosed in brackets [...] are optional for most of the commands.*

You must signal that you have completed entry of a command by pressing [Return] at the end of every command.

Command Name   Any valid UNIX command or utility program functions as a *command name*. Under UNIX, commands and utilities are different; however, in this text, the word *command* includes both of them.

UNIX is a case-sensitive system and only accepts command names in lowercase.

Arguments   *Arguments* are commands that perform some sort of operation, such as printing a file or displaying information. Commands often need to operate on something, which means that you must provide additional information. The additional information the command needs to operate on is called an *argument*. For example, if the command is **print**, then you have to tell UNIX what to print (the name of a file) and where to find the file you want to print (somewhere on the disk). The name of the file plus where the file is located on the disk is an example of *argument field*.

Options   *Options* are variations on the command. If they are included in the command line, they are usually preceded by a minus sign (-). Most options are designated by a single lowercase letter, and more than one option can be specified on one command line. This text does not describe all possible options for every command.

3.2.3   Date and Time Display: The *date* Command

The **date** command displays the current date and time on the screen (see figure 3–10). The date and time are set by the system administrator; users cannot change them.

Show the current date and time.

The **date** *command displays the day of the week, month, day, and time (Eastern Daylight Time), followed by the year. UNIX uses a 24-hour clock.*

Figure 3–10
The date command.

```
$ date
Sat Nov 29 14:00:52 EDT 2001
$ _
```

3.2.4   Names of Users Display: The *who* Command

The **who** command lists the login names, terminal lines, and login times of the users who are currently logged on the system. You can use the *who* command to check the level of activity in the system or to find out whether a particular person is on the system (see figure 3–11).

Figure 3–11
The **who** command.

```
$ who
david    tty04   Nov  28 08:27
daniel   tty10   Nov  28 08:30
$ _
```

Who is logged in the system?

1.   *The first column shows the login name of the user.*

2.   *The second column identifies the terminal being used.*

3.   *The tty number gives you some indication about the location of the terminal.*

4.   *The third and fourth columns show the date and time that each user logged in.*

If you type **who am I** or **who am i**, UNIX displays who the system thinks you are (see figure 3–12).

Who am I?

Figure 3–12
The **who** command with **am i** argument.

```
$ who am i
 david   tty04   Nov 28 08:48
 $ _
```

who Options

Table 3–1 lists some of the **who** command options. Other options are available, but let's practice these few options and not get carried away with details.

1.   There must be a space between the command field and the option field.

2.   Options are preceded by a minus sign.

3.   There is no space between the minus sign and the option letter.

Table 3–1
The **who** command options.

Option	Operation
-q	The quick who; just displays the name and number of users.
-H	Displays heading above each column.
-b	Gives the time and date of the last reboot.
-s	Displays just the name, line, and time columns.

4. Option letters must be typed as they are indicated, uppercase or lowercase.

Examples Using Options

The following examples show how the use of options in the command line can change the output format and level of details displayed.

 Display columns headers, the **-H** option.

Figure 3–13
The **who** command with **-H** option.

```
$ who -H
NAME      LINE      TIME
david     tty04     Nov 28 08:27
daniel    tty10     Nov 28 08:30
$ _
```

 Get a quick list and user count, the **-q** option.

Figure 3–14
The **who** command with **-q** option.

```
$ who -q
david daniel
# users=2
$ _
```

Show time and date of the last boot, the **-b** option.

Figure 3–15
The **who** command with **-b** option.

```
$ who -b
system boot Nov 27 08:37
$ _
```

3.2.5 Display a Calendar: The *cal* Command

The **cal** command displays the calendar for the specified year. If year and month are both specified, just that month is displayed. Month and year are examples of command line arguments. The default argument for the **cal** command is the current month (figure 3–16).

Display the calendar for November 2001.

Figure 3–16
The **cal** command output.

```
$ cal 11 2001
November 2001
 S  M Tu  W Th  F  S
             1  2  3
 4  5  6  7  8  9 10
11 12 13 14 15 16 17
18 19 20 21 22 23 24
25 26 27 28 29 30
$ _
```

1. *Type the specified year in full year value. For example, type* **cal 1998** *(not* **cal 98***).*

2. *Use the month number (01 to 12) and not the month name.*

3. *The* **cal** *command without arguments displays calendar of the current month.*

4. *The* **cal** *command with year argument but without month argument displays a calendar for the specified year.*

3.3   GETTING HELP

UNIX has not left novices or forgetful experienced users in the cold! The **learn** and **help** commands are two programs that provide assistance for using the UNIX operating system. These programs are designed to be user-friendly and are intended to be used, even by novices, without assistance. However, these commands vary from one system to another, and they may or may not be installed on your system.

3.3.1   Using the *learn* Command

The **learn** command brings up a computer-aided instruction program that is arranged in series of courses and lessons. It displays the menu of the courses and guides the user to select courses, presents description of the courses, and so on.

To use the **learn** command, type **learn** on the command line and press [Return]. If the **learn** program is installed on your system, the **learn** main menu is displayed (see figure 3–17); otherwise, you see an error message similar to the following:

    learn: not found

Figure 3–17
Learn utility main menu.

```
$ learn
These are the available courses
    files
    editor
    vi
    more files
    macros
    eqn
    C
If you want more information about the courses, or if you have never used
'learn' before, press RETURN; otherwise type the name of the course you want,
followed by RETURN
```

3.3.2   Using the *help* Command

The **help** program is more popular than the **learn** program and is installed on more UNIX systems. The **help** command presents you with the hierarchy of menus, and a series of menu selections and questions lead you to a description of the most commonly used UNIX commands. To use the **help** command, type **help** on the command line and press [Return]. UNIX displays the **help** main menu (see figure 3–18). If **help** is not installed on your system, you see the following error message:

    help: not found

Figure 3–18
Help utility main menu.

```
$ help

help: UNIX System On-line Help

        Choices        description


           s        starter: general information
           l        locate: find a command with keyword
           u        usage: information about command
           g        glossary: definition of terms
           r        redirect to a file or a command
           q        Quit
        Enter choice
```

3.3.3   Getting More Information: The UNIX Manual

You can find a detailed description of the UNIX system in a large document called *User's Manual*. Your installation may have a printed copy of this manual. The electronic version of the manual is stored on disk and is called the on-line manual. If the on-line manual is installed on your system, you can easily display pages from system documentation on your terminal. However, the UNIX user's manual is tersely written and difficult to read. It is more like a reference guide than a true user's manual and is most helpful to experienced users who know the basic use of a command but have forgotten exactly how to use it.

3.3.4   Using the Electronic Manual: The *man* Command

The **man** (manual) command shows pages from the on-line system documentation. To get information about a command, type **man** followed by name of the command. As you begin to learn new commands, you may want to use **man** to get the details about the commands. For example, to find more information about **cal** command, type **man cal** and then press [Return]. UNIX responds by showing a page similar to figure 3–19. Be patient; sometimes the system takes a while to find your desired command.

Figure 3–19
man utility display of **cal**.

```
CAl(1)            User Environment Utilities       CAL(1)



NAME
      cal - print calendar
SYNOPSIS
      cal [ [ month ] year ]
DESCRIPTION


      cal prints a calendar for the specified year. If a month
      is also specified, a calendar just for that month is
      printed.  If neither is specified, a calendar for the present
      month is printed. Year can be between 1 and 9999. The year is
      always considered to start in January even though this is
      historically naive.    Beware that "cal 83" refers to the
      early Christian era, not the 20th century.
      The month is a number between 1 and 12.
      The calendar produced is that for England and the United
      States.
EXAMPLES



      An unusual calendar is printed for September 1752. That is
      the month 11 days were skipped to make up for lack of leap
      year adjustments. To see this calendar, type: cal 9 1752
```

showing a page similar to figure 3–19. Be patient; sometimes the system takes a while to find your desired command.

The UNIX user's manual is organized into sections, and the number in parentheses after command name is referring to the section number in the manual that contains the description. For example "CAL(1)" refers to section 1, the User Command section. The other sections include System Administration Commands, Games, etc.

3.4   CORRECTING TYPING MISTAKES

Even the most talented typists make mistakes or change their minds when typing commands. The shell program interprets the command line after you press [Return]. As long as you have not ended your command line (by pressing [Return]), you have the opportunity to correct your typing mistakes or to cancel the whole command line.

systems. Try them on your system; if they do not work, ask the system administrator for assistance.

If you mistype a command name and end the command line by pressing [Return], UNIX displays a generic error message (see figure 3–20). It responds with the same error message if you type a command that is not installed on your system.

 The date command is mistyped.

Erasing Characters Use [Back Space] for erasing characters. When you

Figure 3–20
UNIX error message.

```
$ daye
daye: not found
$ _
```

press [Back Space], the cursor moves to the left, and the character it moves over is erased. An alternative way to backspace is [Ctrl-h]; press it once for each character you intend to erase. For example, if you type **calendar** and then press [Back Space] five times, the cursor moves over the last five characters and **cal** remains on the screen. Then you can press [Return] to execute the **cal** command. The character that erases the command line a character at a time is called the *erase character*.

Erasing an Entire Line You can erase an entire line any time before typing [Return] to end the command line. When you press the [Ctrl-u] character, the entire command line is removed and the cursor moves to a blank line. For example, suppose you type **passwd** and then you decide not to change your password. You can press [Ctrl-u], and the **passwd** command is erased. The character that erases the entire line is called the *kill character.*

 [Ctrl-u] is considered a single character although it involves two keys.

Terminating Program Execution If you have little time, and the running program takes a long time to perform its task, then you may want to terminate the execution of the program. The character that terminates your running program is called the *interrupt character*. On most systems, [Del] or [Ctrl-c] is assigned as the interrupt character. The interrupt character stops the running program and causes the shell prompt ($) to be displayed.

3.5   USING SHELLS AND UTILITIES

Much of UNIX's strength and flexibility comes form its shells. *Shell* is a program that handles user interaction with the UNIX system. The UNIX commands are processed by a shell that lies between the user and the other parts of the operating system. Each time you type a command and press [Return], you send a command to the shell. The shell analyzes the line you typed and then proceeds to carry out your request. Shell is a command interpreter. If you type the **date** command, shell locates where the program date is kept and runs it. So you, the user, are actually addressing the shell and, technically speaking, not UNIX.

Shell Commands   Some commands are part of the shell program; these *built-in commands* are recognized by shell and are executed internally.

Utility Programs   Most UNIX commands are executable programs (utilities) that shell locates and executes.

 In this book, the word *command* is used to refer to both shell commands and utility programs.

3.5.1   Kinds of Shells

The shell is just a program. Like other programs, shell has no special privileges on the system. This is one reason various flavors of the shell programs exist. If you are a professional programmer, with some effort and devotion you can create your own shell program. Two main varieties of shells are in widespread use: the Bourne Shell and the C Shell.

Bourne Shell   Bourne Shell comes with the standard Bell Labs release of UNIX. This book assumes that you have a Bourne Shell and the prompt for Bourne Shell is the dollar sign ($).

C Shell   C Shell was developed at the University of California at Berkeley and is part of BSD (Berkeley Software Distribution) package. The prompt sign for C Shell is the percent sign (%).

3.6   MORE ABOUT THE LOGGING IN PROCESS

When you boot (bootstrap) the UNIX system, the resident part of the operating system (kernel) is loaded into the main memory. The rest of the operating system programs (utilities) remain on the system disk and are brought into memory only when you request the command be executed. The shell program is also loaded into memory for execution whenever you log in. Learning about the sequence of events that occur when you log in will help you gain a better understanding of the UNIX internal operation.

Figure 3–21
getty displays the **login:** prompt.

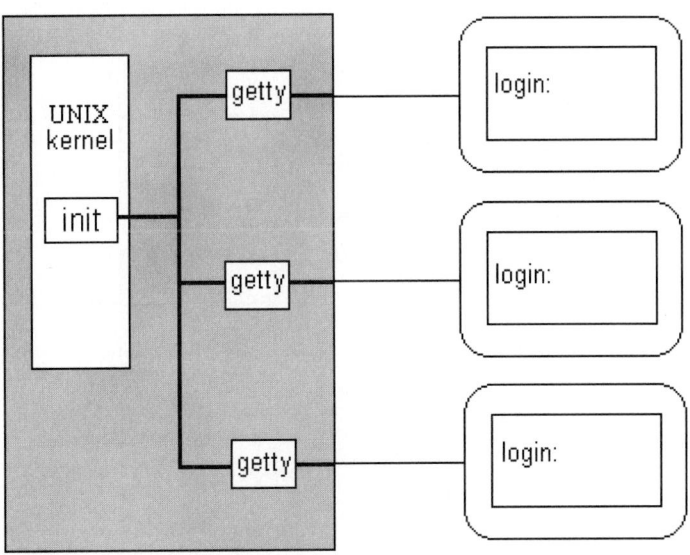

After UNIX completes the boot procedures, a program called *init* activates a program called *getty* for each terminal port on the system. The getty program displays the **login:** prompt at the assigned terminal, and then waits for you to type your User Id (see figure 3–21).

When you enter your User Id, the getty reads it and starts another program, called *login*, to complete the logging in process. It also gives the login program the characters you typed at the terminal, the characters presumed to be your User Id (login name). Next, the login program begins execution and dis-

Figure 3–22
Login displays the **password:** prompt.

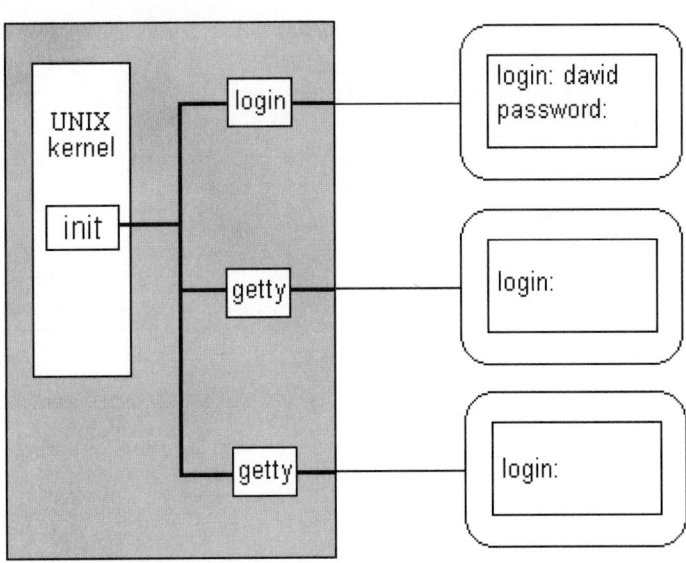

Figure 3–23
Shell displays the $ prompt.

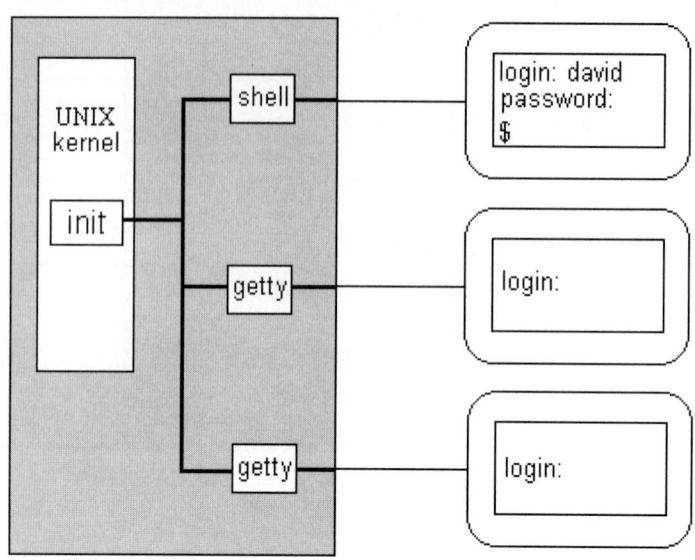

plays the **password:** prompt at the terminal. The login program waits for you to enter your password (see figure 3–22).

After you have typed in your password, the login program verifies your User Id and password. Next it checks for the name of a program to execute. In most cases, this will be the shell program. The shell program, if it is the Bourne Shell (standard shell), displays a **$** prompt. Now shell is ready to accept your commands (figure 3–23).

When you log off the system, the shell program is terminated and the UNIX system starts up a new getty program at the terminal and waits for someone to log in. This cycle continues as long as the system is up and running (figure 3–24).

Figure 3–24
Logging in and logging off cycle.

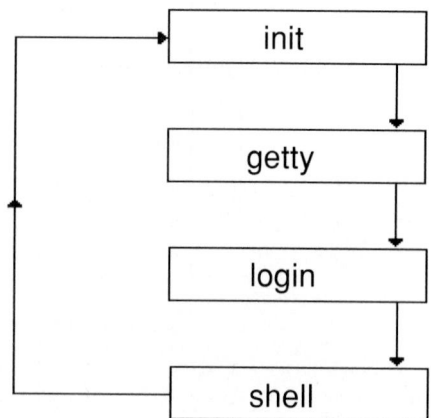

Command Summary

The following UNIX commands (utilities) were discussed in this chapter. To refresh your memory, the command line format is repeated in Figure 3–25.

Figure 3–25
The command line format.

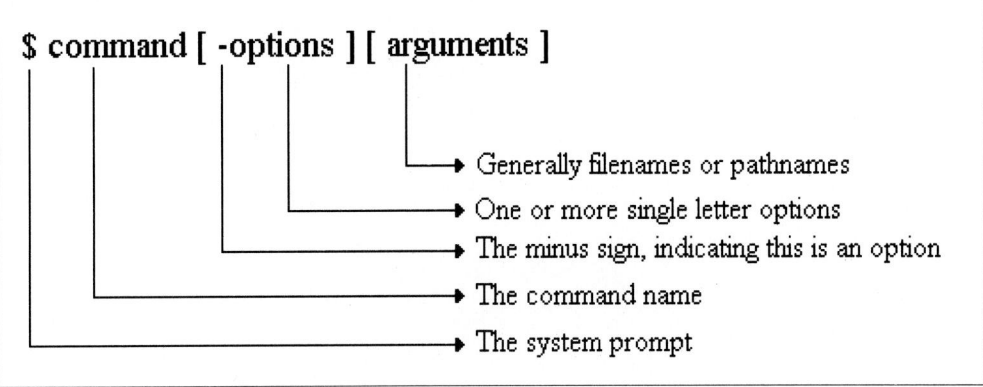

---

date
Displays the day of the week, month, date, and time.

---

cal
Displays the calendar for specified year, or month of a year.

---

who
Lists the login name, terminal lines, and login times of the users who are on the system.

Option	Operation
-q	The quick who; just displays the name and number of users.
-H	Displays a heading above each column.
-b	Gives the time and date of the last reboot.
-s	Displays just the name, line, and time columns.

---

learn
A computer-aided instruction program that is arranged in series of courses and lessons. It displays the menu of courses and lets you select your desired lesson.

---

help
Brings to the display a series of menus and questions that lead you to the description of the most commonly used UNIX commands.

man
This command shows pages from the on-line system documentation.

passwd
This command changes your login password.

Review Exercises

1. What is the logging in process?

2. What is the logging out process?

3. Why are you assigned a login name?

4. What are the sequence of events that comprise the UNIX internal operation at startup (boot) time?

5. What is the shell program, and what is its role in UNIX environment?

Terminal Session

Before starting your first terminal session, spend a few minutes to determine the following information about your system.

Find out your login name (User Id).

If your system requires a password to log in, then find out your password.

Find out which keys are assigned as the following:

- the erase key
- the kill key
- the interrupt key

Now that you are ready, start by turning on your terminal and wait for **login:** prompt.

1. Using your User Id and password, log in to the system. Take notice of the messages appearing on the screen.

2. Check the prompt sign and find out what shell variety you are using.

3. Use the **who** command to find out who is currently logged in the system.

4. Use the **who** command options to find out the number of users in the system and the last time the system was booted.

5. Find out what help utilities are available in your system.

6. Use the **date** command to see the current date and time.

7. Use **cal** command to find the day of your birth date.

8. Look at the calendar for the year 2001.

9. Use **passwd** command to change your password.

10. Try new passwords that do not meet the password format, so you become familiar with type of the error messages that UNIX displays.

11. After you have successfully changed your password, log out and log in again, using your new password.

12. Try to correct your typing mistakes using the erase key.

13. Try to terminate a line of command using the kill key.

14. Log off to end your session.

The vi Editor: First Look

Chapter 4 is the first of the two chapters that discuss the UNIX operating system vi editor (*vi* is pronounced *vee-eye*); chapter 6 is the second. Chapter 4 starts with an explanation of editors in general and then discusses the types of editors and their applications. After a brief description of the editors supported by UNIX, the chapter introduces the vi editor. The rest of the chapter presents the basic commands necessary to do a simple editing job in the vi editor. Basic concepts and operations with the vi editor are explained:

- the different modes of the vi editor
- memory buffers
- the process of opening a file for editing
- saving a file
- quitting vi

In This Chapter

4.1   WHAT IS AN EDITOR?

Editing a text file is one of the most frequently used computer operations. In fact, most of the things you want to do require some sort of file editing sooner or later.

An editor (text editor) is a tool that facilitates the creation of files or modification of the existing files. Files may contain notes, memos, program source code, and so on. An editor is a washed down, vanilla sort of word processor. It does not have the typographical features (bold, center, underline, etc.) that word processors do.

At least one editor program is supplied with every operating system software. There are two general types of editors:

- line editors
- full screen editors

The Line Editor   In a *line editor*, most of the changes are applied to a line or group of lines at a time. To make a change, you must first specify the line number in the text, and then you must specify the change itself. Line editors are usually difficult to use because you cannot see the scope and context of your editing task. Line editors are good for global operations like search, replace and copy large blocks of text in your file.

The Screen Editor   A *screen editor* displays a screenful of the text that you are editing and allows you to move the cursor around the screen and make changes. Any changes you make are applied to the file, and you get an immediate feed back on the screen. You can easily view the rest of the text one screen full at a time. The screen editors are more user-friendly than line editors; they are preferred for everyday editing jobs.

4.1.1   UNIX-Supported Editors

The UNIX operating system supports a number of both line-oriented and screen-oriented editors, so you can create or alter a file easily and efficiently. To name a few, *emacs* and *ex* are line editors, and *vi* is a screen editor under UNIX.

A line editor called *ed* is an old editor supplied with the early versions of the UNIX operating systems. Currently, the ex family of editors is supplied with most UNIX operating systems. The ex editor originally provided a display facility that showed a screenful of text and let you work with a full screen instead of one line at a time. In order to use this capability, you had to give ex the **vi** (for *visual*) command; however, the use of visual mode of the ex editor became so popular that the developers of the ex editor now provide a standalone vi editor. This means you can use **vi** without having to start the ex editor.

See page xxii for an explanation of icons used to highlight information in this chapter.

Table 4–1
Some of the editors supported by UNIX.

Editor	Category
ed	The original line-oriented editor
ex	A more sophisticated superset of the ed editor
vi	A visual, screen-oriented editor
emacs	A public-domain, screen-oriented editor

The Text Formatter   The UNIX editors are not text formatting programs. They do not provide functions like centering a line or setting up margins, things that are readily available with any word processing program. To format text, UNIX supports utilities like *nroff* and *troff*.

Text formatters are usually used to prepare documents. Input to these programs are text files that you create using editors like the vi editor. Output from text formatters is paginated, and you can display the formatted text on the screen or send it to the printer. Table 4–1 shows some of the UNIX operating system editors and their categories.

4.2   THE vi EDITOR

The vi editor is a screen-oriented text editor available on most UNIX operating systems, which provides some of the flexibility and ease of the word processing programs. Because vi is based on the line editor ex, it is possible to use ex commands from within vi. When you use vi, changes to your file are reflected on the terminal screen, and the position of the cursor on the screen indicates the position within your file. More than one hundred vi commands are available, providing many capabilities and also the challenge of learning them! Do not panic. Only a few of the commands are necessary to do a simple editing task.

Two versions of vi, the *view editor* and the *vedit editor*, are tailored for specific tasks or users. These versions are the same as the vi editor except that certain flags (options) are preset. Not every system has these versions on it. By end of the two vi chapters in this book you will have learned to customize the vi environment according to your own needs.

The view Editor   The *view editor* is the version of the vi editor with the read-only flag set in it. The view editor is useful when you want to look only at the contents of your file and not modify it. The view editor prevents you from inadvertently changing your file, and your file remains intact.

The vedit Editor   The *vedit editor* is the version of the vi editor with several flags set. The vedit editor is intended for beginners; its flag settings make it easier to learn how to use vi.

4.2.1   The vi Modes of Operation

The vi editor has two basic modes of operation: command (edit) mode and text input mode. Some commands are applicable only to the command mode, and others work only in the text input mode. During a vi editing session, you change from one mode of vi to another to do the editing job.

Command Mode   When you start the vi editor, it comes up in command mode. In command mode, key entries (any key or sequence of keys you press) are interpreted as commands. The keys are not echoed on the screen, but the commands associated with the specified key or keys are carried out. While the vi editor is in the command mode, by pressing a key or sequence of keys you can delete lines, search for a word, move the cursor on the screen, and perform a number of other useful operations.

Certain commands in the command mode start with the colon [**:**], forward slash [**/**] or question mark [**?**]. The vi editor displays these commands on the last line on the screen; to signal the end of the command line for these types of commands, you press [Return].

Text Input Mode   In text input mode, the keyboard becomes your typewriter. vi displays any key or sequence of the keys you press, and keys are interpreted not as a command but as text that you want to write into your file.

Status Line   The bottom line on the screen, usually line 24, is used by vi to give you some feedback about your editing operation. Error messages and other informative messages are displayed on status line. vi also displays the commands that start with **:**, **/**, or **?** on line 24.

4.3   BASIC vi EDITOR COMMANDS

The basic editing job usually involves the following operations:

- Creating a new file or modifying an existing file (open file operation)
- Entering text
- Deleting text
- Searching text
- Changing text
- Saving the file and quitting the editing session (close file operation)

The following sections walk you through a few editing sessions, exploring the vi editor's way of working, and show you some of the necessary editing commands from both text input mode and command mode.

Relying solely on the textbook to learn the vi editor (or any other editor) is not a good idea. It is highly recommended that after an initial reading of this chapter, you practice the examples and terminal session exercises on your system.

Assumptions   In order not to repeat the setup of examples in every section, the general assumptions that are applicable to all examples are summarized here.

- The *current line* is the line that the cursor is on.
- The double underline (_) indicates the position of the cursor on the line.
- The myfirst file is used to show the operations of different keys and commands. When necessary, examples are illustrated on screens. If there are multiple screens, the top one shows the current state of the text, and the subsequent ones show the changes on the screen after the specified keys or commands are applied on the text.
- To save space, only the relevant part of the screens is shown.
- The examples are not continuous; the editing changes are not carried over from one example to another.

4.3.1   Access to the vi Editor

As with any other software program, with vi the first step is to learn how to start and end the program. This section shows how to invoke the vi editor to create a small text file and then save the file.

Starting vi

To start the vi editor, type **vi**, press [Spacebar], type the name of the file (in this example, **myfirst**), and then press [Return].

If a myfirst file already exists, vi displays the first page (23 lines) of the file on the screen. If myfirst is a new file, vi clears the screen, shows the vi blank screen, and positions the cursor at the upper left corner of the screen. The screen is filled with tildes (~) in the first column. The vi editor is in command mode and is ready to accept your commands. Figure 4–1 shows the vi editor blank screen.

1. *The status line shows the file name and the fact that it is a new file.*

2. *To save space, screens shown in this book are not shown in full size (24 lines).*

In order to input your text, you must put the vi editor in the text input mode. Make sure Caps Lock is off, and then press [i] (for insert). vi does not display the letter *i* but enters into the text input mode. Now type the lines shown in

Figure 4–1
The vi editor blank screen.

```
    ~
    ~
    ~
    ~
    "myfirst" [new file]
```

Figure 4–2
The vi editor display screen.

The vi history
vi is an interactive text editor that is supported by most of the
UNIX operating systems.

~

~

~

~

~

~

"myfirst" [new file]

figure 4–2. The vi editor displays everything you type on the screen. Use [Back Space] to erase characters, and press [Return] at the end of each line to go to the next line. Do not be overly concerned about the syntax and spelling of the text; the goal here is to create a file and save it.

 Make sure Caps Lock is off because uppercase and lowercase letters have different meanings in the command mode.

1. *While the vi editor is in the command mode, most commands are initiated as soon as you press the key; there is no need to use [Return] to indicate the end of the command line.*

2. *The vi editor provides no visual feedback indicating the mode it is in. (This problem is explored in chapter 6.)*

3. *If your file does not fill the whole screen, the vi editor fills the first column of the remaining lines with tildes (~).*

4. *If your screen is not similar to the one shown, your terminal type is probably not set or set incorrectly. (This problem is explored in chapter 8.)*

Ending vi

In order to save a file that you've created or edited with vi, you must first place vi in command mode. To do so, press [Esc]; if the sound on your terminal is activated, you hear a beep that indicates vi is in the command mode. The save file and quit vi both are commands that start with the colon [:]. Press [:] to put the cursor on the last line of the terminal screen. Then type **wq** (for *write* and *quit*) and press [Return]. The vi editor saves your file (which you called "myfirst") and passes control back to the shell. Shell displays the dollar sign prompt. The **$** signals that you are out of the vi editor and back to the shell; the system is ready for your next command. Figure 4–3 shows the vi editor display after you enter **:wq.**

Figure 4–3
The vi editor screen after **wq** command.

```
    The vi history
    vi is an interactive text editor that is supported by most of the
    UNIX operating systems.
    ~
    ~
    ~
    ~
    :wq
    "myfirst" 3 lines 106 characters
    $ _
```

The vi editor feedback appears on the last line of the screen. It shows the file name followed by the number of lines and number of characters in the file.

4.3.2   Text Input Mode

You must be in text input mode in order to type text into your file. However, each key enters the vi text input mode in a slightly different manner. The location of the text in your file depends on the place of the cursor on the screen and the key you choose to place vi in the text input mode.

Table 4–2 summarizes the keys that change the vi editor from the command mode to the text input mode. For example, let's use **myfirst**, the file created in the previous section. Suppose you have it on the screen and want

Table 4–2
The vi change mode keys.

Key	Operation
i	Inserts the text you enter before the character that the cursor is on.
I	Places the text you enter at the beginning of the current line.
a	Appends the text you enter after the character that the cursor is on.
A	Places the text you enter after the last character of the current line.
o	Opens a blank line below the current line and places the cursor at the beginning of the new line.
O	Opens a blank line above the current line and places the cursor at the beginning of the new line.

to enter **999** in your file. (There is nothing special about **999**; it is to illustrate the location of the text you enter relative to the position of the cursor on the screen. You can type anything you wish.) Also assume the cursor is on the letter *m* of the word *most* as indicated by the double underline. Depending on what key you choose to enter in the text input mode, the **999** that you type will be put in a different location in your file.

Inserting Text: Using [i] or [I]

Pressing [i] or [I] places the vi editor in text input mode. However, each puts you in a different place in the file: pressing [i] places the text you enter before the cursor position, and pressing [I] places your text at the beginning of the current line. Do the following things to experiment with [i]:

☐ Press [i]; vi enters in the text input mode.
☐ Press [9] three times; *999* appears before the *m*.

> The vi history
> The vi editor is an interactive text editor that is supported by <u>m</u>ost of the UNIX operating systems.

> The vi history
> The vi editor is an interactive text editor that is supported by 999<u>m</u>ost of the UNIX operating systems.

The cursor remains on the letter *m*, and the vi editor remains in text input mode until you press [Esc] to return to command mode.

Do the following things to experiment with [I]:

☐ Press [I]; vi enters in the text input mode and moves the cursor to the beginning of the current line.
☐ Press [9] three times; *999* appears at the beginning of the current line, and the cursor moves to the *T*.

> The vi history
> The vi editor is an interactive text editor that is supported by <u>m</u>ost of the UNIX operating systems.

> The vi history
> 999<u>T</u>he vi editor is an interactive text editor that is supported by most of the UNIX operating systems.

The cursor remains on the *T*, and the vi editor remains in text input mode until you press [Esc] to return to command mode.

Adding Text: Using [a] or [A]

Pressing [a] or [A] places the vi editor in text input mode. However, each puts you in a different place in the file: pressing [a] places the text you enter after the cursor position, and pressing [A] adds the text you enter to the end of the current line. Do the following things to experiment with [a]:

◻ Press [a]; vi enters in the text input mode, and the cursor moves to the *o*, the next letter on the right.
◻ Press [9] three times; *999* appears after the *m*.

> The vi history
> The vi editor is an interactive text editor that is supported by most of the
> UNIX operating systems.

> The vi history
> The vi editor is an interacive text editor that is supported by m999ost of the
> UNIX operating systems.

The cursor remains on the *o*, and the vi editor is in the text input mode until you press [Esc] to return to the command mode.

Do the following things to experiment with [A]:

◻ Press [A]; the vi editor enters in text input mode, and the cursor moves to the end of the current line.
◻ Press [9] three times; *999* appears after the *e* of the word *the*, the last character on the current line.

> The vi history
> The vi editor is an interactive text editor that is supported by most of the
> UNIX operating systems.

> The vi history
> The vi editor is an interactive text editor that is supported by most of the999
> UNIX operating systems.

The cursor moves to the end of the line, and the vi editor remains in text input mode until you press [Esc] to return to the command mode.

Opening a Line: Using [o] or [O]

Pressing [o] or [O] places the vi editor in text input mode. Pressing [o] opens a blank line above the current line, and pressing [O] opens a blank line bellow the current line. Do the following things to experiment with [o]:

□ Press [o]; the vi editor enters in text input mode, opens a line below the current line, and moves the cursor to the beginning of the line.

□ Press [9] three times; *999* appears on the new line.

> The vi history
> The vi editor is an interactive text editor that is supported by most of the
> UNIX operating systems.

> The vi history
> The vi editor is an interactive text editor that is supported by most of the
> 999_
> UNIX operating systems.

The cursor moves to the end of the new line, and the vi editor remains in text input mode until you press [Esc] to return to command mode.

Do the following things to experiment with [O]:

□ Press [O]; the vi editor enters in text input mode, opens a line above the current line, and moves the cursor to the beginning of the line.

□ Press [9] three times; *999* appears on the new line.

> The vi history
> The vi editor is an interactive text editor that is supported by most of the
> UNIX operating systems.

> The vi history
> 999_
> The vi editor is an interactive text editor that is supported by the most of the
> UNIX operating systems.

The cursor moves to the end of the new line, and the vi editor remains in text input mode until you press [Esc] to return to command mode.

 Avoid the use of the arrow keys in text input mode. On some systems, the arrow keys are interpreted as regular ASCII characters, and their ASCII codes are inserted into your file.

Using [Spacebar], [Tab], [Back Space] and [Return]

While in text input mode, the vi editor displays on the screen the letters you type, but not all keys on the keyboard produce a displayable character. For example, when you press [Return], you intend to move the cursor to the next line, and you do not expect to see a [Return] symbol on the screen. As you know by now, depending on the vi editor's mode, keys have different meanings. Consider the use of these keys in text input mode.

[Spacebar] and [Tab]   Pressing [Spacebar] always produces a space character before the cursor position. Pressing [Tab] usually produces eight spaces. The tab size is changeable and can be set up to any number of spaces. (See chapter 6.)

[Back Space]   Pressing [Back Space] moves the cursor one character to the left over the currently typed text.

[Return]   Pressing [Return] always opens a new line. Depending on the position of the cursor on the current line, it opens a line above or below the current line:

- If the cursor is at the end of the line or there is no text to the right of it, then pressing [Return] opens an empty line below the current line.
- If the cursor is on the very first character of the current line, then pressing [Return] opens an empty line above the current line.
- If the cursor is somewhere on the line with text to the right of it, then pressing [Return] splits the line, and the text on the right of the cursor moves to the new line.

 The above explanation applies only when the vi editor is in the text input mode.

4.3.3   Command Mode

When you start the vi editor, it enters command mode. If vi is in text input mode and you want to change to command mode, press [Esc]. To make sure vi is in command mode, you can press [Esc] twice. If you press [Esc] while the vi editor is in the command mode, nothing happens, and vi remains in the command mode.

Cursor Movement Keys

In order to delete text, correct text, or insert text, you need to move the cursor to the specific location on the screen. While in command mode, you use the arrow keys (cursor control keys) to move the cursor around on the screen. On some terminals, the arrow keys do not work as explained or are not available. In these cases, you can use the [h], [j], [k], and [l] letter keys to move the cursor left, down, right, and up, respectively. Pressing any of the cursor movement keys moves the cursor position one space, one word, or one line at a time.

Table 4–3 summarizes the cursor movements keys and their applications. Each key application is explained in the examples and the terminal sessions. Figure 4–4 shows the effect of these cursor movement keys on the screen.

[j] and [k]   The [j] or [Down Arrow] key moves the cursor one line down to the same position as it was on the previous line. The [k] or [Up Arrow] key moves the cursor one line up. When there is no line below the current line (end of the file), or the current line is the first line (top of the file), then you hear a beep, and the cursor remains on the current line. These keys do not wrap around.

Table 4–3
vi's cursor movement keys.

Key	Operation
[h] or [Left Arrow]	Moves the cursor position one space to the left.
[j] or[Down Arrow]	Moves the cursor position one line down.
[k] or [Up Arrow]	Moves the cursor position one line up.
[l]or [Right Arrow]	Moves the cursor position one space to the right.
[$]	Moves the cursor position to the end of the current line.
[w]	Moves the cursor position forward one word.
[b]	Moves the cursor position back one word.
[e]	Moves the cursor position to the end of the word.
[0] (zero)	Moves the cursor position to the beginning of the current line.
[Return]	Moves the cursor position to the beginning of the next line.
[Spacebar]	Moves the cursor position one space to the right.
[Back Space]	Moves the cursor position one space to the left.

Figure 4.4
The movement of the cursor on the screen.

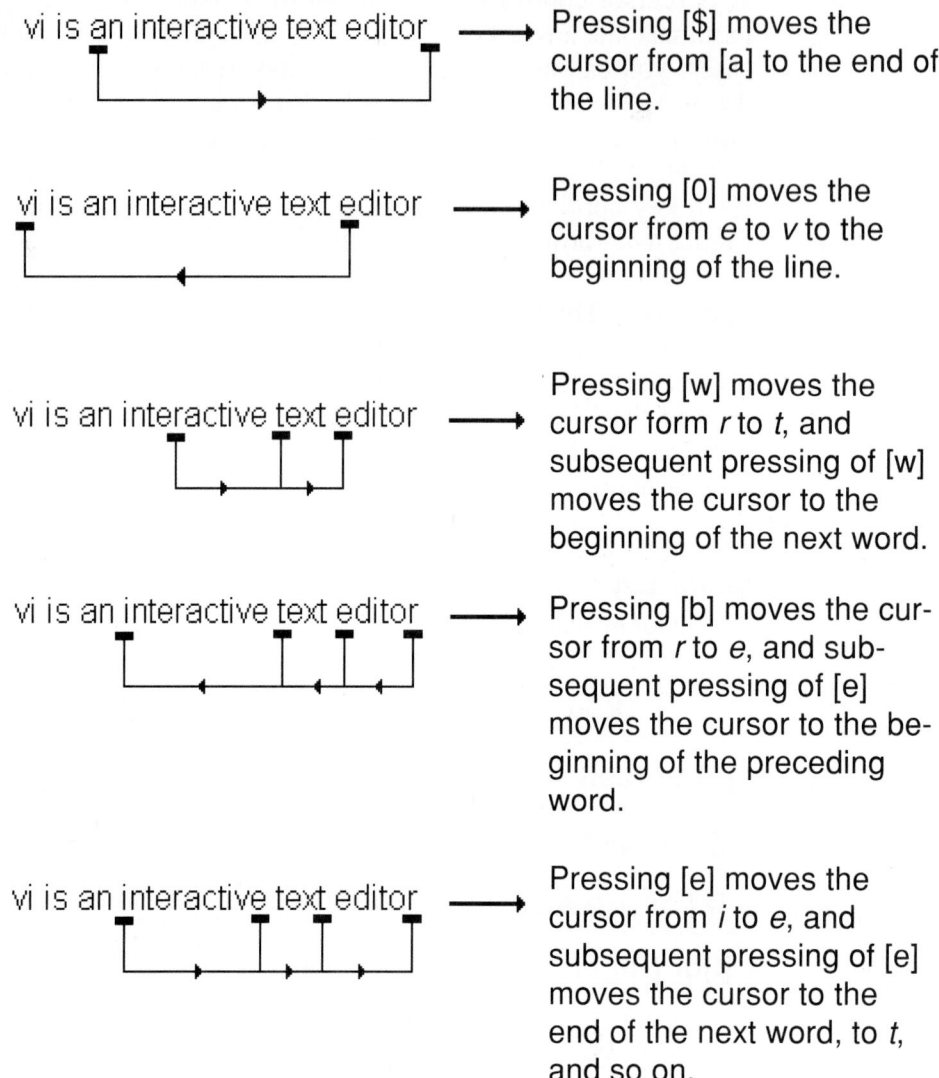

Pressing [$] moves the cursor from [a] to the end of the line.

Pressing [0] moves the cursor from *e* to *v* to the beginning of the line.

Pressing [w] moves the cursor form *r* to *t*, and subsequent pressing of [w] moves the cursor to the beginning of the next word.

Pressing [b] moves the cursor from *r* to *e*, and subsequent pressing of [e] moves the cursor to the beginning of the preceding word.

Pressing [e] moves the cursor from *i* to *e*, and subsequent pressing of [e] moves the cursor to the end of the next word, to *t*, and so on.

[h] and [l]   Each time you press the [h] or [Left Arrow] key, the cursor moves one character to the left until it is on the first character of the current line; then it beeps, indicating it cannot move farther to the left. The [l] (lowercase L) or [Right Arrow] key moves the cursor to the right in the similar manner. These keys do not wrap around.

[$] and [0]   Pressing [$] moves the cursor to the end of the current line. This key cannot be repeated; when the cursor is at the end of the line, pressing [$] does not change anything. Pressing [0] (zero) moves the cursor to the beginning of the current line in a similar manner.

Table 4–4
The vi editor keys for correcting text.

Key	Option
[x]	Deletes the character specified by the cursor position.
[d][d]	Deletes the line specified by the cursor position.
[u]	Undoes the most recent change.
[U]	Undoes all the changes on the current line.
[r]	Replaces a character that the cursor is on.
[R]	Replaces characters starting from he cursor position. Also enters in the text mode.
[.]　(dot)	Repeats the last text changes.

[w], [b], and [e]　Each time you press [w], the cursor moves to the beginning of the next word. Pressing [b] moves the cursor left (back) to the beginning of the preceding word, and pressing [e] moves the cursor to the end of the word. These keys wrap around and, if necessary, move the cursor to the next line.

[Return]　Each time you press [Return], the cursor moves to the beginning of the next line below the current line, until you reach the end of the file.

Text Correction

While in command mode, you can replace (overwrite) characters, and delete characters, a line, or a number of lines. You can also recover from some of your mistakes by using the undo command. As the name implies, it disregards your most recent command. These text correcting commands apply only when vi is in command mode, and most of them do not change the vi mode. Table 4–4 summarizes the delete text keys and their applications.

Character Deletion: Using [x]

Suppose you have the myfirst file on the screen and want to correct some text in the file. The cursor is positioned on the letter *m* of the word *most*. Using [x], you can delete characters starting from the cursor position:

> The vi history
> The vi editor is an interactive text editor that is supported by m̲ost of the UNIX operating systems.

□ Press [x]. The vi editor deletes the *m*, and the cursor moves to *o*, the next letter to the right. The **vi** editor remains in command mode.

> The vi history
> The vi editor is an interactive text editor that is supported by o̲st of the
> UNIX operating systems.

□ Press [x] three more times. The vi editor deletes *o*, *s*, and *t*, respectively, as you press [x] repeatedly.

> The vi history
> The vi editor is an interactive text editor that is supported by ̲of the
> UNIX operating systems.

The vi editor remains in command mode and the cursor moves to the space before the *o*. If you want to delete more than one character in one command, you can use the **n[x]** command, where *n* is an integer immediately followed by the letter *x*. For example, the command **5x** deletes five characters starting from the cursor position.

The repeating factor can be used with other vi commands. For example, **dd** *deletes one line, and* **3dd** *deletes three lines.*

Deletion and Recovery: Using [d][d] and [u]

Using [d] twice you can delete a line, starting from the current line:

> The vi history
> The vi editor is an interactive text editor that is supported by m̲ost of the
> UNIX operating systems.

> **The vi history**
> U̲NIX operating systems.

□ Press [d] twice. The vi editor deletes the current line, regardless of the cursor position on the line.
□ The vi editor is in command mode, and the cursor moves to the beginning of the next line. Press [u], and the vi editor undoes your last delete.

> The vi history
> T̲he vi editor is an interactive text editor that is supported by most of the
> UNIX operating systems.

The vi editor remains in command mode, and the cursor moves to the beginning of the line. If you want to delete more than one line in one command, you can use the **n[d][d]** command where *n* is an integer number followed immediately by two presses of [d]. For example, the command **5dd** deletes five lines starting from the current line.

Text Replacement: Using [r], [R], and [U]

Using [r] or [R], you can replace a character, or characters, starting from the cursor position. However, pressing [R] puts the vi editor in text input mode, and you must press [Esc] to return to command mode.

To learn about [r], do the following:

☐ Press [r] to replace (overwrite) the character that cursor is on.
☐ Press [9]. The vi editor responds by changing the *m* to *9*. The vi editor remains in command mode, and the cursor stays on the same position.

> The vi history
> The vi editor is an interactive text editor that is supported by most of the
> UNIX operating systems.

> The vi history
> The vi editor is an interactive text editor that is supported by 9ost of the
> UNIX operating systems.

To learn about [R] and [U], do the following:

☐ Press [R] to replace the characters starting from the cursor position. The vi editor enters text input mode.
☐ Press [9] three times. The vi editor responds by adding *999* after the cursor position, overwriting *ost*. The **vi** editor remains in text input mode.

> The vi history
> The vi editor is an interactive text editor that is supported by 9999 of the
> UNIX operating systems.

☐ Press [Esc] to change to command mode.
☐ Press [U] to undo your changes on the current line.

The vi editor responds by restoring the current line to its previous state.

> The vi history
> The vi editor is an interactive text editor that is supported by most of the
> UNIX operating systems.

Pattern Search: Using [/] and [?]

The vi editor provides operators to search a file for a specified pattern. The forward slash [/] and question mark [?] are the keys used to search forward and backward, respectively, through your file. If you are editing a large file, you can also use these operators to position the cursor at a specific place in the file. For example, if you want to look for the word UNIX in your file, press [Esc] (to make sure vi is in command mode) and then type /**UNIX** and press [Return].

When you press [/], vi shows the / at the bottom of the screen and waits for the rest of the command. After you press [Return], the vi editor starts searching forward for the character string *UNIX* from the current position of the cursor. If the *UNIX* is present in your file, vi positions the cursor on the first occurrence of it.

You can move the cursor to the next occurrence by pressing [n] (for next). Every time you press [n], vi shows the next occurrence of the pattern you are searching for, until the vi editor reaches the end of the file; then it goes back to the beginning of the file and continues the process (it wraps around).

If you prefer to search backward through the file, type ?**UNIX** and press [Return]. The vi editor continues to search backward as long as you press [n] after each finding of the word *UNIX*.

Repeating of the Previous Change: Using [.]

The [.] (dot) key is used in command mode to repeat the most recent previous text changes. This feature is quite useful when you want to do a lot of repetitive changes in a file.

To experiment with [.], try the following:

☐ Press [d][d] to delete the current line.

> The vi history
> The vi editor is an interactive text editor that is supported by most of the
> UNIX operating systems.

> The vi history
> UNIX operating systems.

☐ Use the cursor movement keys to position the cursor on another line.

> The vi history
> ~
> ~
> ~

☐ Press [.]; the vi editor repeats the previous text change and deletes the current line. The cursor moves to the next line, and vi remains in command mode.

Leaving the vi Editor

There is only one way to enter **vi**, but there are several ways to leave it. The vi editor gives you a selection depending on what you intend to do with your file after editing. Table 4–5 summarizes the vi editor quit commands.

The :wq Command   Most of the time at the end of an editing session you use the **:wq** command, which saves the file and exits the vi editor. UNIX displays the $ prompt, indicating that the shell has returned. The **:ZZ** command (uppercase *z*) works just the same: it saves your file and quits the vi editor.

The :q Command   If you use the vi editor to look at the contents of a file without doing any editing, then the **:q** command exits the vi editor. However, if you have changed something in your file and use this command to exit, vi responds by showing the following message at the bottom line on the screen—a typical UNIX, terse message—and the vi editor remains on the screen:

    No write since last change (:q! overrides).

The :q! Command   If you change something in a file and then decide not to save the changes, use the **:q!** command to leave the vi editor. In this case, the original file remains intact and changes are abandoned.

The :w Command   Use the **:w** command to save your file periodically during the course of a long editing session; you do not want to lose your work accidentally. The **:w** command accepts a new file name to save your changes in a new file, if you do not want to write over the original file.

Table 4–5
The vi editor save and quit commands.

Key	Operation
[w][q]	Writes (saves) the contents of the buffer and quits the vi editor.
[w]	Writes (saves) the contents of the buffer but stays in the editor.
[q]	Quits the editor.
[q][!]	Quits the editor and abandons the contents of the buffer.
[Z][Z]	Writes (saves) the contents of the buffer and quits the vi editor.

Figure 4–5
The vi editor mode of operations.

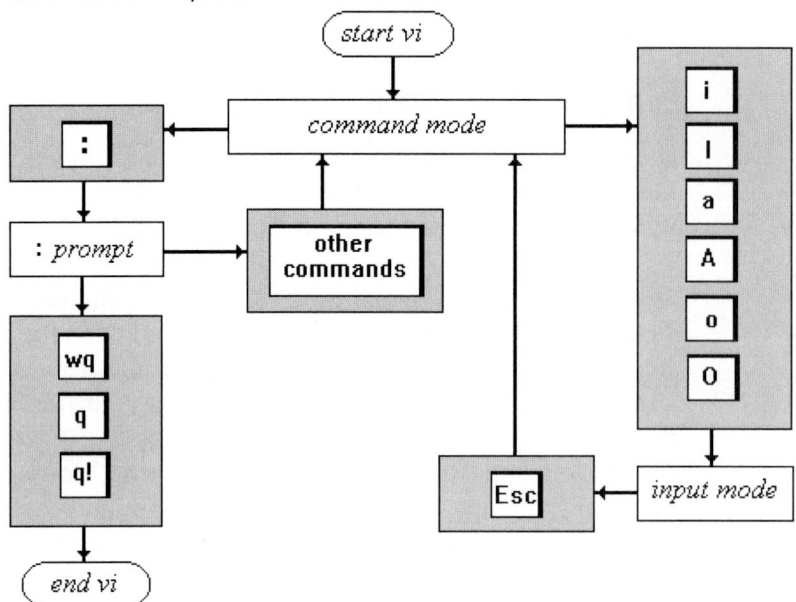

The ZZ Command   Use the **ZZ** (uppercase z) command for a quick save and exit the vi editor.

*The **ZZ** command is not preceded by [:], and you do not press [Return] to complete the command. Just **ZZ**, and the job is done.*

Figure 4–5 shows the vi editor modes of operation and the key sequences or commands that change vi mode from one mode to another.

1. Most of the commands just discussed start with [:].

2. Pressing [:] positions the cursor on the last line on the screen; then vi displays on the same line any key you press to complete the command.

3. Remember to press [Return] to signal the completion of a command.

4.4   THE MEMORY BUFFER

The vi editor creates a temporary workspace for a file that you want to create or modify. If you are creating a new file, vi opens a temporary workspace for your file. If the specified file is an existing file, vi copies the original file into temporary workspace and the changes you make are applied to that copy and not the original file. This temporary workspace is called a *buffer* or *work buffer*. The vi editor uses several other buffers to manage your file during an editing session. If you want to keep the changes you have made, you must save the altered file (the copy in the buffers) to replace the original file. Changes are not saved automatically; you save your file by issuing a write command.

When you open a file for editing, vi copies the file into a temporary buffer and displays the first 23 lines of the file on the screen. A window of 23 lines over the text in the buffer is what you see on the screen (see figure 4–6 A). By moving this window up and down over the buffer, vi displays other parts of the text. When you use the arrow keys or other commands to move the window down, say, to line 10, the first nine lines on the screen are scrolled out (disappearing from the screen) and you see lines 10 to 32 of the text (figure 4–6 B). Using arrow keys and other commands, you can move the window up or down over any portion of the file.

 You must remember to write (save) your changes before quitting the vi editor; otherwise, your changes are discarded.

Figure 4–6
The vi editor temporary buffer.

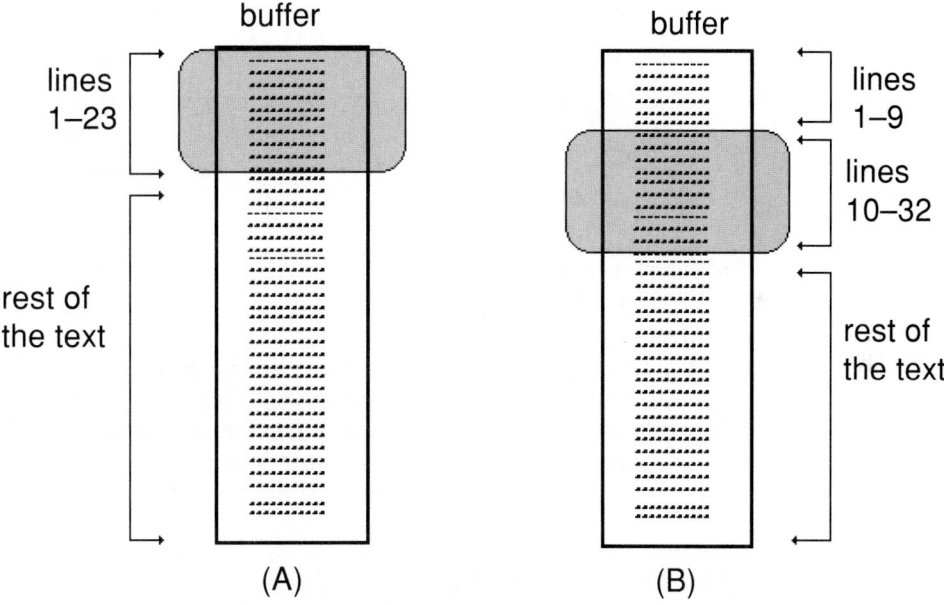

window of 23 lines over buffer

Command Summary

The following vi editor commands and operators were discussed in this chapter. To refresh your memory, figure 4–7 shows the vi editor mode of operation.

Figure 4–7
The vi editor mode of operations.

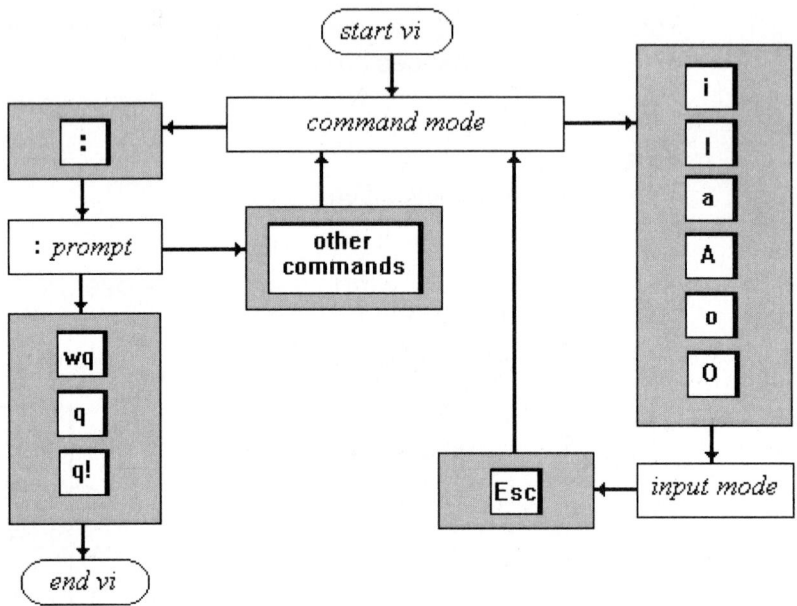

The vi editor
vi is a screen editor you can use to create files. vi has two modes: command mode, and text input mode. To start vi, type **vi**, press [Spacebar], and type the name of the file. Several keys place vi in text input mode, and [Esc] returns vi to the command mode.

The save and quit commands
With the exception of the ZZ command, the rest of these commands start with [:], and you must end your command line with [Return].

Key	Operation
[w][q]	Writes (saves) the contents of the buffer and quits the vi editor.
[w]	Writes (saves) the contents of the buffer but stays in the editor.
[q]	Quits the editor.
[q][!]	Quits the editor and abandons the contents of the buffer.
[Z][Z]	Writes (saves) the contents of the buffer and quits the vi editor.

Key	Operation
[h] or [Left Arrow]	Moves the cursor position one space to the left.
[j] or[Down Arrow]	Moves the cursor position one line down.
[k] or [Up Arrow]	Moves the cursor position one line up.
[l]or [Right Arrow]	Moves the cursor position one space to the right.
[$]	Moves the cursor position to the end of the current line.
[w]	Moves the cursor position forward one word.
[b]	Moves the cursor position back one word.
[e]	Moves the cursor position to the end of the word.
[0] (zero)	Moves the cursor position to the beginning of the current line.
[Return]	Moves the cursor position to the beginning of the next line.
[Spacebar]	Moves the cursor position one space to the right.
[Back Space]	Moves the cursor position one space to the left.

The change mode keys
These keys change vi from command mode to text input mode. Each key places vi in the text input mode in a different manner. [Esc] places vi in command mode.

Key	Operation
[i]	Places the text you enter before the character that the cursor is on.
[I]	Places the text you enter at the beginning of the current line.
[a]	Places the text you enter after the character that the cursor is on.
[A]	Places the text you enter after the last character of the current line.
[o]	Opens a blank line below the current line and places the cursor at the beginning of the new line.
[O]	Opens a blank line above the current line and places the cursor at the beginning of the new line.

Keys for correcting text
These keys are all applicable in command mode only.

Key	Operation
[x]	Deletes the character specified by the cursor position.
[d][d]	Deletes the line specified by the cursor position.
[u]	Undoes the most recent change.
[U]	Undoes all the changes on the current line.
[r]	Replaces a character that the cursor is on.
[R]	Replaces characters starting from he cursor position. Also enters in text mode.
[.]	Repeats the last text changes.

The search commands
These keys allow you to search forward or backward in your file for a pattern.

Key	Operation
[/]	Searches forward for a specified pattern.
[?]	Searches backward for a specified pattern.

Review Exercises

1. What is an editor?

2. What is a text formatter?

3. Name the editors that the UNIX operating system supports.

4. Name the vi modes.

5. Name the keys that place the vi editor in text input mode.

6. Explain how the vi editor uses buffers.

7. Name the command that saves your file and quits the vi editor.

8. Name the command that just saves your file and remains in the vi editor.

9. Name the key that places the vi editor in command mode.

10. Name the operator that deletes one line of text and the operator that deletes five lines of text.

11. Name the operator that deletes a character and the operator that deletes ten characters.

12. Name the key that repeats your most recent text change.

Terminal Session

In this terminal session, you create a small text file and practice the editing keys that vi provides. Use your imagination. Do not limit yourself to the small file in this exercise.

Try to use all the keys that are explained in this chapter.

1. Use the vi editor to create a file called **test** and type in the text shown on screen 1.

2. Save this file.

Screen No. 1

```
The vi history
The vi editor was developed at the University of california, berkeley
as part of the berkeley unix system.

~

~

"test" [new file ]
```

3. Open the test file again, and add text to make it to look like the text shown on screen 2.

4. Save this file again.

5. Open the text file once more and edit the text to make it to look like the text on screen 3.

Screen No. 2

> The vi history
> The vi editor was developed at the University of california
> berkeley as part of the berkeley unix system.
> At the beginning the vi editor was part of another editor
> The vi part of the ex editor was often used and became very.
> This popularity forced the developers to come up with a stand alone
> vi editor.
> now the vi editor is independent of the ex editor and is available on
> most of the UNIX operating system.
> The vi editor is a good editor for everyday editing jobs.

Screen No. 3

> The vi history
> The vi editor was developed at the University of California
> Berkeley as part of the Berkeley UNIX system.
> At the beginning the vi (visual) editor was part of the ex editor
> and you had to be in the ex editor to use the vi.
> The vi part of the ex editor was often used and became
> very popular. This popularity forced the developers to come up
> with a stand alone vi editor.
> Now the vi editor is independent of the ex editor and is available
> on most of the UNIX operating systems.
> The vi editor is a good, efficient editor for everyday editing jobs
> although it could have been more user friendly.
> ~
> ~
> ~
> ~

CHAPTER **5**

Introduction to the UNIX File System

This is the first of two chapters that discuss the file structure of the UNIX system; chapter 7 is the second. Chapter 5 describes the basic concepts of files and directories, and their arrangement in a hierarchical tree structure. It defines the terminology used in the UNIX file system. It discusses commands that facilitate the manipulation of the file system, explains the naming convention for files and directories, and shows a practical view of the file system and its associated commands (in terminal session exercises).

In This Chapter

5.1   DISK ORGANIZATION

The information a computer uses is stored in files. The memos you write, the programs you create, and the text you edit are all stored in files. But where are the files stored? How do you keep track of them? You give each file a name, and files are usually saved on a particular section of the disk. But considering the capacity of disks, how do you keep track of the whereabouts of the files on the disk? You divide your disk into smaller units and subunits, name each of them, and store related information in a particular unit.

UNIX follows the same idea in handling your disk. While you are working on a computer, the files you work with are stored in the computer's random access memory (RAM) or what in general is called *main memory*. UNIX uses RAM for short-term storage; your files are usually stored on hard disk for permanent, long-term storage. (Hard disk is the most common file storage media; however, you can store your files on other storage media such as floppy disks or tape.)

UNIX allows you to divide the disk into many units (called *directories*), and subunits (called *subdirectories*), thereby nesting directories within directories. UNIX provides commands to create, organize, and keep track of directories and files on disk.

5.2   FILE TYPES UNDER UNIX

For the UNIX operating system, a file is a sequence of bytes. UNIX does not support other structures (such as records or fields), as some other operating systems do. UNIX has three categories of files:

Regular Files   Regular files contain sequences of bytes that could be programming code, data, text, and so on. The files you create using the vi editor are regular files, and most of the files you manipulate are this type of file.

Directory Files   In most respects, a directory file is a file like any other file, and you name it as you name a file. However, it is not a standard ASCII text file. The directory file itself is a file that contains information (like filename) about other files. It consists of a number of records in a special format defined by your operating system.

Special Files   Special files (device files) contain specific information corresponding to peripheral devices such as printers, disks, and so on. UNIX treats I/O (input and output) devices as files, and every device in your system—the printer, floppy disk, terminal, and so on—has a separate file.

See page xxii for an explanation of icons used to highlight information in this chapter.

Figure 5–1
Directory structure.

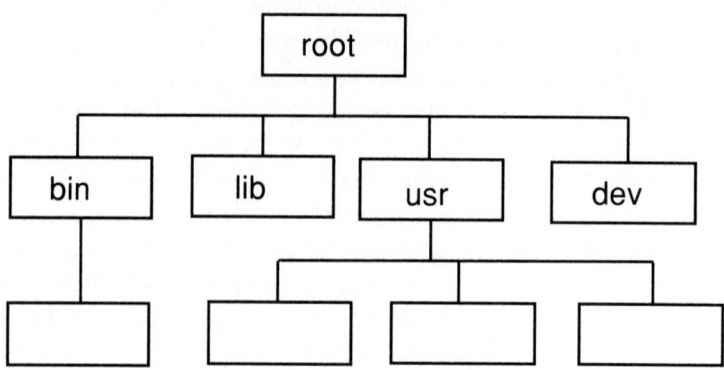

5.3   ALL ABOUT DIRECTORIES

Directories are the essential feature of the UNIX file system. The directory system provides the structure for organizing files on disk. To visualize a disk and its directory structure, think of your disk as a file cabinet. A file cabinet may have several drawers, which can be compared to disk directories. A drawer may be divided into several sections, which are comparable to subdirectories.

In UNIX, the directory structure is organized in levels; it is known as a hierarchical structure. This structure allows you to organize files so you can easily find any particular one. The highest level directory is called the *root* and all other directories branch directly or indirectly from it. Directories do not contain your information but instead provide a reference path to allow

Figure 5–2
Parents and child relationship.

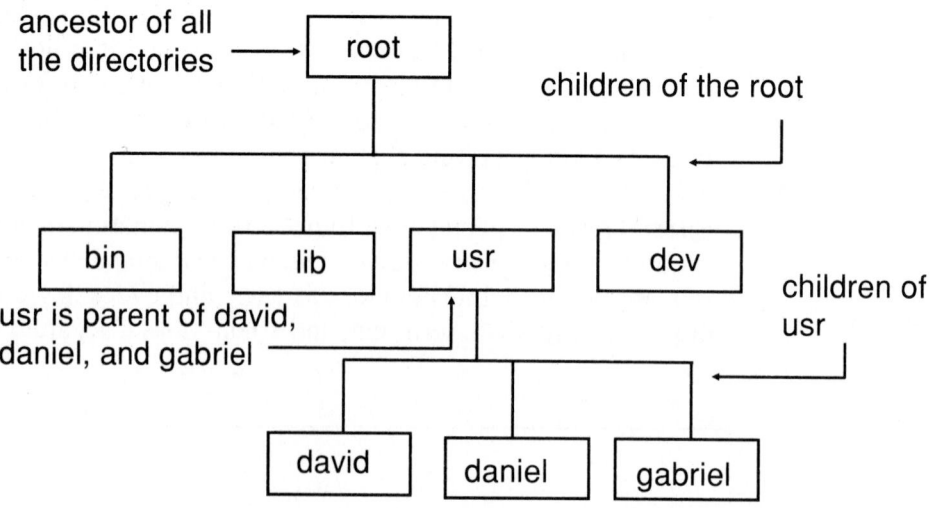

you to organize and find your files. Figure 5–1 shows the root and some other directories.

One example of hierarchical structure is your family's lineage tree. A couple may have a child, that child may have several children, and each of those children may have more children. The terms *parent* and *child* describe the relationship between levels of the hierarchy. Figure 5–2 shows this relationship. Only the root directory has no parents. It is the ancestor of all the other directories.

A hierarchical directory structure is often illustrated as a tree. The tree representing the file structure is usually pictured upside down, with its root at the top. Using this tree analogy, the tree's root represents the root directory, the branches the other directories, and the leaves are the files.

The Home Directory

The system administrator creates all user accounts on the system and associates each user account with a particular directory. This directory is the *home directory*. When you log on to the system, you are placed automatically into your home directory. From this single directory (your home directory), you can expand your directory structure according to your needs. You can add as many subdirectories as you like, and by dividing subdirectories into additional subdirectories, you can continue expanding your directory structure. Figure 5–3 shows that the directory called usr has three subdirectories called

Figure 5–3
Directories, subdirectories, and files.

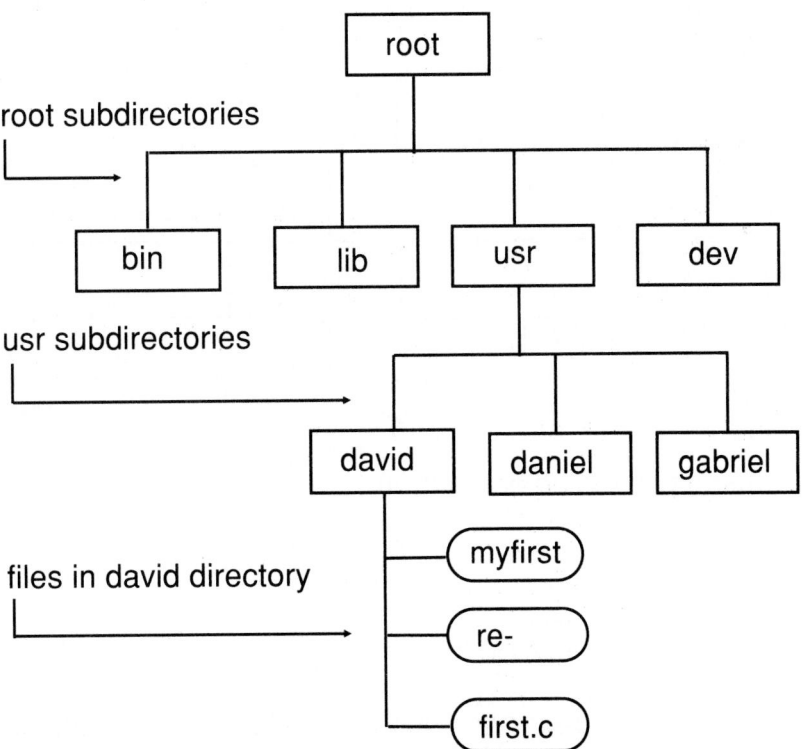

david, daniel, and gabriel. The directory david contains three files, but the other directories are empty.

1. *Figure 5–3 is not the standard UNIX file structure, and file structure setup varies from one installation to another.*

2. *Your login name and your home directory name are usually the same. Your login name and home directory are assigned by the system administrator.*

3. *The root directory is present in all UNIX file structures.*

4. *The name of the root directory is always the forward slash (/).*

The Working Directory

While you are working on the UNIX system, you are always associated with a directory. The directory you are associated with, or working in, is called the *working directory* or the *current directory*. Several commands allow you to view or change your working directory.

5.3.1   Understanding Paths and Pathnames

Every file has a pathname. The pathname locates the file in the file system. You determine a file's pathname by tracing a path from the root directory to the file, going through all intermediate directories. Figure 5–4 shows the hierarchy and

Figure 5–4
Pathnames in a directory structure.

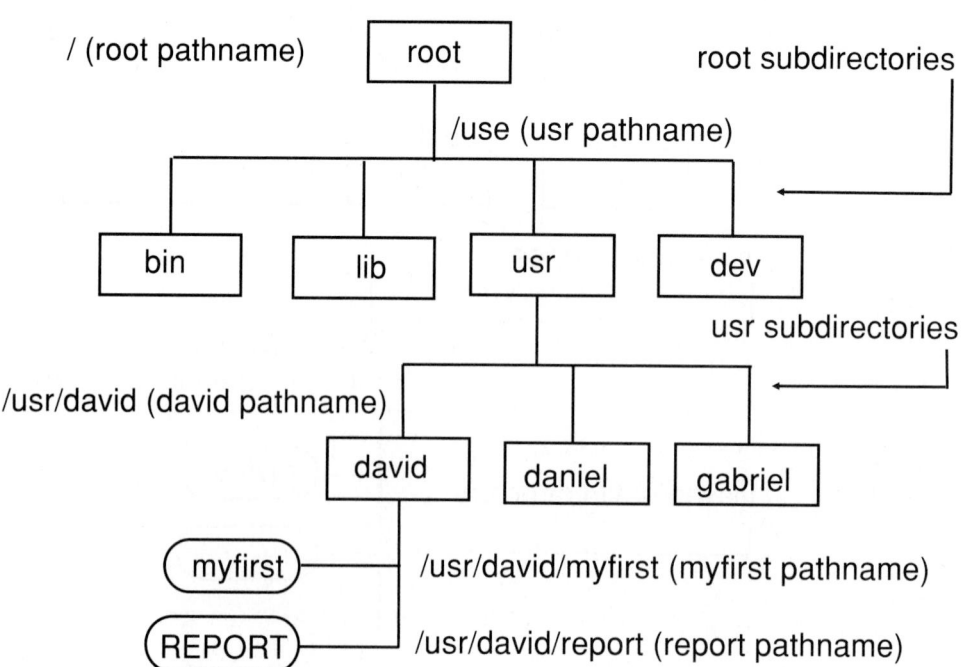

the pathnames of directories and files. For example, using figure 5–4, if your current directory is *root*, then the path to a file (say, myfirst) under the david directory is /usr/david/myfirst.

At the end of each path is an ordinary file (called *file*) or a directory file (called *directory*). Ordinary files are at the ends of paths and cannot have further directories; as in the tree analogy, a leaf cannot have branches. Directory files are the points in the structure that can support other paths, just as tree branches can have other branches.

1. *The forward slash (/) at the very beginning stands for the root directory.*

2. *The other slashes serve to separate the names of other directories and files.*

3. *Files in your working directory are immediately accessible. To access files in another directory you need to specify the particular file by its pathname.*

Absolute Pathname   An *absolute pathname* (full pathname) traces a path from the root to the file. An absolute pathname always begins with the name of the root directory, forward slash (/). For example, if your working directory is usr, the absolute pathname of the file called myfirst under the directory david is /usr/david/myfirst.

1. *Absolute pathname specifies exactly where to find a file, thus it can be used to specify file location in the working directory or any other directory.*

2. *Absolute pathnames always start from the root directory and therefore have a slash (/) at the beginning of the pathname.*

Relative Pathname   A *relative pathname* is a shorter form of the pathname. It traces a path from the working directory to a file. Like absolute pathname, relative pathname can describe a path through many directories. For example, if your working directory is usr, the relative pathname to the file called REPORT under the david directory is david/REPORT.

There is no initial slash (/) for a relative pathname. It always starts from your current directory.

5.3.2   Using File and Directory Names

Every ordinary and directory file has a filename. UNIX gives you much freedom in naming your files and directories. The maximum length of the filename depends on the UNIX version and system manufacturer. All UNIX systems allow a filename to be at least 14 characters, and most support much longer filenames, up to 255 characters.

You name a file using a combination of characters or numbers. The only exception is the root directory, which is always named / (forward slash) and referred to by this single character. No other file can use this name.

There are characters that have a special meaning to the shell you are using. If those characters are used in a filename, the shell interprets them as part of a command and acts on them. Although there are ways to override this interpretation of special characters, a better choice is to avoid using them. In particular, avoid using the following characters in file names:

```
< > . . . . . . . . . . . . . . . . less than and greater than signs
( ) . . . . . . . . . . . . . . . open and close parentheses
[ ] . . . . . . . . . . . . . . . . open and close brackets
{ } . . . . . . . . . . . . . . . . open and close braces
* . . . . . . . . . . . . . . . . asterisk or star
? . . . . . . . . . . . . . . . . question mark
" . . . . . . . . . . . . . . . . double quotation mark
' . . . . . . . . . . . . . . . . single quotation mark
- . . . . . . . . . . . . . . . . minus sign
$ . . . . . . . . . . . . . . . . dollar sign
^ . . . . . . . . . . . . . . . . caret
```

You avoid confusion if you choose characters from the following list:

```
uppercase letters . . . . . . . . . . (A–Z)
lowercase letters . . . . . . . . . . (a–z)
numbers . . . . . . . . . . . . . . . (0–9)
underscore . . . . . . . . . . . . . ( _ )
dot (period) . . . . . . . . . . . . . (.)
```

UNIX uses spaces to tell where one command or filename ends and another begins. Use a period or underline where you normally would use a space. For example, if you want to give a name MY NEW LIST to a file, you may call it MY_NEW_LIST or MY.NEW.LIST instead.

The filename you choose should mean something. Names like *junk*, *whoopee*, or *ddxx* are correct filenames but are poor choices because they do not help you recall what you stored in the file. Choose a name as descriptive as possible and associate the filename with the contents of the file. The following filenames have correct syntax and also convey information about the contents of the file:

```
REPORTS     Jan_list    my_memos
shopping.lis  Phones     edit.c
```

The UNIX operating system is case-sensitive: uppercase letters are distinguished from lowercase letters. You can use a mixture of uppercase and lowercase letters in any sequence within your filename. Keep in mind, however, that files named MY_FILE, My_File, and my_file are considered three different files.

UNIX makes no distinction between names that can be assigned to ordinary files and those that can be assigned to directory files. Hence, it is possible to have a directory and a file with the same name, for example, the found+lost directory could have a file in it called found+lost.

Referring to the parent and child analogy, like children of one parent, no two files in the same directory can have the same name. It makes good sense for parents to give their children different names, but in UNIX it is mandatory. However, like children of different parents, files in different directories can have the same names.

 You must avoid using spaces in any part of a filename.

Filename Extensions   The filename extension helps to further categorize and describe the contents of the file. Filename extensions are part of the filename following a period and in most cases are optional. Some programming language compilers, like C language, depend on a specific filename extension. (Compilers are explained in chapter 10.) In figure 5–5, first.c in the source directory with extension .c is a typical file extension for C programming language.

You can use several periods within the same filename. The following examples show some filenames with extension.

```
report.c        report.o
memo.04.10
(use of more than one period)
```

5.4   DIRECTORY COMMANDS

Now that you are familiar with some of the basic file concepts and definitions, it is time to learn to work with files and directories. The following examples and command sequences show the use of commands that let you manipulate your files and directories.

In the following examples, assume your login name is david, figure 5–5 is your directory structure, and your home directory is david.

5.4.1   Displaying Directory Pathname: The *pwd* Command

The **pwd** (print working directory) command displays the pathname of your working (current) directory. For example, when you first log in on a UNIX system, you are in your home directory. To display the pathname of your home directory, which at this point is also your working directory, you use the **pwd** command just after you log in.

 Log in and show the pathname of your home directory.

```
login: david [Return] ....... Enter your login name (say, david).

password: ............... Enter your password.

welcome to UNIX!

$ pwd [Return]. .......... Display your home directory path.

/usr/david

$ _ .................... Prompt for next command.
```

1. /usr/david is your home directory pathname.

2. /usr/david is also your current or working directory pathname.

3. /usr/david is an absolute pathname, because it begins with /, tracing the path of your home directory from the root.

4. david is your login name and your home directory name.

Locating a File in Your Working Directory   Your working directory is david, and figure 5–5 shows that you have five files plus a directory called source, which has one file in it. You want to locate the file called myfirst. The pathname for myfirst, which is in the david directory is /usr/david/myfirst. This is the absolute pathname to the file. However, when a file is in your working directory, you do not need a pathname to refer to it. The name of the file (in this case, myfirst) by itself is sufficient.

Locating a File in Another Directory   When a file is in a directory different from your working directory, you need to specify which directory the file is in. Suppose your working directory is usr. The pathname for the file called first.c in your source directory is david/source/first.c

david/source/first.c *is what is called a* relative pathname. *It does not start from the root directory.*

Figure 5–5
The directory structure used in examples.

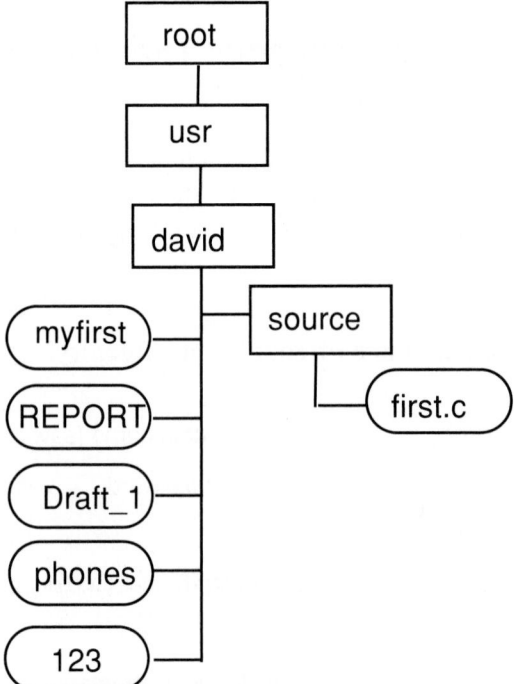

5.4.2　Changing Your Working Directory: The *cd* Command

You are not going to work in your home directory all the time. You are likely to change your working directory from one directory to another. The **cd** (change directory) command makes the specified directory your working directory.

To change your working directory to the source directory, do the following:

> **$ pwd [Return]**. . . . . Check your current directory.
>
> /usr/david
>
> **$ cd source [Return]** . . . . Changes to source directory.
>
> **$ pwd [Return]** . . . . Display your working directory.
>
> /usr/david/source

Assuming you have permission, change your working directory to daniel by doing the following:

> **$ cd /usr/daniel [Return]** . . . . Change to daniel directory.
>
> **$ pwd [Return]**. . . . . Check your working directory.
>
> /usr/daniel
>
> **$ _** . . . . Prompt for next command.

Returning to Your Home Directory　　When you have levels of directories and your working directory happens to be a few levels deep in the nested directory structure, then it is convenient to be able to return to your home directory without too much typing. You use the **cd** command with **$HOME** (a variable that holds your home directory pathname) as the directory name. You can also type just the **cd** command followed by [Return]; the default is your home directory.

Use the following command sequence to practice the use of the **cd** command:

> **$ cd $HOME [Return]** . . . . Return to home directory.
>
> **$ cd source [Return]** . . . . Change to source directory.
>
> **$ cd [Return]** . . . . No directory name is specified;
> default is your home directory.
>
> **$ pwd [Return]**. . . . . Check if you are in your home directory.
>
> /usr/david
>
> **$ cd xyz [Return]** . . . . Change to directory called xyz. It does not
> exist, so you get the following message:
>
> xyz: not a directory
>
> **$ _** . . . . Prompt for next command.

5.4.3 Creating Directories

The very first time you log on to the UNIX system, you begin work from your home directory, which is also your working directory. Probably no file or subdirectory exists in your home directory at this point, and you will want to build your own subdirectory system.

Advantages of Creating Directories

There are no restrictions on directory structure in UNIX; if you want to keep all your files under your home directory, you can. Although creating an effective directory structure takes some time, it also provides many advantages. Particularly when you have a large number of files, the advantages of creating a directory structure become apparent. The following lists some of the advantages of using directories:

* Grouping related files in one directory makes it easier to remember and access them.
* Displaying a shorter list of your files on the screen enables you to find a file more quickly.
* You can use identical file names for files that are stored in different directories.
* Directories make it feasible to share a large-capacity disk with other users (perhaps other students), with a well-defined space for each.
* You can take advantage of the UNIX commands that manipulate directories.

Figure 5–6
The directory structure used in examples.

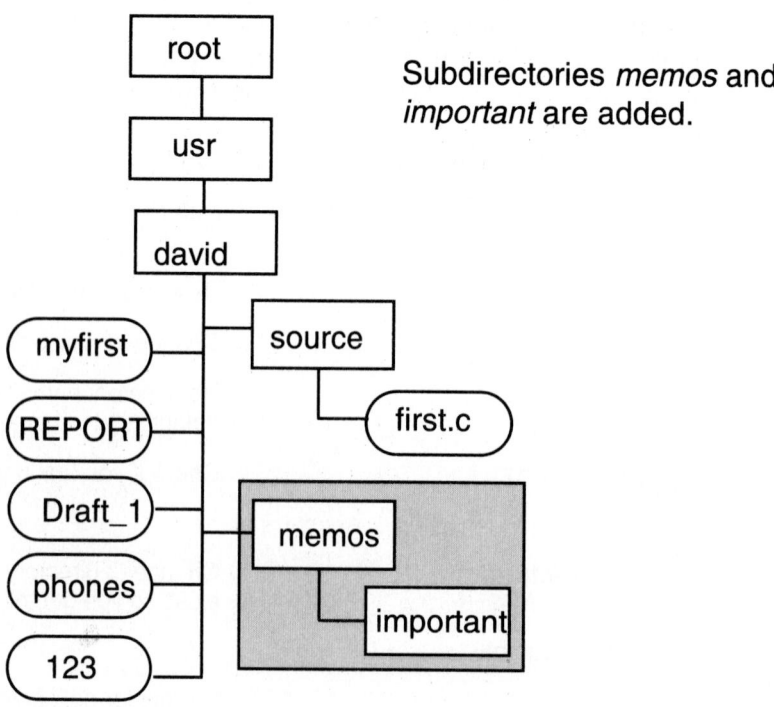

Subdirectories *memos* and *important* are added.

Using directories requires careful planning. If you logically group your files into manageable directories, your plan will pay off handsomely. If you haphazardly create and fill directories, then you may have difficulty finding your files or require more time to recognize them.

Directory Creation: The mkdir Command

The **mkdir** (make directory) command creates a new subdirectory under your working directory or any other directory you specify as part of the command. For example, the following command sequences show how to create subdirectories under your home or other directories. Figure 5–6 shows your directory structure after you add the new directories.

To create a directory called memos under your home directory, do the following:

$ **cd [Return]** . . . . Make sure you are in your home directory.

$ **mkdir memos [Return]** . . . . Create a directory called source.

$ **pwd [Return]** . . . . Check where you are.

/usr/david

$ **cd memos [Return]** . . . . Changes to new directory.

$ **pwd [Return]** . . . . Check where you are.

/usr/david/memos

$_ . . . . Your current directory is memos.

While you are in your home directory, create a new subdirectory called important in the memos directory.

$ **cd [Return]** . . . . Make sure you are in your home directory.

$ **mkdir memos/important [Return]** . . . Specify the new directory pathname.

$ **cd memos/important [Return]** . . . . . . Change to new directory.

$ **pwd [Return]** . . . . Check your working directory.

/usr/david/memos/important

$_ . . . . Now your working directory is important.

A directory structure can be created to your specific needs.

-p Option   You can create a whole directory structure using a single command line. You use the **-p** option to create levels of directories under your current directory. For example, suppose you want to create a directory structure three levels deep, starting in your home directory. The following command sequences shows how to do it, and figure 5–7 depicts the directory structure after these commands sequences are applied.

Figure 5–7
The directory structure used in examples.

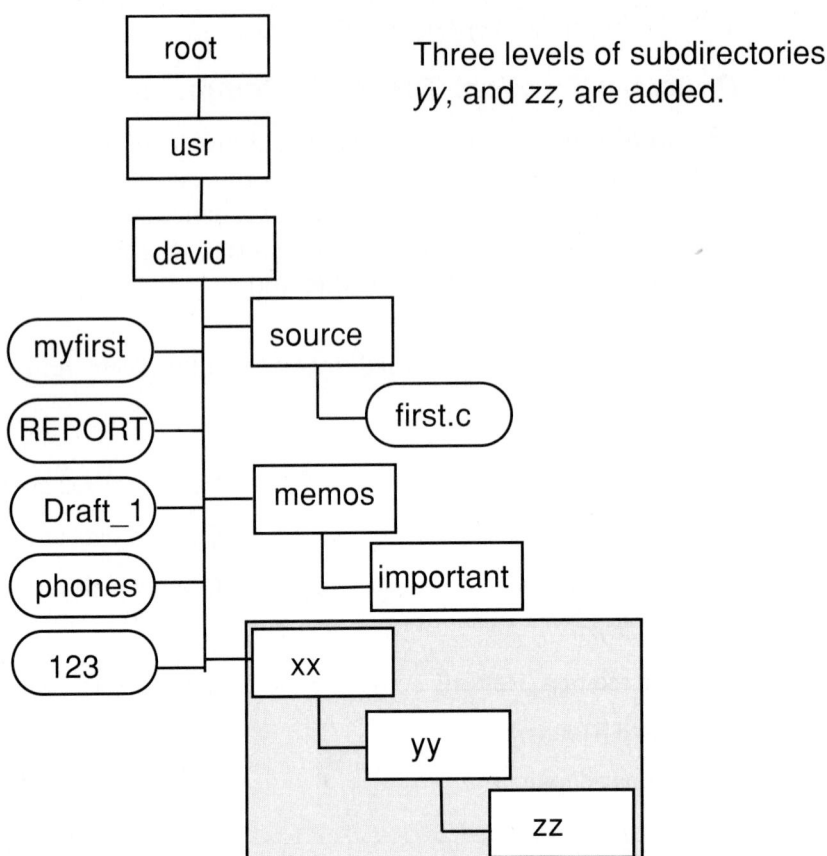

Three levels of subdirectories, *xx*, *yy*, and *zz,* are added.

   While in your home directory, create a directory structure with three levels by doing the following:

$ **cd [Return]** . . . . Make sure you are in home directory.

$ **mkdir -p xx/yy/zz [Return]** . . . . Create a directory called xx; in
                                                                     xx create a directory called yy, and in yy
                                                                     create a directory called zz.

$ _ . . . . Ready for next command.

1. The parent directory must be nonexistent. In the above example, you should not have a directory called zz in your current directory.

2. You do not have to be in the parent directory to create a subdirectory. As long as you give the pathname for the new directory, you can issue the command from any level of directories.

5.4.4 Removing Directories: The *rmdir* Command

Sometimes you find that you have no more use for a directory, or maybe you created a directory by mistake. In both cases, you want to remove the unwanted directory, and UNIX has the command for you!

The **rmdir** (remove directory) command removes (deletes) the specified directory. However, it only removes empty directories—directories that contain no other subdirectories or files other than the dot (.) and dot dot (..) directories (which are explained later in this chapter).

To remove the important directory in your memos directory, do the following:

$ **cd memos [Return]** . . . . Change your working directory to memos.

$ **pwd [Return]**. . . . . Make sure you are in memos.

/usr/david/memos

$_ . . . . Yes, you are.

$ **rmdir important [Return]** . . . . Remove the important directory.

$_ . . . . Ready for next command.

1. *The* important *subdirectory could be removed because it was an empty directory.*

2. *You must be in a parent directory to remove a subdirectory.*

From the david directory, try to remove the source subdirectory by doing the following:

$ **cd [Return]** . . . . Change to david directory.

$ **rmdir source [Return]** . . . . Remove the source directory.

rmdir: source: Directory not empty

$ **rmdir xyz [Return]** . . . . Remove a directory called xyz.

rmdir: xyz: Directory does not exist

$_ . . . . Ready for next command.

1. *You could not remove the* source *subdirectory because it was not an empty directory. Files are located in it.*

2. **rmdir** *returns an error message if you give a wrong directory name or if it cannot locate the directory name in the specified pathname.*

3. *You must be in the parent or higher level of directory to remove subdirectories (children).*

5.4.5   Listing Directories: The *ls* Command

The **ls** (list) command is used to display the contents of a specified directory. It lists the information in alphabetical order by file name, and the list includes both file names and directory names. When no directory is specified, the current directory is listed. If instead of a directory name a file name is specified, then **ls** shows the file name with any other information requested.

Figure 5–8 is used in examples and command sequences as the directory structure, and subsequent figures show the effect of the example commands on your files and directories. Please follow the figures for better understanding of the examples.

1. *Remember, a directory listing contains only the name of the files and subdirectories. Other commands let you read the contents of a file.*

2. *If no directory name is specified, the default is your current directory.*

3. *Filename does not indicate whether it is a file or a directory.*

4. *By default, the output is sorted alphabetically; numbers come before letters, and uppercase letters before lowercase letters.*

Figure 5–8
The directory structure used in examples.

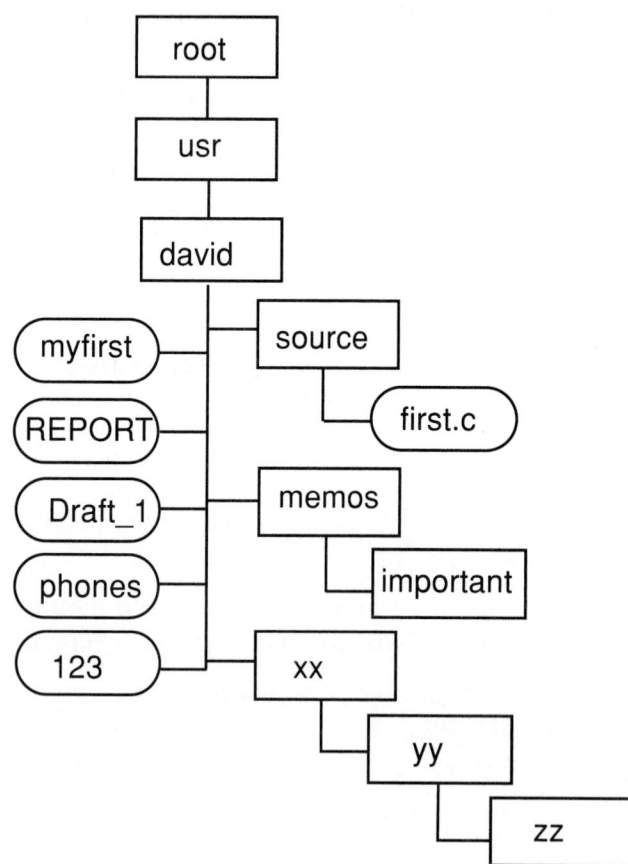

Assuming your current directory is david, show the contents of your home directory by typing **ls**. You may want to list the contents of directories other than your current directory. You can also list a single file to check whether it exists in the specified directory.

```
$ ls
123
Draft_1
REPORT
memos
myfirst
phones
source
xx
$ _
```

While in your home directory david, list files in the source directory by doing the following:

$ **cd [Return]** . . . . Make sure you are in the david directory.

$ **ls source [Return]** . . . . While in david, display list of files in the
                                      source directory.

first.c

$ _ . . . . Ready for next command.

While in your home directory check whether first.c exists in the source directory.

$ **ls source/first.c [Return]** . . Display the first.c filename in the source directory to
                                      see whether it exists. It does exist, so the filename is
                                      displayed.

first.c

$ **ls xyz [Return]** . . . . Display a file called xyz if it exists.
                                      It does not exist; you get the error message.

source/xyz: No such a file or directory

$ _ . . . . You get the prompt sign back.

ls Options   When you need more information about your files or you want the listing in a different format, use the **ls** command with options. These versatile options provide capabilities for listing your files in column format, showing a file's size, or distinguishing between files and directory names.

Table 5–1
The **ls** command options.

Option	Operation
-a	Lists all files, including the hidden files.
-C	Lists files in multicolumn format. Entries are sorted down the columns.
-F	Puts a slash (/) after each filename, if that file is a directory, and an asterisk (*) if it is an executable file.
-l	Lists files in a long format, showing detailed information about the files.
-m	Lists files across the page, separated by commas.
-p	Puts a slash (/) after each filename if it is a directory name, and an asterisk (*) if it is an executable file.
-r	Lists files in reverse alphabetic order.
-R	Recursively lists the contents of the subdirectories.
-s	Shows size of each file in blocks.
-x	Lists files in multicolumn format. Entries are sorted across the line.

Table 5–1 shows most of the **ls** command options. Let's use some of these options and observe their outputs on the screen.

1. *Every option letter is preceded by a hyphen.*

2. *There must be a space between the command name and the option.*

3. *You can use pathnames to list files in a directory other than your working directory.*

4. *You can use more than one option in a single command line.*

The most informative option is the **-l** (long format) option. The listing produced by the **ls** command and **-l** option shows one line for each file or subdirectory and displays several columns of information for each file.

List the files in your current directory in long format by doing the following:

☐ Type **cd** and press [Return]; then type **ls -l** and press [Return].

The first output line in figure 5–9 shows the total size of the displayed files. The size indicates the number of blocks, which is usually 512 bytes.

Figure 5–9

The **ls** command, and the **-l** option.

```
$ cd
$ ls -l
total 11
- rw- r– r–      1    david        student        1026    Jun 25   12:28    123
- rw- r– r–      1    david        student         684    Jun 25   12:20    Draft_1
- rw- r– r–      1    david        student         342    Jun 25   12:28    REPORT
drw- r– r–       1    david        student          48    Jun 25   12:28    memos
- rw- r– r–      1    david        student         342    Jun 25   12:28    myfirst
- rw- r– r–      1    david        student         342    Jun 25   12:28    phones
drw- r– r–       1    david        student          48    Jun 25   12:28    source
drw- r– r–       1    david        student          48    Jun 25   12:28    xx
$ _
```

Figure 5–10

The ls command long format.

1	2	3	4	5	6	7
- rwx rw----1		**david**	**student**	**342**	**Jun 25 12:28**	**myfirst**

Column 1 . . . . Consists of 10 characters. The first character indicates the file type and the rest indicate file access mode.

Column 2 . . . . Consists of a number indicating the number of the links.

Column 3 . . . . Indicates the owner's name.

Column 4 . . . . Indicates the group name.

Column 5 . . . . Indicates the size of the file in bytes.

Column 6 . . . . Shows the date and time of last modification.

Column 7 . . . . Shows the name of the file.

Figure 5–10 gives you a general idea about the columns. Look at each column and see what type of information it conveys.

File Type   The first column consists of 10 characters and the first character in each line indicates the type of file. The following summarizes the file types.

-	indicates an ordinary file
d	indicates a directory file
b	indicates a block oriented special (device) file, such as disks.
c	indicates a character oriented special (device) file, such as printers.

Table 5–2

The file's permission characters.

Key	Permission Settings
[r]	Read permission granted.
[w]	Write permission granted.
[x]	Execute permission granted (permission to run the file as a program).
[-] (hyphen)	Permission is not granted.

File Access Mode   The next 9 characters, which consist of three sets of the the letters *r, w, x,* and/or hyphens (-), describe the access mode of each file. They tell how every user in the system can access a particular file, and they are called *file access,* or *permission mode.* Within each set, the letters *r, w, x,* and hyphens (-) are interpreted as described in table 5–2.

1. *The execute permission (x) makes sense if the file is an executable file (a program).*

2. *If a hyphen appears instead of a letter, then the permission is denied.*

3. *If file is a directory file, then x is interpreted as permission to search the directory for a specific file.*

Each set of letters grants or denies permission to a different group of users. The first set of the *rwx* letters grants read, write, and execute permission to *owner* (user), the second *rwx* is for *group,* and the third one is for *others.* By setting the access letters for different groups of users, you can control who can have permission for your files and what type of access they have. For example, suppose you are in david directory, and you issue the following command:

$ ls -l myfirst [Return] . . . . List myfirst in long format.

- rwx rw----   1   david   student   342   Ju 25   12:28   myfirst

The output shows that myfirst is an ordinary file; the first letter is a hyphen. The first group of letters (rwx) means the *owner* has read, write and execute permission. The second group of letters (rw-) means the *group* has read and write permission, but execute permission is denied. The last three characters (---), three hyphens, show that *others* are denied all access rights.

Number of Links   The second column shows a number that indicates number of links. Links (ln command) is discussed in chapter 7. In our example the number of links for myfirst is 1.

File Owner   The third column shows the owner of the file. Usually this name is the same as user id of the person who created it, in this case, **david**.

File Group   The fourth column shows the user group. Every UNIX user has a user id and a group id. Both are assigned by the system administrator. For example, people who are working on a project get the same group id. In our example the file's group is **student**.

File Size   The fifth column shows the file size, this is the number of bytes (characters). In our example, the file size is 342 bytes.

Date and Time   The sixth column shows the date and time of the last modification. In our example, myfirst was last modified on Jun 25, 12:10.

Filename   The seventh column (finally) shows the name of the file, in our example, myfirst.

While you are in david, list the files in the source directory in long format by doing the following:

$ **cd [Return]** . . . . Make sure you are in your home directory.

$ **ls -l source [Return]** . . . . List files in source directory.

- rwx rw- - - -   1   david   student 342   Jun 25   12:28   first.c

$ _ . . . . Back to the prompt.

1.   *You are in your home directory, listing files in the* source *directory.*

2.   *You have only one file in the* source *directory.*

3.   *Your file,* first.c, *is an ordinary file, indicated by a hyphen (-).*

4.   *You have read, write, and execute permission (rwx). User group has read and write permission, indicated by (rw). The permission is denied to others, indicated by (--).*

5.   first.c *has one link.*

6.   *The owner name is **david**, and group name is **student**.*

7.   first.c *file is 342 bytes large.*

8.   first.c *was last modified on Jun 25 12:28.*

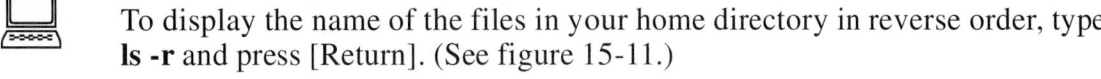

To display the name of the files in your home directory in reverse order, type **ls -r** and press [Return]. (See figure 15-11.)

Notice the option is the lowercase *r*.

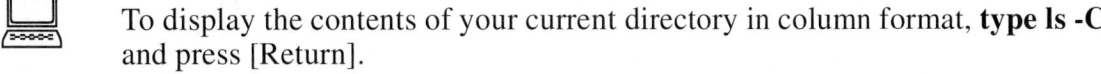

To display the contents of your current directory in column format, **type ls -C** and press [Return].

Figure 5–11
The **ls** command with the **-r** option.

```
$ ls -r
xx
source
memos
myfirst
phones
REPORT
Draft_1
123
$_
```

Figure 5–12
The **ls** command with the **-C** option.

```
$ ls -C]
123            Draft_1        REPORT        memos
myfirst        phones         source        xx
$ _
```

The columns are alphabetically sorted across the screen. (See figure 5–12.)

To display the contents of your current directory, separated by commas, type **ls -m** and press [Return]. (See figure 5–13.)

Figure 5–13
The **ls** command and the **-m** option.

```
$ ls -m
123, Draft_1, REPORT, memos, myfirst, phones, source, zz
$ _
```

Invisible Files

A filename beginning with a period is called an *invisible file*, or a *hidden file*, and directory listing commands normally do not display them. Startup files are usually invisible (named with the dot at the beginning) so that they do not clutter your directory. (Startup files are discussed in chapter 7.)

You can create your own invisible file in your home, or any other subdirectories you wish. Just start the file name with [.]. Two special invisible entries, a single and double dot (. and ..), appear in every directory except the root directory.

The . and .. Directory Entries   The **mkdir** (make directory) command automatically puts two entries in every directory you create. They are a single and double period, representing the current and one level higher directories respectively. Using the parent and child analogy, dot dot (**..**) represents the parent directory and dot (**.**) is the child directory.

These directory abbreviations can be used to refer to the parent and current directories in the UNIX commands when the pathname is required.

List all files in source, including the hidden files, by doing the following:

☐ Type **cd source** and press [Return] to change to the source directory.

☐ Type **ls -a** and press [Return] to list all files including the invisible files:

```
.

..
first.c
```

1.   At this point dot (.) means your current directory (/usr/david/source).

2.   At this point dot dot (..) means your parent directory (/usr/david).

Change your working directory to the parent directory, by doing the following:

$ cd .. [Return]. . . . . Change to the parent directory (/usr/david).

$ pwd [Return]. . . . . Check where you are.

/usr/david

$_ . . . . Prompt is back, and you are in /usr/david directory.

1.   At this point, the dot (.) represents the current directory which is (/usr/david).

2.   At this point the dot dot (..) represents the parent directory which is (/usr).

List the files in the parent directory of david, separated by commas, by doing the following:

$ cd [Return] . . . . Back to david.

$ **ls** **-m** **..** **[Return]** . . . . List the files in the parent directory of david, which
                                is usr; show filenames across the screen,
                                separated by commas.

david, daniel, gabriel

$_ . . . . Ready for the next command.

Using Multiple Options

You can use more than one option in a single command line. For example, if
you want to list all files, including invisible (**-a** option) files, in long format
(**-l** option), and filenames in reverse alphabetic order (**-r** option), you type
ls -mar or **ls -m -a -r** and press [Return].

1. *You can use one hyphen to start options, but no space between the
    option letters.*

2. *The sequence of the option letters in the command line is not important.*

3. *You can use one hyphen for each option, but there must be a space
    between option letters.*

List your home directory across the screen and indicate each directory name
with a slash (/).

```
$ cd
$ ls  -m  -p
123, Draft_1, REPORT, memos/, myfirst, phones, source/, xx/
$_
```

*Two options are used, **-m** to produce filenames across the screen, and **-p** to
place a slash (/) at the end of the directories filenames.*

To show all filenames in reverse order, separated by commas, and to indicate
the directory files with a slash and executable files with an asterisk, do the
following:

```
$ cd
$ ls  -amF
./, ../, 123, Draft_1, REPORT, memos/, myfirst, phones, source/, xx/
$_
```

1. *Three options are used, **-a** to show hidden files, **-m** to produce filenames
    across the screen, and **-F** to indicate directories and executable files by
    placing a slash (/) or an asterisk at the end of the filenames respectively.*

2. *The two invisible files are directory files, indicated by the slash at the
    end of filenames.*

List all the files in your home directory, in column format, in reverse order.

```
$ ls -arC
xx          phones      memos         REPORT     123     .
source    myfirst       Draft_1                  .
$_
```

 List files in **david**, separated by commas, and show size of each file.

```
$ ls -s -m
total 11,  3 123,  2 Draft_1, 1  REPORT, 1  memos, 1  myfirst, 1  phones,
1 source, 1  xx
$_
```

1. *The first field (total 11) shows total size of files, usually in blocks of 512 bytes.*
2. *The option -s produces the file size; each file is at least 1 block (512 bytes), regardless of how small the file may be.*

 List all files (including hidden files) in **david** in column format and also show file sizes.

```
$ ls -a -x
total 13        3 123      1  memos 1 source
1 .             3 Draft_1 1  myfirst  1 xx
1 ..            1 REPORT         1  phones
$_
```

1. *The total size is 13 blocks, as the size of the two hidden files is added.*
2. *The -x option formats the columns in a slightly different manner than -C. Each column is alphabetically sorted.*

 Show the directory structure under **david** in column format.

```
$ cd
$ ls -R -C
123          Draft_1     REPORT    memos     myfirst      phones
source      xx
./memos:
./source:
first.c
./xx:
yy
./xx/yy
zz
./xx/yy/zz:
$_
```

The command's options are uppercase letters *R* and *C*.

1. *The **-R** option lists filenames in the current directory* **david**, *which has three subdirectories:* **memos**, **source**, *and* **xx**.

2. *Each subdirectory encountered is shown by its pathname followed by the (:) (./memos:), and then lists the files in that directory.*

3. *The pathnames are relative pathnames, starting with your current directory (the current directory sign is the dot at the beginning of the pathnames).*

5.5   DISPLAYING FILE CONTENTS

So far in this book you have learned file manipulation commands to scan directories to locate files and look at a list of filenames. What about looking at the content of a file? You can always print a file to obtain a hard copy of its contents, or use the vi editor to open a file and look at it on the screen. You can also use the **cat** command for this purpose.

You can use the **cat** (for concatenation) command to display a file (or files), to create files, and to join files. In this chapter, only the display capability of the **cat** command is discussed. For example, to display a file called myfirst, you type **cat myfirst** and press [Return].

If myfirst exists in your current directory (no pathname is specified, the default is your current directory), the **cat** command displays the contents of myfirst on the screen (standard output device). If you specify two filenames, then you see contents of the two files (one after another in the same sequence specified in the command line). For example, type **cat myfirst yourfirst** and press [Return] to display contents of two files, myfirst and yourfirst, on the screen.

If the file is long, all you see on the screen is the last 23 lines of the file; the rest of the lines scroll up before your eyes. Unless you are a fast reader, this is not much use. You can stop the scrolling process by pressing [Ctrl-s]. To continue scrolling, press [Ctrl-q].

It is rather inconvenient to look at contents of a file in this manner. Please be patient; the best is yet to come. UNIX has other commands that show a long file a page at a time.

 Every [Ctrl-s] must be canceled by a [Ctrl-q]. Otherwise the screen remains locked, and your input from the keyboard is ineffective.

5.6   PRINTING FILE CONTENTS

You can look at the contents of a file on the screen, using the vi editor or **cat** command. However, there are times when you want a paper copy of your file.

UNIX provides commands to send your file to the printer, gives you the status of your print job, and lets you cancel your print job if you change your mind. Lets investigate these commands.

5.6.1   Printing: The *lp* Command

The **lp** command sends a copy of a file to the printer for producing a hard (paper) copy of your file. For example, suppose you want to print the contents of the myfirst file, type **lp myfirst** and press [Return].

UNIX confirms your request by displaying the request id, similar to the following message:

> request id is lp1-8054 (1 file)

As always, there is a space between the command (**lp**) and the argument (filename).

If you specify a filename that does not exist, or that UNIX cannot locate, then **lp** returns a message like to the following:

> lp: can't access file "xyz"
> lp: request not accepted

You can specify several files on one command line.

> $ **lp myfirst REPORT phone [Return]** . . Print myfirst, REPORT, and phone files.
>
> request id is lp1-6877 (3 files)
>
> $_ . . . . Ready for the next command.

Table 5–3
The **lp** command options.

Option	Operation
-d	Prints on a specific printer.
-m	Sends mail to the user mailbox at completion of the the print request.
-n	Prints specified number of copies of the file.
-s	Suppresses feedback messages.
-t	Prints a specified title on the banner page of the output.
-w	Sends a message to the user's terminal after completion of the print request.

Only one banner page (first page) is produced for this request. However, each file is printed beginning at the top of a page.

Each print request is associated with an id number. You use the id number to refer to the print job, such as when you want to cancel a print request. Table 5–3 shows the options you can use to make your print request more specific.

-d *Option*   Your system may be hooked up to more than one printer. Use **-d** option to specify a particular printer. If the printer is not specified, the default printer (the system printer) is used.

The following command sequence shows an example of the **-d** option.

   $ lp -dlp2 myfirst [Return]. . . . . Print myfirst on lp2 printer.

   request id is lp2-6879 (1 file)

   $_ . . . . Ready for the next command.

The names of the printers are not standardized and are different from one installation to another.

There is no space between the option letter **-d** and the printer's name **lp2**.

-m *Option*   Upon normal completion of your print request, the **-m** option sends a mail to your mailbox. (Mail and mailbox are discussed in chapter 9.)

The following command sequence shows an example of the **-m** option.

   $ lp -m myfirst [Return] . . . . Print the myfirst file, and send mail at the
                                                   completion of the print request.

   request id is lp1-6869 (1 file)

   $_ . . . . Ready for the next command.

Upon completion of the print request, you receive mail similar to the following message in your mailbox.

   From LOGIN:
   printer request lp1-6869 has been printed on the printer lp1

-n *Option*   Use the **-n** option when you need more than one copy of your file to be printed. The default is one copy.

The following command sequence shows an example of the **-n** option.

$ **lp -n3 myfirst [Return]** . . . . Print 3 copies of myfirst on the
                                              default printer.

request id lp1-6889 (1 file)

$_ . . . . Ready for the next command.

-w Option   The **-w** option writes a message on your terminal after completion of the print request. If you are not logged in, it informs you by sending a
mail to your mailbox.

The following command sequence shows an example of the **-w** option.

$ **lp -w myfirst [Return]** . . . . Print myfirst, and show a message when
                                              job is done.

request id lp1-6872 (1 file)

$_ . . . . Ready for the next command.

Upon completion of the print job, the system usually beeps to draw your attention and displays a message similar to the following:

lp: printer request lp1-6872 has been printed on the printer lp1.

-t Option   The **-t** option prints the specified string on the banner page (first
page) of the output.——

The following command sequence shows an example of the **-t** option.

$ **lp -thello myfirst [Return]**. . . . . Print myfirst, and print "hello" on
                                              the banner page.

request id lp1-6889 (1 file)

$_ . . . . Ready for the next command.

5.6.2   Cancelling a Printing Request: The *cancel* Command

You use the **cancel** command to cancel unwanted printing requests. If you send
a wrong file to the printer or decide not to wait for a long printing job, then the
UNIX **cancel** command helps. To use the **cancel** command, you need to specify
the id of the printing job, which is provided by **lp**, or the printer name.

The following command sequences illustrate the use of the cancel command.

$ **lp myfirst [Return]** . . . . Print myfirst on the default printer.

request id lp1-6889 (1 file)

$_ . . . . Ready for the next command.

$ **cancel lp1-6889 [Return]** . . Cancel the specified printing request.

Request "lp1-6889" canceled

$_ . . . . Ready for the next command.

$ **cancel lp1 [Return]**. . . . . Cancel the current requests on the printer "lp1."

request "lp1-6889" canceled

$ **cancel lp1-85588 [Return]** . . . . Cancel the print request; wrong print request id; the system displays an error message.

cancel: request "lp1-85588" non-existent

$ **cancel lp1 [Return]**. . . . . Cancel the request that is currently on the printer "lp1"; if there is no printing job on the printer, the system informs you.

cancel: printer "lp1" was not busy

$_ . . . . Ready for the next command.

1. *Specifying printing request id cancels the printing job even if it is currently printing.*

2. *Specifying the printer name only cancels the request which is currently printing on the specified printer. Your other printing jobs in the queue will be printed*

3. *In both cases the printer is freed to print the next job request.*

5.6.3   Getting the Printer Status: The *lpstat* Command

You use the **lpstat** command to obtain information about printing requests and the status of the printers. You can use the **-d** option to find out the name of the default printer on your system.

Try the following command requests to practice use of this command:

$ **lp source/first.c [Return]** . . . . Print first.c in the source directory.

request id lp1-6877 (1 file)

$ **lp REPORT [Return]**. . . . . Print REPORT file on the default printer.

request id lp1-6878 (1 file)

$ **lpstat [Return]** . . . . Show status of the printing requests.

lp1-6877   student   4777   jun 11 10:50 on lp1
lp1-6877   student   4777   jun 11 10:50 on lp1

$ **cancel lp1-6877 [Return]** . . . . Cancel specified printing request.

request "pl1-6877" canceled

$ **lpstat -d [Return]** . . . . Show the name of the default printer.

system default destination: lp1

$ **cancel lp1 [Return]**. . . . . Cancel printing request that is currently printing.

 *If you do not have any printing request in the queue or currently printing on the printer, the **lpstat** does not show anything, and $ prompt is displayed.*

5.7 DELETING FILES

You know how to create files and directories. You know how to remove empty directories. But what if the directory is not empty? You must remove all the files and subdirectories. How do you remove (delete) files?

Use the **rm** (remove) command to delete files that you do not want to keep any more. You specify the filename to delete the file from your working directory, or specify pathname to the files you intend to delete if it is in another directory. Figure 5–14 shows how your directory structure looks after the files deletions.

Figure 5–14
The directory structure used in examples.

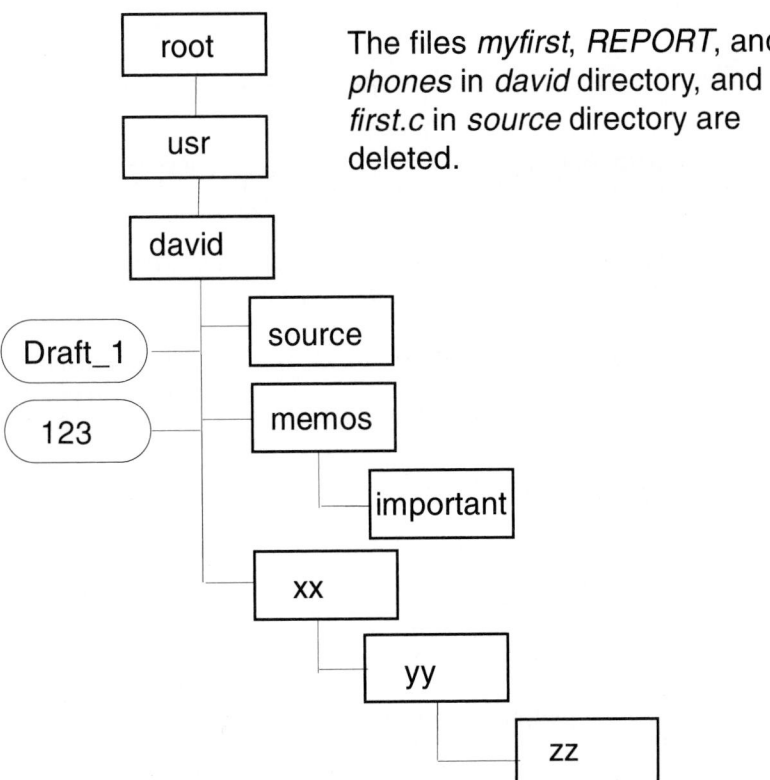

The files *myfirst*, *REPORT*, and *phones* in *david* directory, and *first.c* in *source* directory are deleted.

The following command sequences show how to use the **rm** command.

$ **cd [Return]** . . . . Change to your home directory.

$ **rm myfirst [Return]**. . . . . Delete myfirst from your home directory.

$ **rm REPORT phones [Return]** . . . . . . Delete 2 files, REPORT and phones.

$ **rm xyz [Return]**. . . . . Delete xyz; if file does not exist, the
system complains by showing an error
message.

rm: file not found

$_ . . . . Ready for next command.

The **rm** command does not give you any warning, and when a file is deleted, it
is deleted for good!

rm Options

Like most UNIX commands, **rm** has options. The **rm** options modify the capabilities of the **rm** command in opposite ways. Table 5–4 summarizes the **rm**
options.

-i Option   The **-i** option gives you more control over the delete operation. If
you use **-i** option, **rm** prompts you for confirmation before deleting each file.
You press [y] for yes, if you are sure you want to delete the specified file, or
[n], if you do not want to delete the file. This is the safest way to remove
files.

The following commands sequences show examples of using the **-i** option:

$ **pwd [Return]**. . . . . Check where you are.

/usr/david

$ **ls source [Return]** . . . . List files in the source directory.

first.c

$ **rm -i first.c [Return]** . . . . Delete first.c; the sytem displays the
confirmation prompt before deletio
Press [y] for yes.

Table 5–4
The **rm** command options.

Option	Operation
-i	Asks confirmation before deleting any file.
-r	Deletes the specified directory and every file and subdirectory in it.

Figure 5–15
The directory structure used in examples.

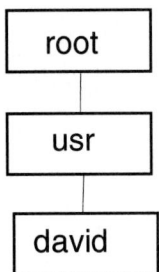

Everything under david, files and subdirectories, is deleted.

rm: remove first.c? **y**

$ **ls source [Return]** . . . . Check whether the file was deleted.

$_ . . . . No files in the source directory.

-r Option   The **-r** option deletes every file and all subdirectories in a directory. You can delete an entire directory structure using **rm** with **-r** option. Commands like this are what make UNIX an operating system for grownups!

Let's look at a command sequence using **-r** option. Figure 5–15 shows your directory structure afterward.

$ **cd [Return]** . . . . Change to home directory.

$ **rm -r [Return]** . . . . Remove all there is under david
                                                                    (home) directory.

$ **ls [Return]** . . . . List files in david.

$_ . . . . Sorry, nothing under david;
                                                                    they are all deleted.

1. *Use the* **-i** *option to get the confirmation prompt.*

2. *Use the* **-r** *option sparingly, and when it is absolutely necessary.*

3. *Use* **rmdir** *to remove directories.*

5.7.1   Before Removing Files

Under UNIX, deleting files and removing directories is quite easy. However, unlike other operating systems, UNIX does not give you any feedback or warning messages. Before you know it, files are deleted, and the remove command is irreversible. Thus before typing **rm**, consider the following points:

1. Make sure it is not 2 o'clock in the morning when you start a major delete operation.

2. Make sure you know what file you want to delete, and you know what the content of the file is.

3. Think twice before pressing [Return] to complete the command.

Command Summary

This chapter introduced the following UNIX commands.

pwd (print working directory)
Displays the pathname of your working directory, or any other directory you specify.

cd (change directory)
Changes your current directory to another directory.

ls (list)
Lists the contents of your current directory, or any directory you specify.

Option	Operation
-a	Lists all files, including the hidden files.
-C	Lists files in multicolumn format. Entries are sorted down the columns.
-F	Puts a slash (/) after each filename, if that file is a directory, and an asterisk (*) if it is an executable file.
-l	Lists files in a long format, showing detail information about the files.
-m	Lists files across the page, separated by commas.
-p	Puts a slash (/) after each filename if it is a directory name, and an asterisk (*) if it is an executable file.
-r	Lists files in reverse alphabetic order.
-R	Recursively lists the contents of the subdirectories .
-s	Shows size of each file in blocks.
-x	Lists files in multicolumn format. Entries are sorted across the line.

mkdir (make directory)
Creates a new directory in your working directory, or in any other directory you specify.

Option	Operation
-p	Lets you create levels of directories in a single command line.

lp (line printer)
Prints (provides hard copy) the specified file.

Option	Operation
-d	Prints on a specific printer.
-m	Sends mail to the user mailbox at completion of the the print request.
-n	Prints specified number of copies of the file.
-s	Suppresses feedback messages.

rm (remove)
Removes (deletes) files in your current directory, or any other directory you specify.

Option	Operation
-i	Asks confirmation before deleting any file.
-r	Deletes the specified directory and every file and subdirectory in it.

lpstat (line printer status)
Provides information about your printing request jobs, including printing request id number that you can use to cancel a printing request.

cancel (cancel print requests)
Lets you cancel print requests that are in queue waiting to be printed or are currently printing.

Review Exercises

1. What is the difference between a directory file and an ordinary file?

2. Can you use the / (slash) character in a filename?

3. What are the advantages of organizing your files in directories?

4. What is the difference between a relative and an absolute pathname?

5. Match the commands shown on the left column to the explanation shown on the right.

1. ls	a.	displays the contents of the xyz file on the screen.
2. pwd	b.	deletes the xyz file.
3. cd	c.	asks for confirmation before deleting a file.
4. mkdir xyz	d.	prints the xyz file on the default printer.
5. ls -l	e.	deletes the xyz directory.
6. cd ..	f.	cancels the printing jobs on the lp1 printer.
7. ls -a	g.	displays the status of the default printer.
8. cat xyz	h.	lists contents of the current directory.
9. lp xyz	i.	creates a directory xyz in the current directory.
10. rm xyz	j.	displays the pathname of the current directory.
11. rmdir xyz	k.	lists the current directory in long format.
12. cancel lp1	l.	changes the working directory to the parent of the current directory.
13. lpstat	m.	lists all files, including the invisible files.
14. rm -i	n.	changes the current directory to the home directory.

6. Determine which one of the following is an absolute pathname, relative pathname or a filename:

   a. REPORTS
   b. /use/david/temp
   c. david/temp
   d. .. (dot dot)
   e. my_first.c
   f. lists.01.07

Terminal Session

Log on to the system, and try the following commands. Observe the output and the command feedback (error messages and so on) on the screen.

Create a directory structure in your home directory, and try different commands until you feel comfortable with directories and files manipulation commands.

1. Show your current directory.

2. Change to your home directory.

3. Identify your home directory.

4. List contents of your current directory.

5. Create a new directory called xyz under your current directory.

6. Create a file called xyz in xyz directory

7. Identify the directories in your working directory.

8. Show the contents of your current directory:

    a. In reverse alphabetical order.
    b. In long format.
    c. In horizontal format.
    d. Show the invisible files in your current directory.

9. Print the xyz file in xyz directory.

10. Check the printer status.

11. Cancel the printing request.

12. Delete xyz in your xyz directory.

13. Delete the xyz directory in your current directory.

CHAPTER **6**

The vi Editor: Last Look

The discussion of the vi editor began in chapter 4 and continues in this chapter. Chapter 6 describes more of the vi editing power and flexibility, introducing more advanced commands. It explains the commands' scopes and their usage in combination with the other commands, discusses the vi editor's manipulation of temporary buffers, and shows some of the ways the vi editor can be customized to your needs. By the end of this chapter, you will be well equipped to use vi to do your editing jobs.

In This Chapter

6.1   MORE ABOUT THE vi EDITOR

The vi editor is part of the *ex family* of editors. vi is the screen-oriented part of the ex, and it is possible to switch between vi and ex editors. In fact, vi commands that start with [:] are ex editor commands. While in vi's command mode, pressing [:] displays the colon prompt at the bottom of the screen and causes vi to wait for your command. When you complete your command line by pressing [Return], ex executes the command and, upon completion, returns control to vi.

To change to the ex editor, type **:Q** and press [Return]. If you have intentionally or accidentally changed to ex editor, type **vi** to get back to the **vi** editor, or type **q** to exit the ex editor and return to the shell prompt.

6.1.1   Invoking the vi Editor

In chapter 4, you learned how to start vi, how to save a file, and how to quit vi. Expanding on those commands, let's explore other ways the vi editor can be invoked and ended.

You can start the vi editor without providing the file name. In this case, you use the write (**:w**) or write and quit (**:wq**) command to name your file.

The following command sequences show you how to do this:

- □ Type **vi** and press [Return] to invoke the vi editor without the file name.
- □ Type **:w myfirst** and press [Return] to save the contents of the temporary buffer into the myfirst file, and stay in the vi editor.
- □ Type **:wq myfirst** and press [Return] to save the contents of the temporary buffer into the myfirst file and quit the vi editor.

If your current editing file does not have a name and you type **:w** or **:wq** without giving a file name, vi displays the following message:

    No current filename

The vi editor normally prevents overwriting an existing file. Thus if you type **:w myfirst** and press [Return], and myfirst already exists, then vi warns you by showing the following message:

    "myfirst" File exists - use ": w! to overwrite "

If you want to overwrite an existing file, use the **:w!** command.

The write command (**:w**) is also useful if you want to save your file or part of it under another name and to keep the original file intact. The following command sequences show ways you can name a file or change the name of the current editing file.

- □ Type **vi myfirst** and press [Return] to invoke vi and copy the myfirst file into the temporary buffer.

See page xxii for an explanation of icons used to highlight information in this chapter.

□ Type **:w yourfirst** and press [Return] to save the contents of the temporary buffer (myfirst) into the yourfirst file. Your current editing file remains myfirst. The display shows this message:

"yourfirst" [New file] 3 lines, 106 characters

□ Type **:wq yourfirst** and press [Return] to save the temporary buffer into
the yourfirst file and quit the vi editor. The original myfirst file remains intact.

6.1.2   Using the vi Invocation Options

The vi editor provides flexibility from the very start. You can invoke vi with
certain invocation options that you type as part of the command line.

The Read-Only Option   The **-R** (for read-only) option makes a file a read-
only file and allows you to step through the contents of the file without risk-
ing accidental changes. To use this option with the myfirst file, type **vi -R
myfirst** and press [Return]. The vi editor shows the following message on the
bottom line of the screen:

"myfirst" [Read only] 3 lines, 106 characters

If you try to save the read-only file using the **:w** or the **:wq** command, vi displays the following message:

"myfirst" File is read only

The Command Option   The **-c** (for command) option allows you to give specific vi commands as part of the command line. This option is useful to position the cursor or search for a pattern in a file before you begin editing. To
use this option with the myfirst file, type **vi -c /most myfirst** and press [Re-
turn]. You are giving a search command (**/most**) as part of the command line.
The vi editor copies the myfirst file into the temporary work buffer and
places the cursor on the line with first occurrence of the word *most*.

6.1.3   Editing Multiple Files

You can start vi and give it a list of filenames instead of one filename. Then,
when you finish editing one file, you start the next file without reinvoking the vi
editor. You press [:][n] (for next) to invoke the next editing file. When you issue
the **:n** command, vi replaces the contents of the working buffer with text from
the next file. However, if you have modified the current text, vi displays a message like the following:

No write since last change (:next ! overrides)

You can use the **n!** command to override this protection. In this case, the
changes you have made in your current editing file are lost.

To see the list of the filenames, you use the **:ar** command. vi responds by showing the list of the filenames and also indicates the current editing filename.

The following command sequences show examples of specifying more than one filename in a command line.

☐ Type **vi file1 file2** and press [Return] to invoke vi with two editing files, file1 and file2; vi responds:

    2 files to edit
    "file1" 10 lines, 410 characters

☐ Type **:w** and press [Return] to save file1.

☐ Type **:ar** and press [Return] to display the names of the files. vi indicates the filename of the current file by enclosing it in brackets:

    [file1] file2

☐ Type **:n** and press [Return] to start file2 for editing; vi responds:

    "file2" 100 lines, 700 characters

Editing Another File   Another way to edit multiple files is to use the **:e** (for edit) command to switch to a new file. While in the vi editor, type **:e** followed by the name of the file and press [Return]. Usually, you save the current editing file before bringing in a new file, and unless you have made no changes, the vi editor warns you to write the current file before switching to the next file.

Try the following command sequences to experiment with changing files.

☐ Type **vi** and press [Return] to Tinvoke vi without specifying the filename.

☐ Type **:e myfirst** and press [Return] to call in the myfirst file. Your current editing file is myfirst; vi shows the name, and size of myfirst:

    "myfirst" 3 Lines, 106 characters

Reading Another File   The vi editor lets you read (import) a file into your current editing file. While in the vi editor command mode, type **:r** followed by name of the file and press [Return]. The **:r** command places a copy of the specified file into the buffer after the cursor position. The specified file becomes part of your current editing file.

Use the following command sequence to import (read) another file into your current working buffer.

☐ Type **vi myfirst** and press [Return] to invoke the vi editor and edit myfirst.

☐ Type **:r yourfirst** and press [Return] to add the contents of yourfirst to the current editing file. vi shows the name and size of the imported file:

"Yourfirst" 10 lines, 212 characters

The **:r** *command adds a copy of the specified file to your current editing file, and the specified file remains intact.*

Writing to Another File   The vi editor lets you write (save) a part of your current editing file into another file. You indicate the range of the lines you intend to save and use the **:w** command to write them. For example, if you want to save the text from line 5 to 100 into a file called temp, type **:5,100 w temp** and press [Return]. vi saves line 5 through 100 in a file called temp and shows a message similar to the following:

"temp" [New file] 96 lines, 670 characters

If the filename already exists, then vi displays an error message. Then you can give a new filename or use the **:w!** command to overwrite the existing file.

6.2   REARRANGING TEXT

Deleting, copying, moving, and changing text are collectively referred to as *cut-and-paste operations*. Table 6–1 summarizes the operators that are used in combination to rearrange text in a file and to do cut-and-paste operations. All of the commands are applicable when vi is in command mode. With the exception of the change command, after completion of the command the vi editor remains in the command mode. The change command places the vi in text input mode, which means that you must press [Esc] to return vi to command mode.

Assuming that you have the myfirst file on the screen and the cursor on the *m*, the following examples show the cut-and-paste applications.

Table 6–1
The vi editor cut and paste keys.

Key	Operation
[d]	Deletes a specified portion of the text and stores it in a temporary buffer. This buffer can be accessed by using the put operator.
[y]	Copies a specified portion of the text into a temporary buffer. This buffer can be accessed by using the put command.
[p]	Places the contents of a specified buffer above the cursor position.
[P]	Places the contents of a specified buffer below the cursor position.
[c]	Deletes text and places vi in text input mode. This is a combination of delete and insert operators.

6.2.1 Moving Lines: [d][d] and [p] or [P]

Using the *delete* and then the *put* keys, you can move text from one part of a file to another.

- Press [d][d]; vi deletes the current line, saves a copy of it in the temporary buffer, and cursor moves to the *U*.
- Press [p]; vi places the deleted line below the current line.

> The vi history
> The vi editor is a text editor which is supported by most of the
> UNIX operating systems.

> The vi history
> UNIX operating systems.

> The vi history
> UNIX operating systems.
> The vi editor is a text editor which is supported by most of the

- Use the cursor movement keys, and place the cursor on any character on the first line.
- Press [P]; vi places the deleted line above the current line.

> The vi editor is a text editor which is supported by most of the
> The vi history
> UNIX operating systems.
> The vi editor is a text editor which is supported by most of the

The deleted text remains in the temporary buffer, and you can move a copy of it to different places in the file.

6.2.2 Copying Lines: [y][y] and [p] or [P]

Using the *yank* and then the *put* operators, you can copy text from one part of the file to another.

- Press [y][y]; vi copies the current line into a temporary buffer.
- Use the cursor movement keys to place the cursor on the first line.

☐ Press [p]; vi copies the contents of the temporary buffer below the current line.

> The vi history
> The vi editor is a text editor which is supported by <u>m</u>ost of the
> UNIX operating systems.

> The vi history
> <u>T</u>he vi editor is a text editor which is supported by most of the
> The vi editor is a text editor which is supported by most of the
> UNIX operating systems.

☐ Use the cursor movement keys to move the cursor to the last line.
☐ Press [P]; vi copies the contents of the temporary buffer above the current line.

> The vi history
> The vi editor is a text editor which is supported by most of the
> The vi editor is a text editor which is supported by most of the
> <u>T</u>he vi editor is a text editor which is supported by most of the
> UNIX operating systems.

The copied text remains in the temporary buffer until the next delete or copy operation, and you can copy the contents of this buffer to anywhere in the file and as many times as you wish.

6.3   SCOPE OF THE vi OPERATORS

In chapter 4, you learned the basic vi commands; however, many vi commands operate on a block of text. A block of text can be a character, a word, a line, a sentence, or some other specified collection of characters. Using the vi commands in combination with the scope keys gives you more control over your editing task. The format for these type of commands can be represented this way:

    command = operator + scope

There is no specific scope key to indicate the entire line. In order to indicate the entire line as the scope of a command, you press the operator key twice. For example, [d][d] deletes a line and [y][y] yanks a line. Table 6–2 summarizes some of the common scopes used in combination with other commands.

The following examples demonstrate the use of the commands formed by the scope operators. To follow these examples, begin with the **myfirst** file on the screen. Using the delete, yank, and change operators on this file gives you a practical view of these commands.

Table 6–2
Some of the vi scope keys.

Scope	Operation
$	The scope is from the cursor position to the end of the current line.
0	(zero) The scope is from just before the cursor position to the beginning of the current line.
e	The scope is from the cursor position to the end of the current word.
b	The scope is from the letter before the cursor backward to the beginning of the current word.

6.3.1   Using the Delete Operator with Scope Keys

To delete text from the current cursor position to the end of the current line:

☐ Press [d][$]; vi deletes text starting from the cursor position to the end of the current line and moves the cursor to the space after the word *by*.

> The vi history
> vi is a text editor which is supported by <u>m</u>ost of the
> UNIX operating systems.

You can use [u] or [U] to undo your most recent text changes.

> The vi history
> vi is a text editor which is supported by_
> UNIX operating systems.

To delete to the beginning of the current line, press [d][0]; vi deletes text starting from the cursor position to the beginning of the current line, and cursor remains on the letter *m*.

> The vi history
> vi is a text editor which is supported by <u>m</u>ost of the
> UNIX operating systems.

> The vi history
> <u>m</u>ost of the
> UNIX operating systems.

To delete a word after the cursor position, press [d][w]; vi deletes the word *most* and the space after it, and moves the cursor to the letter *o*.

> The vi history
> vi is a text editor which is supported by m̲ost of the
> UNIX operating systems.

> The vi history
> vi is a text editor which is supported by o̲f the
> UNIX operating systems.

To delete more than one word after the cursor position (for example, three words), press [3][d][w]; vi deletes three words, *most*, *of*, and *the*, and the space after it, and moves the cursor to the space after word *by*.

> The vi history
> vi is a text editor which is supported by m̲ost of the
> UNIX operating systems.

> The vi history
> vi is a text editor which is supported by_
> UNIX operating systems.

To delete to the end of the word, press [d][e]; vi deletes the word *most* and moves the cursor to the space before the letter *o*.

> The vi history
> vi is a text editor which is supported by m̲ost of the
> UNIX operating systems.

> The vi history
> vi is a text editor which is supported by _of the
> UNIX operating systems.

To delete to the beginning of the pervious word, press [d][b]; vi deletes the word *by*, and the cursor remains on the space before the letter *o*.

> The vi history
> vi is a text editor which is supported _of the
> UNIX operating systems.

6.3.2   Using Yank Operator with Scope Keys

The yank operator can use the same scopes as the delete operator. The [p] operator is used to place the yanked text in other places in the file, showing what portion of the text is yanked using the scope keys.

To copy text from the current cursor position to the end of the current line, do the following:

☐ Press [y][$]; vi copies the text starting from the cursor position to the end of the current line to the temporary buffer.

☐ Use the cursor movement keys to move the cursor to the end of the last line.

☐ Press [p]; vi copies the yanked text right after the cursor position.

> The vi history
> vi is a text editor which is supported by m̲ost of the
> UNIX operating systems.

> The vi history
> vi is a text editor which is supported by most of the
> UNIX operating sytems.m̲ost of the

To copy text from the current cursor position to the beginning of the current line, do the following:

☐ Press [y][0]; vi copies the text starting from the cursor position to the beginning of the current line, and the   cursor remains on the letter *m*.

☐ Use the cursor movement keys to place the cursor on the letter *v* on the first line.

☐ Press [P]; vi copies the yanked text from the temporary buffer to right before the cursor position.

> The v̲i history
> vi is a text editor which is supported by most of the
> UNIX operating systems.

> The vi is a text editor which is supported by_vi history
> vi is a text editor which is supported by most of the
> UNIX operating systems.

6.3.3   Using Change Operator with Scope Keys

The change operator, [c], can use the same scope keys as delete and yank operators. The difference in the [c] operator's function is that it changes vi from command mode to text input mode. After pressing [c], you can enter text, beginning from the cursor position, and the text moves to the right. It wraps around when necessary to make room for the text you are entering. You return vi to command mode, as always, by pressing [Esc]. The change operator deletes the portion of the text indicated by the scope of the command and also places the vi editor in text input mode.

Some versions of the vi editor have a marker to mark the last character to be deleted. This marker is usually a dollar sign [$], which overwrites the last character to be deleted.

The following example shows how to use the change text operator with the scope key to change a word.

□ Press [c][w]; vi places a marker at the end of the current word, overwrites the letter *t*, and changes to text input mode. The cursor remains on the letter *m*, the first character scheduled for change.

□ Type **all** to change the word *most* to *all*.

□ Press [Esc] to return vi to command mode.

> The vi history
> vi is a text editor which is supported by <u>m</u>ost of the
> UNIX operating systems.

> The vi history
> vi is a text editor which is supported by <u>m</u>os$ of the
> UNIX operating systems.

> The vi history
> vi is a text editor which is supported by <u>a</u>ll$ of the
> UNIX operating systems.

6.4   USING BUFFERS IN vi

The vi editor has several buffers used for temporary storage. The temporary buffer (work buffer) that holds a copy of your file was discussed in chapter 3, and when you use the write command, the contents of this buffer is copied to a permanent file. There are two categories of temporary buffers, called *numbered buffers* and *named buffers* (or *alphabetic buffers*), that you can use for storing your changes and later retrieving them.

6.4.1   The Numbered Buffers

The vi editor uses nine temporary buffers numbered from 1 to 9. Every time you delete or yank text, it is placed in these temporary buffers, and you can access any of the buffers by specifying the buffer number. Each new deletion or yanking of the text replaces the pervious contents of these buffers. For example, when you give the [d][d] command, vi stores the deleted line in the buffer 1. When you use [d][d] again, to delete another line, vi bumps the old contents up one buffer, in this case to buffer 2, and then stores the new material in the buffer 1. This means that buffer 1 always holds the most recently changed material. The contents of the numbered buffers change every time you issue a delete or yank command. After a few text changes, of course, you lose track of what is stored in each of the numbered buffers. But keep on reading; the best is yet to come!

The contents of the numbered buffers can be recovered by using the put operator, prefixed with the buffer number. For example, to recover the material from buffer 9, you type **"9p**. The command **"9p** means copy the contents of the buffer 9 to where the cursor is. The format for specifying the buffer number can be presented as follows:

> double quotation mark + *n* (where *n* is the buffer number from 1 to 9) + ([p] or [P])

The temporary numbered buffers are depicted in figures 6–1 through 6–5. The examples explain the vi's sequence of events when you change text in the file.

 Assume that your screen looks like the screen in the figure 6–1, with five lines of text, and the numbered buffers are empty, as you have not yet done any editing operation.

☐ Position the cursor on the first line and use the delete command to delete the current line. The vi editor saves the deleted line in the buffer 1, and the screen and buffers look like figure 6–2.

Figure 6–1
The vi editor's nine numbered buffers.

```
AAAAAAAAAA                          ┌──────────────┐ 1
2222222222222                       └──────────────┘
BBBBBBBBBB                          ┌──────────────┐ 2
333333333333333                     └──────────────┘
CCCCCCCCCC                          ┌──────────────┐ 3
~                                   └──────────────┘
                                       ~   ~
                                         ~
                                    ┌──────────────┐
                                    └──────────────┘ 9
```

Figure 6–2
The screen and buffers after first delete.

□ Delete two lines, using the delete command. The vi editor responds by deleting the two lines from your text, and moves the contents of temporary buffers one buffer up, to empty buffer 1. Then it saves the deleted lines in buffer 1. The screen and buffers look like figure 6–3.

1. *The two lines deleted are saved in one buffer. The numbered buffers are not storage for a line but for any size of text you have changed, 1 line or 100 lines are saved in one buffer.*

2. *When all nine buffers are full, and vi needs buffer 1 for new material, the contents of buffer 9 are lost.*

□ The portion of the text that you yank is also saved in the temporary buffers. Place the cursor on the first line and then type **yy** and press [Return]. vi responds by copying the line you yanked into buffer 1. Remember that vi has to move all the buffers contents to the next buffer to empty buffer 1, and then the new material is copied into buffer 1. Refer to figure 6–4.

□ Now, if you remember what you have in the numbered buffers, you can have access to each of them by specifying its number as part of a

Figure 6–3
The screen and buffers after second delete.

Figure 6–4
The screen and buffers after yank.

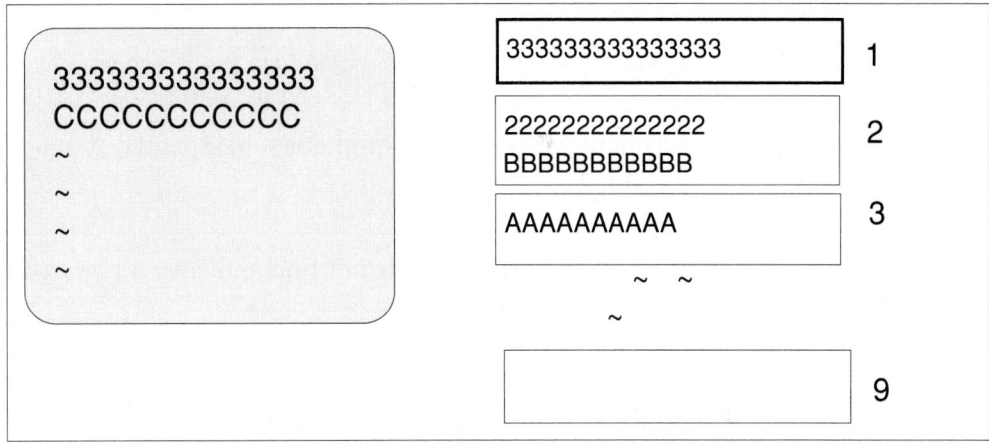

command. For example, to copy the contents of buffer 2 to the end of the file, type **"2p**, and vi copies the contents of buffer 2 to right after the cursor position. Figure 6–5 shows the screen and contents of the buffers after the put command.

Accessing the buffers does not change their contents.

6.4.2 The Alphabetic Buffers

The vi editor also uses 26 named buffers. These buffers are named from *a* through *z*, and you can refer to them by specifying their names explicitly. These buffers are similar to the numbered buffers, except the vi editor does not automatically change the contents of them every time you delete or yank from a file. It gives you more control over the operation. You can store deleted or copied text into a specified buffer, and later copy text from the named buffer to other places in your text, using the put operator. The text in a numbered buffer re-

Figure 6–5
The screen and buffers after put command.

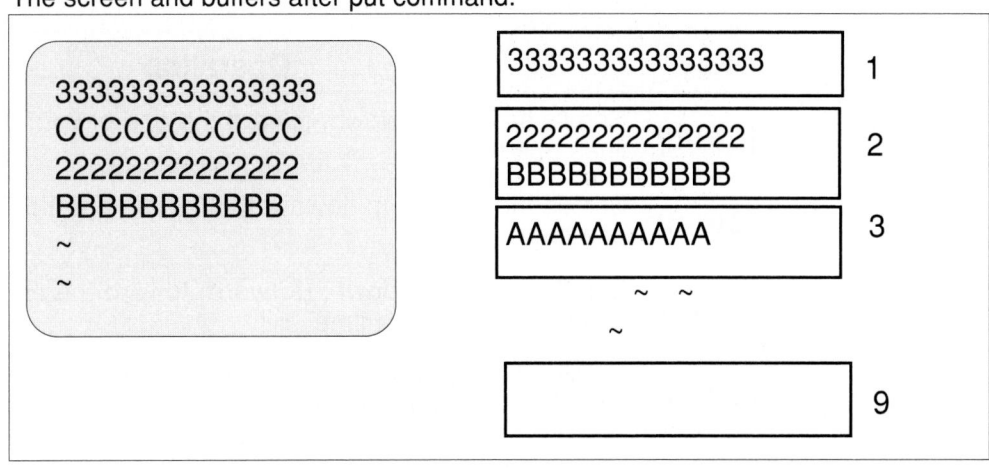

mains unchanged until you specify the buffer in a delete or yank operation. The format for specifying a specific buffer in your command can be presented as follows:

double quotation mark + buffer name (*a* to *z*) + the command

To experiment with using commands to specify a named buffer, do the following things:

☐ Type **"wdd** to delete the current line and save a copy of it in named buffer w.

☐ Type **"wp** to copy the contents of named buffer w to the location indicated by the cursor position.

☐ Type **"z7yy** to copy seven lines into named buffer z.

☐ Type **"zp** to copy the contents of named buffer z (7 lines) to the location indicated by the cursor position.

1. These commands are not displayed on the screen.

2. The alphabetic buffers are named in lowercase letters from *a* to *z*.

3. These commands do not require the [Return].

6.5   THE CURSOR POSITIONING KEYS

The screen displays 24 lines of text at a time, and if your file contains more than 24 lines, you use the cursor movement keys to scroll a new line up or down into view. If your file contains one thousand lines of text, to bring line 999 into view on the screen, you need about 999 key strokes. This is cumbersome and not practical. To overcome this problem, you use the vi editor's *paging operators*. Table 6–3 summarizes the paging operators and their capabilities.

Table 6–3
The vi's paging keys.

Key	Operation
[Ctrl-d]	Scrolls the cursor down, toward the end of your file, usually 12 lines at a time.
[Ctrl-u]	Scrolls the cursor up, toward the top of your file, usually 12 lines at a time.
[Ctrl-f]	Scrolls the cursor down, (forward) toward the end of your file, usually 24 lines at a time.
[Ctrl-b]	Scrolls the cursor up (backward), toward the top of your file, usually 24 lines at a time.

[Ctrl-d] means simultaneously holding down [Ctrl] and [d]; it is the same for other control keys.

Other Cursor Positioning Keys

If you have a really large file, even the scrolling commands are not practical to position the cursor. Another way to position the cursor is to use [G], prefixed with the line number on which you want to place the cursor.

 To make line number 1000 the current line, do the following:

☐ Type **1000G** to move the cursor to line 1000.
☐ Type **1G** to move the cursor to the first line.
☐ Type **G** to move the cursor to the end of the file.

Another useful command is [Ctrl-g], which tells you the line number of the current line. For example, if you press [Ctrl-g] while in command mode, the vi responds by showing a message similar to the following:

"myfirst" line 30 of 90 — 30%

6.6   CUSTOMIZING THE vi EDITOR

The vi editor has many parameters (they are also called *options* or *flags*) that you can set, enable, or disable to control your working environment. These parameters have default values but are adjustable, and they include things like the tab setting, the right margin setting, and so on.

In order to see on the screen the complete list of parameters and how they are currently set in your system, while in command mode type **:set all** and press [Return].

Your terminal screen shows options similar to figure 6–6. Your system may have other options set.

Figure 6–6
Screen showing vi's options.

```
  ~
  ~
  ~
  :set all
  noautoindent          number              terms=wyse50
  nobeautify            readonly            noterse
  hardtabs=8            reports=10          windows= 23
  noignorecase          shiftwidth= 8       wrapmargin= 0
  magic                 showmode
  [Hit return to continue]
```

6.6.1   The Options Formats

The set command is used to set the options, and the general format of the options falls into three categories, each set in a different manner:

- Boolean (toggle)
- numeric
- string

Assuming there is an option called X, the following examples show how to set up the three categories of options.

The Boolean Options

The *Boolean options* work like a toggle switch: you can turn them on or off. These options are set by typing the option name and are disabled by adding the word *no* in front of the option name. Typing **set X** enables option X, and typing **set noX** disables option X.

There is no space between the word <u>no</u> and the option's name.

The Numeric Options

The *numeric options* accept a numeric value, and depending on the option, the range of the numeric value is different. Typing **set X=12** assigns value 12 to option X.

The String Options

The *string options* are similar to the numeric options, but they accept a string value. Typing **set X=PP** assigns string PP to option X.

There is no space on either side of the equal sign.

The Set Command

The set command is used to set the different vi environment options, list them, or get the value of a specified option. The basic formats of the set command are as follows; each command is completed by pressing [Return]:

     :set all

shows all the options on the screen.

     :set

shows only the changed options.

     :set X?

shows the value of the option X.

6.6.2 Setting the vi Environment

The behavior of the vi editor can be customized by setting the edit parameters to new values, and there are different methods you can use to set them. The direct method of changing these values is to use the vi set command to set the values as desired. In this case, vi must be in the command mode before you can issue the set commands. You can set every option using this method; however, the changes are temporary, and they are in effect for your current editing session. When you quit the vi editor your options settings are abandoned.

This section describes some useful vi parameters (listed alphabetically), and table 6–4 summarizes these options. Most of the option names have abbreviations, and you can use the full or abbreviated names in the set command.

autoindent Option The *autoindent* (**ai**) *option* aligns each new line you type in text mode with the beginning of the pervious line. This option is useful for writing computer programs in C, Ada, or other structured programming languages. You use [Ctrl-d] to backspace one level of indentation; each [Ctrl-d]

Table 6–4
Some of the vi's environment options.

Option	Abbreviation	Operation
autoindent	**ai**	Aligns the new lines with the beginning of the previous ones.
ignorcase	**ic**	Ignores the uppercase, lowercase difference in search operations.
magic	-	Allows use of the special characters in search.
number	**nu**	Displays line number.
report	-	Informs you of the number of lines affected by your last command.
scroll	-	Sets number of lines to scroll when [Ctrl-d] command is given.
shiftwidth	**sw**	Sets number of spaces to indent. Used with autoindent option.
showmode	**smd**	Displays the vi editor modes on the right corner of the screen.
terse	-	Shortens the error messages.
wrapmargin	**wm**	Sets the right margin to the specified number of characters.

backs up the number of columns specified by the *shiftwidth* option. The default value for this option is set to **noai**.

ignorecase Option   The vi editor performs case-sensitive searches—i.e., it differentiates between uppercase and lowercase letters. In order to make the vi editor ignore the letter cases, type **:set ignorecase** and press [Return].

To restore vi to the case-sensitive search, type **:set noignorecase** and press [Return].

magic Option   Certain characters (like bracket pairs [ ]) have a special meaning when you use them in search strings. When you toggle this option to **nomagic**, these characters no longer have special meaning. Default for this option is **magic**.

number Option   The vi editor does not ordinarily display the line numbers associated with each line. There are occasions when you want to refer to a line by line number, and sometimes having the line numbers on the screen gives you a better feel for the size of a file and what part of the file you are editing. To display the line numbers, type **:set number** and press [Return].

When you decide you do not want the line numbers to be displayed, type **:set nonumber** and press [Return].

 The line numbers are not part of the file; they only appear on the screen while you are using the vi editor.

report Option   The vi editor does not give you any feedback on your editing job. For example, if you type **5dd**, vi deletes five lines starting from the current line but does not show any confirmation message on the screen. If you want to see feedback related to your editing, use the report parameter of the set command. This parameter is set to the number of lines that must be changed before the vi editor displays a report of the number of lines affected.

To set the report option to affect two-line edits, type **:set report=2** and press [Return]. Then if your editing job affects more than two lines, vi displays a report on the status line. For example, deleting two lines (**2dd**),or copying two lines (**2yy**) produces the following reports on the bottom line, respectively.

```
2 lines deleted
2 lines yanked
```

scroll Option   The *scroll option* is set to the number of lines that you want the screen to scroll when using [Ctrl-d]. For example, to have the screen scroll five lines, type **:set scroll=5** and press [Return].

shiftwidth Option   The *shiftwidth* (**sw**) *option* sets the number of spaces used by [Ctrl-d] key when the autoindent option is in effect. The default setting for this option is **sw=8**. To change the setting to 10, for example, type **:set sw=10** and press [Return].

***showmode* Option**   The vi editor does not display any visual feedback to indicate whether it is in text input mode or command mode. This can be confusing, especially for beginners. You can set the showmode option to provide the visual feedback on the screen.

To toggle on the showmode option, type: **:set showmode** and press [Return]. Then, depending on what key you use to change from command mode to text input mode, vi displays a different message at the lower right side of the screen. If you press [A] or [a] to change mode, vi displays APPEND MODE; if you press [I] or [i], vi shows INSERT MODE; and if you press [O] or [o], vi displays OPEN MODE, and so on.

These messages remain on the screen until you press [Esc] to change to command mode. When there is no message on the screen, vi is in command mode.

To turn off the showmode option, type **:set noshowmode** and press [Return].

***terse* Option**   The *terse option* makes the vi editor display shorter error messages. The default for this option is **noterse**.

6.6.3   Line Length and Wraparound

Your terminal screen usually has 80 columns. When you type text and reach the end of the line (pass the 80th column), the screen starts a new line; that is what is called *wraparound*. The screen also starts a new line when you press [Return]. Thus, the length of a line on the screen could be any length from 1 to 80 characters. However, the vi editor starts a new line in your file only when you press [Return]. If you type 120 characters before pressing [Return], on the screen your text appears in two lines, but in your file it is one line of 120 characters.

Long lines can be a problem when you print a file, and it is confusing to relate the number of lines on the screen to the actual number of lines in the file. The simplest way to limit the length of a line is by pressing [Return] any time before reaching the end of the line on the screen. Another way to limit the line length is to set the wrapmargin parameter and let the vi editor insert returns automatically.

***wrapmargin* Option**   The *wrapmargin option* causes the vi editor to break the text you are entering when it reaches the specified number of characters from the right margin. To set the wrapmargin to 10 (where 10 is the number of the characters from the right side of the screen), type **:set wrapmargin=10** and press [Return]. Then, when what you are typing reaches column 70 (80 minus 10), the vi editor starts a new line, just as if you had pressed [Return]. If you are typing a word as the characters pass column 70, vi moves the whole word to the next line. This means the right margin will probably be uneven. But remember, the vi editor is not a text formatter or a word processor.

The default value for the wrapmargin option is 0 (zero). To turn wrapmargin off, type **:set wrapmargin=0** and press [Return].

6.6.4   Abbreviations and Macros

The vi editor provides you with some shortcuts to make your typing faster and simpler: **:ab** and **:map** are two commands that serve this purpose.

The Abbreviation Operator   The **ab** (for *abbreviation*) command lets you assign short, abbreviated words to any string of characters. This helps you to speed up your typing. You pick an abbreviation that you will remember for text that you often type, and after you have set up that abbreviation in the vi editor, you can use the abbreviated word instead of typing the whole text. For example, to abbreviate the words *UNIX Operating System*, which is used often in this text, type **:ab uno UNIX Operating System** and press [Return].

In this example, *uno* is the abbreviation assigned to *UNIX Operating System*; thus when vi is in text input mode, any time you type **uno** and then a space, vi expands *uno* to *UNIX Operating System*. If *uno* is part of another word, such as unofficial, no expansion occurs. It is the space before as well as after the *uno* that makes the vi editor recognize *uno* as an abbreviation and expand it.

To remove an abbreviation, you use the **uab** (for *unabbreviate*) operator. For example, to remove the *uno* abbreviation, type **:unab uno** and press [Return].

To list which abbreviations are set, type **:ab** and press [Return].

1.   The abbreviations are assigned in the vi editor command mode, and are used while you are typing in the text input mode.

2.   The abbreviations set up are temporary; they remain in effect only during the current editing session.

Try setting up some some abbreviations as follows:

- ❑ Type **:ab ex extraordinary adventure** and press [Return] to assign *ex* to the string *extraordinary adventure*.
- ❑ Type **:ab 123 one, two, three, etc.** and press [Return] to assign *123* to the string *one, two, three, etc.*
- ❑ Type **:ab** and press [Return] to display all the abbreviations:

       ex   extraordinary adventure
       123   one, two, three, etc.

- ❑ Type **:unab 123** and press [Return] to remove the *123* abbreviation.

The Macro Operator   The macro operator (**map**) lets you assign key sequences to a single key. As abbreviation gives you a shortcut in text input mode, **map** gives you shortcuts in command mode. For example, to assign the command **5dd** (delete five lines) to [q], type **:map q 5dd** and press [Return]. Then, while vi is in command mode, each time you press [q], vi deletes five lines of text.

To remove a map assignment you use the **unmap** operator. Type **:unmap q** and press [Return].

To look at the list of the map keys and their assignments, type **:map** and press [Return].

The vi editor uses most of the keys on the keyboard for commands. This leaves you with a limited number of keys and escape keys to assign to your key sequences. Available keys are [K] [q], [V], [Ctrl-e], and [Ctrl-x].

You can also assign the function keys of your terminal with the **map** command. In this case, you type **#n** as the key name, where *n* refers to the function key number. For example, to assign **5dd** to [F2], type **:map #2 5dd** and press [Return].

Then, if you press [F2] while in command mode, vi deletes five lines of text.

The following examples show some key assignments.

□ Type **:map V /unix** and press [Return] to assign [V] to the search command, searching for *unix*.

□ Type **:map #3 yy** and press [Return] to assign [F3] to yank a line.

□ Type **:map** and press [Return] to display the map key assignments.

```
V     /unix
#3    yy
```

Suppose you want to find the word *unix* in your file and replace it with "UNIX". Follow this key sequence:

□ Type **:/unix** and press [Return] to search for the word *unix*.

□ Type **cwUNIX** and press [Esc] to change the word *unix* to *UNIX* and return vi to command mode.

In map key assignment, you press [Ctrl-v][Return] to represent [Return], and [Ctrl-v][Esc] to represent the [Esc] key in the command line. Thus, to map the preceding command sequences to a single key, say [v], type **:map v /unix** and press [Ctrl-v][Return] and type **cwUNIX** and press [Ctrl-v][Esc]. This command line uses unprintable characters ([Ctrl-v] and [Esc]), so what you see on the screen is the following:

```
:map v /unix ^McwUNIX ^[
```

1. The map keys you create in the vi editor are temporary; they are in effect only for the current editing session.

2. The map keys are assigned and used while vi is in command mode.

You must precede [Return] and [Esc] with [Ctrl-v] if they are part of a map key assignment.

6.6.5   The .exrc File

All the options that you set up while in the vi editor are temporary; they disappear when you exit vi. To make the options permanent, and save yourself the trouble of retyping them for every editing job, you can save the options settings in a file called .exrc.

Files starting with a . (dot) are called hidden files; you learned all about them in chapter 5.

When you start the vi editor, it automatically checks for the existence of the .exrc file in your current (working) directory, and sets up the edit environment according to what it finds in the file. If vi does not find the .exrc file in the current directory, it checks your home directory, and sets up options according to the .exrc file it finds there. If vi does not find a .exrc file, it assumes the default values of the options.

The way vi checks for the existence of the .exrc file gives you a powerful tool to create specialized .exrc file for your different editing needs. For example, you may create a general-purpose .exrc file under your home directory, and a different .exrc file for your C programs under the directory in which you keep your C programs, and so on. You can use the vi editor to create a .exrc file or to modify it, if it already exists.

To create a .exrc file, type **vi .exrc** and press [Return]. Then enter the set and other commands you want to use (perhaps like those on the following screen).

```
set showmode
set nu
set wm=10
:ab uop UNIX Operating System
:map q 5dd
```

Do not forget the . (dot) at the beginning of the filename.

If you create this file under your home directory, each time you use vi, the edit environment has been established. Under the settings shown, vi displays what mode it is in; shows the line number; sets the right margin at 10 characters (line length is 70); inserts *UNIX Operating System* into your file every time you type **uop** followed by a space; and deletes five lines every time you press [q].

1.   *.exrc belongs to a group of files called startup files.*

2.   *There are other utilities that use startup files similar to the .exrc file.*

6.7   THE LAST OF THE GREAT vi COMMANDS

Before concluding this discussion of the vi editor, we must consider one more vi operator. You know enough vi editor commands and other particulars so that you can easily and efficiently create or modify files. However, that is not all that vi can do. The vi editor has more than 100 commands and numerous variation on them that when combined with the scope of the commands give you detailed control over your editing job. Refer to Appendix F for other books which help to expand your vi skills.

6.7.1   Running Shell Commands

You can run UNIX shell commands from the vi command line. This handy feature lets you temporarily put the vi aside and go to the shell commands. The [!] (exclamation mark) signals vi that the next command is a UNIX shell command. For example, to run the date command while in the vi editor, type **:! date** and press [Return]. The vi editor clears the screen, executes the command **date**, and you see lines similar to the following on the screen:

    Sat Nov 29 14:00:52 EDT 2001
    [Hit any key to continue]

Pressing a key returns the vi editor to the screen, and you can continue editing where you left off. If you want, you can also read the result of the shell commands and add it to your text. You use the **:r** (read) command, followed by [!] to incorporate the command's result into your editing file.

 To read the system's date and time, type **:r ! date** and press [Return]; **vi** responds by putting the current date and time under the current line.

The vi editor remains in command mode.

> The vi history
> The vi editor is a text editor which is supported by <u>m</u>ost of the
> UNIX operating systems.

> The vi history
> The vi editor is a text editor which is supported by <u>m</u>ost of the
> Sat Nov 29 14:00:52 EDT 1993
> UNIX operating systems.

 The following command sequence shows the use of [!].

- □ Type **:! ls** and press [Return] to list the files in the current directory.
- □ Type **:! who** and press [Return] to show who is on the system.
- □ Type **:! date** and press [Return] to show the date and time of day.
- □ Type **:! pwd** and press [Return] to list the contents of the working directory.
- □ Type **:r ! date** and press [Return] to read the results of the **date** command and place it after the cursor position.
- □ Type **:r ! cal 1 2001** and press [Return] to read the calendar of the January 2001 and place it after the cursor position.
- □ Type **:! vi mylast** and press [Return] to invoke another copy of vi to edit the mylast file.

6.7.2   Joining Lines

Use [J] to join two lines together. The [J] command joins the line below the current line to the current line, right after the cursor position. If the joining of the two lines resulted in a long line, vi warps it around the screen.

To join two lines together, do the following:

Use the cursor movement keys to place the cursor at the end of the first line.
- □ Press [J]; vi joins the line below the current line to the current line.

```
The vi history_
vi is a text editor which is supported by most of the
UNIX operating systems.
```

```
The vi historyThe vi is a text editor which is supported by most of the
vi is a text editor which is supported by most of the
UNIX operating systems.
```

6.7.3   Searching and Replacing

There are occasions when you want to change a word in a file. If the file is a long one, then to go through the text, finding each occurrence of a specific word and change it is cumbersome. Additionally, the chances are good that you will miss one or two occurrences of the word. A better way is the use of the vi search commands (/ and ?) in combination with other commands to do the job.

The following command sequences demonstrate the vi search and replacement capability:

- □ Type **:/UNIX** and press [Return] to search forward to find the first occurrence of the word *UNIX*.
- □ Type **cwunix** and press [Return] to change *UNIX* to *unix*.
- □ Type **n** to find the next occurrence of the word UNIX.
- □ Press [.] to repeat the last change: *UNIX* to *unix*.
- □ Type **:?unix** and press [Return] to search backward from the current line, to find the first occurrence of the word *unix*.
- □ Type **dw** to delete the word *unix*.
- □ Type **n** to find the next occurrence of the word *unix*.
- □ Press [.] to repeat the last command (**dw**) and delete the word *unix*.

Command Summary

The following vi editor commands and operators were discussed in this chapter. These commands complement the commands you learned in Chapter 4.

Cut-and-paste keys
These keys are used to rearrange text in your file.
These keys are applicable in the vi's command mode.

Key	Operation
[d]	Deletes a specified portion of the text and stores it in a temporary buffer. This buffer can be accessed by using the put operator.
[y]	Copies a specified portion of the text in a temporary buffer. This buffer can be accessed by using the put command.
[p]	Places the contents of a specified buffer above the cursor position.
[P]	Places the contents of a specified buffer after the cursor position.

Scope keys
Using the vi commands in combination with the scope keys gives you more control in your editing task.

Scope	Operation
$	The scope is from the cursor position to the end of the current line.
0 (zero)	The scope is from just before the cursor position to the beginning of the current line.
e	The scope is from the cursor position to the end of the current word.
b	The scope is from the letter before the cursor backward to the beginning of the current word.

Paging keys
The paging keys are used to scroll a larger portion of your file.

Key	Operation
[Ctrl-d]	Scrolls the cursor down, toward the end of the file, usually 12 lines at a time.
[Ctrl-u]	Scrolls the cursor up, toward the top of the file, usually 12 lines at a time.
[Ctrl-f]	Scrolls the cursor down, (forward) toward the end of the file, usually 24 lines at a time.
[Ctrl-b]	Scrolls the cursor up (backward), toward the top of the file, usually 24 lines at a time.

Setting the vi environment
You can customize the behavior of the vi editor by setting the vi environment options. You use the set command to change the options values.

Option	Abbre-viation	Operation
autoindent	**ai**	Aligns the new lines with the beginning of the previous ones.
ignorcase	**ic**	Ignores the uppercase, lowercase difference in search operations.
magic	**-**	Allows the use of the special characters in search.
number	**nu**	Displays line number.
report	**-**	Informs you of the number of lines affected by the last command.
scroll	**-**	Sets number of lines to scroll when [Ctrl-d] command is given.
shiftwidth	**sw**	Sets number of spaces to indent. Used with autoindent option.
showmode	**smd**	Displays the vi editor modes on the right corner of the screen.
terse	**-**	Shortens the error messages.
wrapmargin	**wm**	Sets the right margin to the specified number of characters.

Review Exercises

Match the commands shown on the left column to the explanations shown on the right. All the commands are applicable only in command mode:

1.	[G]	a.	Replace the character under the cursor with the letter *x*.
2.	/most	b.	Place the cursor on the last line in the file.
3.	[Ctrl-g]	c.	Copy four lines in the buffer x.
4.	2dw	d.	Move cursor down one line.
5.	[k]	e.	Show line number of the current line.
6.	"x4yy	f.	Position the cursor on line 66.
7.	[$]	g.	Delete the character under the cursor.
8.	[0] (zero)	h.	Retrieve the contents of buffer 1.
9.	66G	i.	Delete two words.
10.	[x]	j.	Position the cursor at the end of the current line.
11.	rx	k.	Find the word *most*.
12.	"1p	l.	Position the cursor at the beginning of the current line.

Terminal Session

In this terminal session, create a file called **garden** and practice using the editing keys discussed in this chapter. Create this file as shown in Screen 1. Then use cut-and-paste, cursor positioning, and other commands to make it look like the Screen 2. Finally, apply the following commands to your **garden** file.

1. Create an abbreviation of your name and add it at the top of your file.

2. Create a map key that finds a line with specific word and delete that line.

3. Undo the previous text changes.

4. While in vi, list your file in your current directory.

5. Read the date and time of the day, and place it after your name in the **garden** file.

6. Read another file (import), and add it to the end of the **garden** file.

Screen 1

Everywhere the trend is toward a simpler, and easy to care
garden. Few advises might help you to have less trouble with
your gardening. I am sure you have heard them before, but
 listen once more. Gardening: The easy approach
visit the plant nurseries, it is good for your soul.
Let me tell you that There is no easy to care garden.
Use plants which are suitable for your climate. Native plants
are good CHOICE. Before planting, choose the right site. Use your
imagination, plants grow faster than what you think.
Gardening can be made easier and more enjoyable
if you hire a gardener to do the job. Use mulches to reduce weeds
and save time in watering the plants. Do not use too much chemicals to
kill every weed insight. You are the only one who sees the weeds, let them
grow. They keep the moisture and prevent soil erosion.

Screen 2

Gardening: The easy approach
Everywhere the trend is toward making simpler, and easy- to -care for
gardens.
However, let me tell you that there are no easy-to-care gardens.
Gardening can be made easier and more enjoyable if you hire a
gardener to do the job.
Some advice might help you to have less trouble with your gardening.
I am sure you have heard them before, but listen once more
1: Before planting, choose the right site.
    Use your imagination. plants grow faster than
 you think.
2: Visit the plant nurseries; it is good for your soul.
3: Use mulches to reduce weeds and save time in watering
4: Use plants which are suitable for your climate.
    Native plants are a good choice.
5: Do not use too many chemicals to kill every weed in sight.
    Probably you are the only one who sees the weeds.
    Let them grow.
    They keep moisture and prevent soil erosion.

CHAPTER 7

The UNIX File System Continued

This is the second chapter that discusses the UNIX file system and its associated commands; it complements the material discussed in chapter 5. Chapter 7 presents more commands for manipulating files, including copying files, moving files, and looking at the content of a file. The chapter also explains the shell input/output redirection operators and file substitution metacharacters.

In This Chapter

7.1   FILE READING

Chapter 5 explained how you can use the vi editor or the **cat** command to read files. To refresh your memory, you can use vi with the read-only option to read files, or you can use **cat** to view a small file. Using the **cat** command to view a large file, [Ctrl-s] to stop screen output, and [Ctrl-q] to resume screen output is very inconvenient. Try the following examples to get the feel of it. Doing so will make you appreciate the other file reading commands that let you view files one screen at a time.

 Assume that your working directory is david and you have a file (say 20 pages long) called large_file in it.

☐ To read large_file using the vi editor, type **vi -R large_file** and press [Return]. This opens large_file for read only. Contents of large_file are displayed on the screen, and you can use vi commands to view the other pages.
☐ To read large_file using the **cat** command, type **cat large_file** and press [Return]. Contents of large_file are displayed and scroll before your eyes. You can use [Ctrl-s] and [Ctrl-q] to stop and resume scrolling.

7.1.1   Reading Files: The *pg* command

You use the **pg** command to view files one screen at a time. A prompt sign (:) is produced at the bottom of the screen, and you press [Return] to continue view-

Table 7–1
The **pg** command options.

Option	Operation
-n	Does not require [Return] to complete the single letter commands.
-s	Displays messages and prompts in reverse video.
-num	Sets the number of lines per screen to the integer num. The default value is 23 lines.
-p*str*	Changes the prompt : (colon) to the string specified as *str*.
+*line-num*	Starts displaying the file from the line specified in *line- num*.
+/*pattern/*	Starts viewing at the line containing the first occurrence of the specified *pattern*.

See page xxii for an explanation of icons used to highlight information in this chapter.

ing the rest of the file. The **pg** command shows EOF (End Of the File) on the last line of the screen when it reaches the end of your file. You press [Return] at this point to get to the **$** prompt.

Using the **pg** command options gives you more control over the format and the way you want to view your file. Table 7–1 summarizes these options.

Unlike other commands' options, some **pg** options start with the plus sign (**+**).

Assuming you have a file called large_file in your working directory, use the **pg** command to read it by doing the following:

☐ Type **pg large_file** and press [Return]. This is a simple way of looking at large_file one screen at a time.

☐ Type **pg -pNext +45 large_file** and press [Return] to view large_file starting from line 45 and show the prompt **Next** instead of the normal prompt **:** (colon).

Two options are used, **-p** to change the default prompt from **:** to **Next**, and **+** to start viewing from line 45.

Use no space between the option **-p** and the string *Next*. Use no space between the **+** and the line number (45).

☐ Type **pg -s +/hello/ large_file** and press [Return] to show prompt and other messages in reverse video, and start viewing from the first line that contains the word *hello*.

Two options are used, **-s** to show prompt and other messages in reverse video, and **+/hello/** to search for first occurrence of the word *hello*.

When the **pg** command displays the prompt sign **:** (or any other prompt if you have used the **-p** option), you can give commands to move forward or backward a specified number of pages or lines to view different parts of the text. Table 7–2 summarizes some of these commands.

Table 7–2
The **pg** command key operators.

Key	Operation
+*n*	Advances *n* screen where *n* is an integer number.
-*n*	Backs up *n* screen where *n* is an integer number.
+*n*l	Advances *n* lines where *n* is an integer number.
-*n*l	Backs up *n* screen where *n* is an integer number.
n	Goes to *n* screen where *n* is an integer number.

7.1.2　Specifying Page or Line Number

You can specify a page number or line number from the beginning of the file or relative to the current page number. Use unsigned integers to indicate that the reference is the beginning of the file. For example, type **10** to go to page 10, or **60l** (that's *six, zero, lowercase letter l*) to go to the line 60 in the file.

Use signed integers to indicate that the reference is relative to the current page. For example, type **+10** to move forward 10 pages, or type **-30l** (*three, zero, lowercase letter l*) to move backward 30 lines. If you only type **+** or **-** without any numbers, the command is interpreted as **+1** or **-1**, respectively.

 These operators are only applicable while you are viewing your file, and **pg** is displaying the prompt sign.

 *If you use **pg** with the **-n** option, then you do not need to press [Return] for single-letter operators.*

7.2　SHELL REDIRECTION

One of the most useful facilities that shell provides is the *shell redirection operators*. Many UNIX commands take input from the standard input device and send the output to the standard output device. This is usually the default setting. Using the shell redirection operators, you can alter where a command gets its input and where it sends its output. The command's standard (default) input/output device is your terminal.

The shell redirection operators allow you to do the following things:

- Save the output of a process in a file.
- Use a file as input to a process.

1.　*A process is any executable program. This could be an appropriate shell command, an application program, or a program you have written.*

2.　*The redirection operators are instructions to the shell and not part of the command syntax. Accordingly, they can appear anywhere on the command line.*

3.　*Redirection is temporary and effective only with the command using it.*

7.2.1　Output Redirection

Output redirection allows you to store the output of a process in a file. There you can edit it, print it, or use it as input to another process. The shell recognizes the greater than sign (>), and double greater than sign (>>) as output redirection operators.

The format is as follows:

command > filename

or

command >> filename

For example, to get the list of the filenames in your working directory, you use the **ls** command. Type **ls** and press [Return]. The shell default output device is your terminal screen (the standard output device). Consequently, you see the list of files on the screen. Suppose you want to save the **ls** command output (the list of filenames in the directory) in a file. One way to do that is to redirect the output of the **ls** command from screen to a file, as follows:

ls > mydir.list

This time the **ls** command output is not sent to the terminal screen, but it is saved in a file called **mydir.list**. If you open the **mydir.list** file, you see the list of files.

1. *If the specified filename already exists, then it is written over, and contents of the existing file are lost.*

2. *If the specified filename does not exist, then shell creates one.*

The double greater than sign (**>>**) redirection operator works the same as the greater than sign (**>**) operator, except it appends the output to the specified file. If you type **ls >> mydir.list**, the shell adds the filenames in the working directory to the end of the file called **mydir.list**.

1. *If the specified file does not exist, then shell creates one to save the output in it.*

2. *If the specified filename does exist, then shell adds the output to the end of the file, and the previous contents of the file remain intact.*

The following command sequences show more examples of the output redirection operators.

To obtain a hard copy of filenames in your home directory, do the following:

$ **cd [Return]** . . . . Change to your home directory.

$ **ls -C [Return]** . . . . List filenames in the david directory in column format. You have two files:

myfirst   yourlast

$ **ls -C > mydir.list [Return]** . . . . Save the output in mydir.list.

$ _ . . . . Done. Prompt is back.

$ **cat mydir.list [Return]** . . . . Check what you have in mydir.list.

myfirst   yourlast

$ **lp mydir.list [Return]** . . . . Print the list.

request id is lp1-8056 (1 file)

$ _ . . . . Ready for next command.

To append the list of the users on the system to mydir.list, do the following:

$ **who >> mydir.list [Return]** . . . . Append the list of the users on the
                                                            system to mydir.list. Now mydir.list
                                                            contains the list of filenames, and list of
                                                            users currently logged in.

$ **date > mydir.list [Return]** . . . . Save the output of the command **date** in
                                                            mydir.list. This time the previous contents
                                                            of the mydir.list is lost, and all you have in
                                                            it is the results of the last command.

$ _ . . . . Ready for the next command.

To save the current year calendar in this_year, print it, and then remove it, do the following:

$ **cal > this_year [Return]** . . . . Save output of **cal** in this_year.

$ **lp this_year [Return]** . . . . Print it.

request id lp1-6889 (1 file)

$ **rm this_year [Return]** . . . . Remove it.

$_ . . . . Ready for next command.

7.2.2   Input Redirection

The input redirection allows you to issue commands or run programs that get their input from a specified file. The shell recognizes the less than sign (<) as the input redirection operator. The format is as follows:

    command < filename

or

    command << *word*

For example, to send mail to another user, you use the **mailx** command (mailx is discussed in chapter 9) and type **mailx daniel < memo**. This command means send mail to the user called *daniel* (his user id). The input to **mailx** is not coming from the standard input device, your terminal, but from the file called memo. Thus, the input redirection operator (<) is used to indicate where the input comes from.

Try using the **cat** command with the input redirection operator.

□ Type **cat < mydir.list** and press [Return] to display the contents of mydir.list; UNIX responds:

myfirst   yourlast

Using the **cat** command with the input redirection operator gives you the same result as the **cat** command with the filename as an argument. There are other commands which work in the same manner. If you specify a filename on the command line, the command takes its input from the specified filename. If you do not specify any argument, the command takes its input from the default input device (your terminal), and if you have the input redirection operator to specify where the input comes from, then command takes its input from the file you specify. Let's look at an example.

Try using the **lp** command with input redirection operator.

The redirection operator (<<) is used mostly in script files (shell programs) to provide standard input to other commands. (This topic is discussed in more detail in chapter 10.)

7.2.3   The *cat* Command Revisited

Now that you know about the shell redirection capabilities, we can explore the **cat** command in more detail. The **cat** command was introduced in chapter 5, where it was used to show contents of a small files on the screen. However, the **cat** command can be use for many things other than displaying files.

Creating Files

Using the **cat** command with the output redirection operator (>), you can create a file. For example, if you want to create a file called myfile, type **cat > myfile**. This command means that the output of the **cat** command is redirected from the standard output device (your terminal) to a file called myfile. The input comes from the standard input device—your terminal (keyboard). In other words, you type the text, and **cat** saves it in the myfirst file. You signal the end of the file by pressing [Ctrl-d].

This feature of the **cat** command is useful for creating small files quickly. Of course, you can also use it to create long files, but you must be a very accurate typist because after you press [Return], you cannot edit the text you have typed. The following command sequences show how to create a file using the **cat** command.

Try using the **cat** command with the output redirection operator to create a file.

$ **cat > myfile [Return]** . . . . Create a file called myfile.

_ . . . . Cursor ready for your input. Let's say you type the following:

**I wish there were a better way to learn
UNIX. Something like having a daily UNIX pill.**

[Ctrl-d] . . . . End your typing.

$ _ . . . . Ready for the next command.

$ cat myfile [Return] . . . . Check if myfile is created; display it
on the screen.

I wish there were a better way to learn
UNIX. Something like having a daily UNIX pill.

$ _ . . . . Ready for the next command.

1. *If* myfirst *does not exist in your working directory, then* **cat** *creates it.*

2. *If* myfirst *already exists in your working directory, then* **cat** *overwrites it. The contents of the old* myfirst *are lost.*

3. *If you do not want to overwrite a file, use the (>>) operator.*

Try appending text to the end of myfile in your current directory.

$ cat >> myfirst [Return] . . . . Create a file called myfirst.

_ . . . . Type your text.

However, for now, we have to suffer and read all these boring UNIX books.

[Ctrl-d-d] . . . . Signal the end of the input text.

$ _ . . . . Back to the prompt.

$ cat myfile [Return] . . . . Display the contents of myfile.

I wish there were a better way to learn
UNIX. Something like having a daily UNIX pill.
However, for now, we have to suffer and read all these boring UNIX books.

1. *If* myfirst *does not exist in your working directory, then* **cat** *creates the file.*

2. *If* myfirst *exists, then* **cat** *appends the input text to the end of the existing file. In this example, your one line of input is appended to* myfirst. *Thus the three lines of text are displayed.*

Copying Files

You can use the **cat** command with output redirection operator to copy files from one place to another. The following command sequences show how this capability of the **cat** command works.

Try copying myfile in the david directory to another file called myfile.copy.

$ **cd [Return]** . . . . Make sure you are in your home directory.

$ **cat myfirst > myfirst.copy [Return]** . . Copy myfirst to myfirst.copy.

$ _ . . . . Ready for the next command.

The input to the **cat** *command is* myfirst *file, and the output from the* **cat** *command (the contents of the* myfirst*) is saved in* myfirst.copy.

Now copy myfirst in the david directory to the source directory, and call it myfirst.copy.

$ **cat myfirst > source/myfile.copy [Return]** . . Copy myfirst to myfirst.copy and place it in the source directory.

$ **ls source/myfirst.copy [Return]**. . . . . Check whether it is copied.

myfirst.copy

$_ . . . . Yes, myfirst.copy is in the source directory.

Because you are in your home directory, the pathname to the myfirst.copy *in* source *directory must be specified in both* **cat** *and* **ls** *commands.*

Next, use the **cat** command to copy two files into a third file.

$ **cat myfirst myfirst.copy > xyz [Return]**. . . . . Copy myfirst and myfirst.copy into xyz.

$_ . . . . Ready for the next command.

1. The previous contents of the xyz, if any, are lost.

2. There is a space between each filename in the list of filenames.

Appending Files

You can use the **cat** command with the output redirection append operator (**>>**) to add a number of files together into a new file.

Append two files to the end of the third file.

$ **cat myfirst myfirst.copy >> xyz [Return]**   Append myfirst, myfirst.copy to the end of the file called xyz.

$ _ . . . . Prompt is displayed.

1. Using the (>>) redirection operator saves the previous contents of xyz, *if any, and the two files are added to the end of* xyz.

2. You may have more than two filenames in the filename list, but they must be separated by a space.

3. The files are appended to the specified output file in the same sequence in which the input files are specified.

7.3 ENHANCED FILE PRINTING

The **lp** command sends your file to the printer as is; it does not change the appearance or format of your file. You can improve the appearance of output by formatting it. For example, adding page numbers, page headings, and double-spaced lines to a document before sending it to the printer or viewing it on the screen.

You use the **pr** command to format a file before printing or viewing it. The **pr** command with no options formats the specified file into pages 66 lines long. It puts a 5-line heading at the top of the page that consists of 2 blank lines, 1 line of information about the specified file, and 2 more blank lines. The information line includes current date and time, the name of the specified file, and the page number. The **pr** command also produces 5 blank lines at the end of each page.

 Try using the **pr** command to format myfirst.

☐ Type **pr myfirst** and press [Return] to format a file called myfirst. (See figure 7–1.)

The **pr** command output is displayed on your terminal, the standard output device. But most of the time you want to format files for hard copy printout. One way to do that is to use the output redirection operator. There are other ways to send formatted files to printer, such as using the pipe operator (|) (which is explained in chapter 8).

 Let's save the formatted version of myfirst in another file and then print it.

Figure 7–1
File printed with page formatting: 5-line heading and 5-line blank footing.

```
                                        [2 blank lines]

    Nov 28  16:30  2001  myfirst  Page 1
                                        [2 blank lines]

    The vi history

    The vi editor is a text editor which is supported by most of the UNIX operating
    systems. However, . . .

    rest of the page . . .
                                        [5 blank lines at bottom of page]
```

Table 7–3
The **pr** command options.

Option	Operation
+*page*	Starts displaying from the specified *page*. The default is page 1.
-*columns*[1]	Displays output in the specified number of *columns*. The default is 1 column.
-a[2]	Displays output in columns across the page, one line per column.
-d	Displays output in double space.
-h*str*	Replaces the filename in the header with the specified string *str*.
-l*number*	Sets the page length to the specified *number* of lines. The default is 66 lines.
-m[1]	Displays all the specified files in multiple columns.
-p	Pauses at the end of each page and sounds the terminal bell.
-*character*	Separates columns with a single specified *character*. If *character* is not specified, then tab is used.
-t	Suppresses the five lines header and five lines trailer.
-w*number*	Sets line width to the specified *number* of characters. The default is 72.

1. The **-m** or **-***columns* is used to produce multi-column output.
2. The **-a** option can only be used with **-***column* option and not **-m**.

$ **pr myfirst > pout [Return]** . . . . Save the formatted copy of myfirst
in a file called pout.

$ **lp pout [Return]** . . . . Print pout.

requested id is lp1-8045 (1file)

$ **rm pout [Return]**. Delete pout if you do not need it.

$_ . . . . Ready for the next command.

pr Options   It is not enough to place five lines at the top and five lines at the bottom of each page and call it formatting. The **pr** options allows you to format a file's appearance with a little more sophistication. Table 7–3 summarizes the **pr** command options.

The following command sequences show the output of the **pr** command using different options.

The examples assume you have two files in your working directory. Let's use **cat** command to create them.

     $ cat > names [Return] . . . . Create a file called names.

     David [Return]
     Daniel [Return]
     Gabriel [Return]
     Emma [Return]
     [Ctrl-d]

     $ cat > scores [Return] . . . . Create a file called scores.

     90 [Return]
     100 [Return]
     70 [Return]
     85 [Return]
     [Ctrl-d]

     $_ . . . . Ready for the next command.

To show the names in column format, and change the heading to *STUDENT LIST*, type **pr -2 -h "STUDENT LIST" names** and press [Return].

                                       [2 blank lines]

Nov 28 2001 14:30 STUDENT LIST"

                                       [2 blank lines]

David   Gabriel
Daniel   Emma

                               [5 blank lines at bottom of page]

The **-h** option changes the heading, but if the specified string has embedded white space, then you must put the string in quotations.

To display names in two columns across the page, and suppress the header, type **pr -2 -a -t names**.

     David   Daniel
     Gabriel   Emma

The difference between options **-2** and **-2 -a** is the order in which the columns are arranged.

To show the files names and scores side by side, type **pr -m -t names scores** and press [Return].

```
David       90
Daniel      100
Gabriel     70
Emma        85
```

The option **-m** shows the specified files side by side in the same order in which the filenames are specified in the command line.

7.4   MORE FILE MANIPULATION COMMANDS

Some of the file manipulation commands were discussed in chapter 5. From that discussion, you know how to create directories (using the **mkdir** command), create files (using the **vi** and **cat** commands), and delete files and directories (using the **rm** and **rmdir** commands). A few more commands will complete your knowledge of file manipulation in UNIX. These commands are used to copy (**cp**), link (**ln**), and move (**mv**) files. The general format of these commands is as follows:

command source target

Where *command* is any of the three commands, *source* is the name of the original file, and *target* is the name of the destination file.

7.4.1   Copying Files: The *cp* Command

The **cp** (copy) command is used to create a copy (duplicate) of a file. You can copy files from one directory to another, make a backup copy of a file, or just copy files for the fun of it!

Suppose you have a file called REPORT in your current directory and want to create a copy of it. To do so, you type **cp REPORT REPORT.COPY** and press [Return].

REPORT is the source file and REPORT.COPY is the target file. If you do not provide the correct pathname/filename for the source or target file, **cp** complains by showing a message similar to the following:

File cannot be copied onto itself
0 file(s) copied

Figure 7–2 shows your directory structure before and after application of the **cp** command.

If target file already exists, then its contents are destroyed.

Figure 7–2
The **cp** command example.

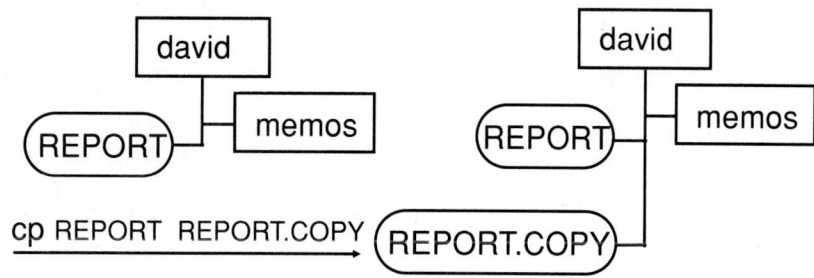

cp Options

Table 7–4 summarizes the **cp** command options.

-i Option The **-i** option protects you from overwriting an existing file. It asks for confirmation if the target file already exists. If your reply is *yes*, it copies the source file, overwriting the existing file. If your answer is *no*, then it quits, and your existing file remains intact.

-r Option It takes a long time and is a tedious job to copy files one by one if you have a long list of files to copy. You use **cp** with the **-r** option to copy directories and all their contents into a new directory.

The following command sequences show how the **cp** command works.

```
$ ls  -C [Return] . . . . . . . . . . . . . . . . . . . . . . . . . List the current directory files.

memos          REPORT

$ cp REPORT   REPORT.COPY [Return]. . . . . Copy REPORT to REPORT.COPY.

$ ls  -C [Return] . . . . . . . . . . . . . . . . . . . . . . . . . See the list of files. REPORT.COPY
                                                              is in the list, as you expected.

memos          REPORT          REPORT.COPY

$ cp REPORT REPORT [Return] . . . . . . . . . . . Source and target filenames
                                                              are the same.

File cannot be copied onto itself
0 file(s) copied

$_ . . . . . . . . . . . . . . . . . . . . . . . . . . . . . . . . . . . . Ready for the next command.
```

Table 7–4
The **cp** command options.

Option	Operation
-i	Asks for confirmation if the target file already exists.
-r	Copies directories to a new directory.

To copy a file from your current directory to another directory, do the following:

> $ **cp REPORT memos [Return]** . . . . . . Create a copy of REPORT in memos.
>
> $ **ls source [Return]** . . . . List files in memos directory, and REPORT is there, as you expected.
>
> REPORT

When the target file is a directory name, then the source file is copied in the specified directory with the same filename as the source filename.

Figure 7–3 shows your directory structure before and after the **cp** command.

Try using the **cp** command with the **-i** option.

> $ **copy -i REPORT memos [Return]** . . . Make a copy of REPORT under memos.
>
> Target file already exists overwrite?. . . . . Shows confirmation prompt, press [y] [Return] for yes or [n] [Return] for no.
>
> $ . . . . Ready for the next command.

Copy files and subdirectories in **david** to another directory called **david.bak** using the **-r** option.

> $ cp -r ./memos ./david.bak . . . . Copy memos directory and all the files in it to david.bak.
>
> $ . . . . Ready for the next command.

1. *If* david.bak *exists in your current directory, then files and directories in* memos *are copied into* david.bak.*.*

2. *If* david.bak *does not exist in your current directory, then it is created and all the files and directories including* memos *itself are copied into* david.bak. *Now, the pathname for files in* memos *under* david.bak *is:* ./david.bak/memos.

Figure 7–3
The **cp** command example.

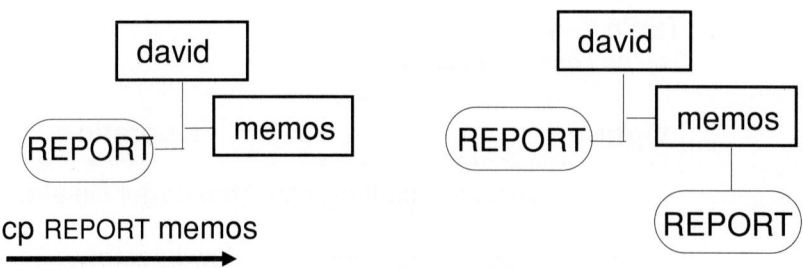

cp REPORT memos

7.4.2   Moving Files: The *mv* Command

You use the **mv** command to move a file from one place to another, or change the name of a file or a directory. For example, if you have a file called RE-PORT in your current directory and you want to change its name to RE-PORT.OLD, you type **mv REPORT REPORT.OLD** and press [Return].

Figure 7–4 shows your directory structure before and after application of the **mv** command to rename REPORT.

Move REPORT to the memos directory.

> **$ mv REPORT memos [Return]** . . . . Move REPORT to memos.
>
> **$_** . . . . Ready for next command.

Figure 7–5 shows your directory structure after application of the **mv** command to move REPORT.

7.4.3   Linking Files: The *ln* Command

You can use the **ln** command to create new links (names) between an existing file and a new filename. This means you can create additional names for an existing file and refer to the same file with different names. For example, assume

Figure 7–4
Using **mv** to rename a file.

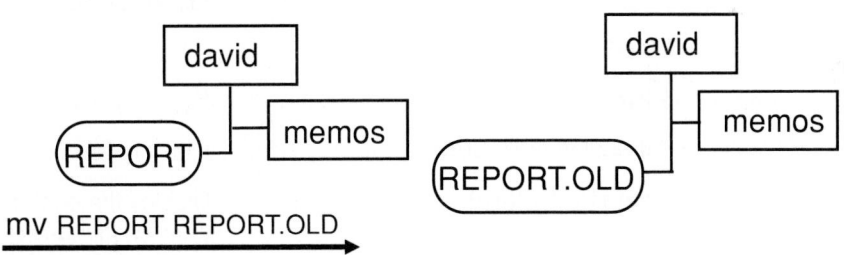

Figure 7–5
Using **mv** to move a file.

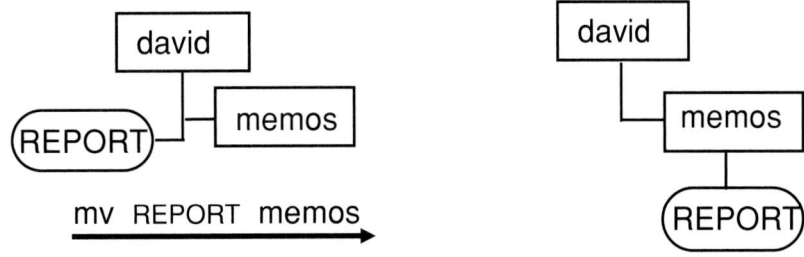

Figure 7–6
Using ln to link filenames.

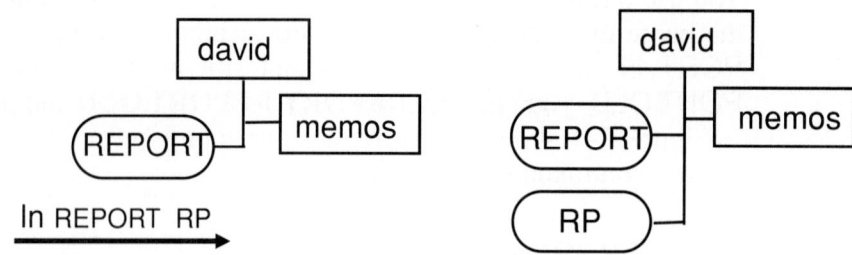

you have a file called REPORT in your current directory, and you type **ln REPORT RP** and press [Return]. This creates a filename RP in your current directory and links that name to REPORT. Now, REPORT and RP are two names for a single file. Figure 7–6 shows your directory structure before and after the **ln** command application.

At first glance, this looks like the **cp** command. However, it is not! The **cp** command physically copies the file into another place, and you have two separate files. Whatever changes you make in one are not reflected in the other. The **ln** command just creates another filename for the same file; no new file is created. If you change anything in any of the linked files, the changes are there in the file regardless of the name you use to refer to it.

 To experiment with **ln**, try the following command sequence.

$ cat > xxx [Return].	Create a file called xxx and type the following line:
Line 1: aaaaaa	
$ [Ctrl-d].	Signal end of the input.
$ ln xxx yyy [Return].	Link yyy to xxx.
$ cat yyy [Return]	Display the contents of the xxx, but use the new filename yyy, and the output is, as you expected, the contents of xxx:
Line 1: aaaaaa	
$ cat >> yyy [Return].	Append a line to the end of yyy, and type the following line:
Line 2: bbbbbbb	
[Ctrl-d]	Signal the end of your input.
$ cat yyy [Return]	Display contents of yyy. You have 2 lines in yyy, as you expected:
Line 1: aaaaaa Line 2: bbbbbbb	

Figure 7–7
Using **ln** to link filenames to a directory.

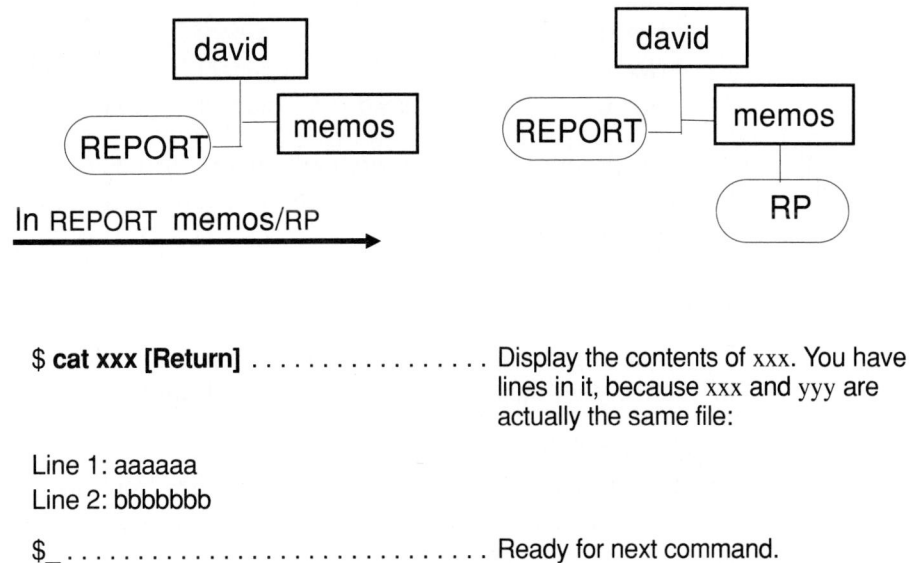

$ **cat xxx [Return]** . . . . Display the contents of xxx. You have
                                             lines in it, because xxx and yyy are
                                             actually the same file:

Line 1: aaaaaa
Line 2: bbbbbbb

$_ . . . . Ready for next command.

If you specify an existing directory name as the new filename, you can access
the file in the specified directory without typing its pathname. For example, suppose you have a file called REPORT and a subdirectory called memos in your
working directory, and you type **ln REPORT memos** and press [Return]. Now
you can access REPORT from the memos directory without specifying its
pathname, in this case ../REPORT.

If you want to specify a different name, type **ln REPORT memos/RP** and
press [Return]. Now RP in the memos directory is linked to REPORT, and
from memos you can use the filename RP to refer to REPORT.

Figure 7–7 shows your directory structure before and after application of
the **ln** command.

Chapter 5 explained that the **ls -l** command lists the filenames in the current directory in a long format and that the second column in the long-format
output shows the number of the links.

List the files in david in long format, type **ls -l** and press [Return].

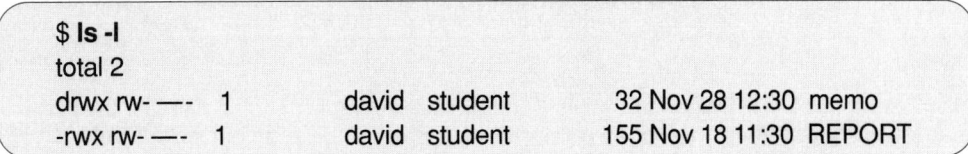

```
$ ls -l
total 2
drwx rw- —-  1       david  student        32 Nov 28 12:30 memo
-rwx rw- —-  1       david  student       155 Nov 18 11:30 REPORT
```

To link REPORT to RP and list the files using the **ls** command with the **-l**
option to see the number of links, type **ln REPORT RP** and press [Return].
Then type **ls -l** and press [Return].

```
$ ln REPORT RP
$ ln -l
total 3
drwx rw----     1      david      student      32    Nov 28   12:30    memo
-rwx rw----     2      david      student     155    Nov 18   11:30    REPORT
-rwx rw----     2      david      student     155    Nov 18   11:30    RP
```

 When you create a file, you also establish a link between the directory and the file. Thus, link count for every file is at least one, and subsequent use of **ln** *adds to the number of links.*

And the Last Words

The three commands **cp**, **mv**, and **ln** all affect the filenames and work in a similar manner, but they are different commands and are used for different purposes:

- **cp** creates a new file.
- **mv** changes the filename or moves files from one place to another.
- **ln** creates additional names (links) for an existing file.

7.4.4 Counting Words: The *wc* Command

You can use the **wc** command to find out the number of lines, words, or characters in a file or list of the specified files.

The following command sequences show the output of the **wc** command, assuming you have myfirst file in your current directory.

 First display the contents of myfirst. Then show number of lines, words, and characters in it.

$ **cat myfirst [Return]** . . . . Display the contents of myfirst.

I wish there were a better way to learn
UNIX. Something like having a daily UNIX pill.
However, for now, we have to suffer and read all these boring UNIX books.

$ **wc myfirst [Return]** . . . . Count number of lines, words, and
characters in myfirst.

4 30 155 myfirst

$ _ . . . . Ready for the next command.

The first column shows number of lines, the second column shows number of words, and the third column shows number of characters.

 A word is considered a sequence of characters with no white space (space or tab character). Therefore, what? *is one word, and* what ? *counts as two words.*

If no filename is specified, then **wc** gets its input from the standard input device (keyboard). You signal the end of input by pressing [Ctrl-d], and **wc** shows the result on the screen.

Use the **wc** command to get the counts of input from the keyboard.

$ wc [Return]. . . . . Invoke the **wc** command with no filename.

_ . . . . The sign is the prompt indicating shell
                                                         is waiting for the rest of the command
                                                         Type the following text:

**The wc command is useful to find out
how large your file is.**

[Ctrl-d] . . . . End your input; **wc** displays the output.

2 13 48

$_. . . . . Ready for the next command.

You can specify more than one filename as argument. In this case, the output shows one line of information for each file, and the last line shows the total counts.

Assume you have two files in your current directory. The following command sequences show the output of the **wc** command specifying the two filenames as arguments.

Count the number of lines, words, and characters in the specified files.

$ **wc myfirst yourfirst [Return]** . . . . Show counts of myfirst and yourfirst.

24	10	400 myfirst
3	100	400 yourfirst
5	104	410 total

$_. . . . . Ready for the next command.

wc Options   You can use the **wc** command with options to get number of lines, words, or characters only, or in any combinations. Table 7–5 summarizes the **wc** command options.

1. *When no option is specified, the default is all options (-**lwc**).*

2. *You can use any combination of the options.*

The following command sequences show the use of **wc** options.

Table 7–5
The **wc** command options.

Option	Operation
-l	Reports number of lines.
-w	Reports number of words.
-c	Reports number of characters.

Count number of lines in myfirst.

> **$ wc -l myfirst [Return]** . . . . Report only the number of lines:
>
> 4 myfirst
>
> $_ . . . . Ready for the next command.
>
> **$ wc -lc myfirst [Return]** . . . . Report number of lines and characters.
>
> 155 4 myfirst
>
> $_ . . . . Prompt is back.

Save the output of the **wc** command in a file and print it.

> **$ wc myfirst > myfirst.count [Return]** . . . . Use output redirection to
> save the **wc** report in
> myfirst.count.
>
> **$ lp -m myfirst.count [Return]** . . . . Print myfirst.count, and report
> when the job is done.
>
> $_ . . . . Ready for the next command.

7.5   FILENAME SUBSTITUTION

Most file manipulation commands require filenames as arguments. When you want to manipulate a number of files, say transferring all files with filename starting with letter *a* to another directory, typing all the filenames one by one is tiring and boring. Shell supports *file substitution*, which allows you to select files whose filenames match a specified pattern. These patterns are created by specifying filenames that contain certain characters that have a special meaning to the shell. The special characters are called *metacharacters* (or *wild cards*). Table 7–6 summarizes the wild cards that can stand for one or more characters in a filename.

File substitution metacharacters (wild cards) can be used in any part of the filename to create a search pattern: at the beginning, middle, or end.

7.5.1   The ? Metacharacter

The question mark (**?**) is a special character that the shell interprets as a single character substitution and expands the filename accordingly.

 Try the following command sequences to see how the **?** special character works.

$ ls -C [Return] . . . . Check filenames in your working directory.
                                                     Assume you have the following files:

report   report1   report2 areport   breport
report32

$ ls -C report? [Return] . . . . Use a single question mark in filename.

report1   report2

$_ . . . . Ready for the next command.

shell expands the filename **report?** to filenames **report** followed by exactly one character, any character. Thus filenames **report1** and **report2** are the only two files that match the pattern.

$ ls report?? [Return] . . . . Use two question marks as
                                                 special characters.

report32

$_ . . . . Ready for the next command.

shell expands the filename **report??** to filenames **report** followed by exactly two characters, any characters. Thus filename **report32** is the only file that matches the pattern.

$ ls -C ?report [Return] . . . . Put ? at the beginning of the filename.

areport   breport

$_ . . . . Ready for the next command.

Table 7–6
The shell file substitution metacharacters.

Key	Operation
?	Matches any single character.
*	Matches any string , including the empty string.
[*list*]	Matches any one of the characters specified in the *list*.
[!list]	Matches any one of the characters not specified in the *list*.

shell expands the filename ?report to filenames report preceded by exactly one character, any character. Thus filenames areport and breport are the only files that match the pattern.

7.5.2   The * Metacharacter

The asterisk (*) is a special character that the shell interprets as any number of characters (including zero characters) of substitution in a filename, and expands the filename accordingly.

 Try the following command sequences to see how the * metacharacter works.

$ **ls -C [Return]** . . . . Check filenames in your working directory.
                                                 Assume you have the following files:

report   report1   report2   areport   breport
report32

$ **ls -C report** [Return] . . . . List all filenames that begin with the word
                                                 report.

report   report1   report2   report32

shell expands the filename report* to filenames report followed by any number of characters, any characters. Thus filenames areport and breport are the only two files that do not match the pattern. The * wild card includes zero character. Thus, filename report followed by no character matches the pattern and is displayed.

$ **ls -C ∗report** [Return] . . . . List all filenames that end with the word
                                                 report.

report   areport   breport
$_   Ready for the next command.

shell expands the filename *report to filenames report preceded by any number of characters, any characters. Thus filenames report, areport, and breport are the only files that match the pattern. The * wild card includes zero character. Therefore, filename report followed preceded by no character matches the pattern and is displayed.

$ **ls -C r∗2** [Return] . . . . List all files that start with *r* and end with *2*.

report2   report32

$_ . . . . Ready for the next command.

shell expands the filename r*2 to filenames r followed any number of characters, but the last character of the filename must be character *2*—any file that starts with *r* and ends with *2*.

7.5.3   The [ ] Metacharacters

The open and close brackets are special characters that surround a list of characters. The shell interprets this list of characters as filenames that contain the specified characters, and expands the filenames accordingly.

Using the **!** before the specified list of characters causes the shell to expand filenames that do not contain the characters in the list at the specified position.

Experiment with the bracket metacharacters by doing the following:

□ To list all the filenames that start with *a* or *b*, type **ls -C [ab]** * and press [Return]; UNIX responds:

    areport   breport

    $_ . . . . Ready for the next command.

shell expands the filename [ab]* to filenames **a** or **b** followed by any number of characters, any characters. Thus **areport** and **breport** are the only two files that match the specified pattern.

□ To list all filenames that do not start with *a* or *b*, type **ls -C [!ab]*** and press [Return]; UNIX responds:

    report   report1   report2   report32

*You can use the **[ ]** special characters to specify a range of characters or digits. For example, **[5-9]** means the digits 5, 6, 7, 8, or 9; and **[a-z]** means all the lowercase letters of alphabet.*

The following command sequences show the use of brackets with a specified alphabet or digits range.

□ Type **ls *[1-32]** and press [Return] to list all the filenames that end with the digits 1 to 32; UNIX responds:

    report1   report2   report32

7.5.4   Metacharacters and Hidden Files

To use the metacharacters for displaying hidden files—filenames starting with **.** (dot)—you must explicitly have the **.** (dot) as part of the specified pattern.

To list all the invisible (hidden) files, type **ls -C .*** and press [Return]; UNIX responds:

.exrc   .profile

shell expands the filename .* to filenames . (dot) followed by any number of characters, any characters. Thus, only the hidden files are displayed.

The pattern is **.*** and there is no space between the dot and the asterisk.

*Wild cards are not limited in use to only the **ls** command. You can use wild cards with other commands that need filename arguments.*

To experiment with some more examples of filename substitution, try the following:

$ rm *.* [Return]. . . . . Delete all the files with filenames that contain at least one dot in their filenames.

$ rm report? [Return] . . . . Delete all filenames that begin with report and end with only one character, any character.

$ cp * backup [Return] . . . . Copy all files from the current directory to the backup directory.

$ mv file[1-4] memos [Return] . . . . . . Move file1, file2, file3, and file4, indicated by the range [1-4], to the memos directory.

$ rm report* [Return]. . . . . Delete all the filenames that start with the string *report*.

$_ . . . . Ready for the next command.

*There is no space between **report** and the asterisk wild card. The **rm report*** command deletes all the files with filenames that begin with* report.

$ rm report * [Return] . . . . Delete all files.

$_ . . . . Ready for the next command.

In the preceding example, there is a space between *report* and the asterisk wild card. This space can have disastrous consequences. The command **rm report *** is interpreted as "delete a file called report, and then delete all the other files." In other words, all files in the current directory are deleted.

$ ls -C [A-Z] [Return] . . . . Show all the single-capital-letter filenames assuming you have some single-letter filenames.

A   B   D   W

$_ . . . . And the prompt.

7.6   UNIX INTERNALS: THE FILE SYSTEM

How does the UNIX file system keep track of your files? How does it know the location of your files on the disk? From your point of view, you create directories to organize your disk space, and directories and files have filenames to identify them. This hierarchical structure of directories and files is a logical view of the file system. Internally, UNIX organizes the disk and keeps track of files in a different manner.

The UNIX file system associates every filename with a number called its *i-node number* and identifies each file with its i-node number. Unix keeps all these i-node numbers in a list, appropriately called *i-node list*. This list is saved on the UNIX disk.

7.6.1   UNIX Disk Structure

Under UNIX, a disk is a standard block device, and a UNIX disk is divided into four blocks (regions):

- boot block
- super block
- i-node list block
- files and directories block

The Boot Block   The *boot block* holds the *boot program*, a special program that is activated at the system boot time.

The Super Block   The *super block* contains information about the disk itself. This information includes the following:

- total number of disk blocks
- number of free blocks
- block size in bytes
- number of used blocks

The i-list Block   The *i-list block* keeps the list of i-nodes. Each entry in this list is an i-node, a 64-byte storage area. The i-node of a regular file or a directory file contains the location of its disk block(s). The i-node of a special file contains the information that identifies the peripheral device. An also i-node contains other information, including the following:

- file access permission (read, write and execute)
- owner and group ids
- file link count
- time of the last file modification
- time of the last file access

- location of blocks for each regular and directory file
- device identification number for special files

The i-nodes are numbered sequentially.

i-nodes and Directories

i-node 2 contains the location of the block(s) that contain the root directory (\). A UNIX directory contains the list of filenames and their associated i-node numbers. When you create a directory, it automatically creates two entries, one for the .. (dot dot) the parent directory and one the . (dot) child directory.

Filenames are stored in directories and not in the i-nodes.

7.6.2   Putting It Together

When you log in, UNIX reads the root directory (i-node 2) to find your home directory and saves your home directory i-node number. When you change your directory using **cd**, UNIX replaces this i-node number with the new directory's i-node number.

When you access a file using utilities or commands (such as **vi** or **cat**) or when a program opens a file, UNIX reads and searches the directory for the specified filename. There is an i-node associated with each filename that points to a specific i-node in the i-node list. UNIX uses your working directory i-node number to begin its search, or if you give a full pathname, it starts from the root directory which always has the i-node 2.

Suppose your current directory is **david**, and you have a subdirectory **memos**, and a file called **report** in **memos**, and you want to access **report**. UNIX starts searching from your current directory, **david** (with a known i-node number), and finds the filename **memo** and its **i-node** number. Next, it reads the **memos** i-node record from the i-node list. The **memos** i-node indicates the block that contains the **memos** directory.

Looking into the block that contains the filenames under **memos**, UNIX finds the **report** filename and its i-node number. UNIX repeats the above process, reads the i-node record from i-node list. Information in this record includes the location of the blocks on the disk that make the **report** file. (See figure 7–8.)

How do you determine what a file's i-node number is? You use the **ls** command with **-i** option. For example, assume your working directory is **david** and you have a subdirectory **memos** and a file called **report** in it.

List filenames and their associated i-node numbers in your current directory.

```
$ ls -i
4311          memos
7446          report
$_
```

Figure 7–8
The directory structure and i-node list.

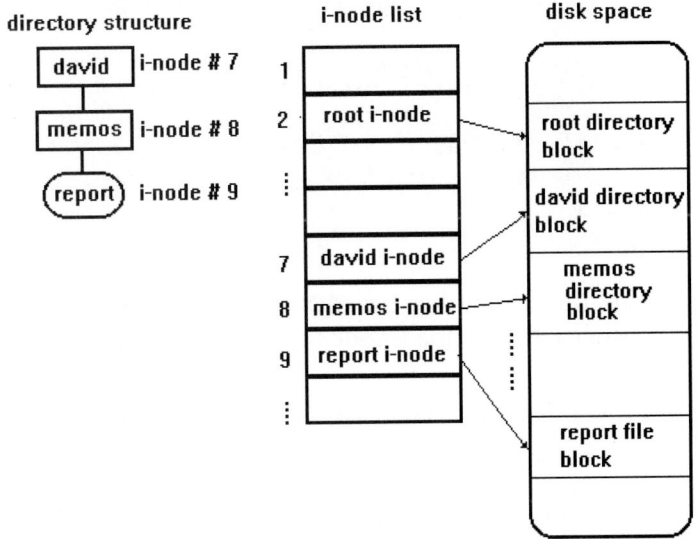

 Make a copy of report, calling it report.old, and then show the i-node numbers.

```
$ cp report report.old
$ ls -i
4311          memos
7446          report
7431          report.old
$_
```

The new i-node number for the report.old indicates that a new file has been created and a new i-node number is associated with it.

 Move the report.old file to the memos directory, and then show the i-node numbers.

```
$ mv report.old memos
$ ls -i
4311          memos
7446          report
$ ls -i memos
7431          report.old
$_
```

report.old is moved to memos directory; its i-node number remains the same, but now it is associated with the memos directory.

Rename report.old in memos to report.sav.

```
$ mv memos/report.old  memos/report.sav
$ ls -i
4311          memos
7446          report
$ ls -i memos
7431          report.sav
$_
```

The i-node number for report.sav remains the same as before; only the name associated with the i-node number is changed.

Link report to a new filename rpt (create another filename for report) and check the i-node changes after the two files are linked, do the following:

```
$ mv memos/report.old  memos/report.sav
$ ls -i
4311          memos
7446          report
$ ls -i memos
7431          report.sav
$_
```

The i-node number for RPT, the new filename, is the same as report. Both the report i-node and the RPT i-node point to the same blocks that comprise the report file.

Command Summary

The following commands and options were discussed in this chapter.

pg
Displays files one screen at a time. You can enter the options or other commands when **pg** shows the prompt sign.

Option	Operation
-n	Does not requires [Return] to complete the single-letter commands.
-s	Displays messages and prompts in reverse video.
-num	Sets the number of lines per screen to the integer num. The default value is 23 lines.
-p*str*	Changes the prompt **:** (colon) to the string specified as *str*.
+*line-num*	Starts displaying the file from the line specified in *line-num*.
+/*pattern/*	Starts viewing at the line containing the first occurrence of the specified *pattern*.

The pg Command Operators
You can use these keys when **pg** is displaying the prompt sign.

Key	Operation
+*n*	Advances *n* screen where *n* is an integer number.
-*n*	Backs up *n* screen where *n* is an integer number.
+*n*l	Advances *n* lines where *n* is an integer number.
-*n*l	Backs up *n* screen where *n* is an integer number.
n	Goes to screen n where n is an integer number.

cp
Copies file(s) in the current directory or from one directory to another.

Option	Operation
-i	Asks for confirmation if the target file already exists.
-r	Copies directories to a new directory.

mv
Renames files or moves files from one location to another.

---

ln
Creates links between an existing file and another filename or directory.
Lets you have more than one name for a file.

---

pr
Formatting your file before printing or viewing on the screen.

Option	Operation
+_page_	Starts displaying from the specified _page_. The default is page 1.
-_columns_	Displays output in the specified number of _columns_. The default is 1 column.
-a	Displays output in columns across the page, one line per column.
-d	Displays output in double spaces.
-h_str_	Replaces the filename in the header with the specified string _str_.
-l_number_	Sets the page length to the specified _number_ of lines. The default is 66 lines.
-m	Displays all the specified files in multiple columns.
-p	Pauses at the end of each page and sounds the terminal bell.
-s_character_	Separates columns with a single specified _character_. If _character_ is not specified, then tab is used.
-t	Suppresses the five lines header and five lines trailer.
-w_number_	Sets line width to the specified _number_ of characters. The default is 72.

---

wc
Counts number of characters, words, or lines in the specified file.

Option	Operation
-l	Reports number of lines.
-w	Reports number of words.
-c	Reports number of characters.

Review Exercises

1. What are the symbols used for the redirection operators?

2. Explain input and output redirection.

3. What are the commands to read a file?

4. What is the difference between moving (**mv**) a file and copying (**cp**) a file?

5. What is the command to rename a file?

6. Is it possible to have more than one name for a file?

7. What are the four regions (blocks) of a UNIX disk? Explain each part.

8. What is an i-node number, and how is it used to locate a file?

9. What is the i-node list, and what is the major information stored in each node?

10. Which of the following commands changes or creates an i-node number?

    a. mv file1 file2
    b. cp file1 file2
    c. ln file1 file2

Match the commands shown on the left column to the explanation shown on the right.

1. wc xxx> yyy

    a. Copy xxx to yyy.

2. cp xxx yyy

    b. Rename xxx to yyy.

3. ln xxx yyy

    c. Copy all filenames that begin with file and exactly 2 characters (any characters) after it.

4. mv xxx yyy

    d. Delete all files in the current directory.

5. rm *

    e. Create another filename for xxx; call it yyy.

6. ls *[1-6]

    f. Display the contents of myfile.

7. copy file?? source

    g. Copy myfile to yyy.

8. pr -2 myfile

    h. Add all files that have exactly one character before the word *file* into one file called yyy.

9. ls -i

    i. Format myfile in 2 columns.

10. pg myfile

    j. List all files having filenames ending with digits 1 to 6.

11. cat myfile

    k. List the current directory filenames and their i-node numbers.

12. cat myfile > yyy   l. Create a file called **yyy** that contains the count of characters in file **xxx**.

13. cat ?file >> yyy   m. View **myfile** one screen at a time.

Terminal Session

In this terminal session, you practice the commands disccussed in this chapter by creating directories and then manipulating files in the directories.

1. Create a directory called **memos** in your home directory.

2. Using the vi editor, create a file called **myfile** in your home directory.

3. Using the **cat** command, append **myfile** a few times to create a large file (say, 10 pages). Call this file **large**.

4. Using the **pg** command and its options, view **large** on the screen.

5. Using the **pr** command and its options, format **large** and print it.

6. Use copy command to copy all files in your home directory to **memos**.

7. Use the **ln** command to create another name for **large**.

8. Using the **mv** command rename **large** to **larg.old**.

9. Using the **mv** command, move **large.old** to **memos**.

10. Use the **ls** command and the **-i** and **-l** options to observe the changes in i-node numbers and number of links when you do the following commands:

    a. Change to the **memos** directory.
    b. Create another name for **myfirst**; call it **MF**.
    c. Copy **myfirst** to **myfirst.old**.
    d. List all files whose filenames start with **my**.
    e. List all files that have extension **old**.
    f. Modify **myfile**. Look at **MF** file; **myfile** modifications are also in **MF** file.
    g. Change to your home directory.
    h. Delete all files in **memos** directory that have the word *file* as part of their filenames.
    i. Delete the **memos** directory with all of the remaining files in it.
    j. List your home directory.
    k. Remove all the files you created in this session.

CHAPTER **8**

Exploring the Shell

This chapter describes the shell and its role in the UNIX system, explaining shell features and capabilities. It discusses shell variables and explains their use and the way they are defined. The chapter introduces more shell metacharacters and ways to make the shell to ignore their special meanings. It also explains UNIX startup files, process, and process management. This chapter continues the introduction of the new commands (utilities), so you can build your vocabulary of the UNIX commands.

In This Chapter

8.1   THE UNIX SHELL

The UNIX operating system consists of two parts: the *kernel* and the *utilities*. The *kernel* is the heart of the UNIX system and is memory-resident (which means that it stays in the memory from the time you boot the system until the system is shut down). All the routines that communicate directly with the hardware are concentrated in the kernel, which is relatively small in comparison with the rest of the operating system.

In addition to the kernel, other essential modules are also memory-resident. These modules perform important functions such as input/output control, file management, memory management, processor time management, etc. Additionally, UNIX maintains several memory-resident tables for housekeeping purposes, to keep track of the system's status.

The rest of the UNIX system resides on the disk and is loaded into the memory only when necessary. Most of the UNIX commands you know are programs (called utilities) that reside on the disk. For those programs, when you type a command (request the program to be executed), the specified program is loaded into the memory.

You communicate with the operating system through a shell, and hardware-dependent operations are managed by the kernel. Figure 8–1 shows the components of the UNIX operating system.

The shell is itself a program (a utility program). It loads into memory whenever you log in to the system. When the shell is ready to receive commands, it displays a prompt. The shell itself does not carry out most of the commands that you type; it examines each command and starts the appropri-

Figure 8–1
The UNIX components.

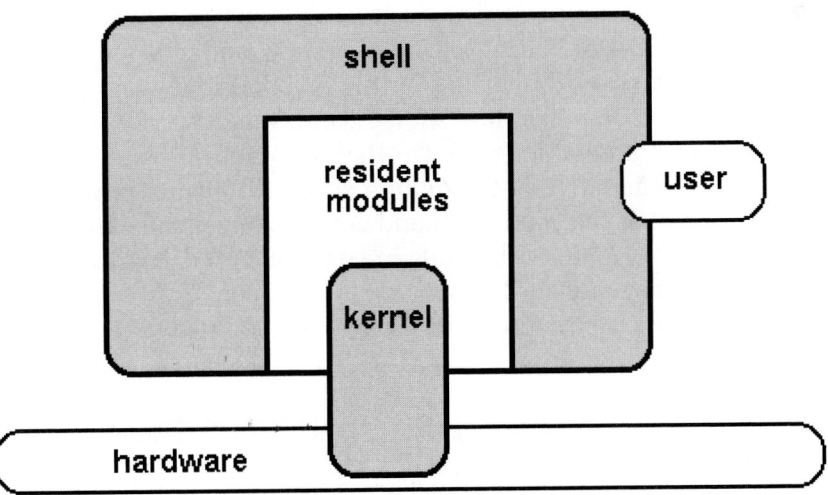

See page xxii for an explanation of icons used to highlight information in this chapter.

Figure 8–2
User interaction with the shell.

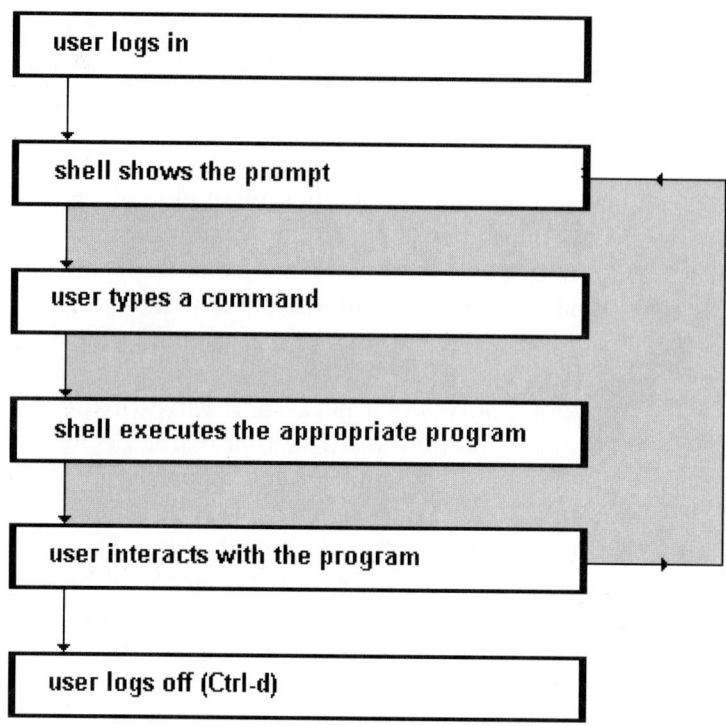

ate UNIX program (utility) that carries out the requested action. The shell determines what program to start (the name of the program is the same as the command you type). For example, when you type **ls** and press [Return] to list current directory files, shell finds and starts a program called **ls**. The shell treats your application programs the same way: you type the program's name as a command, and shell executes the program for you. Figure 8–2 shows the user interaction with the shell program.

The shell also contains several built-in commands. These commands are part of the shell itself and are recognized and executed internally. You already know some of the built-in commands (**cd**, **pwd**, and others).

The standard UNIX system comes with more than 200 utility programs. One of these programs is **sh**, the shell itself.

8.1.1   Understanding the Shell Major Functions

The shell is the most frequently used utility program on the UNIX system. It is a sophisticated program that manages the dialogue between the user and the UNIX system. You interact with it repeatedly during work sessions. The shell is a regular executable C program that is usually stored in /bin directory. One of the the most commonly used shell programs is *Bourne shell*, named after its developer; it is stored under the name sh in the /bin directory. When you log in, an interactive Bourne shell is invoked automatically. However, you can invoke shell (another copy of it) by typing **sh** at the $ prompt.

The shell includes the following major features. You are already familiar with some of these features, and the rest of them are explored in this chapter.

Command Execution   Command (program) execution is a major function of the shell. Just about anything you type at the prompt is interpreted by the shell. When you press [Return] at the end of the command line, the shell starts analyzing your command; if there are filename substitution characters, or input/output redirection signs, it takes care of them, and then executes the appropriate program.

Filename Substitution   If filename substitution (also called *filename generation*) is specified on the command line, then the shell first performs the substitution and then executes the program. The shell program itself is not involved in the substitution process. (The filename substitution characters — metacharacters * and ?—were discussed in chapter 7.)

I/O Redirection   The input/output redirection is handled by the shell. Again the shell program itself is not involved, and the redirection is set up before the command execution. If input or output redirection is specified on the command line, the shell opens the file and connects it to the standard input or standard output of the program respectively. This topic was discussed in chapter 7.

Pipes   Pipes, also called *pipelines*, let you connect simple programs together to perform a more complex task. The vertical line on the keyboard, [I], is the pipe operator.

Environment Control   The shell lets you customize your environment to suit your needs. By setting the appropriate variables, you may change your home directory, prompt sign, or other aspects of the working environment.

Background Processing   The background processing capability of the shell enables you to run programs in the background while doing other jobs in the foreground. This is helpful for time-consuming, noninteractive programs.

Shell Scripts   Commonly used sequences of the shell commands can be stored in files called *shell scripts*. The name of the file can later be used to execute the stored program, enabling you to execute the stored commands with a single command. The shell also includes language constructs that allow you to build shell scripts that perform more complex jobs. Shell scripts are discussed in chapter 11.

8.1.2   Displaying Information: The *echo* Command

You can use the **echo** command to display messages. It displays its arguments on your terminal, the standard output device. Without argument, it produces an empty line, and by default appends a new line to the end of the output. For example, if you type **echo hello there** and press [Return] at the prompt, you will see the following:

    hello there

 The argument string can be any number of characters. However, if your string contains any metacharacters, the string must be enclosed in quotation marks. (This topic is discussed further in this chapter.)

Table 8–1 shows the characters that you can use as part of a string to control the format of the message. These characters are preceded by a backslash (\) and are interpreted by shell to produce the desired output. They are also called *escape characters.*

 The backslash itself is a shell metacharacter. Therefore, if it is used in your string, it must be enclosed in quotation marks.

 The following command sequences show how to use the **echo** command, and the result of incorporating the escape characters in the argument string.

    $ echo Hi, this is a test. [Return] . . . . . Show a simple message on the
                                                 screen.

    Hi, this is a test.

    $ echo Hi, "\n" this is a test. [Return]. . Show the same message in two
                                                 lines.

    Hi,
    this is a test.

    $_ . . . . Prompt.

Table 8–1
The escape characters.

Escape character	Meaning
\n	Carriage return and a linefeed (newline).
\t	Tab.
\b	Backspace .
\r	Carriage return without a linefeed.
\c	Inhibit carriage return.

\n must be enclosed in quotation marks to be interpreted as the *nextline* command.

$ **echo Hi, "\n" this is a test. > test [Return]** . . This time save the output in a file.

$ **cat test [Return]** . . . . Confirm the contents of test.

Hi,
this is a test.

$_ . . . . Prompt.

$ **echo Hi, "\n" this is a test. "\c" [Return]** . . . . This time do not produce the nextline at the end of the message.

Hi,
this is a test.$

The prompt sign (**$**) appears right after the word *test*. That is the effect of **\c** in the argument string.

$ **echo This is a test. [Return]** . . . . . See what happens to the blanks.

This is a test.

The shell interprets the above command line with four arguments, and each argument is separated with a space in the output.

$ **echo "This is a test." [Return]** . . . . . . See the wonders of quotation mark; now the blank spaces are preserved.

This is a test.

$ _ . . . . And the prompt.

8.1.3   Removing Metacharacters' Special Meanings

The shell metacharacters have special meanings to the shell. But sometimes you want to override those meanings. The shell provides you with a set of characters that remove the meaning of the metacharacters. This process of removing the special meaning of the metacharacters is called *quoting* or *escaping*. The set of quoting characters is as follows

- backslash [\]
- double quotation mark ["]
- single quotation mark [']

The **echo** *command is used in most of the following examples to demonstrate how this process works. However, use of quoting is applicable to other commands when you have to use any of the special characters as part of the command's argument.*

Backslash   The backslash [\] is used to make the character that follows it be interpreted as an ordinary alphanumeric character. For example, [?] is a file substitution character (wildcard) and has a special meaning to the shell. But \? is interpreted as the real question mark.

Delete a file called temp? from your current directory.

     $ **rm temp? [Return]** . . . . Remove temp?.

The shell interprets this command as deleting all files whose filenames consist of temp and one character after it. Therefore, it deletes any file that matches this pattern, such as temp, temp1, temp2, tempa, tempo, etc.
    All you wanted to delete was a single file called temp?.

     $ **rm temp\? [Return]** . . . . Try again, using \? to represent the ?

This time shell scans the command line, finds the \, ignores the special meaning of the question mark, and passes the filename temp? to the **rm** program.

Display the metacharacters.

     $ **echo \< \> \" \' \$ \? \& \ | \\ [Return]** . Let's do them all.

     < > " ' $? & | \

     $_ . . . . Ready for the next command.

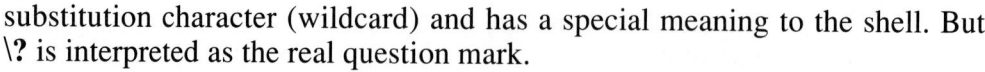

To remove the special meaning of the backslash, precede it with a backslash.

Double Quotation Marks   You can use the double quotation marks ["] to override the meaning of most of the special characters. Any special character between a pair of double quotation marks loses its special meaning, except the dollar sign (before a variable name), the single quotation mark, and the double quotation mark. (You use the backslash to remove their special meaning.)
    Double quotation marks also preserve the white-space characters: the blank space, tab, and new line characters. The use of double quotation marks for this purpose was demonstrated in the **echo** command examples.

The following command sequences show the application of the double quotation marks.

     $ **echo > [Return]** . . . . Display the > sign.

     syntax error: 'newline or ;' unexpected

     $_ . . . . And the prompt.

The shell interprets your command as redirecting the output of the **echo** command to a file. It looks for the filename and because none is specified, it responds with the cryptic error message.

```
$ echo ">" [Return] . . . . . . . . . . . . . .  Enclose the argument with double
                                                 quotation marks. The > is displayed.

>

$ ls -C [Return] . . . . . . . . . . . . . . . .  Check your current directory files.
memos          myfirst       REPORTS

$ echo * [Return] . . . . . . . . . . . . . . .  Use a metacharacter as argument.
memos          myfirst       REPORTS
```

The shell substitutes * with the names of all the files in your current directory.

```
$ echo "*" [Return] . . . . . . . . . . . . . .  Now use the double quotation marks.
*

$_ . . . . . . . . . . . . . . . . . . . . . . . . . . .  And the prompt.
```

No substitution occurs between the double quotation marks. Therefore, the special meaning of the * is removed.

Display the message "The UNIX System".

```
$ echo "\"The UNIX System\"" [Return]
"The UNIX system"
```

A backslash is necessary before a double quotation mark to inhibit the special meaning of the double quotation marks.

Single Quotation Marks   Single quotation marks ['] work very much like the double quotation marks. Any special character between a pair of single quotation marks loses its special meaning, except the single quote mark. (You use \' to remove its special meaning.)

Single quotation marks also preserve the white-space characters. The string between the single quotation marks becomes a single argument, and the space character no longer has its special meaning as argument separator.

The open and close quotation marks for this purpose are the same character, the forward quote. Do not use the back quotation mark (the accent grave character [`]). This distinction is very important. The shell interprets the string inside the back quotation marks as an executable command.

Display special characters using a pair of single quotation marks.

```
$ echo ' <   >   "   $   ?   &   | ' [Return]. . . .  Use the echo command and
                                                      single quotation marks.

 <   >   "   $   ?   &   |

$_ . . . . . . . . . . . . . . . . . . . . . . . . . . . . . . . .  Prompt is back.
```

The spaces between the characters are preserved.

8.2   SHELL VARIABLES

The shell program handles the user interface and acts as a command interpreter. In order for the shell to service all your requests (executing commands, manipulating files, etc.), it needs to have certain information and to keep track of that information: your home directory, terminal type, and prompt sign.

This information is stored in what are called the *shell variables*. *Variables* are named items you set to values to control or customize your environment. The shell supports two types of variables: environment variables and local variables.

Environment Variables   Environment variables are also known as *standard variables*; they have names that are known to the system. They are used to keep track of the essential things and are usually defined by the system administrator. For example, the standard variable TERM is assigned to your terminal type:

TERM= vt100

Local Variables   Local variables are user-defined; they are entirely under your control. You define, change, or delete them as you wish.

8.2.1   Displaying and Removing Variables: The *set* and *unset* Commands

You can use the **set** command to find out what shell variables are set for your shell to use.

Figure 8–3
The output of the set command.

```
$ SET
HOME= /usr/students/david
IFS=
LOGNAME= david
LOGTTY= /dev/tty06
MAIL= /usr/mail/students/david
MAILCHECK= 600
PATH= :/bin:/usr/bin
PS1= "$ "
PS2= ">"
TERM= wyse50
TZ= EST5EDT
$ _
```

Type **set** at the prompt and press [Return], and shell displays the list of the variables. Your list will be similar to but not exactly like that in figure 8–3.

The names of the standard variables on the left of the equal (=) sign are shown in uppercase letters in figure 8–3. This is not a requirement; you can use lowercase, uppercase, or any mixture of them for variable names.

The right side of the equal sign is the value assigned to a variable. You can use characters, digits, and the underscore character in variable names, but the first letter must be a character, not a digit.

 You must specify the exact variable name (including capitalization) when referring to a variable.

You use the **unset** command to remove an unwanted variable. If you have a variable **XYZ=10**, and you want to remove it, type: **$ unset XYZ** and press [Return].

8.2.2　　Assigning Values to Variables

You can create your own variables, and you can also modify the values assigned to standard variables. You assign values to a variable by writing the variable name, followed by an equal (=) sign (the assignment operator), followed by the value you want to assign to the variable, like this:

age=32

or

SYSTEM=UNIX

The shell treats every value that you assign to a variable as a string of characters. In the preceding example, the value of the variable age is the string 32, and not the number 32. If your string contains embedded white-space characters (space, tab, etc.), you must enclose the entire string in pair of double quotation marks, like this:

message= "Save your files, and log off" [Return]

 1.　A shell variable name must begin with a (lowercase or uppercase) letter and not a digit.

2.　The are no spaces on either side of the equal sign.

8.2.3　　Displaying the Values of Shell Variables

To access the value stored in a shell variable, you must precede the name of the variable with a [$]. Using the previous example, age is the name of the variable, and **$age** is 32, the value stored in the age variable.

You use the **echo** command to display the value assigned to the shell variable.

set displays a list of variables; echo shows the specified variable.

Use the **echo** command to display text and values of the shell variables.

$ age= 32 [Return]. . . . . Assign the value **32** to *age*.

$ echo Hi, nice day [Return] . . . . Display the argument string.

HI, nice day

$ echo age [Return]. . . . . Display the argument,
the word *age*.

age

$ echo $age [Return]. Now the argument is **$age**,
the value stored in *age*.

32

$ echo you are $age years old. [Return] . . . . . Add some text to obtain
more meaningful output.

You are 32 years old.

$_ . . . . Ready for the next command.

The shell variables are frequently used as a command argument on a command line, as in the following:

$ all= -lFa [Return]. . . . . Create a variable called *all* and
assign the value (string) **-lFa**
(hyphen, lowercase letter *l*,
uppercase letter *F*, lowercase
letter *a*) to it.

$ file= myfirst [Return] . . . . Create a variable called file, and
assign the string myfirst to it.

$ echo $all $file [Return]. . . . . Show the values of the two
variables.

-lFa myfirst

$ echo "All = $all   File = $file" [Return] . . . . . Add some text so a more
meaningful display is obtained.

All = -lFa   File = myfirst

$ ls $all $file [Return] . . . . Use the two variables as part of a
command line.

command's output

$_ . . . . Prompt is displayed.

Variable names are preceded by [$]. Thus the shell substitutes the variables all and file with the values stored in them -laF and myfirst respectively. After substitutions, the command becomes **ls -lFa myfirst**.

Observe the outputs of the following commands. They show the subtle differences in the way the variables are interpreted between the quotation marks.

$ **echo age= 32 [Return]** . . . . **32** is assigned to variable *age*.

$ **echo $age "$age" '$age' [Return]** . . . Display age.

32 32 $age

$_ . . . . Prompt.

8.2.4   Understanding the Shell Standard Variables

The values assigned to the standard shell variables are usually set by the system administrator. Thus, when you log in, the shell refers to these variables to keep track of things in your environment. You can change the value of these variables. However, the changes are temporary and apply only to the current session. Next time you log in, you have to set them again. If you want the changes to be permanent, place them in a file called .**profile**. The .**profile** file is explained later in this chapter.

HOME

When you log in, shell assigns the full pathname of your home directory to the variable HOME. The HOME variable is used by several UNIX commands to locate the home directory. For example, the **cd** command with no argument checks this variable to determine the pathname to the home directory and then sets the system to your home directory.

To experiment with the HOME variable, try the following command sequence.

$ **echo $HOME [Return]** . . . . Show your home directory pathname.

/usr/david

$ **pwd [Return]**. . . . . Show the current directory pathname.

/usr/david/source . . . . source subdirectory in david.

$ **cd [Return]** . . . . No argument is specified. Default is your home directory.

$ **pwd [Return]**. . . . . Check your current directory. You are in david, your home directory.

/usr/david

$ **HOME= /usr/david/memos/important [Return]**

. . . . Change your home directory pathname. Now your home directory is important.

$ **cd [Return]** . . . . Change to your home directory.

$ **pwd [Return]**. . . . . Display your current directory; your
current directory is important.

/usr/david/memos/important

$_ . . . . And the prompt.

IFS

The Internal Field Separator (IFS) variable is set to a list of characters that are
interpreted by the shell as separators of command-line elements. For example,
to get a long list of the files in your directory, you type **ls -l** and press [Return].
The space character in your command separates the command word (**ls**) from its
option (**-l**).

Other separator characters assigned to the IFS variable are the tab character
([Tab]) and the new line character ([Return]).

The IFS characters are invisible (nonprintable) characters, so you do not see
them on the right side of the equal sign. But they are there!

To change the IFS characters, do the following:

$ **ls -C [Return]** . . . . In this command line, space character is
the delimiter.

memos   myfirst   Report

$ **sav.IFS= $IFS [Return]** . . . . Just to be safe, save the old IFS values.

$ **IFS= ! [Return]** . . . . Change IFS value to exclamation point.

$ **ls!-C [Return]** . . . . In this command, the exclamation point
is the delimiter. It's awkward, but it work
fine.

$ **IFS= $sav.IFS [Return]** . . . . Change the delimiter back to the original
one.

$_ . . . . And the prompt.

MAIL

The MAIL variable is set to the filename of the file that receives your mail. Mail
sent to you is stored in this file, and shell periodically checks the contents of this
file to notify you if there is mail for you. For example, to set your mailbox
to /usr/david/mbox, you would type **MAIL=/usr/david/mbox** and press
[Return].

MAILCHECK

The MAILCHECK variable specifies how often the shell is to check for arrival
of mail in the file set in the MAIL variable. The default for MAILCHECK is
600 (seconds).

PATH

The PATH variable is set to the directory names that the shell searches for the location of the commands (programs) in the directory structure. For example, **PATH=:/bin:/usr/bin**.

The directories in the path string are separated by colons. If the very first character in the path string is a colon, the shell interprets that as **.:** (*dot, colon*), meaning that your current directory is first on the list and is searched first.

UNIX usually stores the executable files in a directory called bin. You can create your own bin directory and store your executable files in it. If you add your bin directory (or any other name you call it) to the PATH, the shell looks there for any commands that it cannot find in the standard directories.

Suppose all of your executable files are located in a subdirectory called mybin that is located in your home directory. To add it to the PATH, you type **PATH=:/bin:/usr/bin:$HOME/mybin** and press [Return].

PS1

The Prompt String 1 (PS1) variable is set to the string used as your prompt sign. The Bourne shell primary prompt sign is set to dollar sign ($).

If you are tired of seeing the $ prompt, you can easily change it by assigning a new value to the shell variable PS1.

$ **PS1= Here: [Return]** . . . . Change your prompt to **Here:**

Here:_. . . . . There you are.

Here: **PS1= "Here: " [Return]** . . . . Add an extra blank space to the end.

Here: _ . . . . It looks nicer!

If your prompt string has embedded spaces, then it must be enclosed in quotation marks.

Here: **PS1= "Next Command: " [Return]**

. . . . Change the prompt sign again.

Next Command: _. . . . . And it is changed.

Next Command: **PS1= "$ " [Return]** . . . Change back to the old **$** prompt.

$_ . . . . And the **$** prompt returns.

PS2

The Prompt String 2 variable assigns the prompt sign that is displayed whenever you press [Return] before completion of the command line and shell expects the rest of the command. You can change the PS2 variable the same way you change the PS1 variable. The Bourne shell secondary prompt defaults to the greater than sign (>).

The following command sequences show examples of the second prompt.

```
$ echo "Good news, UNIX [Return] . . . The command line is not completed,
                                    thus the PS2 prompt sign (>) is displayed.

>  is on video tape." [Return] Now the command line is complete.

Good news, UNIX is on vedio tape.

$ ls \ [Return] . . . . . . . . The command line is not completed. This
                                is signaled by the backslash.

> . . . . . . . . . . . . . . . . . . . . . . . . . . . . . shell displays the second prompt sign,
  . . . . . . . . . . . . . . . . . . . . . . . . . . . . . and waits for the rest of the command.

>  -l [Return] . . . . . . . . . . . . . . . . . . . . . Now the command line is complete.
                                          shell puts it together as ls -l and executes.

$_ . . . . . . . . . . . . . . . . . . . . . . . . . . . . And the prompt is back.
```

CDPATH

The CDPATH variable is set to a list of absolute pathnames, similar to the PATH variable. The CDPATH effects the operation of the **cd** (change directory) command. If this variable is not defined, then **cd** searches your working directory to find the filename that matches its argument. If the subdirectory does not exist in your working directory, then UNIX displays an error message. If this variable is defined, **cd** searches for specified directory according to the pathnames assigned to CDPATH variable. If the directory is found, it becomes your working directory.

For example, if you type **CDPATH=:$HOME:$HOME/memos** and press [Return], the next time you use the **cd** command, it will start searching from your current directory, then your home directory, and eventually the **memos** directory to find a match to the filename specified as the **cd** command argument.

SHELL

The SHELL variable is set to the full pathname of your login shell:

    SHELL= /bin/sh

TERM

The TERM variable sets your terminal type:

    TERM= vt100

TZ

The TZ variable sets the time zone that you are in:

TZ= EST5EDT

It is usually set up by the system administrator.

8.3   MORE METACHARACTERS

As you remember from chapter 7, metacharacters, or special characters, are in-terperated and processed in a special manner by the shell. So far, we have dis-cussed the file substitution and redirection metacharacters. This section explores some more of them.

8.3.1   Executing the Commands: Using Single Back Quotation Marks

The back quotation marks ['] tell the shell to execute the enclosed command and to insert the command's output at same point on the command line. It is also called *command substitution*. The format is as follows:

'command'

where *command* is the name of the command to be executed.

The following command sequences show examples of command substitution.

$ **echo The date and time is: 'date' [Return]** . . Command date is executed.

The date and time is: Mon 16 30:14:14 EDT 2001

$_ . . . . Prompt is back.

The shell scans the command line, finds the back quotation marks, and executes the command date. It replaces the **'date'** on the command line with the output from the date and executes the echo command.

$ **echo List of filename in your current directory:\n 'ls -C' > LIST [Return]**

$ **cat LIST [Return]** . . . . Check what you have stored in LIST.

List of filenames in your current directory:
memos   myfirst   REPORT

$_ . . . . Ready for the next command.

8.3.2   Sequencing the Commands: Using the Semicolon

You can enter series of commands on a command line, separated by semicolons.
The shell executes them in sequence from left to right.

To experiment with the semicolon metacharacter, try the following:

$ **date ; pwd ; ls -C [Return]** . . . . Three commands in sequence.

 Mon Nov 28   14:14:14 EST 2001

/usr/david

memos   myfirst   REPORT

$ **ls -C > list ; date > today ; pwd [Return]** . . . . Three commands in sequence,
                                                 with output of two commands
                                                 redirected to files.

/usr/david

$ **cat list [Return]** . . . . Check contents of *list*.

memos   myfirst   REPORT

$ **cat today [Return]** . . . . Check contents of *today*.

Mon Nov 28   14:14:14 EST 2001

$_ . . . . Your favorite prompt sign.

8.3.3   Grouping the Commands: Using Parentheses

You can group commands together by placing them between a pair of parentheses. The group of commands can be redirected as if they were a single
command.

To experiment with the parentheses as metacharacters, try the following:

$ **(ls -C ; date ; pwd) > outfile [Return]** . . . . Three commands in sequence,
                                                 grouped together, with output
                                               redirected to a file.

$ **cat outfile [Return]** . . . . Check contents of outfile.

 memos   myfirst   REPORT
Mon Nov 28   14:14:14 EST 2001
/usr/david

$_ . . . . And the prompt.

8.3.4   Background Processing: Using the Ampersand

UNIX is a multitasking system; it allows you to execute programs concurrently. Usually, you type a command and within a few seconds the output of the command is displayed on the terminal. What if you run a command that takes minutes to execute? In that case, you have to wait for the command to finish executing before you can proceed with the next job. However, you do not need to wait all those unproductive minutes. The shell metacharacter ampersand (&) provides you the means to run programs in the background, as long as the background programs do not require input from the keyboard. If you enter a command followed by [**&**], then that command is sent to the background for execution, and your terminal is free for the next command.

The following examples show applications of the ampersand metacharacter:

$ **sort data > sorted & [Return]**	Sort data and store the results in sorted.
1348	Process Id is displayed.
$ **date [Return]**.	Prompt is immediately displayed, ready for next command.

The output of the **sort** command is redirected to another file. This prevents **sort** from sending its output to the terminal while you are doing other tasks.

1.   *The background command process id (PID) number identifies the background process and can be used to terminate or obtain its status.*

2.   *You can specify more than one background command on a single command line.*

$ **date & pwd & ls -c & [Return]**	Create three background processes; three PID numbers are displayed.

2215
2217
2216

$ **echo "the foreground process" [Return]**

. . . .	Run **echo** command in foreground.
Mon Nov 28 14:14:14 EST 2001 . .	Output from background process **date**.
the foreground process	Output from foreground process **echo**.
/usr/david	Output from background process **pwd**.
$_	Prompt, and then output from background process **ls -C**.

memos   myfirst   REPORT

$_	Ready for the next command.

By default, the outputs of the background commands are displayed on your terminal. Thus the output of the foreground program is interleaved with the output of the background program and produces quite a confusing display. You can prevent the confusion by redirecting the output of background commands to files.

8.3.5   Chaining the Commands: Using the Pipe Operator

The shell lets you to use the standard output of one process as standard input to another process. You use the pipe metacharacter, [|], between the commands. The general format is as follows:

>   command A | command B

where command A output is introduced as input to command B. You can chain a sequence of commands together, creating what is called a *pipeline*. Let's look at some examples that give you an appreciation of this very useful and flexible shell capability.

Type **ls -l | lp** and press [Return] to send the output of the **ls -l** command to the printer.

To count number of the files in your current directory, do the following:

$ ls -C [Return] . . . . Let's see the files in your current directory.

memos   myfirst   REPORT

$ ls -C > count [Return] . . . . Now save the list of your files in count.

$ wc -w count [Return] . . . . Count the number of words. You have 3 files in your current directory.

3

ls -C | wc -w [Return] . . . . Use the pipe operator to obtain the number of files in your current directory.

3

The output of the command **ls -C** (list of the files in your current directory) is passed as input to the **wc -w** command.

To save number of users logged in the system in a file, do the following:

$ echo " Number of the logged in users: " ' who | wc -l ' > outfile [Return]

$ cat outfile [Return] . . . . Check what is stored in outfile.

Number of the logged in users: 20

In the above command, shell scans the command line, finds the back quotation marks, executes the **who| wc -l** commands, and passes the output of the **who** to the **wc** as input data. If there are 20 users logged on the system, then the output is 20. The shell replaces the **'who | wc -l'** with 20. Then the shell executes the **echo** command that reads *Number of the logged in users: 20* and stores the output in outfile.

8.4   MORE UNIX UTILITIES

These utilities give you more flexibility and control in day-to-day usage of the system. Also, some of the utilities are used in script file (program) examples in chapter 11 and 12.

8.4.1   Timing a Delay: The *sleep* Command

The **sleep** command causes the process executing it to go to sleep for a specified number of seconds. You can use **sleep** to delay the execution of a command for a period of time. For example, if you type **echo sleep 120 ; echo " I am awake!"** and press [Return], the **sleep** command is executed, causes two minutes delay, and then (after two minutes) the **echo** command is executed, and the string argument *I am awake!* is displayed on the screen.

8.4.2   Displaying the PID: The *ps* Command

You use the **ps** (process status) command to obtain the status of the active processes in the system. When used without any options, it displays information about your active processes. This information is arranged in four columns (see figure 8–4) with the following column headings:

- PID: the process ID number
- TTY: your terminal number that controls the process
- TIME: time duration (in seconds) that your process is running
- COMMAND: the name of the command

Figure 8–4
The **ps** command output format.

```
$ ps
PID          TTY        TIME      COMMAND
24059        tty11      0:05      sh
24259        tty11      0:02      ps
$ _
```

Table 8–2
The **ps** command options.

Option	Operation
-a	Displays status of the all active processes, not just the user's.
-f	Displays a full list of information, including the full command line.

ps Options

Only two of the **ps** options are discussed in this book—the **-a** option and the **-f** option—and they are summarized in table 8–2.

-a option   The **-a** option displays status information for all active processes. Without this option, only your active processes are displayed.

-f option   The **-f** option option displays a full list of information including the complete command line under the command column.

Figure 8–5 shows the output of the **ps** command using both **-a** and **-f** options.

To find the process number of a process running in the background, do the following:

$ (**sleep 1200 ; echo "Had a nice long sleep") & [Return]**

24259 . . . . The background process ID number.

$ **ps [Return]** . . . . Show your processes' status.

PID TTY   TIME COMMAND

24059 tty11   0:05 sh. . . . . The login shell.

24070 tty11   0:00 sleep 1200 . . . . The **sleep** command.

24259 tty11   0:02 ps. . . . . The **ps** command.

$ Had a nice long sleep. . . . . Output from the background process.

$_ . . . . And the prompt.

Figure 8–5
Output of the **ps** command with **-a** and **-f** options.

PID	TTY	TIME	COMMAND
24059	tty11	0:05	sh
24259	tty11	0:02	ps
24059	tty11	0:05	sh
24259	tty11	0:02	ps

The **sleep** command delays the execution of the **echo** command for two minutes. The **&** at the end of the command line places the commands in the background.

Separate the commands with semicolons, and group them together by placing them between the parentheses.

8.4.3   Keep On Running: The *nohup* Command

When you log out, your background processes are terminated. The **nohup** command causes your background processes to be immune to terminating signals. This is useful when you want your programs to continue processing after you have logged out.

If you type **nohup (sleep 1200 ; echo "job done") &** and press [Return] and then log out, your command process will continue in the background. Where is the **echo** command output displayed? As you are logged out, the process is not associated with any terminal, and the output is automatically saved in a file called nohup.out.

When you log in, you can check the contents of this file to determine the output of your background processes. Alternatively, you can always redirect the output of your background programs to specified files.

To experiment with the **nohup** command, try the following command sequence.

```
$ nohup(sleep 1200 ; echo "job done") & [Return]
........................................ Create a background job.

12235 .......................... Background job PID.

$ [Ctrl-d]........................ Log out and wait a few minutes.

login: david [Return] .............. Log in again.

password:.......................... Enter your password; it's not echoed to
                                      the screen.

$ cat nohup.out [Return]............ Check the contents of nohup.out file.
job done

$_ ............................. Ready for the next command.
```

8.4.4   Terminating a Process: The *kill* Command

Not all programs behave normally all the time. A program might be in an infinite loop or be waiting for resources that are not available. Sometimes an unruly program locks your keyboard, and then you are in real trouble! UNIX provides you with the **kill** command to terminate the unwanted process (*process* is a running program). The **kill** command sends a signal to the specified process. The signal is an integer number indicating the kill type (UNIX is a morbid language), and the process is identified by the process ID number (PID). In order to use the **kill** command, you must know the PID of the process that you intend to terminate.

Signals   Signals range from 0 to 15 and are mostly implementation-dependent. However, 15 is usually the default signal value and causes the receiving process to terminate.

Some processes protect themselves from the **kill** signals. You use the signal value 9 (sure kill) to terminate them.

The following command sequences illustrate the use of the **kill** and its signals.

To issue a simple **kill** command, try the following:

    $ (sleep 1200 ; echo Hi) & [Return] . . . Create a background process.

    22515 . . . . Process ID number.

    $ ps [Return] . . . . Check the process's status. It is there:

    PID TTY   TIME COMMAND

    24059 tty11   0:05 sh . . . . The login shell.

    22515 tty11   0:00 sleep 1200 . . . . The **sleep** command.

    24259 tty11   0:02 ps . . . . The **ps** command.

    $ kill 2515 [Return] . . . . Terminate the background process.

    job terminated

    $ ps [Return] . . . . Check again. The background process is
                                                        terminated.

    PID TTY   TIME COMMAND

    24059 tty11   0:05 sh . . . . The login shell.

    24259 tty11   0:02 ps . . . . The **ps** command.

    $_ . . . . And the prompt.

No signal number is specified. The default is signal number 15, which causes the receiving process to terminate.

To make sure an unruly process has been terminated, try the following:

    $ (sleep 1200 ; echo Hi) & [Return] . . . Create a background process.

    22515 . . . . Process id number.

    $ kill 22515 [Return] . . . . A simple kill.

```
$ ps [Return] . . . . . . . . . . . . . . . . . . . .  Check the process's status. It is still there:

PID TTY   TIME COMMAND

24059 tty11   0:05 sh. . . . . . . . . . . . . . .  The login shell.

22515 tty11   0:00 sleep 1200 . . . . . . . .  The sleep command.

24259 tty11   0:02 ps. . . . . . . . . . . . . .  The ps command.

$ kill -9 2515 [Return] . . . . . . . . . . . . .  A sure kill; signal value 9 is specified.

$ ps [Return] . . . . . . . . . . . . . . . . . . . .  Check again. Sure enough, the
                                                      background process is terminated.

PID TTY   TIME COMMAND

24059 tty11   0:05 sh. . . . . . . . . . . . . . .  The login shell.

24259 tty11   0:02 ps. . . . . . . . . . . . . .  The ps command.
```

 You can terminate only your own processes. The system administrator is authorized to terminate anybody's processes.

 To terminate all of your processes, do the following:

```
$ (sleep 1200; echo "sleep tight" ; sleep 1200) & [Return]

11234 . . . . . . . . . . . . . . . . . . . . . . . . . .  Sleep PID.

11236 . . . . . . . . . . . . . . . . . . . . . . . . . .  Echo PID.

11237 . . . . . . . . . . . . . . . . . . . . . . . . . .  Sleep PID.

$ kill -90 [Return]. . . . . . . . . . . . . . . . .  You are logged out.
```

 The PID 0 (zero) causes all processes associated with your shell to be terminated. That includes your login shell itself. Accordingly, when you use the 0 signal, you are logged out.

8.4.5 Splitting the Output: The *tee* Command

Sometimes you will want to look at the output of a program on the screen and also to store the output in a file for later reference or obtain a hard copy of the output on the printer. You can always do that this way: first run the command and viewing the output on the screen; then, using redirection operator, save the output in a file or send it to the printer.

Alternatively, you can use the **tee** command to get the same result in less time and with less typing. The **tee** command is usually used with the pipe operator. For example, when you type **sort phone.list | tee phone.sort** and press [Return], the pipe operator passes the output of the **sort** command (the sorted phone.list) to **tee**. Then **tee** displays it on the terminal and also saves it in phone.sort, the specified file.

This is an indispensable command when you want to capture the user/program dialog, running an interactive program.

Table 8–3
The tee command options.

Option	Operation
-a	Appends output to file, not overwriting an existing file.
-i	Ignores interrupts, does not responds to the interrupt signals.

Try viewing the contents of your current directory and saving the output in a file, as follows:

$ **ls -C | tee dir.list [Return]** . . . . Display the current directory filenames and also save the output in dir.list.

memos   myfile   REPORT

$ **cat dir.list [Return]** . . . . Check the contents of dir.list.

memos   myfile   REPORT

$_ . . . . The prompt.

The output of the **ls -C** is piped to **tee**. The **tee** command shows its input on the screen (displays the input on the default output device) and also saves it in a file called dir.list.

> tee Options

Table 8–3 summarizes the two options of the **tee** command.

To view the list of the users currently on the system, and save the list in an existing file called dir.list, type **who | tee -a dir.list** and press [Return]. If dir.list exists, then the output of the **who** command is added to the end of the file. If dir.list does not exist, it is created.

8.4.6   File Searching: The *grep* Command

You can use the **grep** command to search for a specified pattern in a file or list of files. The pattern used by the **grep** command is called *regular expression*, whence the strange name of the command (*Global Regular Expression Print*).

   grep is a file searching and selection command. You specify the filename and the pattern to be looked for in the file, and when **grep** finds a match, the line containing the specified pattern is displayed on the terminal. If no file is specified, the system searches through the input from the standard input device.

Look for the word *UNIX* in myfile.

> $ **cat myfile [Return]** . . . . Check contents of myfile.

I wish there were a better way to learn
UNIX. Something like having daily UNIX pill.

> $ **grep UNIX myfile [Return]** . . . . Find the lines that contain the word *UNIX*.

UNIX. Something like having daily UNIX pill.

You can specify more than one file or use file substitution (wild cards) in filenames.

Look for the string **"# include <private.h>"** in all the C source files.

□ Type **grep "#include <private.h>" *.c** and press [Return] to look for the pattern in all files with extension *c* in the current directory.

The pattern is a string with embedded spaces and metacharacters, so it is enclosed in the quotations.

If you specify more than one file to be searched, **grep** displays the name of the file preceding each line of output.

grep Options   If you do not specify any option, **grep** displays lines in the specified file(s) that contain a match for the specified pattern. The options give you more control over the output and the way pattern search is done. Table 8–4 summarizes the **grep** options.

Assuming you have the following three files in your current directory, the command sequences show examples of **grep** using options.

FILE1	FILE2	FILE3
UNIX	unix	Unix system
11122	11122	11122
BBAA	CCAA	AADD
unix system		

Table 8–4
The **grep** command options.

Option	Operation
-c	Displays only the count of the matching lines in each file that contain the match .
-i	Ignores lowercase or uppercase letters in the search pattern. They both match each other.
-l	Displays the names of the files with one or more matching lines, not the lines themselves.
-n	Displays a line number before each output line.
-v	Displays only those lines that do not match the pattern.

Search for the word *UNIX*.

> $ **grep UNIX FILE1 [Return]** . . . . Search for the word *UNIX* in FILE1.
> UNIX
>
> $_ . . . . And the prompt.

grep matches the exact pattern (uppercase or lowercase), so it finds the word *UNIX* and not *unix*.

Specify more than one file as argument, and use the **-i** option.

> $ **grep -i UNIX FILE? [Return]** . . . . Use the **-i** option.
> FILE1: UNIX
> FILE1: unix system
> FILE2: unix
> FILE3: Unix system
>
> $_ . . . . Your prompt.

The **-i** option tries to match the specified letter pattern, regardless of case. Thus the specified pattern *UNIX* matches *unix*, *Unix*, and so on.

The name of the file is displayed when you specify more than one file as the argument.

Show the lines that do not contain the word *UNIX*.

> $ **grep -vi UNIX FILE1 [Return]** . . . . Use options **-i** and **-v**.
> 11122
> BBAA
>
> $_ . . . . Prompt.

Display how many lines in each file do not contain *11*.

$ **grep -vc 11 FILE? [Return]**. . . . . Show count of the lines in FILE1, FILE2,
and FILE3 that do not contain *11*.

FILE1:3
FILE2:2
FILE3:2

$_ . . . . Prompt.

Find out whether user david is logged in.

$ **who | grep -i david [Return]** . . . . Use **grep** with the pipe operator.

$_ . . . . Prompt.

The pipe makes the output of the **who** to be the standard input to **grep**. Thus
grep scans the output of **who** for lines containing the pattern *david*.
In this example, **grep** did not produce any output. Thus david is not on the
system.

8.4.7   Sorting Text Files: The *sort* Command

You can use the **sort** command to sort the contents of a file into alphabetical or
numerical order. By default, the output is displayed on your terminal, but you
can specify a filename as argument or redirect the output to a file.

The **sort** command sorts the specified file on a line-by-line basis. If the
first characters on two lines are the same, it compares the second characters
to determine the order of the sort. If the second characters are the same, it
compares the third characters, and this process goes on until two characters
differ or the line ends. If two lines are identical, then it does not matter which
one is placed first.

*This command sorts files alphabetically, but the order of the sort might be
different from one computer to another, depending on the computer's code set.
The most commonly used code set in UNIX systems is ASCII.*

Many options can be used to control the sort order, but let's start with a simple
example to explore the **sort** basic functions.

Suppose you have file called junk in your working directory. Figure 8–6
shows contents of junk. Figure 8–7 shows the output of the **sort** command,
sorting the contents of junk.

1. *ASCII values for nonalphanumeric characters (space, dash, backslash,
etc.) are less than those for alphanumeric characters. Thus the line
starting with a blank space is placed at the top of the file.*

2. *Uppercase letters are sorted before lowercase letters. Thus in our example This appears before this.*

3. *Numbers sorted by the first digit. Thus 11 appears before 4.*

sort Options

The **sort** example showed that the result of the **sort** command, the sorted output, is probably not what you consider sorted. The **sort** command options give you freedom to sort files in a variety of orders. Table 8–5 summarizes some of the more useful options.

-b Option   The **-b** option causes **sort** to ignore the leading blanks (tabs and space characters). These characters are usually delimiters (field separators) in your file, and when you use this option **sort** does not consider them in sort comparison.

-d Option   The **-d** option, used for dictionary sorting, uses only letters, digits, and blanks (spaces and tabs) in sort comparison. It ignores the punctuation and control characters.

-f Option   The **-f** option considers all lowercase characters as uppercase characters; it ignores the distinction between them in **sort** comparison.

-n Option   The **-n** option causes numbers to be sorted by their arithmetic values rather than by their first digit. This includes ascribing minus signs and decimal points to their arithmetic meanings.

Figure 8–6
The junk file.

```
This is line one
this is line two
   this is a line starting with a space character
4: this is a line starting with a number
11: this is another line starting with a number
End of junk
```

Figure 8–7
The sorted junk file.

```
   this is a line starting with a space characters
11: this is another line starting with a number
4: this is a line starting with a number
End of junk
This is line one
this is line two
```

Table 8–5
The **sort** command options.

Option	Operation
-b	Ignores leading blanks.
-d	Uses the dictionary order for sorting. Ignores punctuation and control characters.
-f	Ignores the distinction between lowercase and uppercase letters.
-n	Numbers are sorted by their arithmetic values.
-o	Stores the output in the specified file.
-r	Reverses the order of the sort, from ascending to descending order.

-o Option   The **-o** option places the output in a specified file instead of the standard output.

-r Option   This **-r** option reverses the order of the sort, such as *z* to *a*.

Using the junk file again, let's see the effects of the options on the sorted output.

    $ **sort -fn junk [Return]** . . . . Sort junk using the **-f** and **-n** options.

     this is a line starting with a space characters
    End of junk
    This is line one
    this is line two
    4: this is a line starting with a number
    11: this is another line starting with a number

    $_ . . . . Prompt.

    $ **sort -f -r -o sorted junk [Return]** . . . . Sort junk using the **-f**, **-r**, and **-o** options
                                              and save it in sorted.

    $ **cat sorted [Return]** . . . . Display sorted.

    this is line two
    This is line one
    End of junk
    4: this is a line starting with a number
    11: this is another line starting with a number
     this is a line starting with a space characters

    $_ . . . . Prompt.

*A filename (*sorted*) is specified with the -o option. thus the output is saved in* sorted, *and cat is used to display the contents of* sorted.

8.4.8   Sorting on a Specified Field

Real files very seldom contain what is in the example file junk. Usually files you want to sort contain lists of people, items, addresses, phone numbers, mailing lists, and so on. By default, **sort** sorts on a line-by-line basis, you probably will want to sort files on a particular field, such as last name or area code.

You can direct the **sort** to look at a specified field for sort comparison, provided that the file is set up accordingly. You specify the desired field by a number that indicates how many fields **sort** must skip to get to the field by which you want the file sorted. You set up your file by breaking each line into fields. No extra effort is needed, because in most list files each line is already divided into fields.

Create a file called phone.list, which contains a list of people and their phone numbers, following figure 8–8, and then we'll use the file to explore the other capabilities of the **sort** command.

Each line in phone.list consists of four fields, and the fields are separated by space or tab characters. Thus, in line one, David is field 1, Brown is field 2, and so on.

In sorting phone.list, no particular field is specified. Thus list is sorted on a line-by-line basis.

Figure 8–8
Original phone.list file and sorted phone.list file.

```
$ cat .phone.list
David Brown          (703) 281-0014
Emma Redd            (202) 477-9000
Marie Lambert        (202) 444-6666
Susan Bahcall        (202) 668-7800
Steve Fraser         (301) 321-5566
Azi Jones            (202) 231-6500
Glenda Hardison      (301) 743-8822
[Ctrl-d]

$ sort phone.list
Azi Jones            (202) 231-6500
David Brown          (703) 281-0014
Emma Redd            (202) 477-9000
Glenda Hardison      (301) 743-8822
Marie Lambert        (202) 444-6666
Steve Fraser         (301) 321-5566
Susan Bahcall        (202) 668-7800
$_
```

You may not want to sort the file on the first name. To sort the file in order of the last name (field 2), you must instruct **sort** to skip one field (first name) before it starts the sorting process. You specify the number of fields **sort** is to skip as part of the command argument.

To sort phone.list on the last name (field 2), type **sort +1 phone.list** and press [Return]. Figure 8–9 shows the result of sorting the file by last name.

Figure 8–9
Sorted (by last name) phone.list file.

```
$ sort +1 phone.list
Susan Bahcall        (202) 668-7800
David Brown          (703) 281-0014
Steve Fraser         (301) 321-5566
Glenda Hardison      (301) 743-8822
Azi Jones            (202) 231-6500
Marie Lambert        (202) 444-6666
Emma Redd            (202) 477-9000
$ _
```

The **+1** argument indicates that **sort** must skip the first field (first name) before starting the sort process.

If you specify **+2**, then **sort** skips the first and second fields and starts from the third field (in this case, area code).

To sort phone.list on the third field (area code), type **sort +2 phone.list** and press [Return]. Figure 8–10 shows the problem that results.

sort skips two fields but counts the spaces after the second field as part of the third field. Thus the output list seems to be sorted on the order of smallest to largest last names.

To the solve this problem, you must instruct **sort** to ignore blank spaces (with the **-b** option).

Figure 8–10
Sorted (by area code) phone.list file.

```
$ sort +2 phone.list
Azi Jones            (202) 231-6500
Emma Redd            (202) 477-9000
David Brown          (703) 281-0014
Steve Fraser         (301) 321-5566
Susan Bahcall        (202) 668-7800
Marie Lambert        (202) 444-6666
Glenda Hardison      (301) 743-8822
$ _
```

Figure 8–11
Sorted (by area code) phone.list file.

```
$ sort -b +2 phone.list
Azi Jones              (202) 231-6500
Marie Lambert          (202) 444-6666
Emma Redd              (202) 477-9000
Susan Bahcall          (202) 668-7800
Steve Fraser           (301) 321-5566
Glenda Hardison        (301) 743-8822
David Brown            (703) 281-0014
$ _
```

 To sort phone.list on the third field, ignoring blanks, type **sort -b +2 phone.list** and press [Return]. Figure 8–11 shows the results.

8.5   STARTUP FILES

When you log in, the login program verifies your user ID and password against the list of authorized users stored in password file. If the login attempt is successful, the login program brings your home directory up on the system, sets up your user ID, group ID, and finally starts your shell. Before displaying its prompt sign, the shell checks for two special files. These two files are called *profile files*, and they contain shell scripts (programs) that shell can execute.

8.5.1   System Profile

The *system profile* is stored in /etc/profile. The first thing your shell does is execute this file. It typically contains commands that display the message of the day, set up system-wide environment variables, and so on. This file is usually created and maintained by the system administrator, and only the super-users can modify it.

Figure 8–12 shows an example of the system profile. The shell executes the commands in this file, so it displays the current date and time, then the message of the day (stored in /etc/motd file), and finally the recent news items.

Figure 8–12
An example of creating the profile file.

```
$ cat /etc/profile
date
cat /etc/motb
news
$ _
```

Figure 8–13
An example of creating the .profile file.

```
$ cat .profile
    echo "welcome to my super Duper UNIX"
    TERM= vt100
    PS1= "David Brown:"
    export TERM PS1
calendar
du
$ _
```

1. The **echo** command displays its argument, *welcome to my super Duper UNIX.*
2. The standard variable TERM (terminal type) is set to *vt100.*
3. The standard variable PS1 (primary prompt sign) is set to *David Brown.*
4. The **export** command makes variables TERM and PS1 available (exported) to all programs.
5. The **calendar** and **du** commands are explained in chapter 13.

8.5.2   User Profile

Each time you log in, the shell checks for a startup file called .**profile** in your home directory. If the file is found, then the shell commands in .**profile** are executed. Whether or not you have a .**profile** in your home directory, the shell continues its process and displays its prompt.

Figure 8–13 shows an example of a .**profile**. Usually you have a .**profile**, courtesy of the system administrator. You can modify the existing .**profile** or create a new one using the **cat** or **vi** utilities.

1. *The name of the file is .***profile***. The filename starts with a dot; it is a hidden file.*

2. *The .***profile*** must be located in your home directory. This is the only place that the shell checks.*

3. *The .***profile*** is one of the startup files you can use to customize your own UNIX environment. Other startup files exist in UNIX, such as the .***exrc*** file that customizes the **vi** editor (discussed in chapter 6) and the .***mail*** file that customizes your mail environment (discussed in chapter 9).*

More on the export *Command*

The **export** command makes the specified list of shell variables available to subshells. When you log in, the standard variables (and variables you may have defined) are known to your login shell. However, if you run a new shell, these variables are not known to the new shell.

For example, if you want to make variables VAR1 and VAR2 available to the new shell, you specify the variable names as arguments for the export command. To see what variables are already exported, type **export** without any arguments.

Make variables available to other shell programs.

$ **export VAR1 VAR2 [Return]** . . . . Export *VAR1* and *VAR2*.

$ **export [Return]** . . . . Check what variables are exported.
VAR1
VAR2

$ _ . . . . List of variables, then the prompt.

8.6   UNIX PROCESS MANAGEMENT

In chapter 3, we introduced the process of booting the system. Now let's go deeper into the UNIX internal process and see how it manages running programs.

In this chapter, you have encountered the word *process* here and there. The execution of a program is called a *process*; you call it a *program*, and when your program is loaded into the memory for execution UNIX calls it a *process*.

In order to keep track of the processes in the system, UNIX creates and maintains a process table for each process in the system. Among other things, the process table contains the following information:

- Process number
- Process status (ready/waiting)
- Event number process is waiting for
- System data area address

A process is created by a system routine called *fork*. A running process calls **fork**, and in response UNIX duplicates that process, creating two identical copies. The process that calls the fork routine is called *parent*, and the copy of the parent created by fork is called *child*. UNIX differentiates between the parent and the child by giving them different process IDs (PIDs).

The following steps are involved in managing a process:

- The parent calls **fork**, thus starts the process.
- Calling **fork** is a system call. UNIX gets control, and the address of the calling process is recorded in the process table's system data area. This is what is called *return address*, so the parent process knows where to start later when it gets control again.
- **fork** duplicates (copies) the process and control returns to the parent.
- The parent receives the PID of the child, a positive integer number, and the child receives the return code zero. (A negative code indicates an error.)
- The parent receiving a positive PID calls another system routine called **wait** and goes to sleep. Now the parent is waiting for the child process to finish (in UNIX terminology, waiting for the child to die).

Figure 8–14
Events happening when **fork** is called.

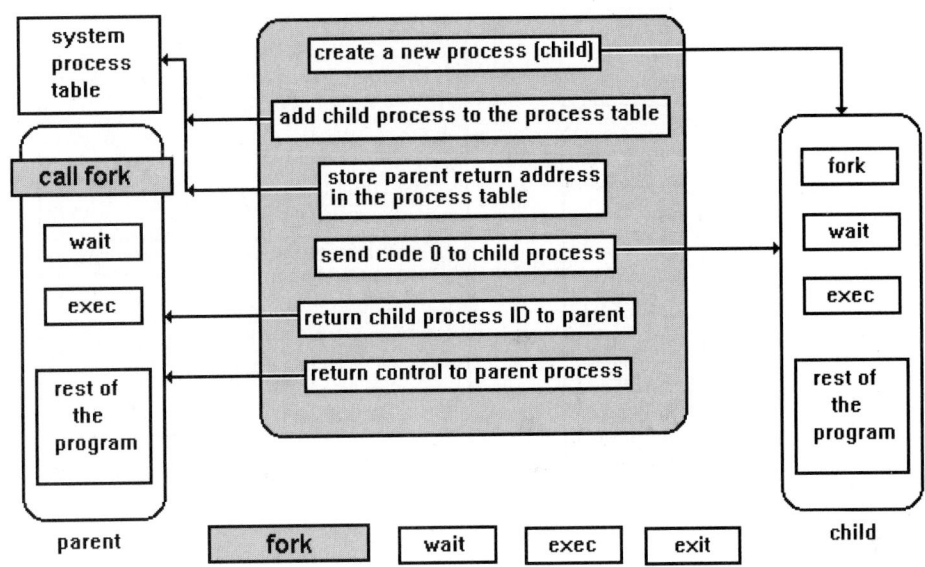

Figure 8–15
Events happening after **wait** is called.

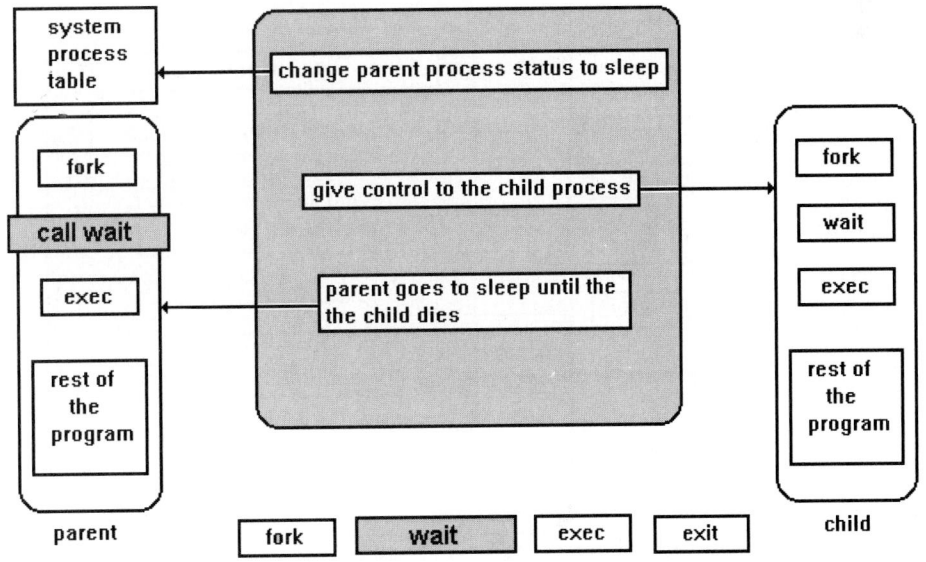

change parent process status to sleep

Figure 8–16
Events happening when **exec** is called.

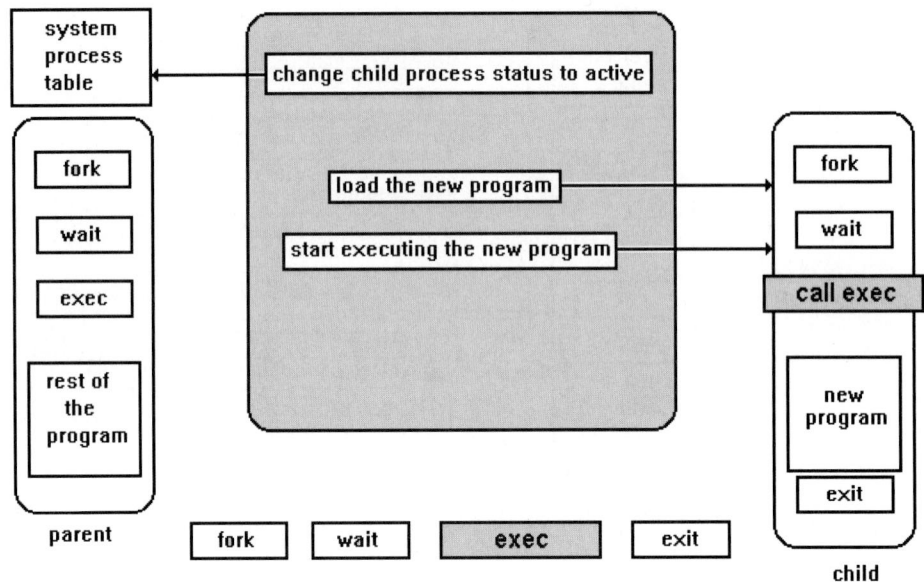

Figure 8–17
Events happening when child calls **exit**.

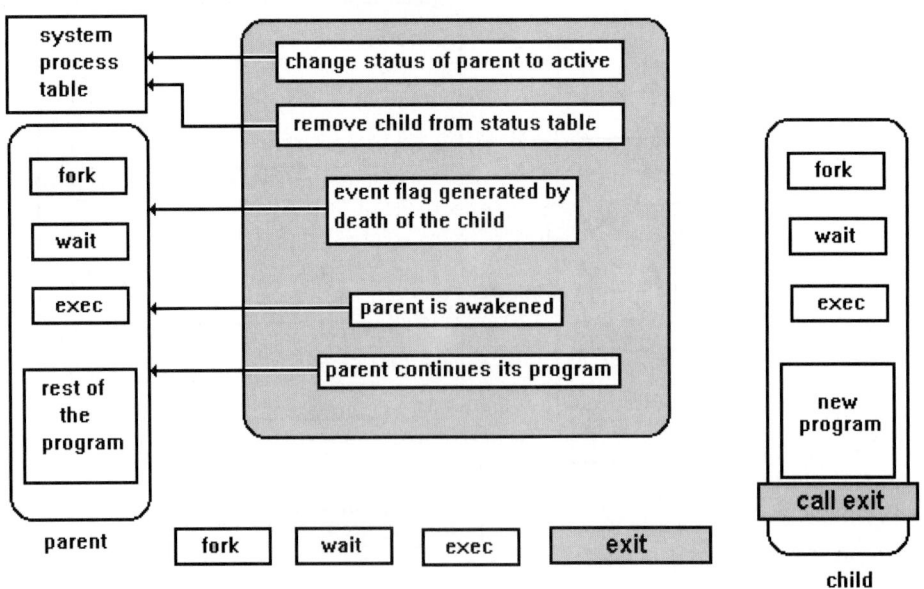

- The child process gets control and begins to execute. It checks the return code; because the return code is zero, the child process calls another system routine called **exec**. The **exec** routine responds by overlaying the child process area with the new program.

- The new program's first instruction is executed. When the new program gets to the end of the instruction, it calls yet another system routine called **exit**, and thus the child process dies. The death of the child awakens the parent, and the parent process takes over.

This process is depicted in figures 8–14 through 8–17. An example is in order to shed some light on this apparently confusing process. Imagine the shell (the **sh** program) is running, and you type a command, say **ls**. Let's explore the steps UNIX takes to run your command:

The shell is the parent process, and when created, the **ls** program becomes the child process. The parent process (shell) calls **fork**. The **fork** routine duplicates the parent (shell) process, and if creation of the child process is successful, assigns it a PID and adds the child process to the system process table. Next, the parent receives the child PID, the child receives code zero, and control is returned to the parent. The shell calls the **wait** routine and goes to wait state (goes to sleep). Meanwhile, the child gets control and calls **exec** to overlay the child process area with the new program—in this case **ls**, the command you typed. Now **ls** carries out the command. It lists your current directory filenames and when finished processing calls **exit**. Thus the child dies. The death of the child generates an event signal. The parent process (shell) is waiting for this event. It is awakened and gets control. The shell program continues, starting execution from the same address before going to sleep. Recall, this address was stored in the process table system data area as return address. And the prompt is displayed.

What happens if the child is a background process? In that case, the parent (shell) does not call the wait routine; it continues in the foreground, and you see the prompt right away.

Who creates the first parent and child processes? When UNIX is booted, the **init** *process is activated. Next,* **init** *creates one system process for each terminal. Thus,* **init** *is the original ancestor to all the processes in the system. For example, if your system supports 64 concurrent terminals, then* **init** *creates 64 processes. When you log in to one of these processes, the login process executes the shell. Later, when you log out (when the shell dies),* **init** *creates a new login process.*

Command Summary

The following UNIX commands were discussed in this chapter.

<table>
<tr><td colspan="2">echo
Displays (echoes) its arguments on the output device.</td></tr>
<tr><th>Escape
character</th><th>Meaning</th></tr>
<tr><td>\n</td><td>Carriage return and linefeed (new line).</td></tr>
<tr><td>\t</td><td>Tab.</td></tr>
<tr><td>\b</td><td>Backspace.</td></tr>
<tr><td>\r</td><td>Carriage return without linefeed.</td></tr>
</table>

<table>
<tr><td>set
Displays the environment/shell variables on the output device. The command unset removes the unwanted variables.</td></tr>
</table>

<table>
<tr><td colspan="2">ps (process status)
Displays the process ID of the programs associated with your terminal.</td></tr>
<tr><th>Option</th><th>Operation</th></tr>
<tr><td>-a</td><td>Displays status of the all active processes, not just the user's.</td></tr>
<tr><td>-f</td><td>Displays a full list of information, including the full command line.</td></tr>
</table>

<table>
<tr><td>nohup
Prevents the termination of the background process when you log out.</td></tr>
</table>

<table>
<tr><td>kill
Terminates the unwanted or unruly processes. You have to specify the process ID number. The process ID 0 kills all programs associated with your terminal.</td></tr>
</table>

<table>
<tr><td>export
Exports the specified list of variables to other shells.</td></tr>
</table>

sleep
Process goes to sleep (waits) for the specified time in seconds.

grep (Global Regular Expression Print)
Searches for a specified pattern in file(s). If specified pattern is found, the line containing the pattern is displayed on your terminal.

Option	Operation
-c	Displays only the count of the matching lines in each file that contain the match.
-i	Ignores case of letters in the search pattern. Uppercase and lowercase match.
-l	Displays only the names of the files with one or more matching lines, and not the lines themselves.
-n	Displays a line number before each output line.
-v	Displays only those lines that do not match the pattern.

sort
Sorts text file(s) in different orders.

Option	Operation
-b	Ignores leading blanks.
-d	Uses the dictionary order for sorting. Ignores punctuation and control characters.
-f	Ignores the distinction between lowercase and uppercase letters.
-n	Numbers are sorted by their arithmetic values.
-o	Stores the output in the specified file.
-r	Reverses the order of the sort, from ascending to descending.

tee
Splits the output. One copy is displayed on your terminal, the output device, and another copy is saved in a file.

Option	Operation
-a	Appends output to file, not overwriting an existing file.
-i	Ignores interrupts; does not respond to the interrupt signals.

Review Exercises

1. What are the major functions of the shell?

2. What is the name of your system shell program, and where is it stored?

3. What are the metacharacters? How does shell interpret them?

4. What are the quoting characters?

5. What are the shell variables?

6. What is the command to display the environment/shell variables?

7. What is the command to remove a variable?

8. Name some of the environment/standard variables.

9. What are the variables, and what role do they play?

10. How do you run a program in the background?

11. How do you terminate a background process?

12. What is the process ID number, and how do you know the process ID of a particular process?

13. What is the pipe operator, and what does it do?

14. How do you prevent termination of your background process after you log off?

15. What is the command for searching for specified pattern in a file?

16. How do you delay the execution of a process?

17. What is the operator that groups the commands together?

18. What is the startup file?

19. What is .profile file, and what is profile file?

20. What are the parent and child in reference to UNIX process management?

21. What is a process?

Terminal Session

In this terminal session, you practice the commands explained in this chapter. The following exercises are only some suggestions of how to use the commands. Use your own examples, and devise different scenarios to master the use of these commands.

1. Use the **echo** command to produce the following outputs:

   a. Hello There
   b. Hello
      There
   c. "Hello There"
   d. These are some of the metacharacters:

      ? * [ ] & ( ) ; > <

   e. File Name: file? Option: all

2. Use the **echo** and other commands to produce the following outputs:

   a. Display the content of your current directory. Have a header that shows a short prompt and the current date and time before listing your directory.
   b. Show the massage " I woke up " with a two-minute time delay.

3. Change your primary prompt sign.

4. Create a variable called *name* and store your first and last names in it.

5. Display the contents of variable *name*.

6. Check whether you have a .**profile** file in your home directory.

7. Create a .**profile** file or modify your existing one to produce the following output every time you log in:

       Hello there
       I am at your service David Brown
       Current Date and TIME: [the current date and time]
       Next Command:

8. Create a background process, check its process ID, and then terminate it.

9. Create a background process. Use the **nohug** command to prevent the termination of the background process.

10. Create a phone list. Let's say you gather the names and phone numbers of ten of your classmates. Use the **sort** command to sort this list in different orders, on first name, on last name, on phone number, in reverse order, etc.

11. Use **grep** and its options to find a particular name in your phone list.

12. Use the **kill** command to log off.

CHAPTER 9

UNIX Communication

This chapter concentrates on the UNIX communication utilities. It describes the commands available for communicating with other users on the system, reading the news about the system, and broadcasting messages to all users. It explains the UNIX electronic mail (e-mail) facilities and shows the commands and options available. This chapter describes how the shell and other variables affect your e-mail environment, and it shows you how to make a startup file that customizes the use of the e-mail utilities.

In This Chapter

9.1   WAYS TO COMMUNICATE

UNIX provides an array of commands and capabilities for communicating with other users. You can have a simple interactive communication with another user, sending and receiving mail through the mail delivery system or broadcasting messages to everyone on the system.

Be sure to follow some basic guidelines for communication with other users in the system:

- Be polite; do not use profanity.
- Think before sending. Do not send mail that you may regret later.

Save a copy of all your outgoing mail.

9.1.1   Using Two-Way Communication: The *write* Command

You can use the **write** command to communicate with another user. This communication is interactive, from your terminal to another terminal, so the receiving terminal must be a logged in user. The message you send appears on the receiving user's screen. Then that user can send you a reply, by issuing the **write** command from his or her terminal. Using the **write** command, two users can effectively have a conversation through their terminals.

Let's follow an example step by step to see how **write** works. Suppose your user ID is **david**, and you want to chit chat with Daniel, whose user ID is **daniel**.

Type **write daniel** and press [Return].

If Daniel is not logged on, you see the message:

    daniel not logged on.

If Daniel is logged on, he sees a message similar to this on his screen:

    Message from david on (tty06) [Thu Nov 9:30:30]

On your terminal, the cursor is placed on the next line, and the system waits for you to type your message. Your message may contain many lines, and each line you type is transmitted to Daniel when you press [Return]. You signal the end of your message by pressing the [Ctrl-d] key at the beginning of a line. This terminates your **write** and sends an EOT (End Of Transmission) message to Daniel.

Figure 9–1 shows screens, depicting a typical conversation. The top screen is David's terminal and the bottom one is Daniel's.

*To use the **write** command, you must know the user ID of the person with whom you want to communicate. You use the **who** command (discussed in chapter 3) to obtain the user ID of the logged in users.*

See page xxii for an explanation of icons used to highlight information in this chapter.

Figure 9–1
Typical screen conversation: top screen is David's; bottom is Daniel's.

```
$ write daniel [Return]
hello Dan [Return]
Is today's meeting still on? [Return]
[Ctrl-d]
<EOT>
$
```

```
Message from david on (tty06 ) [Thu Nov  9:30:30] ....
hello Dan
Is today's meeting still on?
<EOT>
$
```

Daniel can reply by using the **write** command from his terminal, but he does not have to wait for you to finish your message. When he sees the initial message that you are writing to her, if he types **write david** and presses [Return], he can send you messages while you send his messages.

With **write** simultaneously active on both terminals, you and Daniel can carry on a two-way conversation. Sometimes this two-way exchange becomes confusing, so it is useful to establish a protocol for using **write**. The common protocol for UNIX users is to end message lines with the character *o* (for over) to inform the receiving party that a message is finished and you are (possibly) waiting for a reply. When you intend to end conversation, type **oo** (for over and out).

If you are receiving a **write** message from another user, the message appears on your terminal, regardless of what you are doing. If you are using the vi editor and in the middle of an editing job, the write message appears on the screen where the cursor is. But don't be alarmed. This is a terminal-to-terminal communication, and what **write** produces does not damage your editing file. It simply overwrites information on your screen, and you can continue with your editing or whatever other job you were doing.

Nevertheless, receiving messages while you are concentrating on a job is not convenient, not to mention the mess it makes on your screen. You can prevent your terminal from accepting messages coming from the **write** command.

9.1.2   Inhibiting Messages: The *mesg* Command

You can use the **mesg** command as a toggle to stop receiving messages from the **write** command or to reactivate receiving messages. **mesg** without argument shows the current status of your terminal in this respect.

The following command sequence shows how to protect yourself from annoying messages.

$ **mesg [Return]**. . . . . Check status of your terminal.

is y . . . . It is set to YES, accepting messages.

$ **mesg n [Return]** . . . . Set it to NO, deny receiving messages.

$ **mesg [Return]**. . . . . Check again.

is n . . . . Now it is set to NO.

$_ . . . . Back to the prompt.

To practice the communication commands, you usually want to have another user to participate in the exercises. However, you can practice most of these commands by yourself. Using your own user ID, you can send and receive messages.

9.1.3   Displaying News Items: The *news* Command

You can use the **news** command to find out what is happening in the system. **news** gets its information from the system directory where the news files are placed, usually in /usr/news. Without any options, **news** displays all the files you have not seen from the news directory. It refers to and updates a file called .news_time in your home directory. This file is created in your home directory the first time you use the **news** command and remains an empty file. The **news** command uses its access time to determine the last time you gave the **news** command.

1. *You press the interrupt key (usually [Del]) to stop displaying one news item and continue with the next item.*

2. *You press the interrupt key twice to quit (terminate) the* **news** *command.*

To check the latest news, type **news** and press [Return]. Figure 9–2 shows some sample new items.

Figure 9–2
The **news** command.

```
$ news [Return]
david  (root) Wen Nov   28   14:14:14  2001
    Let's congratulate david; he got his B.S. degree.
    Friday night party on second floor. Be there!

books  (root) Wed Nov   28   14:14:14  2001
    Our technical library is growing.
    New set of UNIX books are now available.
$_
```

Table 9–1
The **news** command options.

Options	Operation
-a	Displays all the news items, old or new files.
-n	Lists only the name of the files (headers).
-s	Displays the number of the current news items.

Each news item has a header that shows filename, file owner, and the time that file was placed in the news directory.

news Options

The **news** options are summarized in table 9–1. The options do not update the your .news_time file.

The following command sequences show how the **news** command options work.

□ List the current news items, using the **-n** option: type **news -n** and press [Return]. UNIX shows only the headers of the files that contain the news items. The header shows the name, the owner of the file, and the time it was created. Figure 9–3 shows the output of the command.

□ To display a specified new item, type **news david** and press [Return], for example. Figure 9–4 shows the output of the sample news item.

Figure 9–3
The **news** command with the **-n** option.

```
$ news -n [Return]
    david   (root) Wed Nov    28    14:14:14  2001
    books   (root) Wed Nov    28    14:14:14  2001
$_
```

Figure 9–4
The **news** command with specified news item.

```
$ news david [Return]
david   (root) Wed Nov    28    14:14:14  2001
    Let's congratulate david; he got his B.S. degree.
    Friday night party on second floor. Be there!
$_
```

*The name of a news item is its filename in the **news** directory.*

9.1.4   Broadcasting Messages: The *wall* Command

You can use the **wall** (write all) command to send messages to all currently logged in users. The **wall** command reads from the keyboard (standard input) until you enter [Ctrl-d] at the beginning of a line to signal the end of the message. The **wall** executable file is usually placed in /etc directory and is not defined in the PATH standard variable—which means you have to type the full pathname to invoke it.

The **wall** command is usually used by the system administrator to warn users of imminent events. You may not have access to it.

Assuming your login name is **david** (and you have access to **wall**), send a message to all users:

□ Type **\etc\wall** and press [Return].
□ Type **Alert . . .** and press [Return].
□ Type **Lab will be closed in 5 minutes. Time to log out.** and press [Return].
□ Press [Ctrl-d]. The system responds as shown in figure 9–5.

1. *The message is also sent to its sender, so you see your own broadcast message.*

2. *The **wall** message you send is not received by currently logged in users who set **mesg** to **n**.*

3. *The system administrator can override access denial.*

4. *The messages carry your user ID; and you cannot send an anonymous message.*

Figure 9–5
Invoking the **wall** command.

```
$ /etc/wall [Return]
   Alert ... [Return]
   Lab will be closed in 5 minutes. Time to log out. [Return]
[Ctrl-d]
$_

   Broadcast message from david
       Alert ...
       Lab will be closed in 5 minutes. Time to log out.
```

9.2   ELECTRONIC MAIL

Electronic mail (*e-mail*) is an essential part of the contemporary office environment. E-mail gives you the capability to send and receive messages, memos, and other documents to and from other users. The main difference between sending mail using the e-mail service and using the **write** command is that with the **write** command only you see the messages sent to you if you are logged in. But with e-mail, your mail is automatically kept for you until you issue the command to read it. E-mail service is more convenient and faster than conventional mail service, and it does not interrupt the receiving party the way phone calls do.

Under UNIX, the **mail** or **mailx** command can be used to send or read e-mail. The **mailx** utility is based on Berkeley UNIX mail and has more powerful features, enabling you to manipulate (review, store, dispose of, etc.) your mail easily and efficiently. **mailx** is the e-mail command discussed in this book. It has a large number of features and options; using some of them requires advanced UNIX experience. In this chapter, we describe enough to make you feel comfortable using it and interested in looking for more information about it.

 *Where do you find more information? Well, how about the **man** command? (In case you have forgotten, **man** was discussed in chapter 3.)*

You use the **mailx** command to send mail to other users or read mail that is sent to you. The **mailx** operation involves a number of files; the way it appears and functions depends on the environment variables that are set up in files, and it needs files for storing your mail.

9.2.1   Using Mailboxes

In the UNIX mail system, you have two kinds of mailboxes, a system mailbox and a private mailbox.

Your System Mailbox

Every user of the system has a *mailbox*, which is a file named the same as your login name (user ID). This file is typically stored in /usr/mail. Mail sent to you is stored in this file, and when you read a message, **mailx** reads from your mailbox. Assuming your login name is **david**, the full pathname to your mailbox could be /usr/mail/students/david.

You can use the **set** command (discussed in chapter 8) to see your system mailbox pathname. The variable MAIL is set to the filename that receives your mail.

Your Private Mailbox: The mbox File

After you read your mail, **mailx** automatically appends a copy of it to a file called mbox in your home directory. If an mbox file does not exist, then **mailx** creates one in your home directory the first time you read your mail. This file contains mail that you have read but not deleted or saved elsewhere. The variable MBOX controls the filename. The default value is HOME/mbox. For example, the following command changes the default setting and sets up your private mailbox in EMAIL directory.

MBOX= $HOME/EMAIL/mbox

 The explicit saving of a message or using the **x** (**xit**) command to exit **mailx** disables the automatic saving of your messages.

The Customizable mailx Environment

You can customize your **mailx** environment by setting up appropriate variables in two startup files: the mail.rc file in the system directory and the .mailrc file in your home directory.

When you call **mailx**, it first checks for a startup file called mail.rc. The full pathname to this file is similar to the following:

/usr/share/lib/mailx/mail.rc

This file is usually created and maintained by the system administrator. Variables set in this file are applicable to all the system users.

The second file that **mailx** looks for is a file called .mailrc in your home directory. You can change the **mailx** environment that the system administrator has set up in the mail.rc file by setting variables in your .mailrc file. This file is not necessary, and **mailx** works fine without it, as long as you are happy with the system administrator's arrangement. Ways to customize your **mailx** environment are discussed in more detail in section 9.5.

9.2.2   Sending Mail

In order to send mail to another person, you must know that person's login name. For example, if you want to send mail to a user identified by the login name **daniel**, you type **mailx daniel** and press [Return].

By default, input to the **mailx** (your message) comes from the keyboard (standard input). Depending on how your system environment variables are set, **mailx** may show the **Subject:** prompt. If it does, you type the subject for your message, and **mailx** changes to *input mode* and waits for you to enter the rest of your message. You signal the end of your message by pressing [Ctrl-d] at the beginning of a line. **mailx** shows <EOT> (for End Of Transmission), and your message is transmitted.

While in the input mode, **mailx** provides you with a large number of commands, enabling you to compose your message with ease and efficiency. All input mode commands start with a tilde (~), and they are called *tilde escape comands*. (The tilde escape commands are explained later in this chapter.)

To send a message to Daniel (login name **daniel**), do the following:

$ **mailx daniel [Return]** . . . . Send message to daniel.

Subject: **meeting [Return]** . . . . Enter subject.

Hi, Dan [Return]
Let me know if tomorrow's meeting is still on.[Return]
Dave [Return]

[Ctrl-d] . . . . Signal end of the message.

EOT . . . . End of transmission.

$_ . . . . Back to the prompt.

1. *The subject field is optional. Just press [Return] to skip the* **Subject:** *prompt.*

2. *Signal end of a message by pressing [Ctrl-d] at the beginning of a blank line.*

3. *Mail is delivered to the other user's mailbox regardless of whether he or she is logged in.*

4. *Recipients are informed that they have mail as soon as they log in. The following message appears on their terminal:*

    You have mail

9.2.3   Reading Mail

In order to read your mail, you type **mailx** with no argument. If you have mail in your mailbox, then **mailx** shows two lines of information followed by a numbered list of headers of messages in your mailbox and then the **mailx** prompt, which by default is a question mark. At this point, **mailx** is in command mode, and you can issue commands to delete, save, or reply to messages, etc. You press [q] at the **?** prompt to exit **mailx**.

The list of headers consists of one line for each mail item in your mailbox. The format is as follows:

> status message # sender date lines/characters subject

Each field in the header line conveys certain information about your mail:

*   The > indicates that the message is the current message.
*   The **status** is **N** if the message is new. That means you have not read this mail.
*   The **status** is **U** (unread) if the message is not new. That means you have seen the message header before, but you have not read the mail itself yet.
*   The **message #** indicates the sequence number of the mail in your mailbox.
*   The **sender** is the login name of the person who sent you the mail.

- The **date** shows the date and time that mail arrived in your mailbox.
- The **line/characters** shows the size of your mail, number of lines and number of characters.

Suppose you are Daniel and you have just logged in and you want to read your mail.

□ The system informs you that you have mail:

> You have mail

□ To read your mail, type **mailx** and press [Return]; UNIX responds:

> mailx version 4.0   Type ? for help.
>   "/usr/students/mail/daniel" : 1 message   1 new
>   > N   1   david . . . . Thu Nov 28 14:14 8:126   meeting

1. *The first header line shows your **mailx** version number and informs you that you can press [?] to get help.*

2. *The second header line shows /usr/mail/daniel, your system mailbox, followed by the number and status of your messages. In this case, you have one message, and **N** indicates this is the first time you are reading it.*

The **?** prompt shows that **mailx** is in command mode. You specify the mail you want to read by typing its associated message number. You can also press [Return] to start reading from the current mail (indicated by > sign on the header), and continue reading your mail in sequence by pressing [Return] after the **?** prompt.

> ? . . . . **mailx** in command mode.
>
> **? 1 [Return]** . . . . Display message 1, the only message in
>   your mailbox.
>
> Message 1:
> From: david   Thu, 28 Nov 01 14:14 EDT 2001
> To: daniel
> Subject: meeting
> Status: R
> Hi, Dan
> Let me know if tomorrow's meeting is still on.
> Dave
>
> ? . . . . Ready for next command.
>
> **? q [Return]** . . . . Exit **mailx**.
>
> Saved 1 message in /usr/students/david/mbox
>
> $ _ . . . . Back to the shell.

When you use **q** *to quit from* **mailx**, *it saves a copy of the mail that you have read in* mbox, *your private mailbox in your home directory. (Thus, at this point your system mailbox is empty.)*

Suppose you want to read your mail again. Type **mailx** and press [Return]; UNIX responds:

   No mail for daniel

Check what you have in mbox.

   $ cat mbox [Return] . . . . Check what you have in your mbox.
   From: david   Thu, 28 Nov 01 14:14 EDT   2001
   To: daniel
   Subject: meeting
   Status: RO
   Hi, Dan
   Let me know if tomorrow's meeting is still on.
   Dave

As you expected, mbox contains a copy of your mail.

9.2.5   Exiting *mailx*: The *q* and *x* Commands

You can exit **mailx** by typing **q** (*quit*) or **x** (*exit*) command at the **?** prompt. Although both commands cause exit from the **mailx**, they do so in a different manner.

The **q** command causes the automatic removal of the mail that you have read from your system mailbox. By default, a copy of the removed mail is kept in your private mailbox (any filename assigned to the MAIL variable).

The **x** command does not remove the mail you have read from your system mailbox. In fact, when you use **x**, nothing changes in your mailbox. Even deleted messages remain intact.

mailx Options   Table 9–2 summarizes the **mailx** options. These options are used in the command line when you invoke **mailx** for reading or sending mail. The following command sequences show the use of the **mailx** options.

   $ mailx -H [Return] . . . . Display the message headers only.

   N 1   daniel   Thu ESP 30 12:26 6/103 Room
   N 2   susan   Thu Sep 30 12:30 6/107 Project
   N 3   marie   Thu Sep 30 13:30 6/70   Welcome

   $_ . . . . Back to the shell.

Table 9–2
The **mailx** command options.

Option	Operation
-f [*filename*]	Reads mail from the specified *filename* instead of the system *mailbox*. If no file is specified, it reads from *mbox*.
-H	Displays the list of the message headers.
-s *subject*	Sets the subject field to string *subject*.

Type **mailx -f mymail** and press [Return] to read mail from the specified file mymail instead of your system mailbox; UNIX responds:

> /usr/students/daniel/mymail: No such file or directory

The **mailx** by default reads mail from your system mailbox. With **-f** option, it reads your mail from a specified file, such as your old mail files. In this case, you specified mymail, and the message shows mymail is not in your current directory.

If you type **mailx -f** and press [Return], with no filename specified, UNIX defaults to your private mailbox, so you see a display like the following:

```
mailx version 4.0  Type ? for help.
  "/usr/students/mail/daniel": 1 message  1 new

>  N  1   david           Thu Nov 28  14:14  17/32  meeting
```

To use the **-s** option, set the *subject* string as part of the command line, and send mail to Daniel (whose user ID is **daniel**), do the following:

$ mailx -s meeting daniel [Return]	Send mail to **daniel**; set the *subject* field to the string **meeting**.
_	Compose your message to Daniel.
[Ctrl-d]	End your message.
EOT	mailx shows End Of Transmission.
$_	Back to the shell.

When Daniel reads your message, the subject field shows **Subject: meeting**.

Use quotation marks around the subject string if it contains spaces.

9.3   *mailx* INPUT MODE

While **mailx** is in *input mode* (composing your mail to be sent), a variety of commands are at your disposal. These commands all start with the tilde (~); that lets you temporarily escape from input mode and issue commands, which is why they are referred to as *tilde escape commands*. Table 9–3 summarizes some of these commands.

Some of these commands are quite important. Imagine you want to write a message that contains more than just a few lines. Using the primitive **mailx** editor is cumbersome and just not up to the job. Instead of using it, you can invoke the vi editor, compose your message using all the ease and power of vi, and then, when you have finished composing your message, exit vi and return to the **mailx** input mode. Then you can give other commands or send the message.

1. Tilde escape commands are applicable only when **mailx** is in input mode.

2. All tilde commands must be entered at the beginning of a line.

The following command sequences show the use of the tilde escape commands while **mailx** is in input mode. Assume your login name is **david**, and you are sending mail to yourself.

> $ **mailx -s "Just a Test" david [Return]** . . . . . Send mail to yourself.

mailx is invoked with **-s** option. The quotation marks are necessary because of the embedded space in the specified *subject* string.

> _ . . . . **mailx** is in input mode.

> ~! **date [Return]** . . . . Invoke the **date** command.

> Wed, Nov 28 16:16 EDT 2001

> _ . . . . Ready for input.

At this point you are using **~!** and executing the **date** command. You can execute any command you wish. The output of the command does not become part of the message you are composing.

> ~< ! **date [Return]** . . . . Invoke the **date** command and redirect the output of the **date** command to be included in your message.

> "date" 1/29 . . . . Feedback message.

> _ . . . . Ready.

The feedback message indicates that 1 line consisting of 29 characters (the output of the **date** command) is added to your text.

Table 9–3
The **mailx** tilde escape commands.

Command	Operation
~?	Displays a list of all *tilde escape* commands.
~! *command*	Lets you invoke the specified shell *command* while composing your message.
~e	Invokes an editor. The editor to be used is defined in the mail variable called EDITOR. vi is the default.
~p	Displays the message being composed.
~q	Quits input mode. Saves your partially composed message in the file called *dead.letter*
~ r *filename*	Reads the specified *filename* and adds its contents into your message.
~ < *filename*	Reads the specified *filename* (using the redirection operator) and adds its contents into your message.
~< ! *command*	Executes the specified command; places its output into the message.
~v	Invokes the default editor, the vi editor, or uses the value of the mail variable VISUAL which can be set up for other editors.
~w *filename*	Writes currently composing message to the specified *filename*.

This is a test message to explore mailx. [Return]

~v [Return]. . . . . Now use vi editor to compose the rest of
your message.

At this point, you have invoked the vi editor and your partially composed message is the input file to the vi editor.

<u>W</u>ed, Nov 28 16:16 EDT 2001
This is a test message to explore mailx capabilities.
~
~
~
"/tmp/Re26485" 2 lines, 69 characters

Now all the power and flexibility of the vi editor is at your disposal. You can delete, modify, or save your text. You can execute commands or import another file and continue composing your message.

Wed, Nov 28 16:16 EDT 2001

This is a test message to explore mailx capabilities.

This message is composed using the vi editor.

:wq [Return]. . . . . Exit vi.

3 Lines, 115 characters . . . . . . Vi feedback.

(continue) . . . . Feedback message.

_ . . . . You are back to **mailx** input mode.

~w first.mail [Return] . . . . . . Save your mail in a file called first.mail.

"first.mail" 3/115 . . . . Feedback message.

The feedback message indicates the size of first.mail: It contains 3 lines and 115 characters.

The **~w** is used to save the currently composed message in the specified file first.mail. This is a good habit, so you have a copy of your transmitted messages. If you set the **mailx** record variable, then your outgoing mail is automatically saved.

~q [Return] . . . . Quit **mailx** input mode.

$_ . . . . Back to the shell.

Using **~q** to quit **mailx** input mode also saves your partially composed message in a file called dead.letter in your home directory (or any filename assigned to the DEAD variable).

Let's start again and complete the sending of your mail. At this point the scenario is that: you are **david** and you want to send mail to yourself. You have a copy of your message in a file called first.mail (you used **~w** to save it) and another copy in dead.letter (you used **~q** to exit input mode).

Send first.mail to **david** using the input redirection sign (<) on the command line.

$ mailx david < first.mail [Return] . . . . Send mail.

$_ . . . . Done.

The < sign directs the shell to pass the specified filename (first.mail) as input to the **mailx** command.

You can specify more than one input file.

By default, the Bourne shell checks every ten minutes for your new mail, so you have to wait a while before you can read the mail you just sent to yourself. When there is new mail in your mailbox, UNIX displays the message **you have mail** before the next prompt.

To send first.mail to **david** using the tilde escape command, do the following:

$ **mailx david [Return]**.	Send mail to yourself.
Subject:.	Ready for you to type your message.
~< first.mail [Return]	Read in the first.mail.
"first.mail" 3/115	Feedback message.
[Ctrl-d]	Transmit it.
EOT	**mailx** shows EOT.
$_	Back to the shell.

The ~< reads in the specified file, in this case first.mail, *and adds its contents to the message you are currently composing. You can also use the* ~r *command to achieve the same results.*

Get your partially composed message that **mailx** saved in dead.letter file, complete the message, and send it to **david**.

$ **mailx david [Return]**.	Send message to **david**.
Subject:.	Ready to go.
~r dead.letter [Return].	Read in (import) dead.letter file.
~v [Return].	Invoke the vi editor.

Wed, 28 Nov 01 16:16 EDT 2001
   This is a test message to explore mailx capabilities.
   This message is composed using the vi editor.
   ~
   ~
   "/tmp/Re265" 3 lines and 115 characters. . . . . The vi editor feedback message.

Let's assume you want to add a few lines to your message.

   Wed, 28 Nov 01 16:16 EDT 2001 . . . . . Complete the message.

This is a test message to explore mailx capabilities.
This message is composed using the vi editor.
This is the first time I am using email. Maybe I should save this
text, get a copy of it and frame it!.
~
~

:wq [Return].	Save and quit.
(continue)	Feedback message.

At this point your message is not displayed, but you can see what you have composed before sending it by typing **~p** and pressing [Return]; UNIX displays the whole message one page at a time:

~p [Return]	Display the composed message.

```
Wed, 28 Nov 01  16:16  EDT 2001
This is a test message to explore mailx capabilities.
This message is composed using the vi editor.
This is the first time I am using e-mail. Maybe I should save this
text, get a copy of it and frame it!.
```

[Ctrl-d] . . . . Indicate the end of your message.

EOT . . . . End of transmission.

$ _ . . . . Back to shell.

9.3.1   Mailing Existing Files

You do not have to compose your messages using the **mailx** editor at all. Maybe you have a memo already written that you want to send to another user. In that case, you use the shell input redirection operator to redirect the **mailx** input from the default input device (the keyboard) to the mailbox of the person you want to receive the file.

Send a file called memo to Daniel, whose user ID is **daniel**.

$ **mailx daniel < memo [Return]** . . . . . . Mail memo to **daniel**.

$_ . . . . Back to shell.

Assuming that your message is in a file called memo and you want to send it to the user ID **daniel**, the above command will do the job.

9.3.2   Sending Mail to a Group of Users

What if you want to send your memo file to Daniel and a few others? It would be very inconvenient to type the **mailx** command to send the same message to ten different users. In that case, you specify a list of the user IDs of the people you intend to receive the mail, and **mailx** sends the mail to all of them.

To send memo to user IDs **daniel**, **susan**, and **emma, type mailx daniel susan emma < memo** and press [Return].

The user IDs are separated by spaces.

If you send mail often to a group of people, you can save yourself a lot of typing by defining a name for your list and use the defined name instead of typing the whole list of user IDs every time. To do this, you use the **alias** command, and the format looks like this:

alias [*name*] [*userID01*] [*userID02*] [*userID03*] [*userID04*] [*userID05*] [*userID06*] where *name* is the name you want type when you want to send mail to the people on this list.

For example, if you type **alias friends daniel david marie gabe emma stev** and press [Return], UNIX assigns the name friends to this list of the user IDs. Now instead of typing all those user IDs, you can just type **friends**. If you place **alias** commands like this in your .mailrc file, they become part of your **mailx** environment and you do not need to assign them every time you want to use **mailx**.

Assuming your friends' user IDs are assigned to the name *friends,* mail your memo to your friends by typing **mailx friends < memo** and pressing [Return].

9.4   *mailx* COMMAND MODE

When you are reading mail, **mailx** is in command mode, and the question mark prompt means it is waiting for your commands. While **mailx** is in command mode, a large number of commands are at your service, enabling you to copy, save, or delete your mail. You can reply to the sender of a message or send mail to a specific user without leaving the command mode. Table 9–4 summarizes some of these commands.

Scenario   The command sequences in the following sections show how **mailx** reads your mail and what commands and options are applicable in command mode.They assume that your user ID is **david**, you have three messages in your system mailbox, and you want to read, display, and delete your mail. The **mailx** command provides you the capabilities to manipulate your mail in different ways. Your problem would be the selection of appropriate commands for the job on hand.

9.4.1   Ways to Read/Display Your Mail

The **mailx** command lets you read and display your mail in several different ways: each piece of mail one at a time, a specified range of messages, or a specified single message. Generally, regardless of how you plan to read your mail, you'll want to display the list of mail, which you do simply by invoking **mailx**. Pressing [Return] at the **?** prompt shows the current message.

Read/display your mail.

```
$ mailx [Return]. . . . . . . . . . . . . . . . . . . . . . . Invoke mailx.

mailx version 4.0   Type ? for help.
"/usr/student/mail/david": 3 messages   3 new
```

Table 9–4
The **mailx** commands in command mode.

Command	Operation
!	Lets you execute the shell commands (the shell escape).
cd [*directory*]	Changes to the specified directory, or to home directory if none is specified.
d	Deletes the specified messages.
f	Displays the headlines of the messages.
q	Exits **mailx** and removes the messages from system mailbox.
h	Displays active message headers.
m *users*	Sends mail to specified *users*.
R *messages*	Replies to the sender of the *messages*.
r *messages*	Replies to the sender of the *messages* and all the other recipients of the same *messages*.
s *filename*	Saves (appends) the indicated messages to the *filename*.
t *messages*	Displays (types) the specified *messages*.
u *messages*	Undeletes the specified *messages*.
x	Exits (xit) **mailx**; does not remove messages from system mailbox.

```
> N  1   daniel . . . . . . . . . Thu  Sep 30  12:26   6/103   Room
  N  2   susan . . . . . . . . . Thu  Sep 30  12:30   6/107   Project
  N  3   marie. . . . . . . . . .Thu  Sep 30  13:30   6/79    Welcome
```

? [Return]. . . . . Displays the current message.

Message 1:
From: daniel Thu Sep 30 12:26 EDT 2001
To: david
Subject: Room
Status: R

Room 707 is reserved for your meetings.

? . . . . Ready for the next command.

Pressing [Return] at the **?** prompt shows the current message, in this case message 1.

    ? 3 [Return] . . . . Displays message 3.

Message 3:
From: marie Thu Sep 30 12:30 EDT 2001
To: david
Subject: Welcome
Status: R

Welcome back!

    ? . . . . Ready for the next command.

    ? t 1-3 [Return] . . . . Type messages 1 through 3.

Message 1:
From: daniel Thu Sep 30 12:26 EDT 2001
To: david
Subject: Room
Status: R

Room 707 is reserved for your meetings.

Message 2:
From: susan Thu Sep 30 12:26 EDT 2001
To: david
Subject: Project
Status: R

Your project is in trouble! See me ASAP.

Message 3:
From: marie Thu Sep 30 12:30 EDT 2001
To: david
Subject: Welcome
Status: R

Welcome back!

    ? . . . . Ready for the next command.

The **t** (type) command displays messages one after another. The range of messages is indicated by the low and high limits numbers separated by a hyphen. In this case, **t 1-3** means display message numbers 1, 2, and 3.

    ? t 1 3 [Return] . . . . Display messages 1 and 3.

Message 1:
From: daniel Thu Sep 30 12:26 EDT 2001
To: david
Subject: Room
Status: R

Room 707 is reserved for your meetings.

```
Message 3:
From: marie Thu  Sep  30  12:30  EDT 2001
To: david
Subject: Welcome
Status: R

Welcome back!
```

?_ . . . . Ready for the next command.

*The **t** command also shows any specified mail indicated by the mail sequence numbers. If more than one mail sequence number is indicated, the numbers must be separated by a space. In this case, **t 1 3** means display messages 1 and 3.*

? **n [Return]** . . . . Show the next message.

At EOF . . . . Feedback message.

?_ . . . . Prompt for the next command.

The **n** (next) command shows the next message in your mailbox, just like pressing [Return]. In this case, there is no next message; thus, the **End Of the File** message is displayed.

? **n10 [Return]** . . . . Show the tenth message.

10: invalid message number.

You can indicate a message number if you want a specific message to be displayed. In this case, **n10** means display message 10. But there is no message 10, so the error message is displayed.

? **f [Return]**. . . . . Show headline of the current message.

> 3 marie Thu Sep 30 12:30 EDT 2001

?_ . . . . Prompt is back.

The **f** command shows the headline of your current message, in this case message 3.

? **x [Return]** . . . . Exit **mailx**.

$_ . . . . Back to the shell prompt.

If you use **x** command to exit from **mailx**, all your messages remain intact in your mailbox.

9.4.2   Ways to Delete Your Mail

The **mailx** command lets you delete your mail one message at a time, delete all of the messages at one time, delete a specified range of messages and recover messages you deleted by mistake. Let's look at some examples. The scenario remains the same. You are David, and there are three messages in your system mailbox.

Delete your mail.

$ mailx [Return]. . . . . Read your mail.

```
mailx version 4.0   Type ? for help.
"/usr/student/mail/david": 3 messages  3 new
 > N  1   daniel                  Thu  Sep 30  12:26  6/103  Room
   N  2   susan                   Thu  Sep 30  12:30  6/107  Project
   N  3   marie                   Thu  Sep 30  13:30  6/79   Welcome
```

? d [Return] . . . . Delete the current message.

? d3 [Return] . . . . Delete message 3.

? h . . . . Show only headlines.

```
 > N  2   susan                   Thu  Sep 30  12:30  6/107  Project
```

The **h** command displays the headlines of the messages in your mailbox. You have deleted messages 1 and 3, and the remaining message (message 2) is displayed.

? u1 [Return] . . . . Undelete message 1.

? u3 [Return] . . . . Undelete message 3.

   *The **u** command undeletes the specified message, in this case messages 1 and 3.*

? h [Return] . . . . Check, all messages are in your mailbox.

```
   1   daniel                  Thu  Sep 30  12:26  6/103  Room
   2   susan                   Thu  Sep 30  12:30  6/107  Project
 > 3   marie                   Thu  Sep 30  13:30  6/79   Welcome
```

? d 1-3 [Return] . . . . Delete messages 1 through 3.

? h [Return] . . . . Check whether they are deleted.

No applicable messages

? u* [Return] . . . . Undelete all the deleted messages.

Using the **u** command with the * wild card undeletes all messages in your mailbox.

? d /vacation [Return] . . . . Delete all messages with the word *vacation* in their subject field.

No applicable messages

Using /*string* with delete command, you can delete mail that has the specified string as part of the subject field. In this case, no message in your mailbox matches the string **vacation**, and no message is removed.

? d daniel [Return]. . . . . Delete all messages from **daniel**.

You can specify the sender's user ID with the delete command to delete all the mail sent by the specified person.

? **x [Return]** . . . . Exit **mailx**.
$_   Back to the shell prompt.

There are many ways to delete unwanted mail. However, when you exit from **mailx** using the **x** command, all messages remain in your mailbox, *even the messages you have deleted*. If you use the **q** command to exit **mailx**, then your mailbox is permanentaly updated according to the commands you have issued.

 After you quit **mailx** using **q**, you can no longer use the undelete command to restore deleted messages, so make sure that you have deleted only the messages you intended to delete before you quit **mailx**.

9.4.3   Ways to Save Your Mail

The **mailx** command lets you save your messages in a specified file while you are reading them. You can save all your messages, a single message, or range of messages. Let's look at some examples. The scenario remains as before: **david** is your login name, and there are three messages in your system mailbox.

$ **mailx [Return]**. . . . . Read your mail.

```
mailx version 4.0   Type ? for help.
"/usr/student/mail/david":  3 messages   3 new
 > N  1   daniel              Thu  Sep 30  12:26  6/103  Room
   N  2   susan               Thu  Sep 30  12:30  6/107  Project
   N  3   marie            Thu  Sep 30  13:30  6/79   Welcome
```

? **s mfile [Return]**. . . . . Appends the current message to mfile.

"mfile" [New file] 12/86 . . . . Feedback message.

The **s** command saves your indicated message in the specified file. At this point mfile contains your current message, message 1, indicated by the > sign.

? **s 2 3 mfile [Return]**. . . . . Append messages 2 and 3 to myfile.

"mfile" [Appended] 18/286. . . . . Feedback message.

? **s 1-3 mfile [Return]**. . . . . Append messages 1 through 3 to mfile.

"mfile" [Appended] 18/286. . . . . Feedback message.

? **x [Return]** . . . . Exit, mailbox remains the same.

$_ . . . . Back to the shell prompt.

At this point, all your messages are appended to mfile. You can use **mailx** command option **-f** to read your mail from mfile.

1. *Do not confuse* **mailx** *command option* **-f** *(to which you add a filename to read a specified file) with* **mailx** *command option* **f** *(which displays only the headline of only the current message).*

2. *Do not confuse* **mailx** *command option* **-s** *(which sets the subject field to the specified characters) with* **mailx** *command option* **s** *(which saves your messages in the specified file).*

9.4.4   Ways to Send a Reply

You can send a reply to the sender of a message while reading your mail. This is convenient because you can send a reply right after you read a message.

To send a reply while in **mailx** read mode, do the following:

$ mailx [Return] . . . . Read your mail.

mailx version 4.0   Type ? for help.
"/usr/student/mail/david": 3 messages   3 new
```
>N  1   daniel          Thu  Sep 30  12:26  6/103  Room
 N  2   susan           Thu  Sep 30  12:30  6/107  Project
 N  3   marie           Thu  Sep 30  13:30  6/79   Welcome
```

? R [Return] . . . . Reply to the current message.

Subject: RE: Room . . . . Subject prompt refers to **Room**.

_ . . . . Cursor appears at the beginning of the line, ready for you to type your reply.

Thank you . . . . Compose your reply.

[Ctrl-d] . . . . End your message.

EOT . . . . Message transmitted.

? . . . . Ready for next command.

? R3 [Return] . . . . Respond to message 3.

? r3 [Return] . . . . Respond to message 3 and all the others who received a copy of it.

Reply command **R** sends your reply only to the author (originator) of the message or the specified list of users. Reply command **r** sends your reply to the author of the message and to all others users who have received the same message.

You can also use the **m** command to send mail to other users. The **m** command places **mailx** into input mode so you can compose your mail. With the **m** command, you can specify one user or a list of users to receive your message.

While in **mailx** command mode, send mail to a specific user by doing the following:

? m daniel [Return] . . . . Send mail to **daniel**.

? m daniel susan [Return] . . . . Send mail to **daniel** and **susan**.

? x [Return] . . . . Exit **mailx**.

$_ . . . . The shell prompt.

9.5   CUSTOMIZING THE *mailx* ENVIRONMENT

You can customize the **mailx** environment by setting **mailx** variables in the .mailrc file. To define these variables, you use the **mailx set** command. The **mailx** command also recognizes some of the shell's standard variables.

9.5.1   Shell Variables Used by *mailx*

Some of the standard shell variables are used by **mailx**, and their values affect the **mailx** behavior: *HOME* (which defines your home directory) and *MAIL-CHECK* (which defines the frequency with which **mailx** checks your mail). For example, if you want arrival of mail in your mailbox to be checked once a minute, then you define *MAILCHECK* as follows:

    MAILCHECK=60

MAILRC is another shell variable used by **mailx**. This variable defines the startup file that **mailx** checks each time you invoke it. If this variable is undefined, then the default value of **$HOME/mailrc** is used. For example, you can define *MAILRC* in your .profile (the startup file for your login shell) as follows:

    MAILRC=$HOME/E-mail/.mailrc

The *HOME*, *MAILCHECK*, and *MAILRC* shell variables are used by **mailx**, but you can not change them while in **mailx**.

A large number of **mailx** variables can be manipulated to tailor the **mailx** environment to your wishes. You can set these variables from within **mailx** or set them in .mailrc. You use the **set** command to set up **mailx** variables and the **unset** command to reverse their setting. The format of the **set** command and the way you create and set up your .mailrc file are similar to .exrc (the vi editor startup file).

These variables can be set in the startup file .mailrc or internally from **mailx**.

append When you terminate reading your mail, if the **append** variable is set, then **mailx** appends messages to the end of the mbox file instead of the beginning.

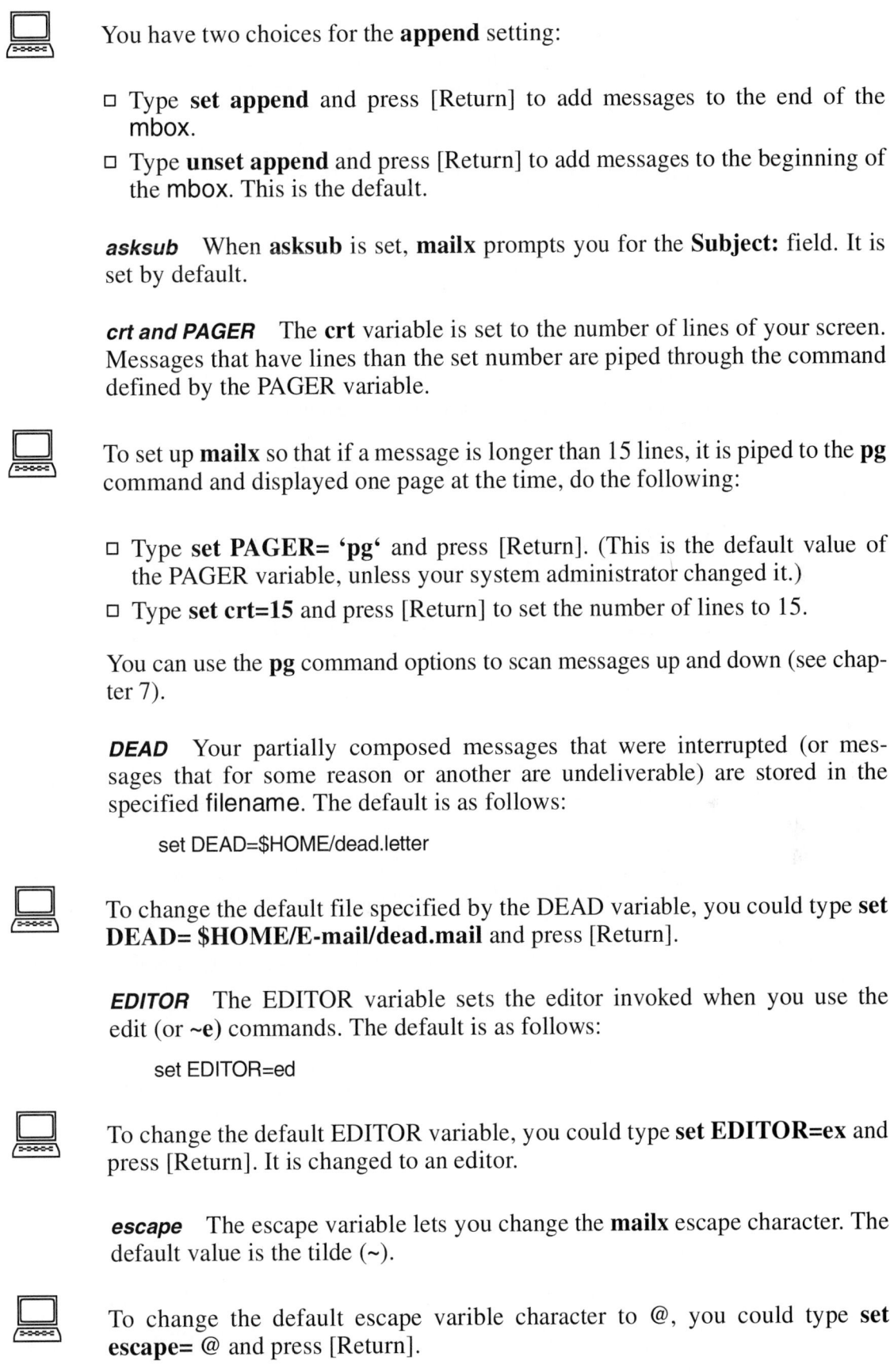

You have two choices for the **append** setting:

□ Type **set append** and press [Return] to add messages to the end of the mbox.
□ Type **unset append** and press [Return] to add messages to the beginning of the mbox. This is the default.

asksub   When **asksub** is set, **mailx** prompts you for the **Subject:** field. It is set by default.

crt and PAGER   The **crt** variable is set to the number of lines of your screen. Messages that have lines than the set number are piped through the command defined by the PAGER variable.

To set up **mailx** so that if a message is longer than 15 lines, it is piped to the **pg** command and displayed one page at the time, do the following:

□ Type **set PAGER= 'pg'** and press [Return]. (This is the default value of the PAGER variable, unless your system administrator changed it.)
□ Type **set crt=15** and press [Return] to set the number of lines to 15.

You can use the **pg** command options to scan messages up and down (see chapter 7).

DEAD   Your partially composed messages that were interrupted (or messages that for some reason or another are undeliverable) are stored in the specified filename. The default is as follows:

    set DEAD=$HOME/dead.letter

To change the default file specified by the DEAD variable, you could type **set DEAD= $HOME/E-mail/dead.mail** and press [Return].

EDITOR   The EDITOR variable sets the editor invoked when you use the edit (or ~e) commands. The default is as follows:

    set EDITOR=ed

To change the default EDITOR variable, you could type **set EDITOR=ex** and press [Return]. It is changed to an editor.

escape   The escape variable lets you change the **mailx** escape character. The default value is the tilde (~).

To change the default escape varible character to @, you could type **set escape= @** and press [Return].

folder   The folder variable makes the specified directory the standard directory for **mailx**. All mail files are saved in the directory specified by the folder variable. There is no default value for folder variable.

To specify the EMAIL file in the HOME directory for mail files, type **set folder= $HOME/EMAIL** and press [Return].

*This command does not create the EMAIL directory. It just assigns the specified directory to the variable folder. You use the **mkdir** command to create the directory.*

header   If the header variable is set, as it is by default, **mailx** displays the header of messages when you are reading mail.

To unset the header variable, type **unset header** and press [Return].

LISTER   The LISTER variable is set to a command that is used to list files in the directory defined in the folder variable. The default command is **ls.**

To change the LISTER variable, type **LISTER= 'ls -l'** and press [Return].

The command is enclosed in a pair of back quotation marks.

MBOX   The MBOX variable saves your read messages automatically in the specified filename. The default filename is $HOME/mbox.

To change the specified filename for read messages, you could type **set MBOX=$HOME/EMAIL/mbox** and press [Return].

*Saving a message in another file or using the **xit** command overrides the automatic saving.*

PAGER   The PAGER variable is set to a paging command and works with the setup of the crt variable. The default paging command is **pg**.

To change the paging command to **more**, type **set PAGER='more'** and press [Return].

record   The record variable is set to the filename that captures all your outgoing mail automatically. There is no default value for this variable.

To save outgoing mail in keep, type **record= $HOME/EMAIL/keep** and press [Return].

*This command does not create the EMAIL directory. It just assigns the specified directory to the record variable. You use the **mkdir** command to create the directory.*

SHELL   The SHELL variable is set to the shell program you intend to use. This is applicable when you use **!** or **~!** to issue a command to the shell while you are in **mailx** environment. The default is the **sh** shell.

To change the default SHELL variable, you could type **set SHELL= csh** and press [Return]. Now shell is changed to c shell.

VISUAL   The VISUAL variable is set to the screen editor you intend to use when **mailx** is in input mode and you use the **~v** command. The default is the vi editor.

9.5.2   Setting Up the *.mailrc* File

The .mailrc startup file in your home directory contains the commands and variables you set to tailor the **mailx** according to your preference. You can use vi or the **cat** command to create a .mailrc file.

Figure 9–6 shows a .mailrc sample file. In the sample file, *friends* and *chess* are the names assigned to two groups of user IDs. The sample file is also set up so that if a message is longer then twenty lines, it is piped to the **pg** command (the default PAGER value). Finally, your private mailbox, as set up in the sample file, is in EMAIL directory, and your outgoing mail is saved in a file called record in EMAIL directory.

Figure 9–6
The *.mailrc* sample file.

```
$ cat .mailrc
alias friends daniel david marie gabe emma stev
alias chess emma susan gabe
set crt=20
set MBOX=$HOME/E-mail/mbox
set record=$HOME/E-mail/record
$ _
```

9.6   COMMUNICATIONS OUTSIDE THE LOCAL SYSTEM

This chapter discussed the UNIX communication utilities that enable you to send mail to users who have login accounts on your local host. You can also send mail to the users on other UNIX computers. If you are on a UNIX network, as big companies and universities usually are, you can use the same commands. However, you must give more information. For example, the destination of your message needs to have the name of the computer (node name on the network) in addition to the user Id of the person on the specified computer. For example, if computer nodes between you and David on the network were named X, Y, and Z, then to send mail to David, you would type the following:

mailx X\!Y\!Z\!david

The details of communicating with other UNIX systems is outside the scope of this book. The commands in this chapter are all the basic skills you need; the rest is just a matter of looking up the commands in a reference book. Appendix F lists some of the books you may find useful for this purpose.

Command Summary

This chapter focused on the UNIX communication utilities and discussed the following commands and options.

---

mesg
This command is set to *n* to prohibit unwanted **write** messages. It is set to *y* to receive messages.

---

mailx
This utility provides the electronic mail system for the users. You can send messages to other users on the system, regardless whether they are logged in.

Option	Operation
-f [*filename*]	Reads mail from the specified *filename* instead of the system *mailbox*. If no file is specified, it reads from *mbox*.
-H	Displays the list of the message headers.
-s *subject*	Sets the subject field to string *subject*.

---

news
This command is used to look at the latest news in the system. It is used by the system administrator to inform others of the events happening.

Options	Operation
-a	Displays all the news items, old or new files.
-n	Lists only the names of the news files (headers).
-s	Displays the number of the current news items.

Wall
This command is used mostly by the system administrator to warn users of some imminent events.

---

write
This command is used for terminal-to-terminal communication. The receiving party must be logged in.

---

mailx tilde escape commands

When you invoke **mailx** to send mail to others, it places itself in input mode, ready for you to compose your message. The commands in this mode start with a tilde (~) and are called tilde escape commands.

Command	Operation
~?	Displays a list of all tilde escape commands.
~! *command*	Lets you to invoke the specified shell *command* while composing your message.
~e	Invokes an editor for editing your message. The editor to be used is defined in the mail variable called *EDITOR*.
~q	Quits input mode. Saves your partially composed message in the file called dead.letter.
~ r *filename*	Reads the specified *filename* and adds its contents to your message.
~ < *filename*	Reads the specified *filename* (using the redirection operator) and adds its contents to your message.
~< ! *command*	Executes the specified command places its output into your message.
~v	Invokes the default visual editor, the vi editor, or uses the value of the mail variable *VISUAL*, which can be set up for other editors.
~w *filename*	Writes currently composing message to the specified *filename*.

mailx command mode
When you invoke **mailx** to read your mail, it places itself in the command mode. The prompt for this mode is the question mark (**?**).

Command	Operation
!	Lets you execute the shell commands (the shell escape).
cd [*directory*]	Changes to the specified directory, or to home directory if none is specified.
d	Deletes the specified messages.
f	Displays the headlines of the current message.
q	Exits **mailx** and removes the messages from the system mailbox.
h	Displays active message headers.
m *users*	Sends mail to specified *users*.
R *messages*	Replies to the sender of the *messages*.
r *messages*	Replies to the sender of the *messages* and all the other recipients of the same *messages*.
s *filename*	Saves (appends) the indicated messages to the *filename*.
t *messages*	Displays (type) the specified *messages*.
u *messages*	Undeletes the specified *messages*.
x	Exits (xit), does not remove messages from system mailbox.

Review Exercises

1. What is the command for terminal to terminal communication? What is the key to signal the end of the communication?

2. What command is usually used by the system administrator to inform users about the everyday events?

3. What command broadcasts the message to everyone on the system?

4. How do you make your terminal immune from unwanted messages?

5. What is the command to read your mail?

6. How do you know you have mail?

Terminal Session

In this terminal session, you practice sending messages to other users. Send the messages to yourself to practice the commands. Then, when you feel comfortable using the commands, select another user as your partner and practice sending mail.

The following exercises are recommended. In order to master the many commands of the UNIX communication utilities, you must spend time at your terminal and try all combinations of the commands.

1. Create a directory **EMAIL** in your home directory.

2. Create a .mailrc file in your home directory. If one already exists, modify it.

3. Set the **mailx** following characteristics:

    a. Use **alias** command to assign names to a group of users.
    b. Set up a file in the **EMAIL** directory to save your outgoing mail automatically.
    c. Set your mbox in the **EMAIL** directory.

4. Send the following mail to yourself.

        So little time and so much to do.
        Could it be reversed?
        So much time and so little to do.

5. While **mailx** is in input mode, use the vi editor to compose your mail.

6. Read the current date and time and append it to the end of your message.

7. Save it in a file before transmitting it.

8. Compose a few more messages in the same manner, using vi and other commands and send it to yourself. This should give you enough messages so you can practice reading your mail.

9. Read your mail.

10. Use all the commands in the **mailx** command mode, including delete, undelete, save, and so on.

11. Read your mail and exit **mailx** using the **x** command Then read your mail and exit **mailx** using the **q** command. Observe the UNIX messages.

12. Use **mailx** and look at your mbox.

13. Now find another partner and have a chat using the **write** command.

14. Set the **mesg** to **n** then to **y** and observe the effect with your partner.

15. Sending mail to others may be one of the less boring parts of learning UNIX. Practice and have fun.

CHAPTER **10**

Program Development

This chapter describes the essentials of program development. It explains the steps in the process of creating a program and provides a general description of the available computer programming languages. It gives an example of a simple C program and walks you through the process of writing source code to make an executable program. The chapter also explains the use of the shell redirection operator to redirect the output and error messages of programs.

In This Chapter

10.1   Program Development

Chapter 1 discussed software and computer programming in general. You learned the important role of software in making computers do all these wonderful things (open to discussion!). You also learned that there are two categories of software: application software and system software.

A *program* consists of instructions that guide the computer to perform its basic arithmetic and logical operations. Each instruction tells the machine to perform one of its basic functions, and usually consists of the operation code and one or more operands. The *operation code* specifies the function to be performed, and *operands* specify the location or data elements to be manipulated. Figure 10–1 shows a typical instruction.

A computer is controlled by programs that are stored in computer memory. Memory storage is capable of storing only zeros and ones, so programs in memory must be in *binary form*. That means programs must be written in zeros and ones or converted to zeros and ones. Do programmers really write programs in zeros and ones? Fortunately, they don't have to any more. Early programmers did not have a choice; they had to code programs in zeros and ones, for which they deserve a lot of respect. Programmers write programs to create both categories of software. To write a program you need a programming language, and there are quite a few you can choose from.

Figure 10–1
The format of a simple instruction.

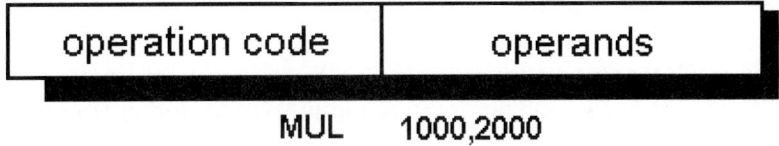

MUL   1000,2000

10.2   Programming Languages

Programming is the process of writing instructions (a program) for a computer to solve a problem. These instructions must be written in a computer programming language. A program can be anything from a simple list of instructions that adds a series of numbers together, to a large and complex structure with many sections that calculate the payroll of a big corporation.

Like computer hardware, programming languages have evolved in generations. Each new generation of languages improved on the previous ones and incorporated more capabilities for programmers.

Figure 10–2 shows the hierarchy and generations of the programming languages. Let's briefly explore the different levels of this hierarchy.

See page xxii for an explanation of icons used to highlight information in this chapter.

Figure 10–2
The hierarchy of the programming languages.

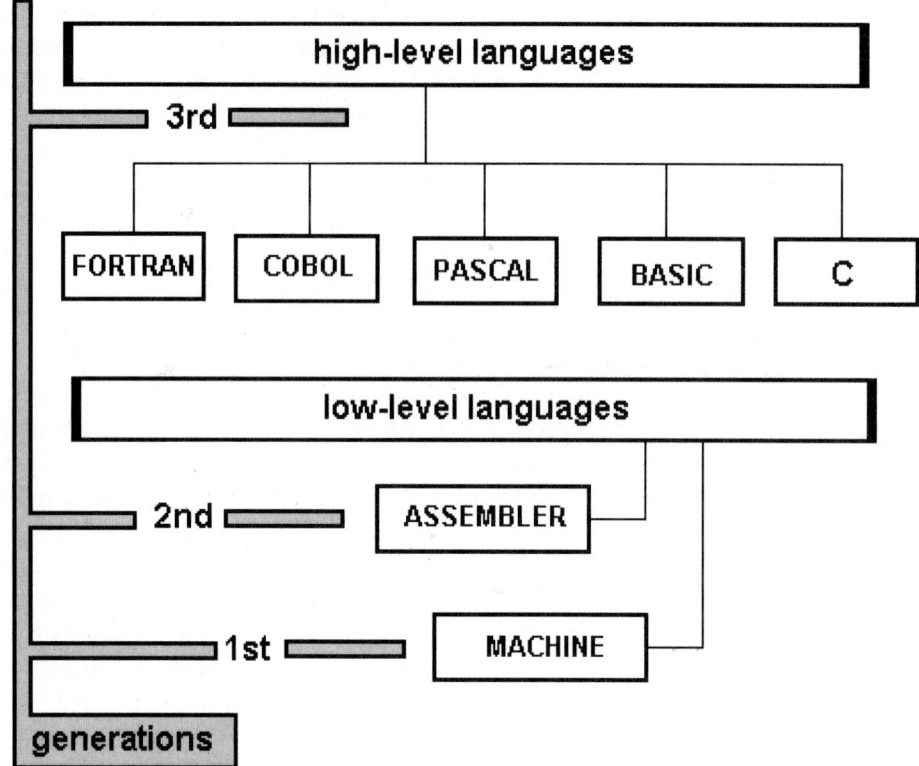

10.2.1   Low-level Languages

Machine Language   In machine language, instructions are coded as a series of zeros and ones. it is cumbersome and difficult to write programs in machine language. Machine language programs are written at the most basic level of computer operation; it is the only language computers understand and execute. Programs written in other programming languages must be translated into the machine language of the computer on which the program is to be executed. (Programs called *compilers* do this translation and are discussed in the next section.)

Assembler Language   Like machine language, assembler language is unique to a particular computer, but the instructions are represented differently. Instead of a series of zeros and ones, assembler language uses some recognized symbols, called *mnemonic* (memory aid), to represent instructions. For example, the mnemonic MUL is used to represent a multiply instruction. Because computers only understand zeros and ones, you must change a program in assembler language to machine language format for execution. This translation is done by invoking a program called *assembler*. Assembler program translates the mnemonics in your program back to the zeros and ones.

10.2.2   High-level Languages

No matter what computer and which high-level language you use to write your program, the program must be translated into machine language before it can be executed. This conversion of a program from a high-level programming language to low-level machine language is the job done by the software programs called *compilers* and *interpreters*. High-level programming languages are simply a programmer's convenience; they cannot be executed in their original form (source code). This section describes a few of the major programming languages.

COBOL   The COBOL (COmmon Business Oriented Language) programming language was introduced in 1959. Developed in response to business community requirements, it was used on mostly the mainframe computers providing data processing services to large companies. More efficient and faster general-purpose computer programming languages exists in the market, but COBOL is going to remain with us, because over half of all business application programs are written in COBOL.

FORTRAN   The FORTRAN (FORmula TRANslator) programming language was developed in 1955. It is most suitable for scientific or engineering programming, and remains the most popular scientific language. Of course, FORTRAN has been modified to meet the demands of new computers. The current version of the FORTRAN is FORTRAN77, which is a general-purpose language capable of dealing with numeric and symbolic problems. As with COBOL, a large body of existing code was written in FORTRAN, and it is still used in engineering and science.

Pascal   The Pascal programming language was developed in 1968 and is named after the seventeenth-century French mathematician Balis Pascal. The idea of good style and habits in programming were around and the buzz word *structured programming* was taking shape when Pascal was created, incorporating the structured programming ideas in it. Pascal was designed as a language to help students learn structured programming and develop good habits in programming. However, the use of Pascal is not limited to educational institutions; it is used in industry to create readable and maintainable codes.

BASIC   The BASIC (Beginners All-purpose Symbolic Instruction Code) programming language was developed in 1964 to help students with no computer background learn about computers and programming. It is accepted as the most effective programming language for instructional purposes. Since then, BASIC has evolved into a general-purpose language, and its use is not limited to the education field. BASIC is widely implemented and is used in business applications.

C   The C programming language was developed in 1972, and it is based on principles practiced in Pascal programming. It was mainly targeted for system programming, creating operating systems, compilers, and so on. Most of the UNIX operating system is written in C. C is a fast, efficient general-purpose language. It is also a portable language; it is relatively machine-independent. A C program written for one type of computer can be run on another with little or no modification. C is by far the language of choice for many programmers developing programs for business, scientific, and other applications.

C++   In the 1980, C++ was developed to add to the C language the tools needed to make it an object-oriented language. Object-oriented programming (OOP) is a relatively new technique in programming. It reduces the program development time.

10.3   Programming Mechanics

To write a program, you have to choose a computer programming language. The choice of programming language depends on the nature of the application. Many general-purpose and specialized programming languages exist that fit any requirement. The exact steps you must follow to produce a program depend on the computer environment.

10.3.1   Steps to Creating an Executable Program

Regardless of the computer operating system and the programming language you use, the following steps are necessary to create an executable program.

1. Creating the source file (*source code*)

2. Creating the object file (*object code/object module*)

3. Creating the executable file (*executable code/load module*)

Source Code   You usually use an editor (such as the vi editor) to write a program and save what you write in a file. This file is the *source code*. The source code is written in the programming language of your choice. By itself, your computer does not understand it. The goal is to convert the source code file to an executable file.

 A source file is a text file, which is also called an ASCII file. You can display it on the screen, modify it using one of the available editors, or send it to the printer to obtain a hard copy of your program's source code.

Object Code   Source code is incomprehensible to the computer. Remember, computers understand only machine language (the pattern of zeros and ones). Thus your source code must be translated to machine-understandable language. This is the job of a compiler or an interpreter. They produce the object code. The *object code* is the machine language translation of your source code. However, it is not an executable file yet; it lacks some necessary parts. These necessary parts are programs that provide the interface between the program and the operating system. They are usually grouped together in files called *library files*.

You cannot send an object file to the printer. It is a file of zeros and ones. If you display it, you may lock your keyboard or hear beeps as some of the zeros and ones are translated into the ASCII codes that represent codes for locking keyboard, beep at your terminal, stop scrolling, and so on.

Executable Code   Your object code might refer to other programs that are not part of your *object module*. Before your program can be executed, these references to other programs must be resolved. This is the job of the *linker* or *link editor*. It creates the *executable code,* the *load module*. The *load module* is a complete, ready-to-be-executed program with all its parts put together.

The load module, like the object file, is not a file to be sent to printer or displayed on your terminal.

In some systems, you invoke the compiler and after the compilation process is completed, you invoke the linker to create the executable file. Other systems have the compiler start the linker automatically. On those systems, you just give the compile command, and if your program does not have any compilation error, then the linker is invoked to link your program.

Exactly how this works varies among systems, depending on the system environment/configuration setup as done by the system administrator.

Figure 10–3
Program development steps.

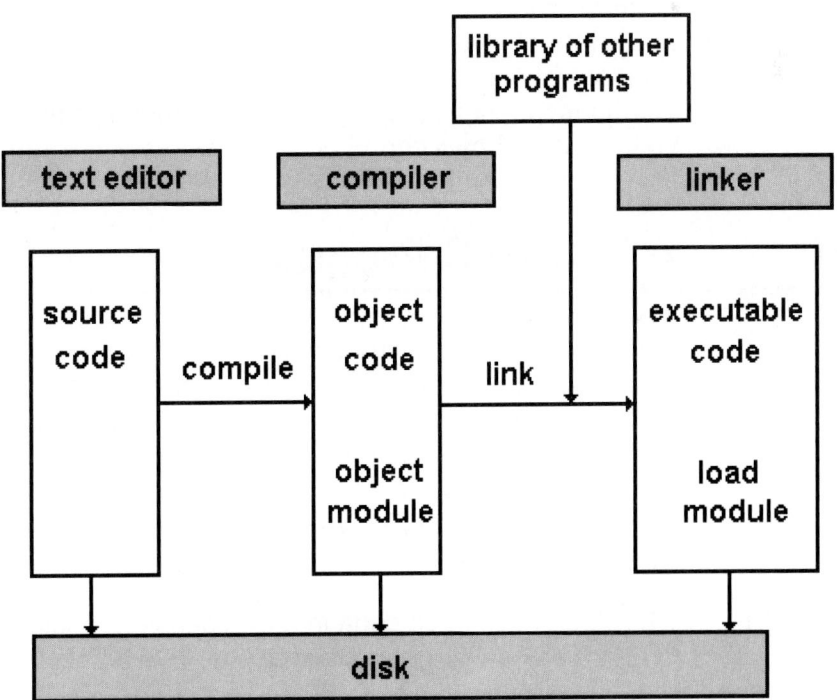

This process, starting from a source file and ending up creating an executable file, is depicted in figure 10–3.

10.3.2   Compilers/Interpreters

The main function of a compiler or an interpreter is to translate your source code (program instructions) to machine code so the computer can understand your instructions. The compiled languages and interpreted languages represent two different categories of computer languages. Each has its advantages and disadvantages.

Compiler   The compiler is a system software program that translates high-level program instructions, such as a Pascal program, into machine language that the computer can interpret and execute. It compiles the entire program at one time and does not give you any feedback until it compiles the entire program.

   A separate compiler is required for each programming language you intend to use on your computer system. To execute C and Pascal programs, you must have a C compiler and a Pascal compiler. Compilers produce a better and more efficient object code than interpreters, so a compiled program runs faster and needs less space.

Interpreter   Like the compiler, the interpreter translates a high-level language program into machine language. However, instead of translating the entire source program, it translate a single line at a time. An interpreter gives you immediate feedback. If the code contains an error, the interpreter picks it up as soon as you press [Return] to finish a line of code. Therefore, you can correct errors during program development. The interpreter does not produce a separate object code file, and it must perform the translation process each time a program is executed. Interpreters are usually used in an educational environment, and the executable code they produce is less efficient than the code produced by a compiler.

10.4   A Simple C Program

Let's write a simple C program and go through the steps to see how this process works. The goal is to understand and practice the compilation process, not to learn C language. However, you'll have to understand some very basic characteristics of C language to be able to write a simple C program and compile it successfully.

   Using the vi editor (or any other editor), create a source file called first.c. Figure 10–4 shows the contents of the file.

1.   Type the source code in lowercase letters. Like UNIX, C language is a lowercase language, and all the keywords must be typed in lowercase.

Figure 10–4
A simple C program.

```
$ cat first.c
/* my first C program */
# include <stdio.h>
main( )
{
    printf ("Hi there!\n");
    printf ("This is my first C program \n");
}
$ _
```

2. In most systems, the extension .c at the end of the source code filename is mandatory.

The next step is to compile your source code. The command is as follows:

> **$ cc first.c [Return]**

The **cc** command compiles your source code, and if you do not have any errors, automatically invokes the linker. The end result is that you have an executable file called **a.out**. By default, **a.out** is the name of the executable file. Now if you want to execute the file to see the program output, you type:

> **$ a.out [Return]** . . . . Execute your program.
>
> Hi there!
> This is my first C program.
>
> $_ . . . . And the prompt.

*The output of **a.out** is displayed on the standard output device, your terminal.*

What if you do not want to call your executable file **a.out**? You can use the **cc** command with the **-o** option to specify the name of the output file.

Compile first.c and indicate the name of the output file. Call it *first*.

> **$ cc first.c -o first [Return]** . . . . Use **cc** with the **-o** option.
>
> $_ . . . . No errors, prompt is back.

Make sure the name of the specified output file and the name of the source code file are different; otherwise, your source code file is overwritten and becomes your executable file—which means your source file is destroyed.

Now your executable file is called first, and any time you type **first** at the prompt, you see program output on the screen.

```
$ first [Return] . . . . . . . . . . . . . . . . . .  Execute first.
Hi there!
This is my first C program.

$_ . . . . . . . . . . . . . . . . . . . . . . . . . . . . .  Ready for the next command.
```

What if you do not want the output on the screen? Maybe you want to store the output of your program in a file. Using the output redirection capability of the shell, you can redirect the program output into another file.

Run **first** and save its output in a file.

```
$ first  > first.out [Return] . . . . . . . . . .  Output is redirected to a file called first.out,
                                                    so it is not displayed on the screen.

$ cat first.out [Return] . . . . . . . . . . . . .  Check the contents of first.out.
Hi there!
This is my first C program.

$_ . . . . . . . . . . . . . . . . . . . . . . . . . . . . .  And the prompt.
```

As you expected, the contents of the first.out file is the output of your C program. The first.out file was created by redirecting the output of your program into it.

Execute **first**, show its output on the screen, and save it in a file.

```
$ first | tee -a first.out [Return] . . . . . . .  Output is displayed on the screen and also
                                                    saved in first.out.
Hi there!
This is my first C program.

$_ . . . . . . . . . . . . . . . . . . . . . . . . . . . . .  The shell prompt.
```

Using the **tee** (split output) command with the **pipe** operator, the output of the program **first** is displayed on the screen and also saved in first.out. The **tee** command **-a** option appends the output to the end of the first.out.

10.4.1   Correcting Mistakes

Assuming you did not make any mistake in writing your first C program, things are fairly simple. You compile and execute your program. But this is not always the case when you write large programs. The chances are good you make syntax and logical mistakes that you have to correct before being able to run a program successfully. The C compiler recognizes syntax errors and displays them on the screen with a line number reference.

Suppose you modify first.c to look like the file in figure 10–5, so that it has no semicolon (;) at the end of the **first printf( )** statement. This time when you compile first.c, the compiler is going to complain.

Figure 10–5
A simple C program with a syntax error.

```
$ cat first.c

/* my first C program */
# include <stdio.h>
main( )
{
    printf ("Hi there!\n")     /* semi colon omitted intentionally.*/
    printf ("This is my first C program \n");
}
$ _
```

Now compile first.c.

$ **cc first.c -o first [Return]** . . . . Compile and call the output file first.

"first.c", line 6: syntax error.
"first.c", line 6: illegal character: 134(octal)
"first.c", line 6: cannot recover from earlier error: goodbye!

$_ . . . . Prompt.

The error messages indicate that you have some sort of syntax error on line 6. The compiler is not clever enough to recognize the exact error and its location; it just directs you to the vicinity of the error in the source code.

At this point, the compiler did not produce an object code file. To correct the errors, you must go back to the source code, first.c, and add the semicolon. Then, to get the correct executable file, you have to recompile the file.

It is easy to look at one or two error lines on the screen, but when you have a large amount of source code, the chances are good that you will have more than a few lines of errors. Remembering the errors and their line numbers when you want to edit your source file to correct the errors is not a trivial task. Therefore, it is desirable to save the compiler error messages in a file for easy reference. The redirection capability of the shell becomes handy again!

The default error device is usually the same as the output device, your terminal, so the errors are displayed on your terminal. Suppose you want to redirect the errors to a specified file.

Compile first.c and save compilation errors, if any, in another file.

$ **cc first.c -o first 2> error [Return]**. . . Recompile.

$_ . . . . The shell prompt.

The digit *2* before the > sign is necessary and indicates the redirection of the standard error device.

Where does the digit *2* come from? The command just shown needs some explanation. Let's go back to the UNIX redirection concept and explore the origins of the digit 2.

10.4.2   Redirecting the Standard Error

The shell interprets the > as standard output redirection. The notation **1>** is the same as > and tells shell to redirect the standard output. The number *1* in **1>** is the file descriptor number; by default, file descriptor 1 is assigned to the *standard output device*. For example, the following two commands do the same job, redirecting the output of the **ls** command to a file.

$ **ls -C > list [Return]**

or

$ **ls -C 1> list [Return]**

File descriptor 2 is assigned to the *standard error device*. The shell interprets the notation **2>** as the redirection of the error output. For example, suppose you do not have a file called Y in your current directory, and issue the following command:

$ **cat Y > Z [Return]** . . . . Copy Y to Z.

cat: cannot open Y . . . . Error message.

The error message appears on the screen. Now redirect the error output to a file.

$ **cat Y > Z 2> error [Return]**   . . . . Copy Y to Z. Keep errors in a file
called error in the current directory.

$_ . . . . No error messages. Prompt is back.

$ **cat error [Return]** . . . . Show the content of the error file.

cat: cannot open Y . . . . As you expected.

$_ . . . . And the prompt.

Now back to your C program and the compilation error, you can redirect the compilation errors to another file by typing:

$ **cc first.c -o first 2> error [Return]** . . . Error message redirected to error file.

$_ . . . . No error is displayed.

$ **cat error [Return]** . . . . Check the compilation errors.

"first.c", line 6: Syntax error.
"first.c", line 6: Cannot recover from earlier error: goodbye!

$_ . . . . Prompt.

10.5　　UNIX Programming Tracking Utilities

Other computer language compilers are available that work in a UNIX environment. You can obtain compilers for nearly every language to run under UNIX.

The goal of this chapter was to introduce you to programming development under UNIX—not to present you with a comprehensive list of languages, compilers, and UNIX programming. However, it is important to know that UNIX provides you with utilities to help you organize your program development process. These utilities become especially useful and important when you are developing large-scale software. The following is a very brief explanation of these utilities and their functions.

10.5.1　　The make Utility

The **make** utility is useful when your program is comprised of more than one file. **make** automatically keeps tracks of the source files that are changed and need recompilation, and relinks your programs if required. The **make** program gets its information from a control file. The *control file* contains rules that specify source files dependencies and other information.

10.5.2　　The SCCS Utility

The **SCCS** (Source Code Control System) is a collection of programs that helps you to maintain and manage the development of your programs. If your program is under **SCCS** control, then you can create different versions of your program easily. The **SCCS** keeps track of all the changes among different versions.

Review Exercises

1. Explain the steps necessary to write a program and produce an executable file.

2. What is a source code?

3. What is the function of a compiler?

4. What is the difference between a compiler and an interpreter?

5. What is the command to compile a C program, and what is the default name of the executable file?

6. Why can't you send your executable file to a printer?

Terminal Session

In this terminal session, you are to write a sample C program. It is not expected that you know C programming. Copy the simple C program example in this chapter or any C programming book. The purpose is to familiarize yourself with the process of program development.

1. Write a simple C program.

2. Compile it.

3. Run the program.

4. Compile it again and specify the executable file.

5. Run it again.

6. Save the output of your program in another file.

7. Modify your source code and make an intentional syntax error.

8. Compile again.

9. Observe the error messages. See if you can decipher them.

10. Recompile your program, save the error messages in a file.

11. Look at the file that contains the compilation errors.

## CHAPTER 11

Shell Programming

This chapter concentrates on shell programming. It explains the capabilities of the shell as an interpretive high-level language. It describes shell programming constructs and particulars. It explores shell programming aspects such as variables and flow control commands. It shows the creation, debugging, and running of shell programs, and it introduces a few more shell commands.

In This Chapter

11.1 UNDERSTANDING UNIX shell PROGRAMMING LANGUAGE: AN INTRODUCTION

Command languages provide the means for writing programs using the sequence of commands, the same commands that you type at the prompt. Most of today's command languages provide more than just the execution of a list of commands. They have features that you find in traditional high-level languages, such as looping constructs and decision-making statements. This gives you a choice of programming in high-level languages or command languages. *Command languages* are interpreted languages, unlike *compiled languages* such as C and FORTRAN. Programs written in a command language are easier to debug and modify than programs written in compiled languages. But you pay a price for this convenience: these programs typically take much longer to execute than the compiled ones.

UNIX shell has its own built-in programming language, and all shells (Bourne shell, cshell, etc.) provide you with this programming capability. The shell language is a command language with a lot of features common to many computer programming languages, including the structured language constructs: sequence, selection, and iteration. Using the shell programming language makes it easy to to write, modify, and debug programs, and this language does not need compilation. You can execute a program as soon as you finish writing it.

The shell program files are called *shell procedures, shell scripts* or simply *scripts*. A *shell script* is a file that contains a series of commands for shell to execute. As you execute a shell script, each command in the script file is passed to the shell to execute, one at a time. When all the commands in the file are executed, or if an error occurs, the script ends.

You do not have to write shell programs. But, as you use UNIX, you will find that sometimes you want to write small scripts to perform functions you want to do that UNIX doesn't have a command for or to perform several commands. UNIX commands are numerous, difficult to remember, and involve a lot of typing. If you do not want to have to remember all that strange UNIX command syntax, or if you are not a good typist, then you may want to write script files.

11.1.1 Writing a Simple Script

You do not need to be a programmer to write simple script files. For example, suppose you want to know how many users are currently on the system. The command and output look like this:

who | wc -l [Return]. . . Type the command.

6 . . . . UNIX will display the number.

The output of the **who** is passed as input to the **wc** command, and the **-l** option counts the lines that indicate the number of current users on the system.

See page xxii for an explanation of icons used to highlight information in this chapter.

Figure 11–1

A simple shell script.

```
# cat won
#
# won
# displays # of users currently logged in
#
who | wc -l
$ _
```

You can write a simple script file to do the same thing. Figure 11–1 shows a simple shell script called won (Who is ON) that uses the **who** and **wc** commands to report the number of people currently logged on the system. The shell scripts are stored in UNIX text files, so you use the vi editor (your favorite text editor) or the **cat** command to create one.

The # at the beginning of a line indicates the line is a remark line and is for documentation. The shell ignores lines starting with the #.

11.1.2   Executing a Script

There are two ways to execute a shell scripts: you can use the **sh** command, or you can make the shell script file an executable file.

Invoking Scripts with sh

You can use the **sh** command to execute script files. Every time you type **sh** you invoke another copy (instance) of the shell. The shell script won is not an executable file, so you must invoke another shell to execute it. You specify the filename, and the new shell reads the script, executes the commands listed in it, and ends when all commands have been executed (or when it reaches an error).

Figure 11–2 shows how the won file can be executed using this method. Typing **sh** to invoke another shell every time you want to execute a script file is not very convenient. However, this method has its advantages, especially when you write complex script applications that need debugging and tracing tools. (These tools are discussed later in this chapter.) Under normal circumstances, the second method of making the script executable is preferred. After all, the less typing the better.

Figure 11–2

Using the sh command to run a script.

```
$ sh  won
6
$_
```

Table11–1
chmod command options.

Character	Who is Affected
u	User/owner.
g	Group.
o	Others.
a	All; can be used instead of the combination of **ugo**.

Character	Permission Category
r	Read permission.
w	Write permission.
x	Execute permission.
-	No permission.

Operator	Specific Action to be Taken on Permission Categories
+	Grants permission.
-	Denies permission.
=	Sets all permissions for a specified user.

Making Files Executable:Using chmod *to Change File Permissions*

The second method of executing a shell program is to make the script file an executable file. In this case, you do not need to invoke another shell; all you type is the name of the script program, just as you do any other shell program (command). This is the preferred method.

What you have to do to make a file executable is change the access permissions for that file. You use the **chmod** command to change the mode of a specified file (for more information about **chmod**, refer to chapter 5). Table 11–1 shows the **chmod** options. Assuming that you have a file called myfile, the following example shows how you can change its access mode.

The following command makes myfile an executable file.

```
$ ls -l myfile [Return] . . . . . . . . . . . . . . Check myfile mode.

- rw- rw- r- -    1         david      student     64 Oct 18 15:45  myfile
```

$ **chmod u+x myfile [Return]** . . . . Change myfile mode.

$ **ls -l myfile [Return]** . . . . Check myfile mode again.

- rwx rw-r- -   1   david   student   64 Oct 18 15:45 myfile

$_ . . . . The shell prompt.

The **ls** command is used to verify the fact that its access mode is changed. The **u** indicates the user access to myfile; the **+x** indicates that myfile access mode is to be changed to executable.

The following command removes the write access for all other users.

$ **chmod o-w myfile [Return]** . . . . Change myfile mode.

$_ . . . . Prompt.

You and members of your group still have read and write access privileges, but others can only read from your file. (You can use the **ls** command to verify the changes.) The letter **o** indicates others, and the **-w** indicates the others do not have write access to myfile.

The following command changes the access privileges for all users (owner, group, and other) to read and write.

$ **chmod a=rw myfile [Return]** . . . . Change myfile mode.

$_ . . . . Prompt.

Now anyone can read or write to myfile. (Again you can use the **ls** command to verify the changes.) The letter **a** indicates all users, and the **=rw** indicates read and write access.

The following command removes all access privileges for the group and other users.

$ **ls -l myfile [Return]** . . . . Display myfile mode.

- rwx rw- r- -   1   david   student   64 Oct 18 15:45 myfile

$ **chmod go= myfile [Return]** . . . . Change myfile mode.

$ **ls -l myfile [Return]**. . . . . Check the mode changes.

- rwx - - - - - - 1   david   student   64 Oct 18 15:45 myfile

$_ . . . . Prompt.

The owner (in this case you) is the only one who has access to myfile. The **ls** command verifies the changes. The **go** command indicates group and others, so the **go=** indicates removal of all access privileges to myfile.

Returning to your won shell script, let's make it to be an executable file.

```
$ ls -l  won [Return]. . . . . . . . . . . . . . . . . . . . . Check mode set for won.

-rw- rw- r- -    1            david      student      64  Oct  18  15:45 won

$ chmod u+x  won [Return] . . . . . . . . . . . . . Change mode.

$ ls -l won [Return] . . . . . . . . . . . . . . Verify the change.

-rwx rw-r- -    1            david      student      64  Oct  18  16:45  won

$ _ . . . . . . . . . . . . . . . . . . . . . . . . . . . . . Prompt.
```

Now won, your shell script file, is an executable file, and you do not need to invoke another shell program to execute it. You execute won like any other command (executable file) by simply typing the filename and pressing [Return].

```
$ won [Return]. . . . . . . . . . . . . . . . . . . Execute won.

6 . . . . . . . . . . . . . . . . . . . . . . . . . . . . . . Output shows there are 6 users.

$ _ . . . . . . . . . . . . . . . . . . . . . . . . . . . . . The shell prompt.
```

11.2   WRITING MORE shell SCRIPTS

Shell programming is relatively simple, and it is a powerful tool at your disposal. You can place any command or sequence of commands in a file, make the file executable, and then execute its contents simply by typing its name at the $ prompt.

Let's modify the won file and add a few more commands to it. Figure 11–3 shows the modified version of the won script file.

Assuming won access mode is changed and it is an executable file, figure 11–4 shows the output of the won second version program.

The output of the won second version is cryptic and certainly can be improved. Let's use a few **echo** commands here and there to make the output more meaningful. Figure 11–5 shows the won script, third version.

Figure 11–3
A shell script sample won program.

```
# cat won
#
# won second version
# displays the current date and time,  # of users currently logged in,
# and your current working directory
#
date
who | wc -l
pwd
$ _
```

Figure 11–4

The output of the won program.

```
$ won
Wed  Nov 29  14:00:52  EDT 2001
     14
$_
```

The **echo** command with no argument is one way to output a blank line. The **echo** command ends its output with a new line. The **-n** option inhibits the default new line code.

Figure 11–6 shows the output of the won version 3. It is more informative and looks better.

Figure 11–5

Another version of the won program.

```
# cat won
#
#  won third version. The user friendly version
#  displays the current date and time, # of users currently logged in,
#  and your current working directory.
#
echo
echo -n "Date and Time: "
date
echo -n "Number of users on the system: "
who | wc -l
echo -n "Your current directory: "
pwd
echo
$ _
```

Figure 11–6

The output of the won shell program.

```
$ won
Date and Time: Wed  Nov 29  15:00:52  EDT 2001
Number of users on the system: 14
Your current directory: /usr/students/david

$_
```

11.2.1   Using Special Characters

As was discussed in chapter 8, the **echo** command recognizes special characters, called *escape characters*. They all start with the backslash (\), and you can use them as part of the **echo** command argument string. These characters give you more control over the format of your output. For example, the following command produces four new lines.

    $ echo "\n\n\n" [Return] . . . . Produces four blank lines.

Three blank lines are produced by the three **\n** codes, and one blank line by the **echo** command default new line at the end of the output string.

Table 11–2 summarizes these escape characters, and the following command sequence shows examples of using the escape characters.

Use the *\n escape* character.

    $ echo "\nHello\n" [Return] . . . . Using \n escape character.

. . . . A blank line produced by the first **\n**.

hello . . . . The word *hello*.

. . . . A blank line produced by the second **\n**.

. . . . A blank line produced by the **echo** command.

    $_ . . . . Prompt.

Beeping Sound   [Ctrl-G] produces a beeping sound on most terminals, and the ASCII code for it is octal number 7. You can use the **\0n** format to sound a beep on your terminal.

Table 11–2
The echo command special characters.

Escape Character	Meaning
\b	A backspace.
\c	Inhibits the default newline at the end of the output string.
\n	A carriage return and a form feed (newline).
\r	A carriage return without a linefeed.
\t	A tab character.
\0n	A zero followed by 1-, 2-, or 3-digit octal number representing the ASCII code of a character.

Use the **\0n** escape code to produce a beeping sound.

> $ **echo "\07\07WARNING" [Return]** . . . Using **\07** for the bell sound.
> WARNING
>
> $_ . . . . Prompt.

You hear the terminal bell sounds twice (beep beep), and the **WARNING** *message is displayed.*

Clearing Screen   When you write scripts, especially interactive ones, you usually need to clear the screen before doing anything else. One way to clear the screen is to use the **\0n** escape character format with the **echo** command to send the clear screen code to the terminal. The code for clearing the screen is terminal-dependent; you may need to ask your system administrator or look it up in the terminal user/technical manual.

Assuming [Ctrl-z] clears your terminal screen (octal number 32), use the **echo** command to clear the screen.

> $ **echo "\032" [Return]** . . . . Clear screen.
>
> $_ . . . . Prompt.

The screen is cleared, and the prompt appears at the left top corner of the screen.

11.2.2   Logging Off in Style

Normally, you press [Ctrl-d] or use the **exit** command to log off and end your session. Suppose you want to change that: you want to type **bye** to log off.

Write a script file called **bye** that contains one line of code, the command **exit**.

> $ **cat bye [Return]** . . . . Show contents of bye.
>
> exit . . . . One line of code.
>
> $_ . . . . Prompt.

Change **bye** to an executable file, and run it to log out.

> $ **chmod u+x bye [Return]** . . . . Change file mode.
>
> $ **bye [Return]** . . . . Log out.
>
> $_ . . . . You are still in UNIX.

Why didn't **exit** work? When you give a command to the shell, it creates a child process to execute the command (as described in chapter 8). Your login shell is the parent process, and your script file bye is the child process. The child process (bye) gets the control and executes the **exit** command that consequently terminates the child process (bye). When the child is dead, control goes back to the parent (your login shell). Therefore the $ prompt is displayed.

To make the bye script work, you must prevent the shell from creating a child process (using the dot command as described in the following section), so that the shell executes your program in its own environment. Then the **exit** command terminates the current shell (your login shell), and you are logged out.

11.2.3   Executing Commands: The dot Command

The dot command (**.**) is a built-in shell command that lets you execute a program in the current shell and prevents the shell from creating the child process. This is useful if you want to test your script files, such as the .profile startup file. The .profile in your home directory contains any command that you want to execute whenever you log in. You do not need to log out and log in to activate your .profile file. Using the dot command, you can execute .profile, and the commands in it are applied to the current shell, your login shell.

Returning to your bye script file, let's execute it again, this time using the dot command.

> **$. bye [Return]** . . . . Using the dot command.
>
> UNIX System V release 4.0
>
> login:_. . . . . Login prompt.

As with other commands in UNIX, there is a space between the dot command and its argument (in this case, your bye program).

Let's try another version of the bye script that does not require the dot command so you can simply type **bye** and press [Return] to log off.

In chapter 10, you learned about the **kill** command. The following command placed in the bye script file means to kill all processes, including the login shell.

> **$ cat bye [Return]** . . . . bye new version.
>
> **kill -9 0** . . . . Command to kill all processes.
>
> $_. . . . . Prompt.

Only one problem remains. You want to be able to use the bye script regardless of your current directory. If bye is in your home directory, you have to either change to your home directory every time you want to execute bye or type the full pathname to the bye file.

Path Modification   You can modify the PATH shell variable and add your home directory to it. Thus your home directory is also searched to find the commands.

 Changing the PATH variable to add your home directory.

      $ **echo $PATH [Return]** . . . . Check the PATH assignment.

      PATH=:/bin:/usr/bin

      $ **PATH=$PATH:$HOME [Return]** . . . . . Add your home directory.

      $ **echo $PATH [Return]** . . . . Check again.

      PATH=:/bin:/usr/bin:/usr/students/david

      $_ . . . . Prompt.

Now everything is ready; type **bye** and press [Return] at the $ prompt, and you are logged off.

 To make your changes permanent, place the new PATH in your .profile file. Then, any time you log in, the PATH variable is set to your desired path.

Command Substitution   You can place the output of a command in the argument string. The shell executes the command surrounded by a pair of back quotation marks (') and then substitutes the output of the command in the string passed to the **echo**. For example, if you type this:

      $ **echo "your current directory: 'pwd' " [Return]**

The output looks like this:

      Your current directory: /usr/students/david

 In this case, **pwd** *is executed, and its output, your current directory name, is placed in a string that is passed to the* **echo** *command.*

11.2.4   Reading Inputs: The *read* Command

One way to assign values to variables is to use the assignment operator, the equals sign (=). You can also store values in variables by reading strings from the standard input device.

You use the **read** command to read the user input and save it in a user-defined variable. This is one of the most common uses of the user-defined variables, especially in interactive programs where you prompt the user for information and then read the user response. When **read** is executed, the shell waits until the user enters a line of text; then, it stores the entered text in one or more variables. The variables are listed after the **read** on the command line, and the end of user input is signaled when the user presses [Return].

Figure 11–7 is a sample script named kb_read that shows how the **read** command works.

Figure 11–7

A shell script sample kb_read.

```
$ cat kb_read
#
# The read command example
#
echo "Enter your name: \c"     # prompt the user
read  name                     # read from keyboard and save the input in name
echo "Your name is $name"      # echo back the inputted data
$ _
```

The **read** command is usually used in combination with **echo**. You use the **echo** to prompt the user for what you want to be entered, and the **read** command waits for the user to enter something.

Invoke the kb_read shell script.

$ **kb_read [Return]** . . . . Run it.

Enter your name _ . . . . User is prompted

david [Return] . . . . Enter a name.

Your name is david . . . . Name is echoed back.

$_ . . . . Prompt.

1. Your input string is stored in the variable name *and then displayed.*

2. It is a good idea to put the variables in quotation marks because you can not anticipate the user input, and you do not want the shell to interpret special characters such as [*], [?], and so on.

The **read** command reads one line from the input device. The first input word is stored in the first variable, the second word in the second variable, and so on. If your input string contains more words than the number of the variables, the left-over words are stored in the last variable.

The characters assigned to the IFS shell variable (see chapter 8) determine the words' delimiters, in most cases the space character.

Figure 11–8 shows a simple script, read_test, that reads the user response and displays it back on the screen.

Let's run the read_test script.

$ **read_test [Return]** . . . . Assuming read_test is an executable file.

Give me a long sentence: . . . . Prompt is displayed.

Figure 11–8
A simple script, read_test, to test the **read** command.

```
$ cat read_test
#
# A simple script to test the read command
#
echo "Give me a long sentence:\c"          # user prompt
read Word1  Word2  Rest                     # read user response
echo " $Word1 \n $Word2 \n $Rest "          # display the content of the variables
echo "End of my act"                        # end the act

$ _
```

Let's test the read command. [Return] Your input.

Let's . . . . Content of the $Word1.

test . . . . Content of the $Word2.

the read command . . . . Content of the $Rest.

$_ . . . . Prompt.

In this example, your input string consists of five words. The **read** has three arguments (variables *Word1*, *Word2*, and *Rest*) to store your entire input. The first two words go to the first two variables, and the rest of the input string is stored in the third and the last variable, *Rest*.

If the **read** in this example had only one parameter, say variable *word1*, the entire input string would have been stored in *word1*.

11.3   EXPLORING THE shell PROGRAMMING BASICS

Now that you know you can place a sequence of commands in a file and create a simple script file, let's explore the shell script as a full-powered programming language that you can use to write applications.

Like any complete programming language, the *shell* provides you with commands and constructs that help you write well-structured, readable, and maintainable programs. This section explains the syntax of these commands and constructs.

11.3.1   Comments

Documentation is important when writing computer programs, and writing a shell script program is no exception. Documentation is essential to explain the purpose and logic of the program, and commands used in the program that are not obvious. Documentation is for you and anybody else who reads your program. If you look at a program a few weeks after you've written it, you will be surprised how much of your code you do not remember.

The shell recognizes # as the comment symbol; therefore, characters after the # are ignored.

The following command sequences show examples of comment line.

     # .... This is a comment.

     # program version 3 .... This is also a comment line.

     date   # show the current date ...... Comment in the middle of the line.

11.3.2   Variables

Like other programming languages, the UNIX shell lets you create variables to store values in them. To store a value in a variable, you simply write the name of the variable, followed by the equals sign and the value you want to store in the variable, like this:

     variable=value

Spaces are not permitted on either side of the equal sign.

The UNIX shell does not support data types (integer, character, floating point, etc.) as some programming languages do. It interprets any values assigned to variables as a string of characters. For example, **count=1** means store character *1* in the variable called *count*.

     The variable names follow the same syntax and rules that are applied to file names as described in chapter 7. Briefly, to refresh your memory, names must begin with a letter or an underscore character (_); you can use letters and numbers for the rest of the name.

     shell is an interpretive language, and the commands or variables you place in your script file can be directly typed at the $ prompt. Of course, this method is a one-time process; if you want to repeat the sequence of commands, you have to type them again.

The following examples are valid variable assignments, and they remain in effect until you change them or log off.

     $ **count=1 [Return]** .... Assign character 1 to count.

     $ **header="The Main Menu" [Return]** .... Store the string in header.

     $ **BUG=insect [Return]** .... Another variable assignment.

If your value string contains embedded white space, then you must place it between quotation marks.

Variables in your shell script stay in the memory until the shell script is finished/terminated, or you can erase the variables using the **unset** command. To do that, you type **unset**, specify the name of the variable you want to erase, and press [Return]. For example, the following command erases the variable called *XYZ*:

> $ **unset XYZ [Return]**

Display of Variables

You know from chapter 7 that the **echo** command can be used to display the contents of variables. The format is as follows:

>   echo $variable

Let's show the contents of the three variables assigned in the above examples.

> $ **echo $count $header $BUG [Return]**   . . . . . Show the value stored in variables.
>
>   1 The Main Menu insect
>
> $_ . . . . The shell prompt.

Command Substitution

You can store the output of a command in a variable. You enclose a command in a pair of back quotation marks ('), and the shell executes the command and replaces the command with its output, like this:

> $ **DATE='date' [Return]**   . . . . Save the output of the **date** command
>   in the variable *DATE*.
>
> $ **echo $DATE [Return]**   . . . . Check what is stored in *DATE*.
>
>   *Wed* Nov 29 14:30:52 EDT 2001
>
> $_ . . . . Prompt.

The output of the **date** *command is stored in the DATE variable, and* **echo** *command is used to display DATE.*

11.3.3   The Command Line Parameters

The shell scripts can read up to ten command line parameters (also called *arguments*) from the command line into the special variables (also called *positional variables*, or *parameters*). *Command line arguments* are the items you type after the command, usually separated by spaces. These arguments are passed to the program and change the behavior of the program or make it act in a specific order. The *special variables* are numbered in sequence from 0 to 9 (no number 10) and are named *$0, $1, $2*, and so on. Table 11–3 shows the list of the special (positional) variables.

Using Special shell Variables

Let's look at examples to understand how these special shell variables are used and arranged. Suppose you have a shell script named BOX, whose mode you

Table 11–3
The shell positional variables.

Variable	Meaning
$0	Contains the name of the script, as typed on the command line.
$1, $2,... $9	Contains the first through ninth command line parameters respectively.
$#	Contains the number of command line parameters.
$@	Contains all command line parameters. "$1" "$2" ...... "$9"
$?	Contains exit status of the last command.
$*	Contains all command line parameters. "$1 $2......$9"
$$	Contains the PID (process ID) number of the executing process.

1. The special variable *$0* always holds the name of the script passed on the command line.
2. Special variables *$1, $2, $3, $4, $5, $6, $7, $8,* and *$9* hold arguments 1 through 9 respectively. Command line arguments after the ninth parameter are ignored.
3. The special variable *$** holds all of the command line arguments passed to the program in a single string. It can store more than nine parameters.
4. The special variable *$@* holds all of the command line arguments, just like the *$**. However, it stores them with quotation around each command line argument.
5. The special variable *$#* holds the count of the command line arguments that are typed on the command line.
6. The special variable *$?* holds the exit status received from the **exit** command in your script file. If you have not coded an **exit**, then it holds the status of the last nonbackground command executed in your script file.
7. The special variable *$$* holds the process-ID of the current process.

Figure 11–9
A shell script file named BOX.

```
$ cat BOX
echo "The following is the output of  $0 script: "
echo "Total number of command line arguments: $# "
echo "The first parameter : $1"
echo "The second parameter: $2 "
echo "This is the list of all the parameters: $* "
$ _
```

have changed to an executable file, using the **chmod** command. Figure 11–9 shows your BOX script file.

The following command sequences show different invocations of the BOX program (with or without the command line arguments), and output of each run is investigated.

Invoke *BOX* with no command line arguments, just type the name of the file.

> $ **BOX [Return]** . . . . No command line arguments.
>
> The following is the output of BOX script:
> Total number of command line arguments: 0
> The first parameter is:
> The second parameter is:
> This is the list of all parameters:
>
> $_ . . . . Prompt.

The variable *$0* holds the name of the script that is invoked. In this case, *BOX* is stored in *$0*. There are no command line arguments, so the *$#* holds 0, and no value is stored in variables *$1, $2,* and *$**. The **echo** command shows the prompt strings.

Invoke *BOX* with two command line arguments.

> $ **BOX IS EMPTY [Return]** . . . . Command line with two arguments.
>
> The following is the output of BOX script:
> Total number of command line arguments: 2
> The first parameter is: IS
> The second parameter is: EMPTY
> This is the list of all parameters: IS EMPTY
>
> $_ . . . . Prompt.

The script name is stored in *$0*; in this case, BOX is stored in *$0*. The first argument is stored in special variable *$1*, the second argument in *$2*, and so on. In this case, **IS** is the first command line argument (stored in *$1*), and **EMPTY** is the second one (stored in *$2*). The *$** holds the list of all the command line arguments. In this case, it holds **IS EMPTY**.

If script is invoked with more than nine command line arguments, any argument after the ninth one is ignored. However, you can capture all of them when you use the special variable *$**.

Assigning Values

Another way to assign values to the positional variables is to use the **set** command. What you type as the **set** command arguments are assigned to the positional variables.

Figure 11–10
The svi script file.

```
$ cat svi
#
# svi: save and invoke vi (svi) program.
#
DIR=$HOME/keep          # assign keep pathname to DIR
cp $1 $DIR              # copy specified file to keep
vi $1                   # invoke vi with the specified filename
exit 0                  # end of the program, exit
$ _
```

 Examine the following examples.

$ **set One Two Three [Return]** . . . . . . Three arguments.

$ **echo $1 $2 $3 [Return]** . . . . Display the values assigned to *$1-$3*.

  One Two Three

$ **set 'date' [Return]** . . . . Another example.

$ **echo $1 $2 $3 [Return]** . . . . Display the positional variables.

Wed Nov 29

$_ . . . . Back to the prompt.

The **date** command is executed, and its output becomes the argument to the **set** command. If the output of the **date** command is:

  Wed Nov 29 14:00:52 EDT 2001

Then, the **set** command has six arguments (space is the delimiter), and the *$1* holds *Wed* (the first argument), *$2* holds *Nov* (the second argument), and so on.

Scenario   Now let's write a script file and make use of these positional variables. Suppose you want to write a script file that stores the specified file in a directory called keep in your home directory, and then invoke the vi editor to edit the specified file. The commands to do this job are:

$ **cp xyz $HOME/keep [Return]** . . . . . . Copy the specified file xyz to keep.

$ **vi xyz [Return]** . . . . Invoke the vi editor.

Figure 11–10 shows the script file called svi that also does the job. Commands in the svi file are the same commands you type at the prompt. The positional variables are used to make svi a versatile program. It saves and edits any specified file passed to it on the command line argument.

If svi works, the xyz file is saved in keep, the vi editor is invoked, and you are able to edit the xyz file. You can use the **ls** command to check if a copy of the xyz is saved in keep.

Scenario Suppose svi mode is changed to be an executable file, and you have a file called xyz in your current directory that you want to edit.

Let's run svi and look at the results.

```
$ svi xyz [Return] . . . . . . . . . . . . . . . . Run svi with a specified filename.

hello . . . . . . . . . . . . . . . . . . . . . . . . . You are in the vi editor, and content of

~ . . . . . . . . . . . . . . . . . . . . . . . . . . . . xyz is displayed.

~ . . . . . . . . . . . . . . . . . . . . . . . . . . . The rest of the vi screen.

"xyz"  1 Line, 5 characters . . . . . . . . . . . vi status line.

$ . . . . . . . . . . . . . . . . . . . . . . . . . . . . Prompt is displayed after you exit vi.
```

What if you do not have the xyz file in your current directory? How does the svi program work if you don't specify a filename? The svi works, but it may not exactly be the way you are expecting. In the first case, the **cp** command fails to find the xyz in your current directory, and the vi editor is invoked with the xyz as a new file. In the second case, the **cp** command fails again, and vi editor is invoked with no filename. In both cases, you do not see the **cp** command's error messages, as vi is invoked before you have a chance to see them.

The svi needs fixing. It must be able to recognize errors, show the appropriate error messages, and not invoke **cp** or vi if the filename is not specified on the command line or the specified file is not in your directory.

Before modifying the svi code to handle the above problems, you need to know other commands and constructs of the shell language.

Terminating Programs: The exit *Command*

The exit command is a built-in shell command that you can use to immediately terminate execution of your shell program. The format of this command is as follows:

```
exit n
```

where **n** is the exit status, what is also called the return code (RC). If no exit value is provided, the exit value of the last command executed by the shell is used. To be consistent with the other UNIX programs (commands) that usually return a status code upon completion, you can program your script to return an exit status to the parent process. As you know, typing **exit** at the $ prompt terminates your login shell and consequently logs you off.

11.4.4   Conditions and Tests

You can specify that certain commands be executed depending on the results of the other commands' executions. You often need this kind of control when writing shell scripts.

Every command executed in the UNIX system returns a number that you can test to control the flow of your program. A command either returns a 0 (zero), which means success (the true condition), or it returns any other number, which indicates failure (the false condition). These true and false conditions are used in the shell programming constructs and are tested to determine the flow of the program. Let's look at these constructs.

The if-then *construct*

The **if** statement provides the mechanism for testing to check whether the condition of something is true or false. Depending on the results of the **if** test, you may change the sequence of command executions in your program. The following shows the **if** statement (construct) syntax:

if [*condition*]

then

    commands

    ...

    last-command

fi

1. *The **if** statement ends with the reserved word **fi** (**if** typed backward).*

2. *The indentation is not necessary but certainly makes the code more readable.*

3. *If the condition is true, then all the commands between the **then** and **fi**, what is called the body of the **if**, are executed. If the condition is false, the body of the **if** is skipped, and the line after the **fi** is executed.*

The square brackets around the conditions are necessary and must be surrounded by white spaces, either spaces or tabs.

Modify the svi script file to include an **if** statement to match figure 11–11. The **if** statement is putting some control over the svi output.

Figure 11–11
Another version of the svi script file.

```
$ cat svi
#
# svi: save and invoke vi (svi) program.
# Adding the if statement
#
if [ $# = 1 ]              # check for number of the command line arguments.
then
      cp $1 $HOME/keep # copy specified file to keep.
fi                        # end of the if statement.
vi $1                     # invoke vi with the specified filename.
exit 0                    # end of the program, exit.
$ _
```

If the count of the command line arguments (*$#*) is one (a filename is specified), then the condition is true and the body of the **if** (the **cp** command) is executed, followed by the vi invocation with the specified filename, no different from the last svi run.

If the count of command line arguments (*$#*) is zero (no filename is specified on the command line), then the condition is false, the body of the if (the **cp** command) is skipped, and only the vi is invoked with no filename.

The if-then-else Construct

By adding the *else* clause to the *if* construct, you can execute certain commands when the test of the condition returns a false status. The syntax of this more complex **if** construct is as follows:

```
if [ condition ]
then
    true-commands
    ...
    last-true-command
else
    false-commands
    ...
    last-false-command
fi
```

1. *If the condition is true, then all the commands between the **then** and **else**, the body of the **if**, are executed.*

2. *If the condition is false, the body of the **if** is skipped and all the commands between the **else** and **fi**; the body of the **else** is executed.*

Modify the svi script file to include the **if** and **else** statements. Figure 11–12 shows this modification.

Figure 11–12
Another version of the svi script file.

```
$ cat svi
#
# svi: save and invoke vi (svi) program.
#  Add if and else statements.
#
if [ $# = 1 ]              # check for number of the command line arguments.
then
    cp $1 $HOME/keep       # copy specified file to keep.
    vi $1                  # invoke vi with the specified filename.
else
    echo "You must specify a filename. Try again."     #display error message
fi                         # end of the if statement
exit 0                     # end of the program, exit.
$ _
```

If the count of the command line arguments (*$#*) is one (a filename is specified), then the condition is true and the body of the **if** (the **cp** and **vi** commands) is executed. Next, the body of the **else** is skipped, and the **exit** command is executed, no different from the previous svi run.

If the count of command line arguments (*$#*) is not one, then the condition is false, the body of the **if** (the **cp** and **vi** commands) is skipped, and the body of the **else** (the **echo** command) is executed. The **echo** shows the error message, and then the **exit** command is executed.

Let's run this new version of the svi.

> **$ svi [Return]** . . . . No command line argument.
>
> You must specify a filename. Try again.
>
> **$**_ . . . . Prompt.

1. *You must specify a filename on the command line; otherwise, you get the error message and the vi is not invoked.*

2. *If you don't specify the filename, then the number of arguments (the value of the positional variable $#) is zero. Therefore, the if condition fails and the body of the if is skipped and the body of the else, the echo command, is executed.*

In this version, the svi script does not check for file existence. If the specified filename is not in the specified directory, the copy command is going to complain, but the vi editor is invoked with the specified filename as a name for a new file.

The if-then-elif Construct

When you have nested sets of **if** and **else** constructs in a script file, you can use the **elif** (short for **else if**) statement. The **elif** combines the **else** and **if** statements. The complete syntax is as follows:

```
if [ condition_1 ]
then
        commands_1
elif [ condition_2 ]
then
        commands_2
elif [ condition_3 ]
then
        commands_3
...
...
else
        commands_n
fi
```

Figure 11–13
The sample script using the **if then elif**.

```
$ cat greetings
#
# greetings
# A program sample using the if-then-elif construct
# This program displays greetings according to the time of the day
#
set 'data'              # set the positional variables to the data string
hour=$4                 # store the part of the date string that shows the hour
if [ "$hour"  -le  12 ]   # check for the morning hours
then
    echo "GOOD MORNING"
elif [ "$hour" -le 18 ]   # check for the afternoon hours
then
    echo "GOOD AFTERNOON"
else
    echo "GOOD EVENING"
fi
$ _
```

The script file in figure 11–13, called **greetings**, outputs greetings according to the time of the day. It shows the **Good Morning** message before noon, **Good Afternoon** if time is between 12:00 and 18:00, and so on. The **if-then elif** construct is used to determine the morning, afternoon, and evening hours.

1. *The* **set** *command is used with the* **date** *as its argument to set the positional variables.*

2. *The* **hour:minute:second** *is the fourth field in the date and time string (the output of the* **date** *command), and it is assigned to the positional variable $4.*

You can write the **greetings** program in many ways depending on the shell commands you know and want to use. For example, instead of using the **set** command and the positional variables, you could use the **date** command capabilities and obtain only the hour field from its output string.

Figure 11–14 shows another version of the **greeting** program. Only the part you have to modify is shown; the rest of the code remains the same.

The line **hour='date +%H'** requires more explanation. The **%H** limits the output of the **date** command to just the part of the date string that shows the hour.

Use the **date** command capabilities.

$ date [Return]. . . . . Display date and time.

Wed Nov 29 14:00:52 EDT 2001

Figure 11–14
The sample script using the **if then elif**.

```
$ cat greetings
#
# greetings Version 2
# A program sample using the if-then-elif construct.
# This program displays greetings according to the time of the day
#
hour='date +%H'          # store the part of the date string that shows the hour
.........                # the rest of the program
```

$ **date +%H [Return]** . . . . Show only hour of the day.

14

$_ . . . . Prompt.

The **date** command has numerous field descriptors that let you limit or format its output. You type a **+** at the beginning of the argument followed by the field descriptors such as **%H**, **%M**, etc. You can use the **man** command to obtain the full list of the field descriptors. Let's look at more examples.

Use the **date** command field descriptors.

$ **date '+DATE: %m-%d-%y' [Return]** . Show only the date separated by hyphens.

DATE: 05-10-99

$ **date '+TIME: %H:%M:%S' [Return]**. . Show only the time separated by colons.

TIME: 16:10:52

1. *The argument must start with the plus sign. It indicates that the output format is under your control. Each field descriptor is preceded by a percent sign (%).*

2. *If the argument contains white space characters, then it must be put inside quotation marks.*

3. *You can add the* greetings *program to your* .profile *file, so every time you log in, the appropriate greeting message is displayed.*

True or False: The test Command

The **test** command is a built-in shell command that evaluates the expression given to it as an argument and returns true if the expression is true (if it returns 0) or, otherwise, false (if it returns non-zero). The expression could be simple, such as testing two numbers for equality, or complex, like testing several commands that are related with logical operators. The **test** command is particularly helpful in writing script files. In fact, the brackets around the condition in the **if** statements are a special form of the **test** command. Figure 11–15 shows the sample script file using the **test** command to test the **if** condition.

Figure 11–15

The shell script file named test.

```
$ cat test
echo "Are you OK?"              # user prompt
echo "Input Y for yes or N for no:\c"     # user prompt
read answer                     # store user response in answer
if test "$answer" = Y           # test if user entered Y
then
    echo"Glad to hear that"     # user entered Y
else
    echo "Go home!"             # user did not enter Y
fi
$ _
```

1. *The test script prompts the user to enter (Y)es or (N)o, and then reads the user answer.*

2. *If the user response is letter Y, the* **test** *command returns zero, and the* **if** *condition is true, then the body of the* **if** *is executed. The message* **Glad to hear that** *is displayed, and the body of the* **else** *is skipped.*

3. *Any input from the user other than a single letter Y makes the* **if** *condition fail; therefore, the body of the* **if** *is skipped and the* **else** *is executed. The message* **Go home** *is displayed.*

Invoking* test *with Brackets   The shell offers you another way to invoke the **test** command. You can use square brackets ([and]) instead of the word **test**. Then the **if** statements can be written as follows:

```
if test "$variable" = value
```

or

```
if [ "$variable" = value ]
```

11.3.5   Testing Different Categories

Using the **test** command, you can test different categories of things, including the following: numeric values, string values, and files. Each of these categories is explained in the following sections.

Numeric Values

You can use the **test** command to test (compare) two integer numbers algebraically. You can also combine expressions comparing numbers with the logical operators. The format is as follows:

test expression_1 *logical Operator* expression_2

Table 11–4
The test command numeric test operators.

Operator	Example	Meaning
-eq	*number1* **-eq** *number2*	is *number1* equal to *number2*?
-ne	*number1* **-ne** *number2*	is *number1* not equal to *number2*?
-gt	*number1* **-gt** *number2*	is *number1* greater than *number2*?
-ge	*number1* **-ge** *number2*	is *number1* greater than or equal to *number2*?
-lt	*number1* **-lt** *number2*	is *number1* less than *number2*?
-le	*number1* **-le** *number2*	is *number1* less than or equal to *number2*?

The logical operators are as follows:

- Logical *and* operator (**-a**): The **test** command returns 0 (condition code true) if both expressions are true.
- Logical *or* operator (**-o**): The **test** command returns 0 (condition code true) if one or both of the expressions are true.
- Logical *not* operator (**!**): The **test** command returns 0 (condition code true) if the expression is false.

The operators available for comparing variables that hold numeric values are summarized in table 11–4.

Scenario Suppose you want to write a script that accepts three numbers as input (command line arguments) and displays the largest of the three. Using the **cat** command, figure 11–16 shows one way of writing this program which is named largest.

1. *When you run the largest program, it waits for you to enter three numbers. Then your input is passed through the **if-then-elif** construct to find the largest number.*

2. *If none of the two first numbers you enter is the largest, then the first **if** statement fails; next, the **elif** also fails, and your program gets to the **else** statement. There is no need of more checking. If the largest number is not the first or the second number, then it must be the third one.*

Figure 11–16
The shell program file named largest.

```
$ cat largest
#
#  largest:
# This program accepts three numbers and shows the largest of them
#
echo "Enter three numbers and I show you the largest of them>> \c"
read num1 num2  num3
if  test "$num1" -gt "$num2" -a   "$num1" -gt "$num3"
then
    echo "The largest number is: $num1"
elif test "$num2" -gt "$num1" -a "$num2" -gt "$num3"
then
    echo "The largest number is: $num2"
else
    echo "The largest number is: $num3"
fi
exit 0
$_
```

 Try a run sample of the largest program.

$ **chmod +x largest [Return]** . . . . Change it into an executable file.

$ **largest 100 10 400 [Return]** . . . . Run it with three arguments.

The largest number is: 400

$_ . . . . Prompt.

Think about how you can improve the largest program. For example, could you make fewer lines of code (do you have to repeat the **echo** command in the body of the **if**, **elif**, and **else**?), error checking (what if you enter two numbers?), etc.

String Values

You can also compare (test) strings with the **test** command. The **test** command provides a different set of operators for the string comparison. These operators are summarized in table 11–5. The following examples show the use of the **test** command with string arguments.

Table 11–5
The test command string test operator.

Operator	Example	Meaning
=	*string1* = *string2*	Does *string1* match *string2?*
!=	*string1* != *string2*	Does string1 not match *string2?*
-n	*-n string*	Does string contain characters (nonzero length)?
-z	*-z string*	Is *string* an empty string (zero length)?

First experiment with the null variable.

> $ **STRING= [Return]** . . . . Declare a null variable.
>
> $ **test -z $STRING [Return]** . . . . Test for zero length.
>
> test: Argument expected . . . . Error message.
>
> $_ . . . . Prompt.

1. *The shell substitutes the null string for $STRING, thus the error message.*

2. *Enclosing a string variable in quotation marks ensures a proper test, even if the variable contains spaces or tabs.*

Now try the variable *$STRING* in quotation marks.

> $ **test -z "$STRING" [Return]** . . . . Test for zero length.

This time the **test** *command returns zero (true), which means the variable $STRING contains a zero length string.*

In another example, the commands are directly typed at the **$** prompt. If the command is not complete, the shell shows the secondary prompt (**>**) and waits for you to complete the command.

> $ **DATE1='date' [Return]** . . . . Initialize *DATE1*.
>
> $ **DATE2='date' [Return]** . . . . Initialize *DATE2*.
>
> $ **if test "DATE1" = "DATE2" [Return]** Test for equality.
>
> > **then [Return]** . . . . The shell shows the second prompt sign as the **if** command is not completed yet.
>
> > **echo "STOP! The computer clock is dead!" [Return]**

> **else [Return]**. . . . . Begin the **else** body.

> **echo "Everything is fine." [Return]**

> **fi [Return]** . . . . End of **if**, as soon as you press
                                               [Return], the program is executed.

Everything is fine. . . . . Output of the program.

$_ . . . . Prompt.

*The result of the above test (**if** condition) is false. Therefore the body of the **else** is executed, and the message is displayed. Can the values stored in DATE1 and DATE2 ever be equal?*

Files

You can use the **test** command to test file characteristics, such as file size, file type, and file permissions. There are more than ten file attributes that can be checked; a few of them are introduced here. Table 11–6 summarizes the file test operators. The following example shows the use of the **test** command in connection with files. The commands are typed directly at the $ prompt.

Assume you have a file called myfile, with only read access to it. Let's type the following commands and see the output.

$ **FILE=myfile [Return]** . . . . Initialize *FILE* variable.

$ **if test -r "$FILE" [Return]**. . . . . Check if myfile is readable.

> **then [Return]** . . . . Secondary prompt.

> **echo "READABLE" [Return]** . . . . . . Show message.

> **elif test -w "$FILE" [Return]** . . . . Check if myfile is writeable.

Table 11–6
The test command file test operators.

Operator	Example	Meaning
-r	**-r** *filename*	Does *filename* exist and is it readable?
-w	**-w** *filename*	Does filename exist and is it writeable?
-s	**-s** *filename*	Does *filename* exist and have a non zero length?
-f	**-f** *filename*	Does *filename* exist, but is not a directory file?
-d	**-d** *filename*	Does *filename* exist and is it a directory file?

> **then** [Return]

> **echo "WRITEABLE"** [Return] . . . . . . Show message.

> **else** [Return]

> **echo "Read and Write access Denied"**

> **fi** [Return]. . . . . End of the **if**.

READABLE

$_ . . . . Back to the primary prompt.

1. *As soon as you type* **fi**, *the end of the* **if** *construct, the shell executes the commands, produces the output, and shows the* **$** *prompt.*

2. *The first* **if** *tests the read access to* myfile. *As you have the read access, the* **test** *command returns 0 (true), and the* **if** *condition is true. So only the body of the first* **if** *is executed, and the message* **READABLE** *is displayed.*

3. *The message* **WRITEABLE** *is echoed if you only have write access to* myfile.

4. *The message* **Read and Write access Denied** *is displayed if you do not have write and read access to* myfile, *and the* **if** *condition and* **elif** *condition fail.*

Figure 11–17 shows yet another version of the svi script file. In this version, the existence of the specified file is checked, and only if the file exists will the **cp** and **vi** commands be executed.

Run this new version of the svi program.

$ **svi xyz** [Return] . . . . Run it, specifying a nonexistent file xyz.

File not found. Try again.

$ **svi** [Return]. . . . . Run it again; no file is specified.

You must specify a filename. *Try again.*

$_ . . . . Prompt.

1. *To check the* **if** *conditions, the word test is used instead of the brackets.*

2. *The above program uses nested* **if** *constructs (***if** *inside another* **if***).*

3. *If the specified file is not found, then it shows the* **File not found. Try again.** *message.*

4. *If the specified file is found then, it copies the file to the* keep *directory and invokes the vi editor.*

5. *If no filename is specified on the command line, the first* **if** *condition fails, and it shows the* **You must specify a filename. Try again.** *message.*

Figure 11–17
Another version of the svi script file.

```
$ cat svi
#
# The save and invoke vi (svi) program.
#  This version checks for the file existence
#
if  test $1 = 1                     # check for # of arguments.
then
        if  test -f $1                  # check for file existence
          then
                cp $1 $HOME/keep  #  copy and invoke vi
                vi $1
        else                          # file not found
           echo " File not found. Try again"
        fi
else                                  # wrong number of arguments
      echo " You must specify a filename. Try again."
fi
$_
```

11.3.6   Parameter Substitution

The shell provides a parameter substitution facility that lets you test the value of a parameter and change its value according to a specified option. This is useful in shell programming, when you want to check whether a variable is set to something. For example, when you issue a **read** command in a script file, you want to make sure the user has entered something before taking any action.

The format consists of a dollar sign ($), a set of braces ({ and }), a variable, a colon (:), an option character, and a word, as follows:

${*parameter:**Option character** word*}

An option character determines what you intend to do with the *word*. The four option characters are specified by -, =, ?, and + signs. These four options perform differently depending on whether the variable is an empty variable.

A variable is an *empty variable* (a *null variable*) if its value is an empty string. For example, all of the following variables are set to a null value, and are empty variables.

EMPTY=. . . . . An empty variable called *EMPTY*.

EMPTY= "" . . . . An empty variable called *EMPTY*.

EMPTY= '' . . . . An empty variable called *EMPTY*.

To create an empty variable, put no blank characters between the quotation marks.

Table 11–7
The shell variable evaluation options.

Variable Option	Meaning
$*variable*	The value stored in *variable*.
${*variable*}	The value stored in *variable*.
${*variable*: -*string*}	The value of *variable* if it is set and not empty, otherwise the value of *string*.
${*variable*: +*string*}	The value of *string* if *variable* is set and not empty, otherwise nothing.
${*variable*: =*string*}	The value of *variable* if it is set and not empty, otherwise *variable* is set to the value of *string*.
${*variable*:?*string*}	The value of *variable* if it is set and not empty, otherwise print the value of *string* and exit.

Table 11–7 summarizes the shell variable substitution (evaluation) options. A brief explanation and example of each type follows.

${parameter} Placing the variable (parameter) inside the braces prevents the conflict caused by the character that follows the variable name. The following example clarifies this matter.

Suppose you want to change the name of a file called memo, specified in the variable called *FILE*, to memoX.

> $ **echo $FILE [Return]** . . . . Check what is stored in *FILE*.
>
>   memo
>
> $ **mv $FILE $FILEX [Return]** . . . . Change memo to memoX.
>
>   Usage: mv
>
> $_ . . . . Prompt.

This command did not work because the shell considers *$FILEX* the name of the variable, which does not exist.

> $ **mv $FILE ${FILE}X [Return]** . . . . Change memo to memoX.
>
> $_ . . . . Job done, prompt is back.

This command worked because the shell considers *$FILE* the variable name and substitutes its value, in this case memo.

${parameter:-word} The - (hyphen) option means if the listed variable (parameter) is set and not empty (non-null), use its value; Otherwise, if the variable is empty (null) or unset, substitute its value with *word*. For example:

$ **FILE= [Return]** . . . . Empty variable.

$ **echo ${FILE:-/usr/david/xfile} [Return]** . . . . . Display *FILE* value.

/usr/david/xfile

$ **echo "$FILE" [Return]** . . . . Check the *FILE* variable.

. . . . It remains empty.

$_ . . . . Prompt.

1. *The shell evaluates the variable FILE; it is empty, so the - option results in substitution of the /usr/david/xfile string, which is passed to the* **echo** *command to display it.*

2. *The FILE variable remains an empty variable.*

${parameter:+word} The + option is opposite of the - option. It means if the listed variable (parameter) is set and is not empty (non-null), then substitute its value with *word*. Otherwise, the variable's value remains the same (empty). For example:

$ **HELP= "wanted" [Return]** . . . . Set *HELP* variable.

$ **echo ${HELP: +" Help is under way"} [Return]**

Help is under way

$ **echo $HELP [Return]** . . . . Check the *HELP* variable.

wanted . . . . It remained the same.

$_ . . . . Prompt.

1. *The shell evaluates the HELP variable; it is set to* wanted. *So the* **+** *option results in substitution of the* **Help is under way** *string, which is passed to the* **echo** *command to display it.*

2. *The value stored in the HELP variable remains the same.*

${parameter:=word} The = option means if the listed variable (parameter) is not set or it is empty (null), then substitute its value with *word*. Otherwise, if the variable is not empty, then its value remains the same. For example:

$ **MESG= [Return]** . . . . Empty variable.

$ **echo ${MESG:= "Hello There!"} [Return]** . . . Display *MESG* value.

Hello There!

$ **echo $MESG [Return]** . . . . Check the *MESG* variable.

Hello There! . . . . It is set the specified sting.

$_ . . . . Prompt.

The *word* can be a string with embedded white spaces. It works as long as you place it in quotation marks.

1. *The shell evaluates the variable MESG. It is empty. So the = option results in setting MESG to the string* **Hello There!**. *Substitution is done, and the* **echo** *command shows the value stored in MESG.*

2. *The value of the MESG is changed and it is not an empty variable any more.*

${parameter:?word}   The **?** option means if the listed variable (parameter) is set and is not empty, then substitute its value. Otherwise, if the variable is empty, print the *word* and exit the current script. If *word* is omitted, then show the preset message **parameter null or not set**. For example:

$ **MESG=[Return]** . . . . *MESG* is an empty variable.

$ **echo ${MESG: ? "ERROR!"} [Return]** . . . . . Does substitution according to the option.

ERROR!

$_ . . . . Prompt.

The shell evaluates the MESG variable; it is an empty variable. So the **?** *option results in substitution of the ERROR string, which is passed to the* **echo** *command to display it.*

You can use this option to show an error message and terminate your shell script if the user just presses [Return] in response to a **read** command. Figure 11–18 shows an example script file called name.

Run the name script.

$ **name [Return]**. . . . . Run name script file.

Figure 11–18
The shell script file called name.

```
$ cat name
#


# Program to test parameter substitution
#
echo "Enter your name: \c"      # prompt the user
read name
echo ${name:?"You must enter your name"}
echo "Thank you. That's all."
exit 0
$ _
```

Enter your name:_ . . . . User prompt.

[Return] . . . . Let's say you just press [Return].

You must enter your name . . . . Feedback to user.

$_ . . . . Script is terminated, and prompt is back.

1. *If you press [Return] in response to the* **read** *command,* name *remains a null variable. The* **?** *option tests the variable; it is a null variable. The specified message is displayed, and the shell program is terminated.*

2. *However, if you enter your name or another word, then the script continues, and the message* **Thank you. That's all** *is displayed.*

11.3.7   The *loop* Constructs

You use the loop constructs in programs when you want to repeat a set of statements or commands. The loop constructs save a lot of time for you, the programmer. Can you imagine writing 100 lines of code to display a simple message 100 times? The shell provides you with three looping constructs: **for** loop, **while** loop, and **until** loop. These loops enable you to repeatedly execute commands for a certain number of times or until certain conditions are met.

The For Loop: The for-in-done Construct

The **for** loop is used to execute a set of commands for a specified number of times. Its basic format is as follows:

```
for variable
in list-of-values
do
    commands
    ...
    last-command
done
```

The shell scans the *list-of-values*, stores the first *word* (value) in the *loop variable*, and commands between the **do** and **done** (what is called the *body* of the loop) are executed. Next, the second word is assigned to the loop variable, and again the body of the loop is executed. The commands in the body of the loop are executed for as many values as the list-of-values contains.

The following command sequences show how the **for** loop works.

$ for count in 1 2 3 [Return] . . . . Set the loop header.

> do [Return] . . . . Waiting for you to complete the command.

> echo "In the loop for $count times" [Return]
. . . . Display message.

> **done [Return]** . . . . End of the **for** loop.

In the loop for 1 times
In the loop for 2 times
In the loop for 3 times

$_ . . . . Prompt.

1. *In this example,* count *is the loop variable, the list-of-values consists of numbers (1, 2, and 3), and the body of the loop is a single* **echo** *command.*

2. *Because three values are listed in the list-of-values, the body of the loop is executed a total of three times.*

3. *The values in the list-of-values are assigned one by one to the* count *variable. Each time through the loop, a new value is assigned until the list-of values is exhausted.*

Scenario　Suppose you want to save the name of the files you print and the time you print them in a file. You write a script file called **slp** (Super LP) that prints your files and saves the information about them in a file called **pfile**. Figure 11–19 shows one way to write a **slp** script.

1. *You can enter more than one filename. Each filename from the list of files in variable filename is assigned to the loop variable FILE. The* **echo** *command takes care of saving the information in* **pfile**, *and the* **lp** *command prints them.*

2. *The* **echo** *command creates* **pfile** *the first time you use this program. On the consequent runs, it appends (the* **>>** *redirection operator) the filenames of the printed files.*

Figure 11–19
The slp script file.

```
$ cat slp
#
# The super line printer program (slp).
#
echo "Enter the name of the file(s)> \c"           # prompt the user
read filename                                      # read input
for FILE in $filename
    echo "\nFilename: $FILE\n Printed: 'date' " >> pfile   # save in pfile
    lp $FILE                                       # print the file
done
echo "\n\07Job done"                               # inform user
exit 0
$_
```

Run the slp program.

$ **slp [Return]**. . . . . Run it.

Enter the name of the file(s)> . . . . Waiting for input.

myfile [Return]. . . . . You enter *myfile*.

lp: request id is lp 1-9223 (f file). . . . . . The lp message.

Job done. . . . . Beep and final message.

$_ . . . . Prompt.

$ **cat pfile [Return]**. . . . . Check *pfile*.

Filename: myfile
Printed: Mon Dec 6   12:01:35 EST   2001

$_ . . . . The shell prompt.

The While Loop: The while-do-done Construct

The second type of looping construct explained here is the **while** loop. Unlike the **for** loop, whose number of iterations depends on the number of values in the list-of-values, the **while** loop continues as long as the loop condition is true. The format is as follows:

```
while [ condition ]
do
    commands
    ...
    last command
done
```

The commands in the body of the loop (between **do** and **done**) are repeatedly executed as long as the loop condition is true (zero). The loop condition must eventually return to false (non-zero); otherwise, your loop is an infinite loop and goes on forever. That is one of those times that you must know the **kill** key on your system, so you can terminate the process.

The following command sequence shows how the **while** loop works.

$ **carry_on=Y [Return]**. . . . . Initials the *carry_on* variable.

$ **while [$carry_on = Y] [Return]**. . . . . Set up the **while** loop.

> **do [Return]**

> **echo "I do the job as long as you type Y:_\b" [Return]**

> **read carry_on [Return]**

> **done [Return]** . . . . Read input.

I do the job as long as you type Y:_. . . . . Waits for input.

Y [Return] . . . . Press [Y] and [Return].

I do the job as long as you type Y:_ . . . . . Waits for input again.

N [Return] . . . . Press [N] and [Return].

$_ . . . . The shell prompt.

In the above example, as long as you press [Y], the loop condition is true, and the body of the loop, the **echo** *and* **read** *commands, is repeated. You stop this program by pressing any character but [Y].*

The Until Loop: The until-do-one Construct

The third type of the looping construct explained here is the **until** loop. The **until** loop is similar to the **while** loop, except that it continues executing the body of the loop as long as the condition of the loop is false (non-zero). The **until** loop is useful in writing scripts whose execution depends on other events occurring. The format is as follows:

```
until [ condition ]
do
   commands
   ...
   last-command
done
```

The body of the loop might never get executed if the loop condition is true (zero) the first time it is executed.

Scenario   You want to check whether a specified user is on the system or, if not, to be informed as soon as the user logs in. Figure 11–20 shows one way to write script file uon (User ON).

   In uon script, the until loop stops as soon as the loop condition is true. If **grep** (chapter 8) does not find the specified user ID in the list of the users, passed to it by the **who** command, then the loop condition remains false

Figure 11–20
The uon script file.

```
$ cat uon
#
# uon: Let me know if xxx is on the system.
#
Until  who | grep "$1" > /dev/null        # redirect the output of grep
do
   sleep  30                              # wait half a minute
done
echo "\07\07$1 is on the system."         # inform user
exit 0
$_
```

(nonzero) and the **until** loop continues executing the body of the loop, the **sleep** command. As soon as **grep** finds the specified user ID in the users list, the loop condition becomes true (zero) and the loop stops. Next, the command after the loop is executed, which informs you, with two beeps, that the specified user is logged in.

1. *The output of the **grep** command is redirected to the null device (never-never land). That means you neither want to see the output nor save it.*

2. *The **sleep** command stops your program for half a minute. The net effect is that the **grep** checks the list of users every half minute.*

There is only one problem left. If you run this program and the specified user is not logged in, then you are at the mercy of the user to log in. You cannot use your terminal while the above program is running. A better idea is to run **uon** in the background.

Running **uon** in the background.

$ uon emma &[Return]	Run it in the background. Check if *emma* is logged in.
4483	Process ID.
$_	Prompt is back.

You can do other work. You will be informed when *emma* logs in.

emma is on the system	Beep beep. You are informed.

You can go on with whatever you were doing.

11.3.8   Debugging shell Programs: The *sh* Command

It is easy to make mistakes when you write long and complex script files. Because you do not compile script files, you do not have the luxury of compiler error checking. Therefore you have to run the program and try to decipher the error messages displayed on the screen. But do not despair!

You can use the **sh** command with one of its options to make the debugging of your script files easier. For example, the **-x** option causes the shell to echo each command it executes. This trace of your script execution can help you to find the whereabouts of the bugs in your program.

sh Options

Table 11–8 summarizes the **sh** command options, and the following examples show how to use them.

Table 11–8
The **sh** command options.

Option	Operation
-n	Reads commands but does not execute them.
-v	Shows the shell input lines as they are read.
-x	Shows the commands and their arguments as they are executed.

If you want to debug the BOX script file, you type the following:

> $ **sh -x BOX [Return]**

You can also place the **sh** options as commands in your script file. Use the **set** command and type the following line at the beginning of your file, or place it wherever you want the debugging to start.

> **set -x**

***-x* Option**   The **-x** option shows the commands in your script file as they look after the parameter and command substitutions have taken place. Using the **sh** command with the **-x** option, let's execute the BOX script file in different ways and explore the possibilities.

Run BOX with the **-x** option, but do not specify command line arguments.

> $ **sh -x BOX [Return]** . . . . Use **-x** option.
>
> + echo The following is the output of the BOX script.
>
> The following is the output of the BOX script
>
> + echo Total number of command line arguments: 0
>
> Total number of command line arguments: 0
>
> + echo The first parameter is:
>
> The first parameter is:
>
> + echo The second parameter is:
>
> The second parameter is:
>
> + echo This is the list of all parameters:
>
> This is the list of all parameters:
>
> $_ . . . . Prompt.

1. *All lines beginning with plus signs (+) are commands that are executed by the shell, and the lines below them show the output of the commands.*

2. *The **echo** commands are displayed after the variable substitutions are done.*

Run BOX using **sh** with the **-x** option, and specify some command line parameters.

> **$ sh -x BOX of candy [Return]** . . . . . . Use **-x** option.
>
> + echo The following is the output of the BOX script.
>
> The following is the output of the BOX script
>
> + echo Total number of command line arguments: 2
>
> Total number of command line arguments:2
>
> + echo The first parameter is: of
>
> The first parameter is: of
>
> echo The second parameter is: candy
>
> The second parameter is: candy
>
> + echo This is the list of all parameters: of candy
>
> This is the list of all parameters: of candy
>
> $_ . . . . Prompt.

-v Option   The **-v** option is similar to the **-x** option. However, it displays the commands before the substitution of the variables and commands are done.

Run the BOX program with the **-v** option, and specify some command line arguments.

> **$ sh -v BOX is full of gold nuggets [Return]**. . Use **-v** option.
>
> echo "The following is the output of the $0 script."
>
> The following is the output of the BOX script
>
> echo "Total number of command line arguments: $#"
>
> Total number of command line arguments: 5
>
> echo "The first parameter is: $1"
>
> The first parameter is: is
>
> echo "The second parameter is: $2"
>
> The second parameter is: full
>
> echo "This is the list of all parameters: $*"
>
> This is the list of all parameters: is full of nuggets
>
> $_ . . . . Prompt

1. *One line shows the command that is executed by the shell, and the line below it shows the output of the command.*

2. *The* **echo** *commands are displayed before the variable substitutions are done. (This is different from the* **-x** *option, which displays the commands after the substitutions are done.)*

You can use the **-x** and **-v** options together on a command line. Using both options enables you to look at the commands in your file before and after execution, plus the output they produce. The following command line shows the **sh** is invoked with both options.

$ sh -xv BOX [Return]

-n **Option**   The **-n** option is used to detect the syntax errors in your script file. Use this option when you want to make sure that you do not have syntax errors in a program before you run it.

For example, suppose you have a script file called check_syntax. Figure 11–21 shows the source code for this program, which has an intentional syntax error.

Run the check-syntax program, using the **-n** option and observe its output.

$ sh -n check_syntax [Return] . . . . Run it.

check_syntax : syntax error at line 8 'else' unexpected

$_ . . . . Prompt.

1. *Using the* **-n** *option, none of the commands in your program are executed. Only the syntax errors are located and recognized.*

Figure 11–21
Source code for the check_syntax program.

```
$ cat check_syntax
#
# check_syntax: Sample program to show the output of the sh n option.
#
echo "$0: Checking the program syntax"
if [ $# -gt 0 ]
 echo "Number of the command line arguments: $# "
else
 echo " No command line arguments
fi

echo " GOOD BYE"
$ _
```

2. *If you use the* **-x** *or* **-v** *option, the program is executed until it reaches the part with the wrong syntax. Then, the error message is displayed and the program is terminated.*

What is wrong at line 8? You have to add the word *then* after the **if** statement to correct the **if-then-else** construct in your program.

What is the output of check_syntax after you fixed the syntax error? The *$0* contains the name of the program, in this case check_syntax. The *$#* contains the number of the command line arguments. If there are command line arguments, the body of the **if** is executed; otherwise, the body of the **else** is executed.

Run check_syntax again.

> $ **check_syntax one two three [Return]** . . . . . Use 3 command line arguments.
>
> check_syntax: checking the program syntax
>
> Number of the command line arguments: 3
>
> $ . . . . Prompt.
>
> $ check_syntax [Return] . . . . No command line arguments
>
> check_syntax: checking the program syntax
>
> No command line arguments
>
> $_ . . . . Prompt.

The **sh** debugging options are mostly useful when you write long and complex shell programs. They will come in handy when you explore the script files presented in chapter 12.

Command Summary

The following commands and options were discussed in this chapter.

---

chmod
This command changes the access permission of a specified file according to the option letters indicating different categories of users. The user categories are: u (for user/owner), g (for group), o (for others), and a (for all). The access categories are: r (for read), w (for write), and x (for executable).

---

sh
This command invokes a new copy of the shell. You can run your script files using this command. Only two of the numerous options are mentioned.

Option	Operation
-n	Reads commands, but does not execute them.
-v	Prints the input to the shell as the shell reads it in.
-x	Prints commands lines and their arguments as they are executed. This option is mostly used for debugging.

. (dot)
This command lets you run a process in the current shell environment, and the shell doesn't create a child process to run the command.

---

exit
This command terminates the current shell program whenever it is executed. It can also return a status code (RC) to indicate the success or failure of a program. It also terminates your login shell if typed at the $ prompt, and logs you off.

---

read
This command reads input from the input device and stores the input string in one or more variables specified as the command arguments.

---

test
This command tests the condition of expression given to it as an argument, and returns true or false depending on the status of the expression. It gives you the capability of testing different types of expressions.

Review Exercises

1. How do you execute a shell script file?

2. What is the command to make a file an executable file?

3. When do you use the **.** (dot) command?

4. What is the command to read input from the keyboard?

5. Explain the command line parameters.

6. What are the shell positional variables?

7. How are the positional variables related to the command line parameters?

8. How do you debug your shell script?

9. Name the command that terminates a shell script.

10. What are the constructs in the shell language?

11. What is the use of the loop construct?

12. What is the difference between the **while** and **until** loops?

Terminal Session

In this terminal session, you are going to write a few script files and improve on the script file samples presented in this chapter.

1. Create a shell script named LL that lists your directory in a long format.

    a. Execute LL using the **sh** command.
    b. Change the LL to an executable file.
    c. Execute LL again.

2. Create a script file that performs the following:

    a. Clears screen.
    b. Skips two lines.
    c. Shows the current date and time.
    d. Shows number of the users on the system.
    e. Beeps a few times and shows the message: **Now at your service**

3. Modify the largest script file from this chapter to recognize number of inputs and display appropriate messages.

4. Write a script file similar to largest that calculates the smallest of the three integer numbers that are read from the keyboard. Make it able to recognize some input errors.

5. Create a script file for each of the script examples in this chapter that were typed at the **$** prompt. Make the appropriate modifications if necessary and run them. Use **sh** with the **-x** and other options to debug, and investigate the way shell scripts are executed.

6. Write a script file that sums the numbers passed to it as arguments on the command line and displays the result. Use the **for** loop construct in your program. For example, if you name this program SUM, and you type:

$ SUM 10 20 30 [Return]

The program displays the following:

10 + 20 + 30 = 60

7. Rewrite the SUM program, this time use the **while** loop.

8. Rewrite the SUM program, this time use the **until** loop.

Review Exercises

1. What are the major functions of the shell?

2. What is the name of your system shell program, and where is it stored?

3. What are the metacharacters? How does shell interpret them?

4. What are the quoting characters?

5. What are the shell variables?

6. What is the command to display the environment/shell variables?

7. What is the command to remove a variable?

8. Name some of the environment/standard variables.

9. What are the variables, and what role do they play?

10. How do you run a program in the background?

11. How do you terminate a background process?

12. What is the process ID number, and how do you know the process ID of a particular process?

13. What is the pipe operator, and what does it do?

14. How do you prevent termination of your background process after you log off?

15. What is the command for searching for specified pattern in a file?

16. How do you delay the execution of a process?

17. What is the operator that groups the commands together?

18. What is the startup file?

19. What is .profile file, and what is profile file?

20. What are the parent and child in reference to UNIX process management?

21. What is a process?

CHAPTER **12**

Shell Scripts:
Writing Applications

This chapter builds on the commands and concepts of the previous chapter and discusses additional shell programming commands and techniques. It also presents a simple application program and shows the process of developing programs using the shell language. It introduces new shell commands when they are used in the shell scripts.

In This Chapter

12.1   WRITING APPLICATIONS

Chapter 11 introduced shell programming basics and mentioned using the shell command language to write application programs. This chapter explains the process of developing application programs. The examples are complete programs, and when necessary new commands or constructs are introduced and explored.

Scenario   You want to protect the access to your terminal (say when you are away from it for few minutes), short of logging off and then logging in again. You can write a script file that when invoked shows a message on the screen and doesn't go away until you enter the correct password. But do you really want to lock your terminal? Yes. The goal here is to learn about commands and programming techniques, and apply them to script files, whether you want to lock your terminal or not.

Figure 12–1
The lock1 script file.

```
 1  #
 2  # name: lock1 (lock version 1)
 3  # definition: This program locks the keyboard, and you must type the
 4  # specified password to unlock it.
 5  # logic:
 6  #      1- Ask the user to enter a password
 7  #      2- Lock the keyboard until the correct password is entered.
 8  #
 9  echo "\032"                              # clear screen
10  echo "\n\nEnter your PASSWORD> "         # ask password
11  read pword_1                             # read password
12  echo "\032"                              # clear screen again
13  echo "\n\n THIS SYSTEM IS LOCKED ...."
14  pword_2=                                 # declare an empty variable
15  until [ "$pword_1" = "$Pword_2" ]        # start of the loop
16  do
17      read pword_2                         # body of the loop
18  done                                     # end of the until loop
19  exit 0                                   # end of the program, exit

file "lock1" 20 lines 166 characters
```

See page xxii for an explanation of icons used to highlight information in this chapter.

12.1.1   The lock1 Program

Figure 12–1 shows a script named lock1 (lock version 1), which does the job by locking your keyboard. The lock1 program is shown using the vi editor, and line numbers are not part of the code. They are produced by the **set nu** option of the vi editor.

Let's look at the lock1 program line by line to see how it works.

Lines 1-8: These lines are all started with the # sign and are documentation lines.

Lines 9 and 12: These lines are commands to clear the screen. Instead of using the **echo** command and the clear screen code, you may use the **tput** command (which is explained later in this chapter).

Line 10: This line prompts you to enter a password. Any sequence of the characters, numbers, and embedded white characters is accepted. The password you enter has nothing to do with your login password.

Line 11: This line reads from the keyboard. When you press [Return], your intended password is stored in the variable called *pword_1*.

Line 13: This line shows the appropriate message on the screen. You can change it to any other message you like.

Line 14: This line declares a variable called *pword_2* which is used to store the inputs from the keyboard.

Lines 15–18: These lines construct the **until** loop. The condition compares the content of the *pword_1* variable (your password) with the content of the *pword_2* variable (what is read from the keyboard). The first time through the loop the contents of the two variables are not equal (*pword_1* contains your password; *pword_2* is empty). Therefore, the body of the **until** loop is executed. Remember, the body of the **until** loop is executed when the loop condition is false. The body of the loop is a **read** command, and it waits to read from keyboard. It doesn't show any prompt; just the cursor is displayed. (After all, you do not want to alert the intruder that your system is waiting for a password.) If you enter anything but the correct password, the **until** loop continues and hangs a read on your keyboard. This **read** command repetition effectively locks your keyboard. It reads, compares, comparison fails, and reads again. When you enter the correct password, the loop condition returns true status (now *pword_1* is equal *pword_2*). The loop stops, and your keyboard is freed.

Line 19: This line exits the lock1 script with zero status, indicating a normal termination of the program.

Problems With the lock1 Program

The lock1 program runs fine, except for some minor problems. There is also some potential for improvement. Let's explore it.

lock1 is not a foolproof program:

- While the keyboard is locked, if you press [Del] (the interrupt key), the lock1 script is terminated, the $ prompt is displayed, and the system is ready to accept commands. So much for protecting your system from intruders! To be effective, the lock1 program must be able to ignore normal interrupt signals.

- The password is displayed. Usually, passwords are not displayed on the screen. On line 10, when the password is requested, whatever you type as your password is echoed on the screen for everyone to see. Displaying of the user response to the password prompt must be prevented.
- The message is hard coded. It always shows **This system is locked**. It is nice to be able to specify the message to be displayed on the command line.

To solve these problems, a few more commands must be explored.

12.2   UNIX INTERNALS: THE SIGNALS

How do you terminate a process? You terminate a process by generating an interrupt signal. What is a signal? A *signal* is a report to your process about a specific condition. For example, [Del], [Break], and [Ctrl-c] are used to send an interrupt signal to a process, so it terminates.

Remember, your process thinks it is working with files and does not know about your terminal. Then how does an interrupt signal that you enter from the keyboard terminate your process? Your interrupt signals go to the UNIX kernel and not your process. It is the kernel that knows about the devices, and it is notified when you press any of the interrupt keys. Then UNIX sends a signal to your process telling it that an interrupt occurred. In response to this signal, your process terminates or takes some other action.

There are several different events that make the kernel send a signal to your process. These signals are numbered to specify the specific event they present. Table 12–1 summarizes some of these signals that are usually used in the script files. The signal numbers may be different in your system. Ask your system administrator, or look it up in your system reference manuals.

Table 12–1
Some of the shell signals.

Signal Number	Name	Meaning
1	**hang up**	Terminal connection is lost.
2	**interrupt**	One of the interrupt keys is pressed.
3	**quit**	One of the quit keys is pressed.
9	**kill**	The kill -9 command is issued.
15	**terminator**	The kill command is issued.

The hang-up *Signal*   Signal 1 is used to tell the process that the system has lost the connection to its terminal. This signal is generated when the cord that runs from your terminal to the computer is disconnected, or when the phone line (your modem connection) is lost. Also, on some systems the hang-up signal is generated when you turn off your terminal.

The interrupt *Signal*   Signal 2 is generated when one of the interrupt keys is pressed. This could be [Ctrl-c], [Del], or [Break].

The interrupt keys in your system might be different. Only one of the keys works on each specific system.

The quit *Signal*   Signal 3 is generated from your keyboard when you press [Ctrl-\]. This causes the process to *core dump* before it terminates.

The kill *Signals*   Signals 9 and 15 are generated by the **kill** (see chapter 8) command. Signal 15 is the default signal, and 9 is generated when the **kill** command option **-9** is used. Both terminate the receiving process.

12.2.1   Trapping the Signals: The *trap* Command

The default action taken by your process when it receives any of the signals is immediate termination. You can use the **trap** command to change the process default action to whatever you specify. For example, you can instruct your process to ignore interrupt signals or instead of termination to execute a specified command. Let's explore the possibilities. The format of the **trap** command is as follows:

     trap '*optional commands*' signal numbers

The *commands* part is optional. When it is present, the commands are executed whenever your process receives one of the signals you have specified to be trapped.

The commands that are specified to the **trap** command must be enclosed in single or double quotation marks.

1. *You can specify more than one signal number to be trapped.*

2. *The signal numbers are the numbers associated with the signals that you want the **trap** command to catch.*

The following command sequences show how the **trap** command works.

     trap " echo I refuse to die! " 15

This command executes the **echo** command and displays the **I refuse to die** message whenever it receives a simple **kill** command. However, your script continues.

     trap " echo Killed by a signal! ; exit " 15

If your process receives a **kill** command (signal 15), the **echo** command is executed and shows the **Killed by a signal** message. Next, the **exit** command is executed, which causes your script to terminate.

    trap ' ' 15

No command is specified. Now, if your process receives the **kill** signal (signal 15), it ignores it, and the script continues.

The quotation marks must be present even if no command is specified. Without the quotation marks the **trap** command resets the specified signals.

12.2.2   Resetting the Traps

Issuing a **trap** command in your script changes the default actions of the signals received by your process. Using the **trap** command, without the optional commands part, changes the specified signals to their default actions. This command is useful when in one part of your script you want to trap a certain signals and in another part you want the signals not to be trapped.

    For example, if you type the following command in your script file:

    $ trap " " 2 3 15

the **interrupt**, **quit**, and **kill** commands are ignored, and if any of their keys is pressed, your script keeps on running. If you type the following command:

    $ trap 2 3 15

the specified signals are reset. That is to say, the **interrupt**, **quit**, and **kill** keys are restored, and if any of them is pressed, your running script is terminated.

12.2.3   Setting Terminal Options: The *stty* Command

You use the **stty** command to set and display terminal characteristics. You can control various characteristics of your terminal, such as the baud rate (rate of transmission between the terminal and the computer), and the functions of certain keys (**kill**, **interrupt**, etc.). The **stty** command without arguments shows a selected group of settings. Use the **-a** option to list all your terminal settings.

    Figure 12–2 shows an example of the terminal settings. Your system might have a different settings.

Figure 12–2
An example of the terminal settings.

```
$ stty
speed  9600  baud; -parity
erase = '^h' ; kill = '^u'
echo
$_
```

Table 12–2
A short list of terminal options.

Option	Operation
echo [-echo]	Echoes [does not echo] the typed characters, the default is echo.
raw [-raw]	Disables [enables] the special meaning of the metacharacters, the default is -raw.
intr	Generates an interrupt signal, usually the [Del] key is used.
erase	(backspace) Erases the preceding character, usually the [#] key is used.
kill	Deletes the entire line, usually [@] or [Ctrl-u] is used.
eof	Generates the (end -of-file) signal from terminal, usually [Ctrl-d] is used .
ek	Resets the erase and kill keys to [#] and [@] respectively.
sane	Sets the terminal characteristic to sensible default values.

Terminals have wide variety of capabilities, and **stty** supports the modification of over a hundred different settings. Some of these settings change the communication mode of your terminal, some change the value assigned to special keys, and yet another group combines settings.

Table 12–2 lists a very small subset of the available options, the most common ones. Use the **man** command to obtain a more detail list of options and the explanation of their functions.

1. *The default settings are usually the best for most of the options.*

2. *Some of the options are enabled by typing the option name and disabled by preceding them with a hyphen.*

Let's look at some examples.

$ **stty -echo [Return]** . . . . Turns echoing off.

$ **stty echo [Return]** . . . . Turns echoing back on.

The **stty echo** command is not displayed on your terminal due to the effect of the previous **stty -echo** command.

Set the **kill** key to [Ctrl-u].

$ **stty kill \^u [Return]** . . . . Now [Ctrl-u] is the the **kill** key.

$_ . . . . Prompt.

*To set a special key, either you press three characters: [\], [^], and the specified letter, or you type the combination keys directly. In the above example, you type \^***u** *or press [Ctrl-u].*

$ **stty sane [Return]**. . . . . Resets options to reasonable values.

$ . . . . Prompt.

When you have changed the options too many times and lost the track of your changes, the **sane** option comes to your rescue.

Change the **kill** and **erase** keys to their default values.

$ **stty ek [Return]**. . . . . Sets the **kill** and **erase** keys.

$_ . . . . Prompt.

This command sets the **kill** key to [@] and the erase key to [#].

12.3   MORE ABOUT TERMINALS

The UNIX operating system supports numerous types of terminals. Each terminal has its own capabilities and characteristics. These capabilities are documented in the terminal user/technical manual along with a set of escape characters to be used that enables you to manipulate the terminal capabilities. Each terminal type has its own set of escape characters. In chapter 11, escape character **\032** was used to clear the screen. The **\032** is the clear screen code for vt100-type terminals. You type the following line to clear the screen:

$ **echo "\032" [Return]** . . . . Clears screen on the vt100-type terminals.

Terminal capabilities are not limited to the clear screen function. There are dozen of other characteristics, such as bold text, blinking, underlining, and so on. You use them to make your display more meaningful, better organized, or simply look nicer.

12.3.1   The Terminals Database: The *terminfo* File

Each terminal supported in your system has an entry in the terminal database (file) called *terminfo* (terminal information). The terminfo database is a single text file that contains descriptions of many types of terminals. For each terminal in the database, there is a list of capabilities associated with that terminal.

12.3.2   Setting the Terminal Capabilities: The *tput* Command

The **tput** utility, which is standard on any system with the terminfo database, lets you print out the values of any single capability. This makes it possible to use terminals' capabilities in shell programming. For example, to clear screen you type:

$ tput clear [Return]

This command works regardless of your terminal type, as long as your system includes the terminfo database and your terminal type is in the database.

Table 12–3 shows some of the terminal capabilities that can be activated using the **tput** command. The **tput** program used with the terminfo database lets you choose particular terminal capabilities and print out their values or store them in a shell variable. By default, **tput** assumes you are using the terminal type specified in the *TERM* shell variable. You can override this by using the **-T** option. For example, you type the following command to specify the terminal type:

$ tput -T wy50 [Return]

Table 12–3
A short list of the terminal capabilities.

Option	Operation
bell	Echoes the terminal's bell character.
blink	Makes blinking display.
bold	Makes bold display.
clear	Clears the screen.
cup *r c*	Moves cursor to the row *r* and column *c*.
dim	Dims the display.
ed	Clears from the cursor position to the end of the screen.
el	Clears from the cursor position to the end of the line.
smso	Starts stand out mode.
rmso	Ends stand out mode.
smul	Starts underline mode.
rmul	Ends underline mode.
rev	Shows reverse video, black on white display.

1. *Usually when you start a mode, it remains in effect until you remove it.*

2. *You can store the character sequences in variables and then use the variables.*

The following command sequences show the use of the **tput** command to change the terminal characteristics.

Using the **tput** command, first clear the screen and then show the message **The terminfo database** in row 10 column 20.

     $ **tput clear [Return]** . . . . Clears screen.

     $ **tput cup 10 20 [Return]** . . . . Positions the cursor.

     $ **echo "The terminfo database" [Return]** . . . . Displays the message.

     The terminfo database

You specify the cursor position before the **echo** *command that displays the message at the specified location on the screen.*

     The above commands can be sequenced together on one line. Commands are separated by colons, as follows:

        $ **tput clear : tput cup 10 20 : echo "The terminfo database" [Return]**

Store a character sequence in a variable and then use it to manipulate the screen displays.

     $ **bell='tput bel' [Return]** . . . . Stores the character sequence for bell in the *bell* variable.

The shell executes the command between the back quotation marks and assigns the command's output, in this case the character sequence for the terminal bell (beep), to the *bell* variable.

     $ **s_uline='tput smul' [Return]** . . . . Stores code for start underline
                                                display.

     $ **e_uline='tput rmul' [Return]** . . . . Stores code for end underline
                                                 display.

     $ **tput clear [Return]** . . . . Clears screen.

     $ **tput cup 10 20 [Return]** . . . . Positions the cursor.

     $ **echo $bell [Return]** . . . . Sounds the terminal bell.

     $ **echo $s_uline [Return]** . . . . Starts underline display.

     $ **echo "The terminfo database" [Return]** . . . . Displays message, underlined.

     <u>The terminfo database</u>

     $ **echo $e_uline [Return]** . . . . Ends underline display.

The **echo** commands can be combined into one command using the assigned variables as follows:

$ **echo " $bell${s_uline}The terminfo database$e_uline" [Return]**

The braces in *${s_uline}* are necessary for the shell to recognize the variable name (see chapter 11, variable substitution).

12.3.3   Solving the *lock1* Program Problems

Let's use the stty, **trap**, and **tput** commands, and modify the lock1 script to fix its problems and create a better user interface. Figure 12–3 shows the new version of the lock script, and the following is the explanation for the modified or added lines.

Line 9: This line traps the signals 2 and 3. This means your script ignores the **interrupt** and **quit** keys when they are received, and continues running.

Line 10: This line disables the echoing capability of the terminal. Therefore the next characters input (in this case the password) are not displayed.

Figure 12–3
The lock2 script file.

```
 1 #
 2 # name: lock2 (lock version 2)
 3 # definition: This program locks the keyboard, and you must  type the
 4 # specified password to unlock it.
 5 # logic:
 6 #             1- Ask the user to enter a password
 7 #             2: Lock the keyboard until the correct password is entered.
 8 #
 9  trap " " 2 3 4                          # ignore the listed signals
10 stty -echo                              # prohibit echoing the input
11 tput clear                              # clear the screen
12 tput  5 10 ;  echo "Enter your PASSWORD> " # ask for password
13 read pword_1                            # read password
14 tput clear                             # clear screen again
15 tput cup 10, 20 ; echo "THIS SYSTEM IS LOCKED ...."
16 pword_2=                               # declare an empty variable
18 until [ "$pword_1" = "$Pword_2" ]      # start of the loop
19  do
20     read pword_2                       # body of the loop
21  done                                  # end of until
22 stty echo                              # enable echo of input characters
23  exit 0                                # end of the program, exit

file "lock2"  23 lines 166 characters
```

Line 11 and 14: These lines clear the screen. Instead of using the **echo** command and the clear screen code, the **tput** command is used.

Line 12: This line issues two commands, separated by the semicolon (**;**). The first command (**tput cup 5 10**) positions the cursor on line 5 column 10. The second command echoes the message at the location of the cursor.

Line 15: This line is similar to the line 12 and issues two commands separated by the semicolon (**;**). The first command (**tput cup 10 20**) positions the cursor on line 10 column 20. The second command echoes the message at the location of the cursor.

Line 23: This line resets (enables) the echoing capability of your terminal. This happens after you have entered the correct key to unlock the keyboard.

Now, if you change the lock2 to an executable file and execute it, by typing the following commands:

> $ **chmod +x lock2 [Return]** . . . . Change the program access mode.

> $ **lock2 [Return]** . . . . Execute it.

your screen looks like the screen depicted in figure 12–4, and you are prompted to enter a password.

Enter any sequence of character or numbers (which are not displayed) as your password. You must remember this password to unlock your keyboard. Next, the terminal screen is cleared and your screen looks like the screen depicted in figure 12–5.

Now the keyboard is locked, and only your password unlocks it. What happens if you forget your password? You cannot use [Del], [Ctrl-c], or other keys to terminate lock2 program. The **trap** command ignores these signals, and the program continues keeping the keyboard locked. You cannot trap the kill signals (9 and 15), but you cannot use your keyboard to issue the **kill** command. The solution is simple: log in using another terminal, and issue a **kill** command to terminate the lock2 from this terminal.

Specifying the Display Message   As mentioned before, you can improve the lock2 program by giving the user freedom of specifying the message to be displayed or choosing the canned (default) message. The specified message must be passed to the program on the command line. For example, you type:

Figure 12–4
The prompt from the lock2 program.

> Enter your PASSWORD> _

Figure 12–5
The message from the lock2 program.

> THIS SYSTEM IS LOCKED

$ lock3 Coffee Break. Will be back in 5 minutes [Return]

You have to modify your lock2 program to accommodate the new changes in our scenario. With the new version (called lock3), you can either enter a message on the command line or execute the program as before without specifying a message. Your program must recognize both cases and show the appropriate message. Figure 12–6 shows the source code for the lock3 program, and the following line explanations clarify how it works.

Lines 11 to 16: These lines make the **if-then-else** construct. The **if** condition checks the value of the positional variable *$#* which contains the number of the line arguments. If *$#* is greater than zero, it indicates that the user has specified a message on the command line, and the body of the **if** is executed. The positional variable *$@* holds the specified message, which is stored in the *MESG* variable.

Figure 12–6
The lock program, third version.

```
 1 #
 2 # name: lock3 (lock program version 3)
 3 # definition: This program locks the keyboard, and you must type the
 4 # specified password to unlock it.
 5 # logic:
 6 #              1: Ask the user to enter a password.
 7 #              2: Lock the keyboard until the correct password is entered.
 8 #
 9 trap " " 2 3 4                          # ignore the listed signals
10 stty -echo                             # prohibit echoing the input
11 if [ $# -gt 0 ]                        # on-line message is specified
12   then
13      $MESG="$@"                        # store the specified message
14 else
15      $MESG=" THIS SYSTEM IS LOCKED "
16 fi
17 tput clear                             # clear the screen
18 tput 5 10 ; echo "Enter your PASSWORD> " # ask for password
19 read pword_1                           # read password
20 tput clear                             # clear screen again
21 tput cup 10, 20 ; echo "$MESG"         # display the message
22 pword_2=                               # declare an empty variable
23 until [ "$pword_1" = "$Pword_2" ]      # start of the loop
24 do
25    read pword_2                        # body of the loop
26 done                                   # end of until
27 stty echo                              # enable echo of input characters
28 exit 0                                 # end of the program, exit

"lock3"  28 lines 166 characters
```

If the *$#* is not greater than zero, then the body of the **else** is executed and *MESG* variable holds the canned message.

Line 21: This line displays the content of the variable *MESG*, either the user-specified message or the canned message.

The remaining lines are the same as the lock2 version of the program, and they carry out the same functions. As before, you change the access mode of your lock3 program to executable mode, and then you can run it with or without specifying a message on the command line.

12.4   MORE COMMANDS

In the next section, we're going to put all our shell programming skills together and write an application that consists of more than just one script file. Before presenting the scenario for this application program, however, we need to examine a few more commands.

12.4.1   Multi-Way Branching: The *case* Construct

The shell provides you with the **case** construct, which enables you to selectively execute a set of commands from the list of commands. You can use the **if-elif-else** construct to achieve the same result, but when you have to use too many **elif** statements (more than two or three, for example), the **case** construct is preferred. Using the **case** construct rather than multiple **elif** statements is a more elegant way to program.

The syntax of the **case** construct is as follows:

```
case variable in
    pattern_1 )
        commands_1 ;;
    pattern_2 )
        commands_2 ;;
    ...
    ...
    *)
    default_commands ;;
esac
```

case, **in**, and **esac** (**case** typed backward) are reserved words (keywords). The statements between the **case** and the **esac** is called the body of the **case** construct.

When your shell executes the **case** statement, it compares the contents of the variable with each of the patterns until either a match is found or the shell reaches the keyword **esac**. The shell executes the commands associated with the matching pattern. The default **case**, represented by ***)**, must be the last

case in your program. The end of each **case** is indicated by two semicolons
(;;).

Let's look at a simple menu program and explore the application of the
case construct. A menu system provides an easy, simple user interface, and
most computer users are familiar with the menu systems. It is easy to implement menus in shell scripts.

You usually expect a menu program to perform the following functions:

- Display the possible options.
- Prompt the user to select a function.
- Read the user input.
- Call other programs according to the user input.
- Display error message if the input is wrong.

The users enters a selection; the menu program must recognize your selection and take action accordingly. This recognition can be easily achieved by
using the **case** construct. For example, assume you have a script called
MENU. The source code for your MENU program is depicted in figure 12–7.
The following command sequences show the running and output of this
program.

Run the MENU program.

$ **MENU [Return]** . . . . Execute the menu program.

Figure 12–7
Source code for a simple menu program.

```
$ cat MENU
#
#  A simple menu program to demonstrate the use of the case construct.
#
echo  " 0: Exit"
echo  " 1: Show Date and Time"
echo  " 2: List my HOME directory"
echo  " 3:  Display Calendar"
echo   "Enter your choice: "          # display the prompt
read  option                          # read user answer
case  $option  in                     # beginning of the case construct
     0 )  echo good bye ;;            # display the message
     1 )  date ;;                     # show date and time
     2 )  ls $HOME ;;                 # display the HOME directory
     3 )  cal ;;                      # show the current month calendar
     *)  echo "Invalid input. Good bye." ;;      # show error message
  esac                                # end of the case construct

  $_
```

0: Exit

1: Show Date and Time

2: List my HOME directory

3: Display Calendar

Enter your choice:. . . . . Waiting for input.

The menu is displayed, and it prompts you to enter your choice. Your input is stored in the variable called *$option*. The variable *$option* is passed to the **case** construct, which recognizes your selection and executes the appropriate commands.

If you enter 0: The *$option* contains 0, which matches the 0 (zero) pattern in the **case** construct. Thus the **echo** command is executed and the message **good bye** is displayed. No other pattern matches and the program ends.

If you enter 1: The *$option* contains 1 which matches the 1 (one) pattern in the **case** construct. Thus the command **date** is executed and date and time of the day is displayed. No other pattern matches, and the program ends.

If you enter 2: The *$option* contains 2 which matches the 2 (two) pattern in the **case** construct. Thus the command **ls** is executed and the contents of your *HOME* directory is displayed. No other pattern matches, and the program ends.

If you enter 3: Similar to the previous selections. The variable *$option* matches the case 3, and output of the **calendar** command is displayed.

If you enter 5: What if you make a mistake and enter 5, or 7? If your **case** construct has a default case (the * matches all), when all other cases fail, the default matches, and its associated commands are executed. In this case, it displays **Invalid input. Good bye.**

12.4.2   Revisiting the *greetings* Program

Let's write another version of the greetings program (which was introduced in chapter 11). In the new version, instead of the **if-elif-else** the **case** construct is used. Figure 12–8 is one way to write this program.

The output of this version is the same as the previous one. It beeps twice, and depending on the hour of the day, it displays appropriate greetings. The *hour* variable (which contains the hour of the day) is passed to the **case** construct. The value stored in *hour* is compared to each of the **case** patterns until a match is found. These patterns need more explanation.

The first pattern **0? | 1 [0-1]** checks for the morning hours (01 to 11). The **0?** represents any two-digit number that consists of a 0 and another digit (0 to 9). Therefore **0?** matches values from 00 to 09. The **1[0-1]** represents any two-digit number that consists of a 1 and another digit (0 to 1). Therefore **1[0-1]** matches values 10 and 11. The | (pipe) is the sign for logical **or**; therefore, the whole expression is true if any of the two patterns matches the value in the *hour* variable. If the value in the *hour* variable is between 01 to 11, the **echo** command displays **Good Morning**.

Figure 12–8
The new version of the greetings program.

```
$ cat greetings2
#   greetings2: greeting program version 2
#   This version uses the case construct to check the hour of the day and to display
#   the appropriate greetings
#
bell='tput bel'              store the code for the bell sound
echo  $bell$bell                 # two beeps
hour='date+%H'                   #  obtain hour of the day
case $hour in
   0? | 1[0-1]  ) echo "Good Morning" ;;
         1[2-7] ) echo "Good Afternoon" ;;
             *  ) echo "Good Evening" ;;
esac
exit 0

$ _
```

The second pattern **1[2-7]** checks for the afternoon hours (12–17). It represents any two-digit number that consists of a 1 and another digit in the range of 2 to 7. Therefore, **1[2-7]** matches values from (12 to 17). If the value in the *hour* variable is between 12 to 17, the **echo** command displays **Good Afternoon**.

The third pattern * (the default) matches any value. If the value in the *hour* variable is between 18 to 23, the first and second patterns fail, and the **echo** command displays **Good Evening**.

12.5   A MENU-DRIVEN APPLICATION

Scenario Suppose you want to write a menu-driven application that facilitates keeping track of your UNIX books. You want to be able to update the list of your books, to know whether any specified book is in your library (or not) and whether a book has been borrowed, who borrowed it, and when it was borrowed.

Of course this is a typical application for a database, but the goal is to practice some of the UNIX commands and to get a feeling about how you can put the commands and constructs together to create useful programs.

12.5.1   The Hierarchy Chart

Figure 12–9 shows the hierarchical chart of a menu-driven UNIX library program called ULIB. When you invoke the ULIB, it shows the main menu and waits for you to enter your choice. Each entry takes you to another level of menus. Like most of the menu-driven user interfaces, the top levels of ULIB's hierarchy chart presents the user interface. In this case, the three programs

Figure 12–9
The ULIB program hierarchy chart.

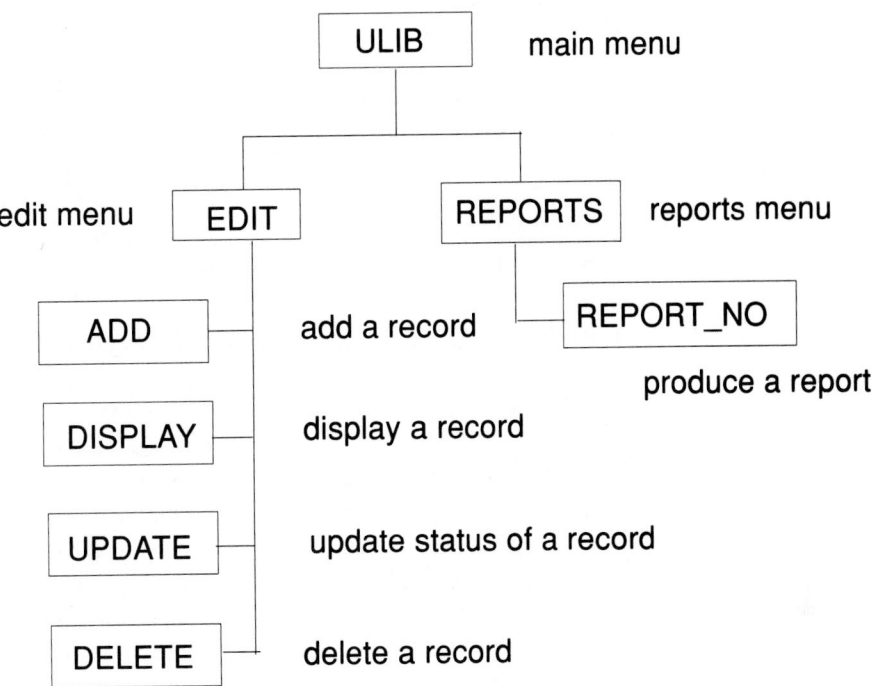

ULIB, EDIT, and REPORTS just show the appropriate menu and wait for the user selection of the items on the menu.

Each box in the hierarchy chart represents a program. Let's start with the first program, the ULIB at the top of the chart. Figure 12–10 shows one way to write this program. The line numbers are not part of the source code. Whenever necessary, these line numbers are referenced to provide more explanation on the commands or logic of the program.

Lines 1–6: These lines are all started with the # sign and are documentation lines.

Line 7: This line stores the terminal code for the bold display in a variable called *BOLD*.

Line 8: This line stores the terminal code for the normal display in a variable called *NORMAL*.

Line 9: This line makes the variables *BOLD* and *NORMAL* available to the sub-shells.

Lines 10–12: These lines are all started with the # sign and are documentation lines.

Line 13: This line clears the screen.

Line 14: This line positions the cursor on the line 5 column 15.

Figure 12–10
The ULIB program source code.

```
 1 #
 2 # UNIX library
 3 # ULIB: This program is the main driver for the UNIX library application program.
 4 #       It shows a brief startup message and then displays the main menu.
 5 #       Invokes the appropriate program according to the user selection.
 6 #
 7 BOLD=`tput smso`               # store code for bold mode in BOLD
 8 NORMAL=`tput rmso`             # store code for end of the bold in NORMAL
 9 export BOLD NORMAL             # make them recognized by subshells
10 #
11 # show the title and a brief message before showing the main menu
12 #
13 tput clear                     # clear screen
14 tput cup 5 15                  # place the cursor on line 5, column 15
15 echo "${BOLD}Super Duper UNIX Library"    # show the title in bold
16 tput cup 12 10                 # place the cursor on line 12, column 10
17 echo "${NORMAL}This is the UNIX library application."   # the rest of the title
18 tput cup 14 10 ; echo "Please enter any key to continue... _\b\c"
19 read answer                    # read user input
20 error_flag=0                   # initialize the error flag, indicating no error
21 while  true                    # loop forever
22   do
23     if [ $error_flag  -eq 0 ]  # check for the error
24       then
26         tput clear             # clear screen
27         tput cup  5 10
28         echo "UNIX Library - ${BOLD}MAIN MENU${NORMAL}"
29         tput cup  7 20 ; echo "0:  ${BOLD}EXIT${NORMAL} this program"
30         tput cup  9 20 ; echo "1:  ${BOLD}EDIT${NORMAL} Menu"
31         tput cup 11 20 ; echo "2:  ${BOLD}REPORTS${NORMAL} Menu"
32         error_flag=0           # reset error flag
33     fi
33         tput cup 13 10 ; echo "Enter your choice _\b\c"
34         read choice            # read user choice
35 #
36 # case construct for checking the user selection
37 #
38         case $choice in        # check user input
39           0 )  tput clear ; exit 0 ;;
40           1 )  EDIT ;;         # call EDIT program
41           2 )  REPORTS         # call REPORT program
41           * )  ERROR  20 10    # call ERROR program
43             tput cup 20 1 ; tput ed          # clear the rest of the screen
44             error_flag=1 ;;    # set error flag to indicate error
45         esac                   # end of the case construct
46 done                          # end of the while construct
```

Line 15: This line displays the message **Super Duper UNIX Library** on the screen. Using the *BOLD* variable makes the message appear in bold.

Line 16: This line positions the cursor on the line 12 column 10.

Line 17: This line displays the rest of the message **This is the UNIX library application** on the screen. Using the *NORMAL* variable deactivates the bold terminal mode, and the rest of the message appears in normal fashion.

 When a terminal mode is set, it remains in effect until it is canceled. Thus if you use the command **tput smso**, your terminal displays text in bold until you cancel the bold mode by typing the command **tput rmso**.

Line 18: This line consists of two commands. The **tput** command positions the cursor on the line 14 column 10, and the **echo** command displays the prompt message.

Line 19: This line waits for input from the keyboard. When you enter a key, the program continues.

This is a good point in the program to stop line explanations and to run it to see what is the output of this part (lines 1 to 19). If you run this program by typing the following command, the ULIB program shows the startup screen and waits for your input to continue the program.

> **$ ULIB [Return]**

Figure 12–11 depicts the startup screen. After displaying the startup screen, the program shows the main menu and waits for the user to specify a selection from the menu. Depending on your selection, the program activates other programs. This process of showing the menu continues until you select the exit function from the menu.

Line 20: This line initializes the **error_flag** to 0 to indicate there is no error yet. The purpose of this flag is to indicate whether the user has made a mistake. Depending on the value of this flag, your program shows the whole menu or just the portion of it that is necessary. This prevents clearing the screen each time the user makes a mistake and makes it less distracting to the user.

Lines 21, 22, and 46: These lines make the **while** loop. The **while** loop condition is set to true. The true condition is always true (succeeds); therefore, the **while** loop continues. That is to say the body of the loop is executed forever,

Figure 12–11
The ULIB program startup screen.

Super Duper UNIX Library

This is the UNIX library Application
Please enter any key to continue..._

and this is exactly what you want, to show the main menu continuously until the exit function is selected.

Lines 23, 24, and 33: These lines make the **if** construct. The **if** condition checks for the state of the **error_flag**. If **error_ flag** is 0, then there is no error, and the condition is true. Therefore the body of the **if** is executed. If the **error_flag** is not 0, the **if** condition fails, and the body of the **if** is skipped.

Line 26: This line clears the screen so the main menu can be displayed. Remember, the startup screen is displayed before the main menu display.

Lines 28–31: These lines show the main menu on the screen.

Line 32: This line resets the **error_flag** to 0 again, initializing it for the next loop iteration.

Lines 33 and 34: These lines display the prompt text and wait for the user to enter a selection.

Let's continue the running of this program. Figure 12–12 shows the main menu. The prompt is displayed and program waits for your input.

*The bold text on the screen is produced by displaying (the **echo** command) the code stored in the BOLD variable.*

Your input is saved in the *choice* variable, and *choice* is passed to the **case** construct to determine the next action according to your input.

Lines 35–37: These lines are all started with the # sign and are documentation lines.

Lines 38–45: These lines make the **case** construct.

If you select 0: The value in the *choice* variable is 0; it matches the 0 pattern and executes the associated commands. In this case, it clears the screen and exits the program. This is the normal way to end this program; choosing the 0 from the main menu.

If you select 1: The value in the *choice* variable is 1; it matches the 1 pattern and executes the associated commands. In this case, it executes the program called EDIT. When the EDIT program is terminated, the control returns to this program, and the program sequentially executes the next lines. Line 45 indicates

Figure 12–12
The ULIB program main menu screen.

> UNIX Library - **MAIN MENU**
>
>   0: **EXIT** this program
>   1: **EDIT** Menu
>   2: **REPORTS** Menu
>
> Enter your choice > _

the end of the **case** construct. Line 46 indicates the end of the **while** loop; therefore, it goes to the line 21 to check the **while** loop condition. The condition is true; hence, the body of the loop is executed and shows the main menu again. This process is repeated until you enter 0 from the main menu.

If you select 2: The value in the *choice* variable is 2; it matches the 2 pattern and executes the associated commands. In this case, it executes the program called REPORTS. Similar to the function 1 selection that was explained above, when the REPORTS program is finished, control returns to this program, and the main menu is displayed, ready for your next selection.

If you make a mistake: If you make a mistake in your selection, inputting any key but the valid 0, 1, and 2 values, the value in the *choice* variable matches the default pattern (the asterisk) and executes the associated commands. In this case, it executes a program called ERROR. The ERROR program shows the error message at the indicated line and column on the screen. The desired line and column are specified on the command line. Therefore, **ERROR 20 10** means showing the error message on line 20 column 10. As before, the control returns to this program when the ERROR program is finished.

Line 43: This line consists of two **tput** commands. The **tput cup 20 1** places the cursor on line 20 column 1, and the **tput ed** clears part of the display between the cursor location and the end of the screen. In this case, lines 20, 21, 22, 23, and 24 are cleared. This erases the error message, but the main menu text remains on your terminal screen.

Line 44: This line sets the **error_flag** to 1, indicating an error has occurred.

Remember **error_flag** *is checked in the* **if** *condition. Because its value is 1, the* **if** *condition fails, and the body of the* **if** *construct is skipped. This means the main menu text is already on the screen and there is no need to redisplay it.*

Figure 12–13 shows the screen when you make a mistake in your selection. The error message and the prompt text are output of the ERROR program. When you press a key to signal your intention to continue the program, the error mes-

Figure 12–13
The ULIB program error message screen.

```
                    UNIX Library - MAIN MENU


                        0: EXIT this program
                        1: EDIT Menu
                        2: REPORTS Menu


                    Enter your choice > 6
                Wrong Input. Try again
           Press any key to continue ...
```

sage is erased and you are prompted again to enter your selection from the menu (as was shown in figure 12–12).

12.5.2   The *ERROR* Program

The ERROR program shows a *canned* (hard coded) error message any time it is called. It accepts the values indicating the location of the cursor (line and column) from the command line. Figure 12–14 shows the source code for this program.

Line 6: This line places the cursor at the specified location on the screen. The row and column values are stored in the two positional variables *$1* and *$2*. These variables contain the first two parameters passed to the program on the command line. Therefore, if you call this program by typing

$ ERROR 10 15 [Return]

the positional variables *$1* and *$2* contain the values 10 and 15 respectively, and the error message will be displayed at row 10 column 15. The ULIB program (figure 12–10) calls the ERROR program, when user input is wrong, to display an error message at line 20 column 10.

Line 7: This line displays the error message.

Line 8: This line displays the prompt.

Figure 12–14
The ERROR program source code.

```
 1 #
 2 # ERROR: This program displays an error message and waits for user
 3 #                 input to continue. It displays the message at the specified
 4 #                 row and column.
 5 #
 6 tput  cup  $1  $2              # place the cursor on the screen
 7 echo "Wrong Input. Try again."   # show the error message
 8 echo "Press any key to continue ....> _\b\c"  # display the prompt
 9 read answer                   # read user input
10 exit  0                       # indicate normal exit
```

Line 9: This line reads the user input. No error checking is performed on the user input; you can enter any key to satisfy the **read** command. Thus control of the program is in the hand of the user, and the user can continue the program by pressing a key.

Figure 12–15
The EDIT program source code.

```
 1 #
 2 # UNIX library
 3 # EDIT: This program is the main driver for the EDIT program.
 4 #        It shows  the edit menu and invokes the appropriate program
 5 #        according to the user selection.
 6 #
 7 error_flag=0                        # initialize the error flag, indicating no error
 8 while  true                         # loop forever
 9   do
10    if [ $error_flag  -eq 0 ]        # check for the error
11      then
12        tput clear ; tput cup  5 10  # clear screen and place the cursor
13        echo "UNIX Library - ${BOLD}EDIT MENU${NORMAL}"
14        tput cup  7 20              # place the cursor
15        echo "0:  ${BOLD}RETURN${NORMAL} To The Main Menu"
16        tput cup   9  20 ; echo "1: ${BOLD}ADD${NORMAL}"
17        tput cup 11 20  ; echo "2: ${BOLD}UPDATE STATUS${NORMAL}'
18        tput cup 13 20  ; echo "3: ${BOLD}DISPLAY${NORMAL}"
19        tput cup 13 20  ; echo "4: ${BOLD}DELETE${NORMAL}"
20      fi
21      error_flag=0                   # reset error flag
22      tput cup 17 10 ; echo "Enter your choice> _\b\c"
23      read choice                    # read user choice
24 #
25 # case construct for checking the user selection
26 #
27 case $choice in                     # check user input
28    0 ) exit 0 ;;                    # return to the main menu
29    1 ) ADD ;;                       # call ADD program
30    2 ) UPDATE                       # call UPDATE program
31    3 ) DISPLAY                      # call DISPLAY program
32    4 ) DELETE                       # call DELETE program
33    * ) ERROR 20 10                  # call ERROR program
34        tput cup 20 1 ;  tput ed     # clear the rest of the screen
35        error_flag=1 ;;              # set error flag to indicate error
36 esac                                # end of the case construct
37 done                                # end of the while construct
```

12.5.3   The *EDIT* Program

The EDIT program is activated whenever you select function 1 from the main menu. This program is a driver for the edit menu and is similar to the main menu program. It shows the edit menu, and according to your selection it activates appropriate programs. It consists of a while loop that covers the whole program.

Figure 12–16
The EDIT menu.

UNIX Library - **EDIT MENU**

0: **RETURN** To The Main Menu
1: **ADD**
2: **DISPLAY**
3: **UPDATE STATUS**
4: **DELETE**

Enter your choice> _

The body of the **while** loop consists of the edit menu display code, and a **case** structure that determines what commands must be executed to satisfy your selection. Essentially this is the logic for any menu program you write: show the menu, read the selection, and act according to the selection.

Figure 12–15 shows the source code for the EDIT program. This program is similar to the main (ULIB) program that was explained in detail in the previous section. Figure 12–16 shows the edit menu. The edit menu is displayed when you choose function 1 from the main menu.

12.5.4   The *ADD* program

This program adds a record to your library file and is activated when you select the add function from the edit menu. It prompts you to enter information, adds the new record to the end of the library file, and asks if you want to add any more records. A yes answer continues the program, appending records to the file. A **no** answer terminates the program and returns the control to the calling program, in this case, the EDIT program, and you are back to the edit menu for your next selection. This program assumes that the library file that holds all the information about your UNIX books is called ULIB_FILE; it further assumes that in the record format the following information is saved for each book in the ULIB_FILE. Each item is stored as a field in the record, and the following lists the field names; this textbook is used as an example to show a possible value for each field.

- Title: UNIX Unbound
- Author: Afzal Amir
- Category: Textbook
  Three valid categories are assumed:
  - System books: abbreviated to *sys*
  - Reference books: abbreviated to *ref*
  - Textbooks: abbreviated to *tb*

- Status: in
  The status indicates whether the book is checked out or is in the library.
  The book's status is determined by the program, and the status field is set
  to **in** (checked in) automatically when you add a book. The status is
  changed to **out** (checked out) when you indicate a book is checked out
  (borrowed) by someone.

- Borrower's name:
  This field remains empty if the status field indicates the specified book is
  in the library (status set to **in**) and is set to the name of the person who
  borrowed the book if the status field shows **out** (checked out).

- Date:
  This field remains empty if the status field indicates the specified book is
  in the library (status set to **in**) and is set to the date that the book is
  checked out if the status field indicates **out** (the book is checked out).

1. *The first time a book record is added to the ULIB_FILE file, the status
   field is set to **in**, and the borrower's name and the date fields remain
   empty.*

Figure 12–17
The ADD program source code.

```
 1 #
 2 # UNIX library
 3 # ADD: This program adds a record to the library file (U_LIB). It asks the
 4 # title, author, and category of the book. After adding the information
 5 # to the U_LIB file, it prompts the user for the next record.
 6 #
 7 answer=y                          # initialize the answer to indicate yes
 8 while  [ "$answer" = y ]          # as long as the answer is yes
 9 do
10     tput clear
11     tput cup  5 10  ; echo "UNIX Library - ${BOLD}ADD MODE"
12     tput cup  7 23  ; echo "Title: "
13     tput cup  9 22  ; echo "Author: "
14     tput cup 11 20  ; echo "Category: "
15     tput cup 12 20  ; echo "sys: system,  ref: reference, tb: textbook"
16     tput cup  7 30  ; read title
17     tput cup  9 30  ; read author
19     tput cup 11 30  ; read category
20     status=in                     # set the status to indicate book is in
21     echo "$title;$author;$category;$status;$bname;$date" >> U_LIB
22     tput cup  14 10 ; echo "Any more to add? (Y)es or (N)o _\b\c"
23     read answer
24     case $answer in               # check user answer
25       [Yy]* ) answer=y ;;         # any word starting with Y or y is yes
26           * ) answer=n ;;         # any other word indicates no
27     esac                          # end of the case construct
```

2. *Subsequently, when someone borrows a book, you update your library by selecting the update function from the main menu. Then, you are asked to enter the name of the person who borrowed the book. The program changes the status field to* **out** *(checked out), and the date field is set to the current date.*

Figure 12–17 shows the source code for this program followed by the line explanations.

Lines 1–6: These lines all start with the # sign and are documentation lines.

Line 7: This line initializes the *answer* variable to the letter *y*, indicating **yes**. As long as this variable indicates **yes**, the **while** loop continues and in each iteration adds one record to the ULIB_FILE file.

Lines 8, 9, and 28: These lines make the **while** loop. The body of this loop is executed as long as the condition of the loop is true—in this case, as long as the value stored in the *answer* variable is the letter *y*.

Line 10: This line clears the screen.

Line 11: This line displays the title of the screen at the indicated cursor position.

Lines 12–14: These lines display the prompts at the specified cursor locations.

Line 15: This line is a help message that explains what abbreviation user must enter in the category field.

Lines 16–20: Each of these lines places the cursor at the specified location on the screen (just after each prompt text), reads the user answers, and stores them in appropriate variables.

Line 20: This line sets the status variable to **in**, indicating the book is in the library.

At this point all the necessary information is obtained, and the next step is to save it in the ULIB_FILE file. If you select the add function from the edit menu, the ADD program is activated. Figure 12–18 shows the screen display produced by the ADD program.

The cursor is placed at the title field. You enter the title of the book followed by [Return], and the cursor moves to the author field. When you enter the last field, the program saves the information and asks you if you want to

Figure 12–18
The ADD program screen format.

```
    UNIX Library - ADD MODE


            Title :
           Author :
         Category :
         sys: system, ref: reference. tb: textbook
```

Figure 12–19
An example of the filled in ADD screen.

UNIX Library - **ADD MODE**

       Title : UNIX Unbound
    Author : Afzal Amir
  Category : tb
    sys: system, ref: reference. tb: textbook

Any more to add? (Y)es or (n)o > _

add another record. Using this textbook as an example, figure 12–19 shows the screen after information has been entered and the record has been saved.

Line 21: This line saves the information in the ULIB_FILE file. By the time the ADD program reaches this line, the variables contain the following values:

- The *title* variable contains **UNIX Unbounded**.
- The *author* variable contains **Afzal Amir**.
- The *category* variable contains **tb**.
- The *status* variable contains the word **in**.
- The *bname* (for borrower's name) variable is empty.
- The *date* (date that the book is checked out) variable is empty.

By default, the **echo** command displays its output on the terminal screen. However, the output of the **echo** command on line 21 is redirected to the ULIB_FILE file. Therefore, the information stored in the specified variables is saved in the ULIB_FILE file.

1. *When you have just added a record, the variable bname (borrower's name) and date (checked out date) remain empty.*

2. *The append sign (>>) is used to write information in the ULIB_FILE file. This is necessary so that each time you add a new record, it is appended to the end of the file and the rest of the records in the file remain intact.*

Delimiter Character

The fields in each record are stored one after another. However, this method of saving makes it difficult to retrieve each field when you want to read and display a record. You must designate a field delimiter and separate the fields in the record by your selected character. Keys that UNIX uses as field separators ([Tab], [Return], and [Spacebar]) are not good choices. Remember, the title of a book or name of the author may contain space characters. If you choose the space character as the delimiter, then the author's name with a space between the first and last names is considered as two fields, while you want your program to see it as one field.

Figure 12–20
The content of the ULIB_FILE file.

```
$ cat  ULIB_FILE
   UNIX Unbounded;Afzal Amir;tb;in;;
$_
```

You can choose [~] or [^] as the delimiter key. In ULIB program, [;] is used as the delimiter character.

The ULIB_FILE file is a text file, and you can use the **cat** command to display its content or use the vi editor to modify it. If the above record is the only record in the file, then the content of the ULIB_FILE file looks like the display in the figure 12–20.

1. *Each record in the file is one line, and fields are separated by semicolons.*

2. *The two semicolons at the end of the line are the placeholders for the two variables bname (when not empty contains the name of the borrower) and date (when not empty contains the date that the book was borrowed).*

Lines 22 and 23: The **echo** command displays the prompt and the **read** command waits for the user answer, which is saved in the *answer* variable.

Lines 23–27: These lines make the **case** construct. The **case** checks for the user answer by matching the value in *answer* to the **case** patterns.

The first pattern is **[Yy]***. This pattern matches all sequences of characters that start with [Y] or [y]. You can type any word that starts with a letter y and the program interprets it as the **yes** answer. The *answer* variable is set to the letter y, the loop condition (line 8) is true, and the the program continues.

The second pattern is [*]. This pattern matches any word that doesn't start with the letter y and interprets it as the **no** answer. The *answer* variable is set to the letter n, the loop condition (line 8) fails, and the program ends.

12.5.5   Record Retrieval

Part of the code in each of the remaining programs in the library application needs to display an existing record on the screen. In order to display a record, you must specify what record you want displayed. For example, if you specify the author's name, the library file is searched to check whether the specified author's name is in the file. If it is found, the record is read (retrieved) and displayed. If the record is not found, an error message is displayed.

12.5.6   The *DISPLAY* Program

The DISPLAY program displays a specified record from the ULIB_FILE file on the screen, and it is activated when you select the display function from the edit menu. It first prompts you to enter the book's title or the author's name. Then, it searches the ULIB_FILE file to find a match for the specified book. If the record is found, it is displayed in a presentable format. If the record is not found, an error message is displayed, and you are prompted for the next input. This process continues until you indicate your intention to end the program. When the DIS-PLAY program ends, the control is returned to the calling program, in this case the EDIT program, and you are back to the edit menu for your next selection.

Figure 12–21 shows the DISPLAY program source code. The following is the line-by-line explanation of this program.

Lines 1–6: These lines are all started with the # sign and are documentation lines.

Line 7: This line copies the value of the environment variable IFS to *OLD_IFS*. You want to save the old values before assigning the new value. Later, you want to be able to restore the IFS variable to its original setup.

Line 8: This line initializes the variable *answer* to the letter *y*. Consequently it forces the first iteration of the **while** loop.

Lines 9, 10, and 45: These lines construct the **while** loop. The body of the loop consists of all the lines between lines 10 and 45. As long as the condition of the **while** loop is true (the *answer* is equal letter *y*), then the body of the loop is executed.

Line 11: This line consists of three commands. It clears the screen, places the cursor on line 5 column 6, and prompts the user to enter the title or the author of the book to be displayed.

Line 12: This line waits for the user input and saves the input in the *response* variable.

Line 13: This line uses the **grep** command (see chapter 8) to find all the lines in the ULIB_FILE file that contain the pattern stored in the *response* variable (the user input), and the output is redirected to the TEMP file. If TEMP file is not empty, it means the specified book record is found, and if TEMP remains an empty file, it means the specified record is not found.

Lines 14, 15, 35, and 37: These lines make an **if-then-else** construct. The **if** condition tests for existence of a nonzero-length file, in this case the TEMP file. If the condition is true (TEMP exists and there is something in it), then the body of the **if** (lines 16-18) is executed. If the condition is false (TEMP is an empty file), then the body of the **else** (line 36) is executed.

Line 16: This line sets the delimiter to the semicolon (;). In this application, the semicolon is the symbol that separates the fields in the records.

Line 17: This line reads each field of the specified book record from the TEMP file.

Lines 18 and 19: These lines place the cursor at the specified location and display the record header.

Line 20: This line consists of two commands. It places the cursor on line 7 column 23 and then displays the title of the book. The *title* variable contains the title of the book as it was read from the TEMP file.

Figure 12–21
The DISPLAY program source code.

```
 1  #
 2  # UNIX library
 3  # DISPLAY: This program  displays a specified record from the ULIB_FILE.
 4  #           It asks the Author/Title of the book, and displays the specified
 5  #           book, or shows error message if the book is not found in the file.
 6  #
 7  OLD_IFS="$IFS"                    # save the IFS settings
 8  answer=y                         # initialize the answer to indicate yes
 9  while [  "$answer" = y  ]        # as long as the answer is yes
10  do
11    tput clear ; tput cup 3  5 ; echo "Enter the Title/Author > _\b\c"
12    read response
13    grep  -i "$response" library > TEMP   # find the specified book in the library
14    if [ -s  TEMP  ]               # if it is found
15      then                         # then
16      IFS=";"                      # set the IFS to semicolon
17      read title author category status bname date  < TEMP
18      tput cup  5 10
19      echo "UNIX Library - ${BOLD}DISPLAY MODE${NORMAL}"
20      tput cup   7 23 ; echo "Title: $title"
21      tput cup   8 22 ; echo "Author: $author"
22      case $category in            # check the category
23             [T t] [Bb] ) word=textbook  ;;
24           [Ss] [Yy] [Ss] ) word=system  ;;
25           [Rr] [Ee] [Ff]  ) word=reference ;;
26                      * ) word=undefined  ;;
27      esac
28      tput cup  9 20 ; echo "Category: $word"         # display the category
29      tput cup 10  22 ; echo "Status: $status"        # display the status
30      if [ "$status" = "out" ]     # if it is checked out
31        then                       # then show the rest of the information
32            tput cup 11 14 ; echo "Checked out by: $bname"
33            tput cup 12 24 ; echo "Date: $date"
34      fi
35    else                           # if book not found
36        tput cup  7 10 ; echo "$response no found"
37  fi
38    tput cup 15 10 ; echo "Any more to look? (Y)es or (N)o _\b\c"
39    read answer                    # read user answer
40    case $answer in                # check user answer
41     [Yy]* ) answer=y ;;           # any word starting with Y or y is yes
42        * ) answer=n ;;            # any other word indicates no
43    esac
45  done                             # end of the while loop
46  IFS=OLD_IFS                      # restore the IFS to its original value
47  exit 0                           # exit
```

Line 21: This line consists of two commands. It places the cursor on line 8 column 22 and then displays the author of the book. The *author* variable contains the name of the author as it was read from the TEMP file.

Lines 22–25: These lines make the **case** construct. The **case** checks the book's category (stored in the *category* variable) and changes the category abbreviations to a full word. For example, category abbreviation *sys* is changed to *system*.

The pattern **[Tt] [Bb]** matches any combination of uppercase and lowercase letters representing the category abbreviation *tb*. The string **textbook** is stored in the *word* variable.

The pattern **[Ss] [Yy] [Ss]** matches any combination of uppercase and lowercase letters representing the category abbreviation *sys*. The string **system** is stored in the *word* variable.

The pattern **[Rr] [Ee] [Ff]** matches any combination of uppercase and lowercase letters representing the category abbreviation *ref*. The string **Reference** is stored in the *word* variable.

If it is none of the above categories, then it matches the default (asterisk) and the string **undefined** is stored in the *word* variable.

Line 28: This line places the cursor on line 9 column 20 and displays the specified book category field (content of the *word* variable).

Line 29: This line places the cursor on line 10 column 22 and displays the specified book status field (content of the *status* variable).

Lines 30 and 34: These lines make an **if-then** construct. If the **if** condition is true (the book is checked out), then the body of the **if** (lines 31-33) is executed. Otherwise, if the status shows the book is **in**, then the body of the **if** is skipped.

Line 32: This line places the cursor on line 11 column 14 and displays the name of the person who has borrowed the book (contents of the *bname* variable).

Line 33: This line places the cursor on line 12 column 24 and displays the date (contents of the *date* variable) the book was checked out.

Line 36: This line is executed when the TEMP file is empty (the specified book not found). It places the cursor on line 7 column 10 and displays the error message.

Similar to the ADD program, the rest of the code is to check the user intention to display another record or to return to the edit menu.

 If you run the ULIB program and select the display function form the edit menu, the following prompt is displayed. Figure 12–22 shows the screen at this point.

Figure 12–22
The prompt displayed by the DISPLAY program.

> Enter the Author/Title > _

Figure 12–23
Sample of the DISPLAY program screen.

```
UNIX Library - DISPLAY MODE

        Title :  UNIX Unbound
       Author :  Afzal Amir
     Category :  textbook
       Status : in

Any more to look? (Y)es or (n)o > _
```

Figure 12–24
Sample screen showing the error message.

```
Enter the Author/Title >XYZ



        XYZ not found

    Any more to look? (Y)es or (N)o >
```

You can enter the author's name or the book's title to specify the book record you want to be displayed. Let's say you enter **UNIX Unbounded**. Figure 12–23 shows the screen that displays your specified record. This screen is very similar to the add screen depicted in figure 12–19. The program prompts you to enter your intention to look at more records or to end the DISPLAY program. When this program ends, control returns to the EDIT program, the edit menu is displayed again, and you can select your next function.

If your specified record is not found, the error message is displayed. Assuming you do not have specified a book titled *XYZ*, figure 12–24 shows the error message and the prompt following it.

12.5.7   The *UPDATE* Program

The UPDATE program changes the status of a specified record in the ULIB_FILE file, and it is activated when you select the update status function from the edit menu. You choose this option when a book is checked out or when a checked out book is checked in. The UPDATE program first prompts you to enter the title or the author of the book whose status you want to change. Then it searches the ULIB_FILE file to find a match for the specified book. If the record is found, it is displayed in a presentable format. If the record is not found, an error message is displayed, and you are prompted for the next input. This process continues until you indicate your intention to end the program. When the UP-

DATE program ends, control is returned to the calling program, in this case the EDIT program, and you are back to the edit menu for your next selection.

Figure 12–25 shows the UPDATE program source code, and a line-by-line explanation of this program follows. The source code for the UPDATE program is longer than that of the previous programs, but most of the lines are copied from the DISPLAY program. The lines of code at the beginning and end of the DISPLAY, UPDATE, and DELETE programs are all the same. All these programs prompt you to specify the author or title of the desired book, and the program either finds the record and displays it or doesn't find the record and displays an error message. At the end of the program, you are prompted to indicate your intention to continue the program or to end it. Therefore, only the new or changed lines are explained here.

Line 12: This line declares three empty variables. These variables store new values when the status of the book is changed from **in** to **out** (checked out) and initialize them to be empty when the status of a book is changed from **out** to **in** (checked in).

- The *new_bname* variable holds the name of the borrower or is empty.
- The *new_status* variable holds the new status, the word *in* or *out*.
- The *new_date* variable holds the current date or is empty.

Lines 33–45: These lines make the **if-then-else** construct. If the **if** condition is true (the *status* variable contains the word *in* indicating the book is in the library), then the body of the **if** (lines 35-39) is executed. If the **if** condition is false (the *status* variable contains the word *out* indicating the book is checked out), then the body of the **else** (lines 41-44) is executed.

Figure 12–25: Part 1
Source code for the UPDATE program.

```
 1 #
 2 # UNIX library
 3 # UPDATE: This program updates the status of a specified book. It asks the
 4 #              Author/Title of the book, and changes the status of the specified
 5 #              book from in (checked in) to out (checked out), or from out to in.
 6 #              If the book is not found in the file, error message is displayed.
 7 #
 8 OLD_IFS="$IFS"              # save the IFS settings
 9 answer=y                    # initialize answer to indicate yes
10 while  [  "$answer" = y ]   # as long as the answer is yes
11 do
12   new_status= ; new_bname= ; new_date=  # declare empty variables
13   tput clear              # clear screen
14   tput clear ; tput cup 3  5 ; echo "Enter the Title/Author > _\b\c"
15   read response
16    grep  -i "$response" ULIB_FILE > TEMP  # find the specified book
```

Figure 12–25: Part 2
Source code for the UPDATE program.

```
17    if [ -s  TEMP  ]                # if it is found
18      then                          # then
19        IFS=";"                     # set the IFS to semicolon
20        read  title author category status bname date  < TEMP
21        tput cup  5  10
22        echo "UNIX Library - ${BOLD}UPDATE STATUS MODE${NORMAL}"
23        tput cup  7  23 ; echo "Title: $title"
24        tput cup  8  22 ; echo "Author: $author"
25        case $category in           # check the category
26               [T t] [Bb] )  word=textbook  ;;
27               [Ss] [Yy] [Ss] )  word=system ;;
28               [Rr] [Ee] [Ff]  )  word=reference ;;
29                          * )  word=undefined  ;;
30        esac
31        tput cup  9  20 ; echo "Category: $word"            # display the category
32        tput cup 10  22 ; echo "Status: $status"            # display the status
33        if [ "$status" = "in" ]     # if it is checked in
34          then                      # then show the rest of the information
35              new_status=out        # indicate the new status
36              tput cup 15  18 ;  echo "New status: $new_status"
37              tput cup  12  24 ;  Checked out by: _ \c "
38              read  new_bname
39              new_date=` date  +%D `
40            else
41              new_status=in
42              tput cup 11 14 ; echo "Checked out by: $bname"
43              tput cup 12 24 ; echo "Date: $date"
44              tput cup  15 18 ; echo  "New status: $new_status"
45        fi
46        grep  -iv "$title;$author;$category;$status;$bname;$date"  ULIB_FILE >
              TEMP
47        mv TEMP  ULIB_FILE
48        echo "$title;$author;$category;$new_status;$new_bname;$new_date" >>
              ULIB_FILE
49      else                          # if book not found
50        tput cup  7 10 ; echo "$response not found"
51    fi
51      tput cup 15 10 ; echo "Any more to update? (Y)es or (N)o > _\b\c"
52      read answer                   # read user answer
53      case $answer in               # check user answer
54        [Yy]* )  answer=y ;;        # any word starting with Y or y is yes
55           * ) answer=n ;;          # any other word indicates no
56      esac
57  done                             # end of the while loop
58  IFS=$OLD_IFS                      # restore the IFS to its original value
59  exit 0                            # exit
```

Lines 35–39: These lines are the body of the **if** and change the status of the record from **in** to **out**. The only item of information needed is the name of the person who checked out the book.

Line 35: This line stores the word *out* in the *new_status* variable, indicating the the book is checked out.

Line 36: This line places the cursor on the specified line and column, and displays the new status. In this case, the new status is **out**.

Line 37: This line prompts the user to enter the name of the person who checked out the book.

Line 38: This line reads the user response and saves it in the *new_bname* variable.

Line 39: This line stores the current date in the *new_date* variable. The **%D** option indicates only the date and not the time in the date string (see chapter 11).

Lines 41–44: These lines are the body of the **else** and change the status of the record from **out** to **in**.

Line 41: This line stores the word *in* in the *new_status* variable, indicating the the book is checked in.

Line 42: This line places the cursor on the specified line and column, and it displays the contents of the *bname* variable, the borrower's name.

Line 43: This line places the cursor on the specified line and column, and displays the contents of the *date* variable, the date that book was checked out.

Line 44: This line places the cursor on the specified line and column, and displays the contents of the *new_status* variable, in this case, the word *in*, indicating the book is checked in.

Line 46: This line saves (copies) every record in the ULIB_FILE file to the TEMP file, except the specified record on the display. It does that by using the **grep** command with the **i** and **v** options (see chapter 8), and redirecting the output of the **grep** from the terminal display to the TEMP file. The **i** option causes the **grep** to ignore the difference between uppercase and lowercase letters. The **v** option causes the **grep** to pick all the lines that do not contain a match for the specified pattern.

Line 47: This line uses the **mv** command (see chapter 5) to rename the TEMP file to ULIB_FILE file. Now the ULIB_FILE file contains every record except the record whose status has been just changed.

Line 48: This line appends the changed record to the ULIB_FILE file. Now the ULIB_FILE file contains the specified record with its updated status.

 Let's continue the running of the program. The terminal display helps you associate the line explanations with the actual output on the screen.

Figure 12–26 shows the UPDATE program display, assuming the update status function is selected from the edit menu and the specified book is **UNIX Unbounded**.

Figure 12–26
The UPDATE program display.

```
            UNIX Library - UPDATE STATUS MODE


               Title :  UNIX Unbounded
              Author :  Afzal Amir
            Category :  textbook
              Status :  in


          New status : out
     Checked out by : Steve Fraser _


     Any more to update? (Y)es or (N)o > _
```

Figure 12–27
The content of the ULIB_FILE file.

```
$ cat  ULIB_FILE
   UNIX Unbounded;Afzal Amir;tb;out;Steve Fraser;12/12/99
$_
```

Figure 12–28
Sample record display.

```
            UNIX Library - DISPLAY MODE


               Title :  UNIX Unbounded
              Author :  Afzal Amir
            Category :  textbook
              Status :  out
     Checked out by : Steve Fraser
                Date : 12/12/99
     Any more to look (Y)es or (N)o > _
```

1. *The status change is reflected on the screen by showing the old status and the new status fields.*

2. *You are prompted to enter the name of the person who checked out the specified book. It is assumed the name* **Steve Fraser** *is entered in response to the* **Checked out by:** _ *prompt.*

Figure 12–27 shows the ULIB_FILE after the change of status. If you compare this display to the figure 12–20 display, you will notice the changes in the fields of the specified record.

Figure 12–28 shows the display produced by the DISPLAY program, showing the same record.

Compare this display (where the status indicates the book is checked out) with the display depicted in figure 12–23 (where status indicates the book is checked in).

12.5.8   The *DELETE* Program

The DELETE program deletes a specified record from the ULIB_FILE file, and it is activated when you select the delete function from the edit menu. It first prompts you to enter the book's title or the author's name. Then it searches the ULIB_FILE file to find a match for the specified book. If the record is found, it is displayed in a presentable format, and the confirmation prompt is displayed. It lets you decide whether the displayed record is the record you want to delete. If the record is not found, an error message is displayed, and you are prompted for the next input. This process continues until you indicate your intention to end the program. When the DELETE program ends, control is returned to the calling program, in this case the EDIT program, and you are back to the edit menu for your next selection.

Figure 12–29 shows the source code for the DELETE program. The length of the program should not worry you. The beginning and the end part of the DELETE program is similar to the DISPLAY and UPDATE programs. The major differences are the code for the confirmation check before deletion of the record and the code for actual removal of the specified record from the ULIB_FILE file.

After the record is found and displayed, the confirmation prompt is displayed. At this point, the program is on the line 36.

Line 36: This line places the cursor on the specified line and column and displays the prompt.

Line 37: This line reads the user response and stores it in the answer variable.

Lines 38-42: These lines make the **if** construct. If the **if** condition is true, then the body of the **if** (lines 40 and 41) is executed. The **if** condition tests for [Y] or

Figure 12–29: Part 1
Source code for the DELETE program.

```
 1 #
 2 # UNIX library
 3 # DELETE: This program deletes a specified record from the ULIB_FILE.
 4 #          It asks the Author/Title of the book, and displays the specified
 5 #          book, and deletes it after confirmation, or shows error message if
 6 #          the book is not found in the file.
 7 #
 8   OLD_IFS="$IFS"                    # save the IFS settings
```

Figure 12–29: Part 2

Source code for the DELETE program.

```
 9   answer=y                              # initialize the answer to indicate yes
10   while [ "$answer" = y ]               # as long as the answer is yes
11   do
12      tput clear ; tput cup 3 5 ; echo "Enter the Title/Author > _\b\c"
13      read response
14      grep -i "$response" library > TEMP   # find the specified book in the library
15      if [ -s TEMP ]                       # if it is found
16         then                              # then
17         IFS=";"                           # set the IFS to semicolon
18         read title author category status bname date < TEMP
19         tput cup 5 10
20         echo "UNIX Library - ${BOLD}DELETE MODE${NORMAL}"
21         tput cup 7 23 ; echo "Title: $title"
22         tput cup 8 22 ; echo "Author: $author"
23         case $category in                 # check the category
24               [T t] [Bb] ) word=textbook ;;
25            [Ss] [Yy] [Ss] ) word=system ;;
26            [Rr] [Ee] [Ff] ) word=reference ;;
27                         * ) word=undefined ;;
28         esac
29         tput cup 9 20 ; echo "Category: $word"        # display the category
30         tput cup 10 22 ; echo "Status: $status"       # display the status
31         if [ "$status" = "out" ]          # if it is checked out
32            then                           # then show the rest of the information
33               tput cup 11 14 ; echo "Checked out by: $bname"
34               tput cup 12 24 ; echo "Date: $date"
35         fi
36         tput cup 9 20 ; echo "Delete this book? (Y)es or (N)o >_\b\c"
37         read answer
38         if [ $answer = y -o $answer=Y ]        # test for Y or y
39            then
40               grep -iv "$title;$author;$category;$status;$bname;$date"
               ULIB_FILE > TEMP
41               mv TEMP ULIB_FILE
42         fi
43   else                                   # if book not found
44      tput cup 7 10 ; echo "$response no found"
45   fi
46      tput cup 15 10 ; echo "Any more to look? (Y)es or (N)o _\b\c"
47      read answer                         # read user answer
48      case $answer in                     # check user answer
49         [Yy]* ) answer=y ;;              # any word starting with Y or y is yes
50            * ) answer=n ;;               # any other word indicates no
51      esac
52   done                                   # end of the while loop
53   IFS=OLD_IFS                            # restore the IFS to its original value
54   exit 0                                 # exit
```

Figure 12–30
The DELETE program display.

```
              UNIX Library - DELETE MODE

                      Title :  UNIX Unbounded
                     Author :  Afzal Amir
                   Category :  textbook
                     Status :  out
              Checked out by :  Steve Fraser
                       Date :  12/12/99


           Delete this book? (Y)es or (N)o > Y


           Any more to delete (Y)es or (N)o > _
```

[y], and the record is deleted. Any other letter fails the test, the body of the **if** is skipped, and the record is not deleted.

Line 40: This line saves (copies) every record in the ULIB_FILE file to the TEMP file, except the specified record which is currently displayed. It does that by using the **grep** command with the **i** and **v** options and redirecting the output of the **grep** from the terminal display to the TEMP file.

Line 41: This line uses the **mv** command to rename the TEMP file to ULIB_FILE file. Now the ULIB_FILE file contains every record except the deleted record.

Figure 12–30 shows a sample of the DELETE program display, assuming the delete function is selected from the edit menu and the specified book exits in the ULIB_FILE file.

12.5.9   The *REPORTS* Program

The other branch of the hierarchy chart (figure 12–9) handles the reports produced by using the information stored in the ULIB_FILE file. The REPORTS program is activated whenever you select function 2 from the main menu. This program is a driver for the reports menu and is similar to the EDIT program. It shows the reports menu, and according to your selection it activates appropriate programs to produce the desired report. It consists of a **while** loop that covers the whole program. The body of the **while** loop consists of the code for the reports menu and a **case** construct that determines what commands must be executed to satisfy your selection.

Figure 12–31 shows the REPORTS program source code. There is no need for line-by-line explanation. You know it all! However, there is another program involved. The program called REPORT_NO is called to produce the desired reports. Depending on the report selection each time, a different report number is specified on the command line. This report number (1, 2, or

Figure 12–31

Source code for the the REPORTS program.

```
 1 #
 2 # UNIX library
 3 # REPORTS: This program is the main driver for the REPORTS menu.
 4 #           It shows the reports menu, and invokes the appropriate program
 5 #           according to the user selection.
 6 #
 7 error_flag=0                      # initialize the error flag, indicating no error
 8 while true                        # loop forever
 9   do
10     if [ $error_flag  -eq 0 ]     # check for the error
11       then
12         tput clear ; tput cup  5 10 # clear screen and place the cursor
13         echo "UNIX Library - ${BOLD}REPORTS MENU${NORMAL}"
14         tput cup  7 20                      # place the cursor
15         echo "0:  ${BOLD}RETURN${NORMAL} To The Main Menu"
16         tput cup  9 20 ; echo "1: Sorted by${BOLD}TITLE${NORMAL}"
17         tput cup 11 20  ; echo "2: Sorted by${BOLD}AUTHOR${NORMAL}"
18         tput cup 13 20  ; echo "3: Sorted by${BOLD}CATEGORY${NORMAL}"
19     fi
20     error_flag=0                  # reset error flag
21     tput cup 17 10 ; echo "Enter your choice> _\b\c"
22     read choice                   # read user choice
23 #
24 # case construct for checking the user selection
25 #
26     case $choice in               # check user input
27        0 ) exit 0 ;;              # return to the main menu
28        1 ) REPORT_NO 1 ;;         # call REPORT_NO program, passing 1 to it
29        2 ) REPORT_NO 2 ;;         # call REPORT_NO program, passing 2 to it
30        3 ) REPORT_NO 3 ;;         # call REPORT_NO program, passing 3 to it
31        * ) ERROR 20 10            # call ERROR program
32            tput cup 20 1 ;  tput ed # clear the rest of the screen
33            error_flag=1 ;;        # set error flag to indicate error
34     esac                          # end of the case construct
35 done                             # end of the while construct
```

Figure 12–32

The REPORTS menu.

```
              UNIX Library - REPORTS MENU


              0: RETURN To The Main Menu
              1: Sorted by the TITLE
              2: Sorted by the AUTHOR
              3: Sorted by the CATEGORY
         Enter your choice> _
```

3) is stored in the *$1* positional variable and is accessed in the REPORT_NO program to identify the desired report.

Figure 12–32 shows the reports menu, assuming the report function is selected from the main menu.

12.5.10   The *REPORT_NO* Program

The REPORT_NO program is activated whenever you select a report number from the reports menu. This program checks the value in the *$1* positional variable and sorts the ULIB_FILE according to this value. If *$1* value is 1, then ULIB_FILE is sorted on the *title* field, the first field in the record. If the *$1* value is 2, then ULIB_FILE file is sorted on the *author* field, the second field in the record, and so on.

The sorted records are saved in the file called TEMP, and it is this file that can be passed to the **pg** or **pr** (see Chapter 8) command to be displayed. However, the report is not nicely arranged and fields in each record are separated by semicolons, similar to figure 12–27. To make the output presentable, records are read from the TEMP file, formatted, and then stored in PTEMP. It is the PTEMP file which is passed to **pg** command to be displayed.

Figure 12–33 shows the REPORT_NO program source code. The line-by-line explanation of some new lines of code in the program follows.

Lines 9, 10, and 11: These lines are the body of the **case** construct. Each of these lines executes a **sort** (see chapter 8) command to sort the ULIB_FILE according to a specified field. The output of the **sort** command is stored in the TEMP file. Let's look at the **sort** options used in each command.

- The **-f** option considers all lowercase letters to be uppercase letters.
- The **-d** option ignores all blanks or nonalphanumeric characters.
- The number option (**+2** and **+3**) sorts the file on the field specified by the field number. In ULIB_FILE, field 1 is the *title* field, field 2 is the *author* field, and field 3 is the *category* field. Those are the three fields of interest in the REPORT_NO program.

Lines 17–33: These lines make the **while** loop that continues until all the records in the TEMP file have been read. The return status of the **read** command is tested, which is 0 (zero) as long as there are records in the TEMP file and is 1 (one) when it reaches the end of the file. The body of the loop is very similar to the DISPLAY program, but the output of the **echo** commands are redirected from the terminal display to the PTEMP file.

Line 33: This line is the end of the **while** loop, and the **< temp** redirects input from the standard input to the TEMP file. This is called loop redirection, and the Bourne shell runs a redirected loop in a subshell. When the loop is ended, the PTEMP contains the sorted and formated report that can be displayed using any number of commands. Here the **pg** command is used.

Line 37: This line displays the PTEMP. The **pg** command shows the report one screenful at a time, and using the **pg** (see chapter 8) options you can scan your report.

Figure 12–33
Source code for the REPORT_NO program.

```
 1  #
 2  #  UNIX library
 3  #  REPORT_NO: This program produces reports from the ULIB_FILE file.
 4  #              It checks for the report number passed to it on the command
 5  #              line, sorts, and produces reports accordingly
 6  #
 7   IFS=";"                                    # set delimiter to ;
 8   case $1 in                                 # check the content of the $1
 9       1 ) sort -f -d  ULIB_FILE > TEMP ;;    # sort on title field
10       2 ) sort -f -d +1 ULIB_FILE > TEMP ;; # sort on author field
11       3 ) sort -f -d +2 ULIB_FILE >TEMP ;;  # sort on category field
12   esac                                       # end of the case

13  #
14  #  read records from the sorted file TEMP. Format and store them in
15  #  PTEMP.
16  #
17   While read title author category status bname date        # read a record
         do
18       echo "       Title: $title"  >> PTEMP                 # format title
19       echo "      Author: $author" >> PTEMP                 # format author
20       case $category in                                     # check the category
21             [T t] [Bb] )  word=textbook  ;;
22             [Ss] [Yy] [Ss] )  word=system ;;
23             [Rr] [Ee] [Ff]  )  word=reference ;;
24                   * )  word=undefined  ;;
25       esac
26       echo "    Category: $word" >> PTEMP                   # format category
27       echo "      Status: $status" >> PTEMP                 # format status
28       if [ "$status" = "out" ]                              # if it is checked out
29          then                                               # then
30             echo "Checked out by: $bname" >>  PTEMP         # format bname
31             echo "              Date: $date\n\n" >> PTEMP   # format date
32          fi
33   done < TEMP                                 # end of the while loop

34  #
35  #  ready to display the formatted records in the PTIME

36
37   pg -c -p "Page %d:"  PTIME                  # display PTIME page by page

38   rm TEMP PTEMP                               # remove files

39   exit 0                                      # end of the program
```

Let's look at the options used in this command.

- The **-c** option clears the screen before displaying each page.
- The **-p** option places the specified string at the bottom of the screen instead of the default colon prompt. Here, the specified string is **Page %d:**. The character sequence *% d* stands for the current screen number.

Line 38: The two files **TEMP** and **PTEMP** are deleted.

Figure 12–34 shows a sample of a report produced by selecting the option 2 from the reports menu. The report is sorted on the second field, the author of the books.

The prompt at the bottom of the screen shows the page number. You can press [Return] to display the next page or type any other **pg** *action command to see your desired part of the report.*

Figure 12–34
A sample report produced by REPORT_NO.

```
              Title: UNIX Unbound
              Author: Afzal Amir
           Category: textbook
               Status: out
   Checked out by: Steve Fraser
              Date: 1/12/99

   Title: UNIX For All
              Author: Brown David
           Category: reference
               Status: in

   Title: A Brief UNIX Guide
              Author: Redd Emma
           Category: reference
               Status: out
   Checked out by: Steve Fraser
              Date: 1/12/99


   Page 1:
```

Command Summary

The following commands were introduced in this chapter.

trap
This command sets and resets the interrupt signals. The following table shows some of the signals you can use to control the termination of your program.

Signal Number	Name	Meaning
1	hang up	Terminal connection is lost.
2	interrupt	One of the interrupt keys is pressed.
3	quit	One of the quit keys is pressed.
4	kill	The kill -9 command is issued.
15	terminator	The kill command is issued.

stty
This command sets options that control the capabilities of your terminal. There are over hundred different settings, and the following table lists only some of the options.

Option	Operation
echo [-echo]	Echoes [does not echo] the typed characters; the default is echo.
raw [-raw]	Disables [enables] the special meaning of the metacharacters; the default is **-raw**.
intr	Generates an interrupt signal; usually [Del] is used.
erase	[Backspace]. Erases the preceding character, usually the [#] key is used.
kill	Deletes the entire line; usually [@] or [Ctrl-u] is used.
eof	Generates the (end -of-file) signal from terminal; usually [Ctrl-d] is used.
ek	Resets the erase and kill keys to [#] and [@] respectively.
sane	Sets the terminal characteristic to sensible default values.

tput
This command is used with the terminfo database, which contains codes for terminal characteristics and facilitates the manipulation of your terminal characteristics such as bold text, clear screen, etc.

Option	Operation
bell	Echoes the terminal's bell character.
blink	Makes blinking display.
bold	Makes bold display.
clear	Clears the screen.
cup *r c*	Moves cursor to the row *r* and column *c*.
dim	Dims the display.
ed	Clears from the cursor position to the end of the screen.
el	Clears from the cursor position to the end of the line.
smso	Starts stand out mode.
rmso	Ends stand out mode.
rmul	Starts underline mode.
rmul	Ends underline mode.
rev	Shows reverse video, black on white display.

Review Exercises

1. What is the **trap** command for?

2. How do you terminate a process?

3. Where do you use the **trap** command?

4. What is the command to display your terminal settings?

5. What is the terminfo database? What information is stored in it?

Terminal Session

The following terminal session gives you the opportunity to practice some of the commands on your terminal and write/modify the programs in this chapter.

1. What type is your terminal?

2. Display a partial listing of your terminal settings.

3. Display a full listing of your terminal settings.

4. Change the setting for the kill key. Check whether it is changed.

5. Change the setting for the erase key. Check whether it is changed.

6. Reset the erase and kill keys to # and @ respectively.

7. Check if you have the **tput** utility on your system.

8. Use the **tput** command to clear the screen.

9. Write a script file named CLS that clears the screen when it is invoked.

10. Write a script file similar to the MENU program. Make your menu show some of the commands you often use but have trouble remembering the exact syntax of, or of those that are long and you are tired of typing.

11. Change the UNIX library program of this chapter to store more information about each book, for example, the price of the book, date of publication, etc.

12. Make the REPORTS program more sophisticated. For example, give the user a choice of reports to be printed or displayed on the terminal.

13. There is lots of room for improvement in the ULIB program. For example, the problem of having more than one book with the same author, or same book title with different authors is not addressed. Can you fix it?

14. The UNIX library program can be used as a prototype for other similar programs. For example, it can be adapted to store names, addresses, and phone numbers of your friends (creating a personal phone directory), or make a database to keep track of your music CDs and records. Use your imagination, and write the code to create an application similar to the UNIX library program that is useful and you can use in your environment.

CHAPTER 13

Farewell to UNIX

Now that we've covered the UNIX basics and you know a little bit about shell programming, it's time to add a few flourishes. The commands discussed in this chapter include disk commands, file manipulation commands, and spelling commands. You have already learned quite a few file manipulation commands, and the new commands in this chapter complement your previous knowledge. The chapter concludes with a few security and system administration commands to help you understand more about the UNIX system and give you a more comfortable feeling about your system.

In This Chapter

13.1   DISK SPACE

There is a limit to number of files you can store on a disk or in a file system. That limit depends on two things:

- the total amount of storage space available
- the amount of space set aside for i-nodes

An i-node number (discussed fully in chapter 7) is assigned to each file in the system; these numbers are kept in the i-node list. An i-node contains specific file information, such as its location on the disk, its size, and so on.

13.1.1   Finding Available Disk Space: The *df* Command

You can use the **df** (disk free) command to find the total amount of disk space or the space available on a specified file system. If you don't specify a particular file system on the command line, then the **df** command reports the free space for all file systems.

Find the total amount of disk space available.

```
$ df [Return] . . . . . . . . . . . . . . . . . . . . No name is specified.

    /           ( /dev/dsk/c0d0s0 ).      14534  blocks      2965  i-nodes

    /usr        ( /dev/dsk/c0d0s2 ).     203028  blocks     51007  i-nodes

$_ . . . . . . . . . . . . . . . . . . . . . . . . . . Ready for the next command.
```

The output shows that this system has three file systems. The first value is the number of free blocks, and the second is the number of free i-nodes. Each block is usually a 512-byte block; some systems use 1024-byte blocks for this report.

-t Option   Using the **-t** option makes the **df** include the total number of blocks in the file system in the output.

Invoke the **df** command with the **-t** option.

```
$ df -t [Return] . . . . . . . . . . . . . . . . . . . Use the -t option.

    /           ( /dev/dsk/c0d0s0 ).      14534  blocks     2965  i-nodes

                              total: 31552  blocks     3936  i-nodes
    /usr        ( /dev/dsk/c0d0s2 ).     203028  blocks    51007  i-nodes
                              total: 539136 blocks    65488 i-nodes

$_ . . . . . . . . . . . . . . . . . . . . . . . . . . Prompt.
```

See page xxii for an explanation of icons used to highlight information in this chapter.

You may want to place the **df** *command in your* .profile *file, so you get a report as soon as you log in.*

13.1.2   Summarizing Disk Usage: The *du* Command

You can use the **du** (disk usage) command to obtain a report that includes each directory in the file system, the number of blocks used by the files in that directory, and its subdirectories. This command is useful when you want to know how the space on a file system is being used.

Obtain a disk usage report on the current directory and its subdirectories.

$ du [Return]. . . . . Report disk usage on current directory.

22	./source/basic
35	./source/c
26	./source
122	./memos
997	.

$_ . . . . Prompt.

The current directory is indicated by dot (.). Here the /source/basic occupies 22 blocks, /source/c occupies 35 blocks, and so on.

The **du** *command can be used to obtain reports on any directory structure.*

du Options

Table 13–1 summarizes the **du** command options, and explanations and examples for each option follow.

-a Option   The **-a** option displays the space used by each file in the specified directory, as well as the directory.

Table 13–1
The **du** command options.

Option	Operation
-a	Displays the directories and file sizes.
-s	Displays only the total blocks for the specified directory: subdirectories are not listed.

Assuming your current directory is source, find the space used by the specified directory. Also list each file in the directory.

$ **du -a basic [Return]** . . . . Use the **-a** option.

2	. /basic/first.bas
65	. /basic/basic.doc
16	. /basic/menu.bas
26	. /basic
5	.

$_ . . . . Ready for the next command.

-s Option   The **-s** option makes **du** report the total amount of the storage used by a directory and suppresses the reports about the subdirectories.

Find the grand total for the current directory, without listing the subdirectories.

$ **du -s [Return]** . . . . Use the **-s** option.

2634

$_ . . . . Ready for the next command.

13.2   FILE MANIPULATION

The following commands facilitate the search to locate a specific file in a crowded hierarchy of directories, and to display a specified portion of a file for a quick look.

13.2.1   Finding Files: The *find* Command

You can use the **find** command to locate files that match a given set of criteria in a hierarchy of directories. The criterion may be a filename or a specified property of a file (such as its modification date, size, or type). You can also direct the command to remove, print, or otherwise act on the file. The **find** command is a very useful and important command that is not used to its full potential. Maybe its unusual command format is discouraging.

The format of the **find** command is different from the other UNIX commands. Let's look at its syntax:

find *pathname   search options   action option*

where *pathname* indicates the directory name that **find** begins its search, and continues down to the subdirectories and their subdirectories and so on. This process of branching search is called *recursive search*. The *search option* part identifies which file you are interested in, and the *action option* part tells what to do with the file once it is found. Let's look at a simple example:

$ **find . -print [Return]**

This command displays the names of all the files in the specified directory and all its subdirectories.

1. *The specified directory is indicated by a dot, meaning the current directory.*

2. *The options after the pathname always start with a hyphen (-). The action option part indicates what to do with the files. In this case* **-print** *means to display them.*

Don't forget the **-print** action key. Without it ,**find** doesn't display any filenames.

Search Options

Table 13–2 shows a partial list of the search options and explanations of the options follows.

-name Option   You use the search option to find a file by its name. You type **-name** followed by the desired filename. The filename can be a simple filename or you can use the shell wild card substitution: [ ], ?, and *. If you use these special characters, place the filename in single quotation marks. Let's look at some examples.

Table 13–2
The **find** command search options.

Operator	Description
-name *filename*	Finds files with the given *filename*.
size ±n	Finds files with the size *n*.
-type *file type*	Finds files with the specified access mode.
-atime ±n	Finds files that were accessed *n* days ago.
-mtime ±n	Finds files that were modified *n* days ago.
-newer *filename*	Finds files that were modified more recently than *filename*.

The **+n** notation in table 13–2 is a decimal number that can be specified as **+n** (meaning more than *n*) or **-n** (meaning less than *n*) or **n** (meaning exactly *n*).

Find some files by name.

> $ **find . -name first.c -print [Return]**. . . Find files named *first.c.*
>
> $ **find . -name ".c" -print [Return]** . . . . Find all files whose names end
>   in *.c.*
>
> $ **find . -name ".?" -print [Return]** . . . . Find all files whose names end
>   with a single character preceded by
>   a period.

1. *In all of the preceding commands, the directory name is the current directory.*

2. *The* **-name** *option identifies the filename. The wild card may be used to generate the filename.*

3. *The action part* **-print** *is to display the name of the file found.*

-size +n Option   You use this search option to find a file by its size in blocks. You type **-size** followed by the number of blocks indicating the size of the file to be checked. The plus or minus sign before the number of blocks indicates greater than or less than, respectively. Let's look at some examples.

Find some files by size.

> $ **find . -name ".c" -size 20 -print [Return]**. . . Find files that are exactly 20 blocks
>   large.

This command finds all files that have filenames that end with *.c* and that are exactly 20 blocks large.

> $ **find . -name ".c" -size +20 -print [Return]** . Find files that are larger than 20
>   blocks.
>
> $ **find . -name ".c" -size -20 -print [Return]** . . Find files that are smaller than 20
>   blocks.

-type Option   You use this search option to find a file by its type. You type **-type** followed by a letter specifying the file type. The *file types* are as follows:

- *b*: a block special file (such as your disk)
- *c*: a character special file (such as your terminal)
- *d*: a directory file (such as your directories)
- *f*: an ordinary file (such as your files)

Find files using the *file type* option.

> $ **find $HOME -type f -print [Return]** . . . . Use the **-type** option.

This command finds all ordinary files and displays their pathnames.

-atime Option You use this search option to find a file by its last access date. You type **-atime** followed by the number of days since the file was last accessed. The plus or minus sign before the number of days indicates greater than or less than, respectively. Let's look at some examples.

Find files by their last access times.

> $ **find . -atime 10 -print [Return]** . . . . . . Find and displays files last
> accessed exactly 10 days ago.

This command displays the name of the files that have not been read for exactly 10 days.

> $ **find . -atime -10 -print [Return]** . . . . . Find and display files last accessed less
> than 10 days ago.

> $ **find . -atime +10 -print [Return]** . . . . . Find and display files last accessed more
> than 10 days ago.

-mtime Option You use this search option to find a file by its last modification date. You type **-mtime** followed by the number of days since the file was last modified. The plus or minus sign before the number of days indicates greater than or less than, respectively. Let's look at some examples.

Find files by their last modification times.

> $ **find . -mtime 10 -print [Return]** . . . . . Find and display files last modified
> exactly 10 days ago.

This command displays the name of the files that are exactly 10 days old.

> $ **find . -mtime -10 -print [Return]** . . . . . Find and display files last modified less
> than 10 days ago.

> $ **find . -mtime +10 -print [Return]** . . . . Find and display files last modified more
> than 10 days ago.

-newer Option You use this search option to find a file modified more recently than a specified filename.

Let's look at an example.

> $ **find . -newer first.c -print [Return]** . . Find and display files modified more
> recently than *first.c* was.

Action Options

The action options tell **find** what to do with files once they are found. Table 13–3 summarizes the three action options.

-print Option   The **-print** action option displays the pathname of the files found that match the specified criterion.

Find pathnames to files called first.c, starting from the home directory.

> **$ find $HOME -name first.c -print [Return]** . . . Find first.c and display the
>   pathnames.
>
> /usr/david/first.c
> /usr/david/source/first.c
> /user/david/source/c/first.c
>
> $_ . . . . Prompt.

The output shows there are three instances of the file first.c *in David's hierarchy of directories.*

-exec Option   The **-exec** action option lets you give a command to be applied to the found files. You type **-exec** followed by the specified command, a space, backslash, and then a semicolon. You can use a set of braces ({}) to represent the name of the files found. An example will help to clarify the sequence.

Find and delete all instances of the first.c file that are 90 days old.

> **$ find . -name first.c - mtime + 90 -exec rm { } \ ; [Return]**
>
> $_ . . . . Prompt.

The search starts from your current directory (represented by .) and is continued through the hierarchy of the directories. The **find** command locates and removes instances of first.c that are 90 days old.

Table 13–3
The find command action options.

Operator	Description
-print	Prints the pathname for every file found.
-exec *command* \;	Lets you give *commands* to be applied to the files.
-ok *command* \;	Asks for confirmation before applying the command.

Two search options are in effect: the **-name** and the **-mtime** options. That means **find** is seeking files that simultaneously satisfy these two search categories.

The command is comprised of many parts, and its syntax is peculiar:

1. the **-exec** option followed by the command (in this case **rm**)
2. a set of braces **{}** followed by a space
3. a backslash (\) followed by a semicolon

All instances of the first.c are deleted. No warning or feedback message is displayed. When you see the $ prompt, the job is done.

-ok Option   The **-ok** action option is just like the **-exec** option, except that it asks for your confirmation before applying the command to the file.

Find and delete all instances of the first.c file, but ask for confirmation before deleting any file.

> $ **find . -name first.c + 90 -ok rm { } \ ; [Return]**
>
> $_ . . . . Prompt.

If a file, for example first.c, satisfies the criterion, then the following prompt is displayed:

> < rm **...** ./source/first.c > ?

If you replay with [Y] or [y], the command is executed (in this case, file.c is deleted); otherwise, your file remains intact.

*You can also use the logical operators **or**, **and**, and **not** to combine the search options. The search starts from your current directory, and it is continued through the hierarchy of the directories.*

13.2.2   Displaying the End of a File: The *tail* Command

You can use the **tail** command to display the last part (the tail end) of a specified file. The **tail** command gives you a quick way to check the contents of a file.

For example, to display the last part of the file called MEMO in your current directory, you type the following:

> $ **tail MEMO [Return]**

By default, **tail** shows the last 10 lines of the specified file. You can override the default value by using one of the available options.

tail Options   The **tail** options are summarized in table 13–4, and they cause the **tail** command to count by blocks, characters, or lines.

Table 13–4
The **tail** command options.

Option	Operation
b	This option causes tail to count by blocks.
c	This option causes tail to count by characters.
l	This option causes tail to count by lines.

1. If a plus sign precedes the option, **tail** counts from the beginning of the file.
2. If a hyphen precedes the option, **tail** counts from the end of the file.
3. If a number precedes the option, **tail** uses that number instead of the default ten lines count.

The following command sequences demonstrate the use of the **tail** command.

$ **tail MEMO [Return]**. . . . . Display the last 10 lines (**no option**).

$ **tail +l MEMO [Return]** . . . . Display the last 10 lines (**+l**).

$ **tail -4 MEMO [Return]** . . . . Display the last 4 lines (**-4**).

$ **tail -10c MEMO [Return]**. . . . . Display the last 10 characters (**-10c**).

You can specify only one filename as an argument.

13.3   MORE UNIX COMMANDS

This section adds to your command repertoire and introduces new commands that help you to manipulate certain aspects of the UNIX environment, create banners, and obtain necessary information about the status of your programs.

13.3.1   Displaying Banners: The *banner* Command

You can use the **banner** command to produce output in large letters. It displays its arguments (10 characters or less) on the standard output, one argument per line. This is useful to create banners, signs, report titles, etc.

Make a **happy birthday** banner.

$ **banner happy birthday | lp [Return]** . Make a banner and send it to the printer.

$_ . . . . Prompt.

The pipe (|) routes the output to the printer. Each word (argument) is printed on a separate line. You can use quotation marks to make two or more words a single argument.

Make a **GO HOME** banner, with both words on the same line.

> $ **banner "GO HOME" | lp [Return]**
>
> $_ . . . . Prompt.

13.3.2   Running Commands at a Later Time: The *at* Command

You use the **at** command to run a command or list of commands at a later time. This is useful if you want to run your programs when the computer is less busy, or when you want to send mail on a certain date. You can specify the time and date part of the command in various formats, and the syntax is quite flexible.

On any given UNIX system, there may be restrictions on who can use the **at** command. The system administrator can limit the access to the **at** command to only a few users. You can try it; if you are not authorized, the following message is displayed:

> at: You are not authorized to use at. Sorry.

1. *You specify on the command line the time and date on which you want your command to be carried out.*

2. *You don't have to be logged in when the commands are scheduled to run.*

Specifying the Time

If the time part of the **at** command is one or two digits (HH format), then it is interpreted as the time in hours. Thus, 04 and 4 both mean four o'clock in the morning. If the time part is four digits (HHMM format), then it is interpreted as time and minutes. Thus 0811 is 08:11. You can also specify the time by typing the word *noon*, *midnight*, or *now* in the time part of the command.

UNIX assumes a 24-hour clock, unless you specify am or pm suffix. Accordingly, 2011 is 08:11 pm.

Specifying the Date

The date part of the **at** command can be a day of the week such as Wednesday or Wed (three-letter abbreviation). It can be in month, day, and year format such as Aug 10, 2001. It can also consist of the special word *today* or *tomorrow*. Here are some examples of legal **at** time and date formats.

> $ **at 1345 Wed [Return]** . . . . Run a job on Wednesday at 1:45 p.m.
>
> $ **at 0145 pm Wed [Return]** . . . . Run a job on Wednesday at 1:45 p.m.

$ at 0925 am Sep 18 [Return] . . . . Run a job on September 19 at 9:25 a.m.

$ at 11:00 pm tomorrow [Return] . . . . Run a job tomorrow at 11 p.m.

The following commands sequences show how to use the **at** command and specify time and date in different formats.

Run a job at 4 a.m. the next day.

$ at 04 tomorrow [Return]. . . . . Specify time and date.

$ sort BIG_FILE [Return] . . . . Sort BIG_FILE.

$ [Ctrl-d] . . . . Indicate end of the input.

user= david . . . . 75969600.a . . . Wed Jan 26 14:32:00

$_ . . . . Ready for the next command.

The **sort** command is invoked tomorrow morning at 4 o'clock. The job ID number is (75969600.a).

What does **at** do with the possible output produced by your command—in this case, the output of **sort**? If you don't specify an output file, the output is mailed to you, and you can find it in your mailbox.

Run a job using output redirection.

$ at 04 tomorrow [Return]. . . . . Specify time and date.

$ sort BIG_FILE > BIG_SORT[Return] . . . . . Save output in BIG_SORT.

$ [Ctrl-d]. . . . . Indicate end of the command list.

user= david   75969600.a   Wed Jan 26 14:32:00

$_ . . . . Prompt.

The output of the **sort** command is redirected to the BIG_FILE.

You can use **cat**, **vi**, *or any of the pagination commands to look at the* BIG_FILE *file.*

Run a job using input redirection.

$ at noon Wed [Return] . . . . At noon on Wednesday.

mailx david < memo [Return] . . . . Mail to **david** the memo file.

[Ctrl-d] . . . . End list of the commands.

user= david . . . . 75969600.a . . . Wed Jan 26 14:32:00   2001

$_ . . . . Prompt.

This mails your memo to **david** at noon on Thursday. A file called memo must be in your current directory before noon on Thursday.

Execute the script file called cmd_file at 3:30 p.m. on Friday.

```
$ at 1530 Fri < cmd_file [Return] . . . . . Input comes from cmd_file.
user = david . . . . . . . . . 75969601.a . . . Fri Jan 28 14:32:00 2001
$_ . . . . . . . . . . . . . . . . . . . . . . . . . . . . Ready for the next command.
```

at Options   Table 13–5 summarizes the **at** command options.

Show the list of your jobs that are scheduled to run later (submitted to **at**).

```
$ at -l [Return] . . . . . . . . . . . . . . . . . . . . List all jobs.
75969601.a. . . . . . . . . . . . . . at  Fri Jan 26 14:32:00 2001
$_ . . . . . . . . . . . . . . . . . . . . . . . . . . . Prompt.
```

Remove a job from the **at** job queue.

```
$ at -r 75969601.a [Return] . . . . . . . . . . Remove the job.
$ at -l [Return] . . . . . . . . . . . Check the at queue.
$_ . . . . . . . . . . . . . . . . . . . . Nothing in the queue.
```

You must specify the job process ID you intend to remove from the queue. You can remove more than one job from the queue by specifying the jobs' process IDs on the command line, separated by a space.

Table 13–5
The **at** command options.

Option	Operation
-l	Lists all jobs that are submitted with **at**.
-m	Mails you a short message of confirmation at completion of the job.
-r	Removes the specified job numbers from the queue of jobs scheduled by **at**.

13.3.3   Revealing the Command Type: The *type* Command

The **type** command is useful when you want to know more about a command. It shows whether the specified command is a shell program or a shell built-in command. The *built-in commands* are part of the shell, and no child process is created when any of them is invoked.

Let's look at some examples.

$ **type pwd [Return]** . . . . More about the **pwd** command.

pwd is a shell built-in

$ **type ls [Return]**. . . . . And the **ls** command.

ls is /bin/ls

$ **type cat [Return]**. . . . . The **cat** command.

cat is a shell built-in

$_ . . . . Prompt.

13.3.4   Timing Programs: The *time* Command

You can use the **time** command to obtain information about the computer time your command uses. It reports the real time, user time, and system time. You type **time** followed by the command name you want to time.

Real time is the actual time (*elapsed time*) from the moment you enter the command until the command is finished. This includes I/O time, time spent waiting for other users, and so on. The real time can be several times greater than the total CPU time.

User time is the CPU time dedicated to the execution of your command.

System time is the time spent executing UNIX kernel routines to service your command.

CPU time is time in seconds and fractions of seconds that the CPU spends to execute your command.

Report the time it takes to sort BIG_FILE.

$ **time sort BIG_FILE > BIG_FILE.SORT [Return]**

60.8 real   11.4 user   4.6 sys

$ . . . . Ready for the next command.

The reports show that the program will run for 60.8 seconds of real time, using 11.4 seconds of user time, and 4.6 seconds of system time, for a total of 16 seconds of the CPU time.

13.3.5   Reminder Service: The *calendar* Command

You can use the **calendar** command to remind yourself of your appointments and other things you want to do. To use this service, you must create a file called calendar in your HOME or the current directory. It displays those lines in the calendar file that contain today's or tomorrow's date. If your system is set up to run the **calendar** command automatically, then it sends you e-mail that contains appropriate lines from your calendar file. You can also run the **calendar** command at the $ prompt to display lines from your calendar file.

The date in each line can be expressed in various formats. Figure 13–1 shows an example of a calendar file, with each line containing a different format of the date string.

Run the **calendar** command, assuming today is January 22.

$ **calendar [Return]** . . . . Run the command.

1/22 You have dentist appointment.

Meet with your advisor on January 22

The BIG MEETING Jan. 23

$_ . . . . Prompt.

Any line in the calendar file that contains the date 1/22 or 1/23 is displayed.

You can place the **calendar** *command in your* .profile *(startup file) so you are informed of your schedule as soon as you log in.*

Figure 13–1
Example of a calendar file.

```
$ cat calendar

1/20  Call David

Meet with your advisor on January 22

1/22  You have dentist appointment.

The BIG MEETING Jan. 23

3/21  Time to clean up your desk
$_
```

13.4   SPELLING ERROR CORRECTION

You can use the **spell** command to check the spelling of the words in your documents. The **spell** command compares the words in a specified file against a dictionary file. It displays the words that are not found in the dictionary file. You can specify more than one file, but when no file is specified, **spell** gets its input from the default input device, your keyboard. Let's look at some examples.

Run the **spell** command without specifying any filename.

> **$ spell [Return]** . . . . No argument is specified.
>
> **lookin goood [Return]**. . . . . Input is from keyboard.
>
> **[Ctrl-d]** . . . . End of input.
>
> lookin
> goood
>
> $_ . . . . And the prompt.

You signal the end of your input by pressing [Ctrl-d] at the beginning of a line. The **spell** command does not suggest correct spelling, it just displays the suspected words. The output is one word per line.

The **spell** command is case sensitive: it is happy with *David* but complains about *david*.

Assuming you have a file called my_doc, check its spelling and save the output in another file.

> **$ spell my_doc > bad_words [Return]** . . . . . Spell check my_doc.
>
> $_ . . . . Prompt.

The **spell** command output is redirected to the bad_words file. You can use the **cat** command to look at this file.

You can specify more than one file as the **spell** command argument. The specified filenames are separated by at least one space.

Assuming you are in the vi editor, invoke the spell checker.

> : **!spell [Return]** . . . . Invoke the spell checker.
>
> **pervious**. . . . . Type the word whose spelling you are in doubt about.
>
> **[Ctrl-d]** . . . . Indicate end of the input.
>
> pervious . . . . Misspelled word.
>
> [Hit return to continue]

Table 13–6
The **spell** command options.

Option	Operation
-b	Checks for British spelling
-v	Displays words which are not in the spelling list, and their derivation
-x	Displays plausible stems for each word being checked

You can invoke any command from within vi by pressing [!] at the colon prompt followed by the name of the command (see chapter 6).

spell Options

Table 13–6 shows the **spell** command options. Explanations and examples for each option follow.

-b Option   This option makes the **spell** command check your file with British spelling. Words like *colour, centre, programme*, etc., are accepted.

-v Option   This option shows all the words that are not literally in the spelling list and their plausible derivations. The derivation are indicated by the plus sign.

Run the **spell** command with the **-v** option. The input is from the keyboard.

```
$ spell -v [Return] . . . . . . . . . . . . . . . Input is expected from the keyboard.

appointment   looking   worked   preprogrammed [Return]

[Ctrl-d] . . . . . . . . . . . . . . . . . . . . . . . . Signal end of your input.
+ ment            appointment
+ ing             looking
+ ed              worked
+ pre             preprogrammed

$_ . . . . . . . . . . . . . . . . . . . . . . . . . . . . Back to the prompt.
```

-x Option   This option displays plausible stems of each word until a matching word is found, or the list is exhausted. The stems are prefixed by the equals sign.

Run the **spell** command with the **-x** option and input from the keyboard.

$ **spell -x [Return]** . . . . Input is expected from the keyboard.

appointment looking worked preprogrammed [Return]

[Ctrl-d] . . . . Signal end of your input.

= appointment
= appoint
= looking
= looke
= look
= preprogrammed
= programmed
= worked
= worke
= work

$_ . . . . Back to the prompt.

13.4.1   Creating Your Own Spelling List

On most UNIX systems, you can create your own dictionary file that supplements the standard dictionary with additional words. For example, you can create a file that contains correct spelling of the special words and terms that are specific to your site or project. Using the plus sign option, you specify your dictionary file on the command line. The **spell** command first checks its own dictionary and then checks the words against your file. You can use the vi editor to create your own spelling list.

1. *Each word in your dictionary file must be typed on one line.*

2. *Your dictionary file must be sorted alphabetically.*

Assuming you have created your own dictionary file called my_own, specify that file on the command line using the plus sign option.

$ **spell + my_own BIG_FILE > MISSPELLED_WORDS [Return]**

$_ . . . . Prompt.

The +my_own indicates you want to use your own dictionary file called my_own. The **spell** *command lists the words that are not found in either of the two dictionary files, its own and yours. The output is redirected into MISSPELLED_WORDS file.*

Scenario The default spelling list (dictionary) doesn't contain the shell commands or other UNIX specific words. Therefore, in your text, if you have words such as **grep** and **mkdir**, they are displayed as suspicious words.

Figure 13–2
Example of a dictionary file.

```
$ cat U_DICTIONARY
grep
i-node
ls
mkdir
pwd
```

You can create a file similar to the one depicted in figure 13–2, which contains the shell commands or UNIX words with correct spelling.

 Run the **spell** command with and without your spelling list.

$ **spell + U_DICTIONARY [Return]** . . . . With your spelling list.

grep   pwd   mkdir   ls [Return] . . . . Your input.

$_ . . . . No spelling errors, prompt is back.

$ **spell [Return]** . . . . Without your spelling list.

grep   pwd   mkdir   ls [Return] . . . . Your input, same as before.

```
grep
ls
mkdir
pwd
```

$_ . . . . Prompt is back.

13.5   UNIX SECURITY

Information and computer time are valuable resources that require protection. System security is a very important part of multiuser systems. There are various aspects of system security to consider:

- Keeping unauthorized people from gaining access to the system
- Keeping an authorized user from tempering with the system files or other users' files
- Granting some users with certain privileges

Security on the UNIX systems is implemented by using simple commands, and the system security can be as lax or tight as you desire. Let's examine some of the available means to secure your system.

13.5.1   Password Security

All the information the system needs to know about each user is saved in a file called /etc/passwd. This file includes each user password; however, it is encrypted, using an encoding method that makes the deciphering of the passwords a very difficult task. (Encryption is discussed in more detail later in this section.)

The passwd file contains one entry for each user. Each entry is a line that consists of seven fields, which are separated by colons. The following line shows the format of each line in the passwd file, followed by the explanation of each field in the line.

> login-name:password:user-ID:group-ID:user-info:directory:program

login-name: *This is your login name, the name you enter in response to the login prompt.*

password: This is your encrypted password. In System V release 4, the encrypted password is not stored in the passwd file; instead, it is stored in a file called /etc/shadow and the letter x is used as the placeholder for the password field in the passwd file.

 You can print the /etc/passwd file, but /etc/shadow file is not readable by ordinary users.

user-ID: This field contains the user ID number. The user ID is a unique number assigned to each user, and user ID 0 indicates *super-user*.

group-ID: This field contains the group ID. The group ID identifies the user as a member of a group.

user-info: This field is used to further identify the user. Usually, it contains the user's name.

directory: This field contains the absolute pathname of the home directory assigned to the user.

program: This field contains the program that is executed after the user logs in. Usually it is the shell program. If program is not identified, /usr/bin/sh is as-

Figure 13–3
Sample of the passwd file.

```
$cat /etc/passwd
root:x:0:1:admin:/:/usr/bin/sh
david:x:110:255:David Brown:/home/david:/usr/bin/sh
emma:x:120:255:Emma Redd:/home/emma:/usr/bin/sh
steve:x:130:255:Steve Fraser:/home/steve:/usr/bin/csh
$_
```

The user **steve** login shell is **csh**, and all others log in to **sh** shell.

sumed. You can change your login shell to /usr/bin/csh to log in to cshell, or change it to any other program you wish to log in to.

Figure 13–3 shows some sample entries in the passwd file. This file can be printed out by any user on the system.

13.5.2   File Security

File security limits access to the files. The UNIX system provides you with the commands to specify who can access a file and once accessed, what type of operation can be done on the file.

The **chmod** command was discussed in chapter 11; here we'll explore the other way of setting file permission. When you use the **ls** command with the -**l** option (chapter 5), you get your directory listing in full detail. Part of this detailed information is the pattern of **rwx** on each entry, which represents the file permission. The **chmod** command is used to change the file access mode (permission). For example, if you want to give execution permission on my-file to all users, you type the following:

$ **chmod a= x myfile [Return]**

However, you can specify the new mode as a three-digit number that is computed by adding together the numeric equivalents of the desired permission. Table 13–7 shows the numeric value assigned to each permission letter.

Assuming you have a file called mayflies in your current directory, the following examples uses the **chmod** command to change the file permission. You can use the **ls -l** command to verify the changes.

Change mayflies permission to allow **read**, **write**, and **execute** permission (access) to all users.

$ **chmod 777 mayflies [Return]** . . . . . . Change the *mayflies* access mode.

$_ . . . . Done, prompt is back.

The number 777 is the result of adding each column's (owner, group or other) numeric values. Each of the digits represents one of the columns.

Table 13–7
The file permission numeric equivalents.

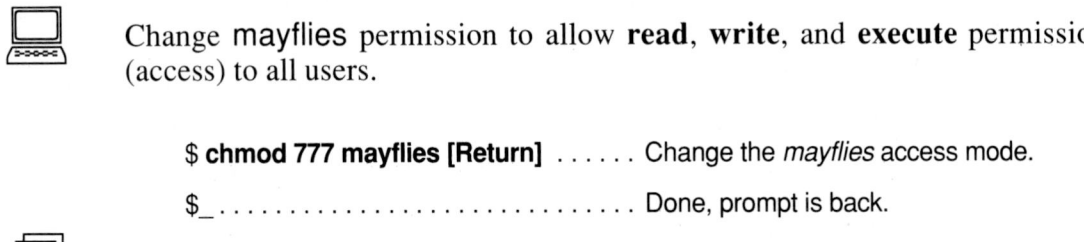

owner			group			other		
r	w	x	r	w	x	r	w	x
4	2	1	4	2	1	4	2	1

Change mayflies permission to allow the **read** access to all but **write** and **execute** access only to the owner.

> $ **chmod 744 mayflies [Return]** . . . . . . Change the *mayflies* access mode.
>
> $_ . . . . Done, the prompt is back.

The digit *7* grants all access to the owner. The first digit *4* grants only the **read** access to the group, and the second digit *4* grants only the **read** access to the other.

Grant all permissions to the owner and group, but only **execute** permission to the others.

> $ **chmod 771 myfile [Return]** . . . . Change the file permission.
>
> $_ . . . . Done, the prompt is back.

The digit *1* grants only the **execute** permission to the other.

13.5.3   Directory Permission

Directories have permission modes that work in a similar manner to file permission modes. However, the directory access permissions have different meanings:

read: The read (**r**) permission in a directory means you can use the **ls** command to list the filenames.

write: The write (**w**) permission in a directory means you can add and remove files from that directory.

execute: The execute (**x**) permission in a directory means you can use the **cd** command to change to that directory or use the directory name as part of a pathname.

Grant access permission for all users on the directory called mybin.

> $ **chmod 777 mybin [Return]**   . . . . Change the access mode of a directory.
>
> $_ . . . . Done, prompt is back.

As with file permissions, each digit stands for one of the user groups (owner, group, and other). Digit *7* means granting write, read, and execute access to a particular group of users.

13.5.4   The Super-user

It is time to know who is the *super-user*, as some of the commands explained in this chapter might be only available to a super-user on your system. The *super-user* is a user who has privileged authority and is not restricted by the file permissions. The system administrator must be a super-user in order to perform administrative tasks such as establishing new accounts, changing passwords, and so on. Usually, the super-user logs in as **root** and can read, write to, or remove any file in the system, or even shut the system down. Super-user status is usually granted to the system administration personnel.

13.5.5   File Encryption: The *crypt* Command

The super-user can access any file regardless of file permissions. How can you protect your sensitive files from others (super-user or not)? UNIX provides the **crypt** command, which encrypts your file and makes it unreadable to others. The **crypt** command changes each character in your file in a reversible way, so you can obtain the original file later. The encoding mechanism relys on simple substitution. For example, the letter *A* in your file is changed to symbol ~. The **crypt** command uses a key to scramble its standard input into an unreadable text that is sent to the standard output.

   The **crypt** command is used for both encryption and decryption. In fact, for decryption of a file, you must provide the same key that you specified its encryption. Let's look at examples.

 Encrypt a file called names in your current directory.

```
$ cat names [Return]. . . . . . . . . . . . . . . . . . . . Display the content of names.

  David     Emma     Daniel     Gabriel     Susan     Marie

$ crypt  xyz  < names > names.crypt [Return] . Use xyz as the encryption key.

$ rm names [Return]. . . . . . . . . . . . . . . . . . . . Remove names.

$ crypt  xyz  < names.crypt > names[Return] . Decode names.crypt.

$ cat names [Return]. . . . . . . . . . . . . . . . . . . . Check content of names.

  David     Emma     Daniel     Gabriel     Susan     Marie

$_ . . . . . . . . . . . . . . . . . . . . . . . . . . . . . . . . . Back to the prompt.
```

The **xyz** is the key used to encrypt the file. The key is actually a password that you use to uncode your file later.

   Using input/output redirection, the input to the command is names, and output is stored in names.crypt.

   Usually, after file encryption, you remove the original copy of the file and leave only the encrypted version, making the information in the file accessible only to someone who knows the encryption key.

Encrypt the names file, not specifying the encryption key on the command line.

> $ **crypt < names > names.crypt [Return]** . . . . . No encryption key is specified.
>
> Key.   . . . . Prompt for entering the key.
>
> $_ . . . . Back to the $ prompt.

If you don't specify the encryption key on the command line, then **crypt** *prompts you to enter one. The key that you enter is not echoed, and this method is preferred over typing the key on the command line.*

If you type the wrong code while entering the password (key) the first time when you encrypt a file, you will not be able to decrypt the file later. As a safety check, you might want to try decrypting the encrypted file before you remove the original.

Command Summary

The following commands were discussed and explored in this chapter.

---

df
This command reports the total amount of the disk space or space available on a specified file system.

---

du
This command summarizes the total space occupied by any directory, its subdirectories, or each file.

Option	Operation
-a	Displays the directories and file sizes.
-s	Displays only the total blocks for the specified directory, and subdirectories are not listed.

---

find
This command locates files that match a given criterion in a hierarchy of directories. With the action options you can tell what to do with the files once they are found.

Search Option	Description
-name *filename*	Finds files with the given *filename*.
size ±*n*	Finds files with the size *n*.
-type *file type*	Finds files with the specified access mode.
-atime ±*n*	Finds files that were accessed *n* days ago.
-mtime ±*n*	Finds files that were modified *n* days ago.
-newer *filename*	Finds files that were modified more recently than *filename*.

Action Option	Description
-print	Prints the pathname for every file found.
-exec *command* \;	Lets you give *commands* to be applied to the files.
-ok *command* \;	Asks for confirmation before applying the command.

---

banner
This command displays its argument, the specified string, in large letters.

---

tail
This command displays the last part (tail end) of a specified file. This is a quick way to check the contents of a file. The options gives the flexibility to specify the desired part of the file.

Option	Operation
b	This option causes tail to count by blocks.
c	This option causes tail to count by characters.
l	This option causes tail to count by lines.

---

spell
This command checks the spelling of the specified document or words entered from the keyboard. It only displays the words not found in the spelling list and does not suggest a correct spelling.

Option	Operation
-b	Checks for British spelling.
-v	Displays words which are not in the spelling list and their derivation.
-x	Displays plausible stems for each word being checked.

---

calendar
This command is a reminder service and reads your schedule from the calendar file in the current directory.

---

at
This command runs your programs at a later time or date. You can specify the time and date in different formats. It executes your commands at the specified time even if you are not logged in.

Option	Operation
-l	Lists all jobs that are submitted with **at**.
-m	Mails you a short message of confirmation at completion of the job.
-r	Removes the specified job numbers from the queue of jobs scheduled by **at**.

chmod
This command changes the access authorities on the files or directories (chapter 9).

crypt
This command encrypts or decrypts your specified file according to a specified key. The encrypted file is not readable, and you must provide the same key used for encrypting the file to decrypt it.

type
This command tells you if the specified command is a built-in command or a shell process.

time
This command times your programs. It reports the real time, user time, and system time for the specified program.

Review Exercises

1. Explain the UNIX system security. What are the ways to secure your file system?

2. Can the super-user delete your files?

3. Can the super-user read your encrypted files?

4. Is the **cd** command a built-in command? How do you find out?

5. What is the command to locate a file and remove it once it is found?

6. Explain *elapsed time*, *user time*, and *system time*.

7. What is the command to look at the last 10 lines of a file?

8. What is the command that reports the disk space?

9. Can you invoke the **spell** command within the vi editor? If so, how?

10. What is the command to use if you want to execute a program at a later time?

11. Do the access modes for files and directories mean the same thing?

Terminal Session

Practice the following commands on your system.

1. Sort a file at 13:00 tomorrow.

2. Send mail to another user at 6 p.m. on Wednesday.

3. Show the last 10 lines of a file.

4. Display the first 5 lines of a file.

5. Save the last 30 characters of a file in another file.

6. Use the **time** command on few commands such as **sort**, **spell**, and so on, and observe the time reports.

7. Change the access mode of your directory to owner only **read**, **write**, and **execute**.

8. Check the spelling in one of your text files.

9. Create your own dictionary file and make the **spell** command use your dictionary file in addition to its own file.

10. Find out the space on the disk.

11. Find out how many blocks are occupied by your home directory and its subdirectories and the files in them.

12. Place the **du** and **df** commands in your .profile file. Observe the reports when you log in.

13. Encrypt a file (if you are authorized). Display the encrypted file on your terminal. Decrypt the file and display it again.

14. Make a banner that shows your initials on the screen.

15. Send your initials banner to the printer.

16. Can you make the system show your initials as soon as you log in?

17. Modify the greetings program (from chapter 12) to show the greetings in large letters.

18. Save the list of all the files that are 7 days old, starting from your home directory.

19. Make a calendar file in your home directory, and type your schedule.

20. Use the **calendar** command to display your current schedule.

21. Place the **calendar** command in your .profile file. Observe the report when you log in.

Appendixes

Command Index

This appendix is a quick index to the commands covered in this book. The commands are in alphabetical order. Numbers after each command indicate the chapter and page numbers.

Command Index
by Category

This appendix is a quick index to the commands covered in this book. The commands are organized according to their functions and in alphabetical order. Numbers after each command indicate the chapter and page numbers.

File and Directory Commands

Communication Commands

Help Commands

Process Control Commands

Line Printer Commands

Information Handling Commands

Terminal Commands

Security Commands

Starting/Ending Sessions

UNIX Editors

Command Summary

The following is a list of the UNIX commands (utilities) in alphabetic order. The numbers after the commands are the chapter and page numbers. To refresh your memory, the command line format is repeated here.

The command line format.

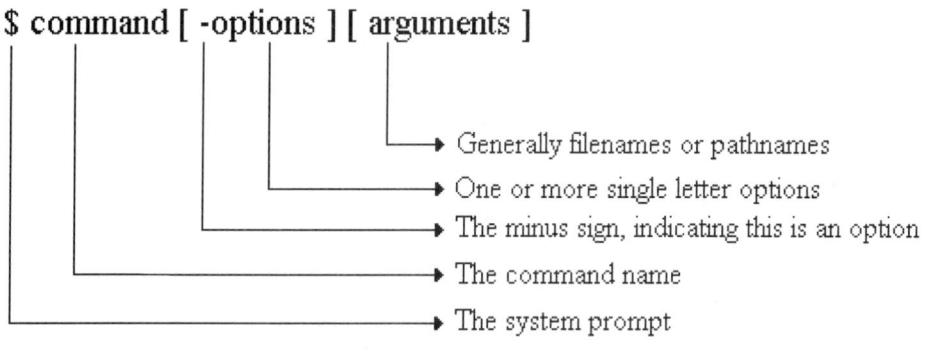

$ command [-options] [arguments]

→ Generally filenames or pathnames
→ One or more single letter options
→ The minus sign, indicating this is an option
→ The command name
→ The system prompt

This command runs your programs at a later time or date. You can specify the time and date in different formats. It executes your commands at the specified time even if you are not logged in.

Option	Operation
-l	Lists all jobs that are submitted with **at**.
-m	Mails you a short message of confirmation at completion of the job.
-r	Removes the specified job numbers from the queue of jobs scheduled by **at**.

banner 385
This command displays its argument, the specified string, in large letters.

cal (calendar) 41
Displays the calendar for specified year, or month of a year.

calendar 386
Reminder service; reads your schedule from the calendar file in the current
directory.

cancel (cancel print requests) 107
Lets you cancel print requests that are in queue waiting to be printed or
are currently printing.

cat (concatenate) 155
Concatenates/displays file(s).

cd (change directory) 89
Changes your current directory to another directory.

chmod (change mode) 280
Changes the access permission of a specified file according to the option
letters indicating different categories of users. The user categories are **u**
(for user/owner), **g** (for group), **o** (for others), and **a** (for all). The access
categories are **r** (for read), **w** (for write), and **x** (for executable).

cp (copy) 162
Copies file(s) in your current directory, or from one directory to another.

Option	Operation
-i	Asks for confirmation if the target file already exists.
-r	Copies directories to a new directory.

crypt 398
Encrypts or decrypts your specified file according to a specified key. The
encrypted file is not readable, and you must provide the same key used for
encrypting the file to decrypt it.

date 38
Displays the day of the week, month, day, and time.

df 377
Reports the total amount of the disk space or space available on a
specified file system.

. (dot) 287
Lets you run a process in the current shell environment, and the shell
doesn't create a child process to run the command.

du 378
Summarizes the total space occupied by any directory, its subdirectories,
or each file.

Option	Operation
-a	Displays the directories and file sizes.
-s	Displays only the total blocks for the specified directory: subdirectories are not listed.

echo 288
Displays (echoes) its arguments on the output device.

Escape character	Meaning
\n	A carriage return and a linefeed (newline).
\t	A tab character.
\b	A backspace.
\r	A carriage return without a linefeed.
\c	Inhibits the carriage return.

exit 286
Terminates the current shell program whenever it is executed. It can also
return a status code (RC) to indicate the success or failure of a program. It
also terminates your login shell if typed at the $ sign prompt, and logs you
off.

export 217
Exports the specified list of variables to other shells.

find 379
Locates files that match a given criterion in a hierarchy of directories. With the action options, you can tell what to do with the files once they are found.

Search Option	Description
-name *filename*	Finds files with the given *filename*.
size ±**n**	Finds files with the size *n*.
-type *file type*	Finds files with the specified access mode.
-atime ±**n**	Finds files that were accessed *n* days ago.
-mtime ±**n**	Finds files that were modified *n* days ago.
-newer *filename*	Finds files that were modified more recently than *filename*.

Action Option	Description
-print	Prints the pathname for every file found.
-exec *command* \;	Lets you give *commands* to be applied to the files.
-ok *command* \;	Asks for confirmation before applying the command.

grep (Global Regular Expression Print) 208
Searches for a specified pattern in file(s). If specified pattern is found, the line containing the pattern is displayed on your terminal.

Option	Operation
-c	Displays only the count of the matching lines in each file that contain the match.
-i	Ignores differntiation between lowercase and uppercase letters in the search pattern. They both match each other.
-l	Displays the names only of the files with one or more matching lines, not the lines themselves.
-n	Displays a line number before each output line.
-v	Displays only those lines that do not match the pattern.

help 43
Presents a series of menus and questions that lead you to the description of the most commonly used UNIX commands.

kill 205
Terminates the unwanted or unruly processes. You have to specify the process ID number. The process ID 0 kills all programs associated with your terminal.

learn 42
A computer-aided instruction program that is arranged in series of courses and lessons. It displays the menu of courses and you can select your desired lesson.

ln (link) 162
Creates links between an existing file and another filename or directory. Lets you have more than one name for a file.

lp (line printer) 104
Prints (provides hard copy) the specified file.

Option	Operation
-d	Prints on a specific printer.
-m	Sends mail to the user mailbox at completion of the the print request.
-n	Prints specified number of copies of the file.
-s	Suppresses feedback messages.
-t	Prints a specified title on the banner page of the output.

lpstat (line printer status) 108
Provides you information about your printing request jobs, including printing request id number that you can use to cancel a printing request.

ls (list) 93
Lists the contents of your current directory or any directory you specify.

Option	Operation
-a	Lists all files, including the hidden files.
-C	Lists files in multicolumn format. Entries are sorted down the columns.
-F	Puts a slash (/) after each filename, if that file is a directory, and an asterisk (*) if it is an executable file.
-l	Lists files in a long format, showing detail information about the files.
-m	Lists files across the page, separated by commas.
-p	Puts a slash (/) after each filename if it is a directory name, and an asterisk (*) if it is an executable file.
-r	Lists files in reverse alphabetic order.
-R	Recursively lists the contents of the subdirectories.
-s	Shows size of each file in blocks.
-x	Lists files in multicolumn format. Entries are sorted across the line.

mailx 234
Provides the electronic mail system for the users. You can send messages to other users on the system, regardless if they are logged in or not. You can read, save, etc. your receiving mail. With many options and commands in different modes, **mailx** gives you plenty of room in regards to the mail manipulation.

Option	Operation
-f [*filename*]	Reads mail from the specified *filename* instead of the system *mailbox*. If no file is specified it reads from *mbox*.
-H	Displays the list of the message headers.
-s *subject*	sets the subject field to string *subject*.

mailx tilde escape commands 236
When you invoke mailx to send mail to others, it places itself in the *input mode* ready for you to compose your message. The commands in this mode starts with a ~ and are called *tilde escape commands*.

Command	Operation
~?	Displays a list of all *tilde escape* commands.
~! *command*	Lets you invoke the specified shell *command* while composing your message.
~e	Invokes an editor for editing your message. The editor to be used is defined in the mail variable called *EDITOR*.
~q	Quits input mode. Saves your partial ly composed message in the file called dead.letter.
~r *filename*	Reads the specified *filename* and adds its contents into your message.
~< *filename*	Reads the specified *filename* (using the redirection operator) and adds its contents into your message.
~<! *command*	Executes the specified command places its output into your message.
~v	Invokes the default visual editor, the vi editor, or uses the value of the mail variable VISUAL which can be set up to other editors.
~w *filename*	Writes currently composing message to the specified *filename*.

man 43
Shows pages from the on-line system documentation.

mesg 230
This command is set to *n* to prohibit unwanted **write** messages. It is set to *y* to receive messages.

mkdir (make directory) 91
Creates a new directory in your working directory, or in any other directory you specify.

Option	Operation
-p	Lets you create levels of directories in a single command line.

mv (move) 165
Renames files or moves files from one location to another.

news 231
Used to look at the latest news on the system. Used by the system
administrator to inform others of the happening events.

Options	Operation
-a	Displays all the news items, old or new files.
-n	Lists only the name of the news files (headers).
-s	Displays the number of the current news items.

nohup 205
Prevents the termination of the background process when you log out.

passwd 34
Changes your login password.

pg (page) 152
Displays files one screen at a time. You can enter the options or other
commands when pg shows the prompt sign.

Option	Operation
-n	Does not require [Return] to complete the single-letter commands.
-s	Displays messages and prompts in reverse video.
-*num*	Sets the number of lines per screen to the integer num. The default value is 23 lines.
-p*str*	Changes the prompt : (colon) to the string specified as *str*.
+*line-num*	Starts displaying the file from the line specified in *line- num*.
+/*pattern*/	Starts viewing at the line containing the first occurrence of the specified *pattern*.

pr (paginating files for printing) 159
Formatting your file before printing or viewing on the screen.

Option	Operation
+*page*	Starts displaying from the specified *page*. The default is page 1.
-*columns*	Displays output in the specified number of *columns*. The default is 1 column.
-a	Displays output in columns across the page, one line per column.
-d	Displays output in double spaces.
-h*str*	Replaces the filename in the header with the specified string *str*.
-l*number*	Sets the page length to the specified *number* of lines. The default is 66 lines.
-m	Displays all the specified files in multiple columns.
-p	Pauses at the end of each page, and sounds the terminal bell.
-s*character*	Separates columns with a single specified *character*. If *character* is not specified, then tab is used.
-t	Suppresses the five lines header, and five lines trailer.
-w*number*	Sets line width to the specified *number* of characters. The default is 72

ps (process status) 203
Displays the process ID of the programs associated with your terminal.

Option	Operation
-a	Displays status of the all active processes, not just the user's.
-f	Displays a full list of information, including the full command line.

pwd 87
Times your programs. It reports the real time, user time, and system time for the specified program.

read 326
Reads input from the input device and stores the input string in one or more variables specified as the command arguments.

sort 211
Sorts text file(s) in different orders.

Option	Operation
-b	Ignores leading blanks.
-d	Uses the dictionary order for sorting. Ignores punctuations and control characters.
-fl	Ignores the distinction between lowercase and uppercase letters.
-n	Numbers are sorted by their arithmetic values.

spell 391
Checks the spelling of the specified document or words entered from the keyboard. It only displays the words not found in the spelling list and does not suggest a correct spelling.

Option	Operation
-b	Checks for British spelling.
-v	Displays words that are not in the spelling list and their derivation.

stty 331
Sets options that control the capabilities of your terminal. There are over hundred different settings, and the following table lists only some of the options.

Option	Operation
echo [-echo]	Echoes [does not echo] the typed characters; the default is echo.
raw [-raw]	Disables [enables] the special meaning of the metacharacters; the default is **-raw**.
intr	Generates an interrupt signal; usually [Del] is used.
erase	Erases the preceding character, usually [#] is used.
kill	Deletes the entire line; usually [@] or [Ctrl-u] is used.
eof	Generates the (end -of-file) signal from terminal; usually [Ctrl-d] is used.
ek	Resets the erase and kill keys to [#] and [@] respectively.

tail 385
Displays the last part (tail end) of a specified file. This is a quick way to check the contents of a file. The options give the flexibility to specify the desired part of the file.

Option	Operation
b	This option causes tail to count by blocks.
c	This option causes tail to count by characters.
l	This option causes tail to count by lines.

tee 207
Splits the output. One copy is displayed on your terminal, the output device, and another copy is saved in a file.

Option	Operation
-a	Appends output to file, not overwriting an existing file.
-i	Ignores interrupts, does not responds to the interrupt signals.

test 301
Tests the condition of expression given to it as an argument, and returns true or false depending on the status of the expression. It gives you the capability of testing different types of expressions.

time 389
Times your programs. It reports the real time, user time, and system time for the specified program.

tput 334
Used with the terminfo database, which contains codes for terminal characteristics and facilitates the manipulation of your terminal characteristics such as bold text, clear screen, etc.

Option	Operation
bell	Echoes the terminal's bell character.
blink	Makes blinking display.
bold	Makes bold display.
clear	Clears the screen.
cup *r c*	Moves cursor to the row *r* and column *c*.
dim	Dims the display.
ed	Clears from the cursor position to the end of the screen.
el	Clears from the cursor position to the end of the line.
smso	Starts stand out mode.
rmso	Ends stand out mode.
smul	Starts underline mode.
rmul	Ends underline mode.
rev	Shows reverse video, black on white display

trap 330
Sets and resets the interrupt signals. The following table shows some of the signals you can use to control the termination of your program.

Signal Number	Name	Meaning
1	hang up	Terminal connection is lost.
2	interrupt	One of the interrupt keys is pressed.
3	quit	One of the quit keys is pressed.
9	kill	The kill -9 command is issued.
15	terminator	The kill command is issued.

type 389
Tells you if the specified command is a built-in command or a shell process.

who 39
Lists the login name, terminal lines, and login times of the users who are on the system.

Option	Operation
-q	The quick **who**; just displays the name and number of users.
-H	Displays heading above each column.
-b	Gives the time and date of the last reboot.
-s	Displays just the name, line and time columns.

wc (word count) 168
Counts number of characters, words, or lines in the specified file.

Option	Operation
-l	Reports number of lines.
-w	Reports number of words.
-c	Reports number of characters.

wall 233
Used mostly by the system administrator to warn the users of some
immediate events.

write 229
Used for terminal-to-terminal communication. The receiving party must be
logged in.

Summary of
vi Editor Commands

This appendix contains a summary of all the vi editor commands covered in this book. For more information refer to chapters 4 and 6.

The vi editor mode of operations.

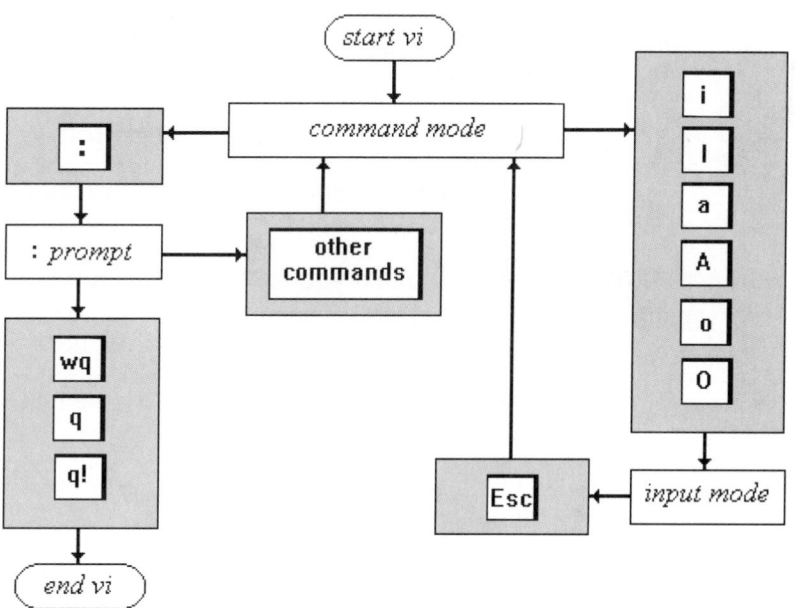

The vi Editor

vi is a screen editor you can use to create files. vi has two modes, command mode and text input mode. To start vi type **vi**, press [Spacebar], and type the name of the file. There are several keys that place vi in text input mode, and [Esc] returns vi to the command mode.

[w][q]	Writes (saves) the contents of the buffer and quits the vi editor.
[w]	Writes (saves) the contents of the buffer but stays in the editor.

Save and Quit Commands

With the exception of the ZZ command, the rest of these commands start with [:], and you must end the command line with [Return].

Key	Operation
[w][q]	Writes (saves) the contents of the buffer and quits the vi editor.
[w]	Writes (saves) the contents of the buffer but stays in the editor.
[q]	Quits the editor.
[q!]	Quits the editor and abandons the contents of the buffer.
[Z][Z]	Writes (saves) the contents of the buffer and quits the vi editor.

Change Mode Keys

These keys change the vi's mode from the command mode to the text input mode. Each key places vi in the text input mode in a different manner. Pressing [Esc] places vi in the command mode.

Key	Operation
[i]	Places the text you enter before the character that the cursor is on.
[I]	Places the text you enter at the beginning of the current line.
[a]	Places the text you enter after the character that the cursor is on.
[A]	Places the text you enter after the last character of the current line.
[o]	Opens a blank line below the current line and places the cursor at the beginning of the new line.
[O]	Opens a blank line above the current line and places the cursor at the beginning of the new line.

Cursor Movement Keys
These keys are all applicable in the command mode only.

Key	Operation
[h] or [left arrow]	Moves the cursor position one space to the left.
[j] or [down arrow]	Moves the cursor position one line down.
[k] or [up arrow]	Moves the cursor position one line up.
[l] or [right arrow]	Moves the cursor position one space to the right.
[$]	Moves the cursor position to the end of the current line.
[w]	Moves the cursor position forward one word.
[b]	Moves the cursor position back one word.
[e]	Moves the cursor position to the end of the word.
[0]	(zero) Moves the cursor position to the beginning of the current line.
[Return]	Moves the cursor position to the beginning of the next line.
[Spacebar]	Moves the cursor position one space to the right.
[Back Space]	Moves the cursor position one space to the left.

Search Commands
These keys allow you to search forward or backward in your file for a pattern.

Key	Operation
[/]	Searches forward for a specified pattern.
[?]	Searches backward for a specified pattern.

Cut and Paste Keys
These keys are used to rearrange text in your file. These keys are applicable in the vi's command mode.

Key	Operation
[d]	Deletes a specified portion of the text and stores it in a temporary buffer. This buffer can be accessed by using the put operator
[y]	Copies a specified portion of the text in a temporary buffer. This buffer can be accessed by using the put command.
[p]	Places the contents of a specified buffer above the cursor position.
[P]	Places the contents of a specified buffer above the after the cursor position.

Scope Keys
Using the vi commands in combination with the scope keys gives you more control in your editing task.

Scope	Operation
[$]	The scope is from the cursor position to the end of the current line.
[0]	(zero) The scope is from just before the cursor position to the beginning of the current line.
[e]	The scope is from the cursor position to the end of the current word.
[b]	The scope is from the letter before the cursor backward to the beginning of the current word.

Keys for Correcting Text
These keys are all applicable in the command mode only.

Key	Operation
[x]	Deletes the character specified by the cursor position.
[d][d]	Deletes the line specified by the cursor position.
[u]	Undoes the most recent change.
[U]	Undoes all the changes on the current line.
[r]	Replaces a character that the cursor is on.
[R]	Replaces characters starting from the cursor position. Also Enters in the text mode.
[.]	(dot) Repeats the last text changes.

Paging Keys
The paging keys are used to scroll a larger portion of a file.

Key	Operation
[Ctrl-d]	Scrolls the cursor down, toward the end of the file, usually 12 lines at a time.
[Ctrl-u]	Scrolls the cursor up, toward the top of the file, usually 12 lines at a time.
[Ctrl-f]	Scrolls the cursor down (forward), toward the end of the file, usually 24 lines at a time.
[Ctrl-b]	Scrolls the cursor up (backward), toward the top of the file, usually 24 lines at a time.

Setting the vi Environment
You can customize the behavior of the vi editor by setting the vi environment options. You use the set command to change the options values.

Option	Abbre-viation	Operation
autoindent	**ai**	Aligns the new lines with the beginning of the previous ones.
ignorcase	**ic**	Ignores the differntiation between uppercase and lowercase in search operations.
magic	-	Allows the use of the special characters in search.
number	**nu**	Displays line number.
report	-	Informs you of the number of lines affected by your last command.
scroll	-	Sets number of lines to scroll when [Ctrl-d] command is given.
shiftwidth	**sw**	Sets number of spaces to indent. Used with autoindent option.
showmode	**smd**	Displays the vi editor modes on the right corner of the screen.
terse	-	Shortens the error messages.
wrapmargin	**wm**	Sets the right margin to the specified number of characters.

ASCII Table

Character/Key	Decimal	Hex	Octal	Binary
CTRL-1 (NUL)	0	00	000	0000 0000
CTRL-A	1	01	001	0000 0001
CTRL-B	2	02	002	0000 0010
CTRL-C	3	03	003	0000 0011
CTRL-D	4	04	004	0000 0100
CTRL-E	5	04	005	0000 0101
CTRL-F	6	05	006	0000 0110
CTRL-G (BEEP)	7	06	007	0000 0111
CTRL-H (BACKSPACE)	8	07	010	0000 1000
CTRL-I (TAB)	9	09	011	0000 1001
CTRL-J (NEWLINE)	10	0A	012	0000 1010
CTRL-K	11	0B	013	0000 1011
CTRL-L	12	0C	014	0000 1100
CTRL-M (RETURN)	13	0D	015	0000 1101
CTRL-N	14	0E	016	0000 1110
CTRL-O	15	0F	017	0000 1111
CTRL-P	16	10	020	0001 0000
CTRL-Q	17	11	021	0001 0001

Character/Key	Decimal	Hex	Octal	Binary
CTRL-R	18	12	022	0001 0010
CTRL-S	19	13	023	0001 0011
CTRL-T	20	14	024	0001 0100
CTRL-U	21	15	025	0001 0101
CTRL-V	22	16	026	0001 0110
CTRL-W	23	17	027	0001 0111
CTRL-X	24	18	030	0001 1000
CTRL-Y	25	19	031	0001 1001
CTRL-Z	26	1A	032	0001 1010
CTRL-[(ESCAPE)	27	1B	033	0001 1011
CTRL-\	28	1C	34	0001 1100
CTRL-]	29	1D	035	0001 1101
CTRL-^	30	1E	036	0001 1110
CTRL-_	31	1F	037	0001 1111
SP (SPACEBAR)	32	20	040	0010 0000
! (EXCLAMATION MARK)	33	21	041	0010 0001
" (DOUBLE QUOTATION MARK)	34	22	042	0010 0010
# (NUMBER SIGN)	35	23	043	0010 0011
$ (DOLLAR SIGN)	36	24	044	0010 0100
% (PERCENT SIGN)	37	25	045	0010 0101
& (AMPERSAND)	38	26	046	0010 0110
' (SINGLE QUOTATION MARK)	39	27	047	0010 0111
((LEFT PARENTHESIS)	40	28	050	0010 1000
) (RIGHT PARENTHESIS)	41	29	051	0010 1001
* (ASTERISK)	42	2A	052	0010 1010
+ (PLUS SIGN)	43	2B	053	0010 1011
, (COMMA)	44	2C	054	0010 1100
- (HYPHEN/MINUS SIGN)	45	2D	055	0010 1101
. (PERIOD)	46	2E	056	0001 1110

Character/Key	Decimal	Hex	Octal	Binary
/ (SLASH)	47	2F	057	0001 1111
0	48	30	060	0011 0000
1	49	31	061	0011 0001
2	50	32	062	0011 0010
3	51	33	063	0011 0011
4	52	34	064	0011 0100
5	53	35	065	0011 0101
6	54	36	066	0011 0110
7	55	37	067	0011 0111
8	56	38	070	0011 1000
9	57	39	071	0011 1001
: (COLON)	58	3A	072	0011 1010
; (SEMICOLON)	59	3B	073	0011 1011
< (LESS THAN SIGN)	60	3C	074	0011 1100
= (EQUAL SIGN)	61	3D	075	0011 1101
> (GREATER THAN SIGN)	62	3E	076	0011 1110
? (QUESTION MARK)	63	3F	077	0011 1111
@ (AT SIGN)	64	40	100	0100 0000
A	65	41	101	0100 0001
B	66	42	102	0100 0010
C	67	43	103	0100 0011
D	68	44	104	0100 0100
E	69	45	105	0100 0101
F	70	46	106	0100 0110
G	71	47	107	0100 0111
H	72	48	110	0100 1000
I	73	49	111	0100 1001
J	74	4A	112	0100 1010
K	75	4B	113	0100 1011
L	76	4C	114	0100 1100

Character/Key	Decimal	Hex	Octal	Binary
M	77	4D	115	0100 1101
N	78	4E	116	0100 1110
O	79	4F	117	0100 1111
P	80	50	120	0101 0000
Q	81	51	121	0101 0001
R	82	52	122	0101 0010
S	83	53	123	0101 0011
T	84	54	124	0101 0100
U	85	55	125	0101 0101
V	86	56	126	0101 0110
W	87	57	127	0101 0111
X	88	58	130	0101 1000
Y	89	59	131	0101 1001
Z	90	5A	132	0101 1010
[(LEFT SQUARE BRACKET)	91	5B	133	0101 1011
\ (BACKSLASH)	92	5C	134	0101 1100
] (RIGHT SQUARE BRACKET)	93	5D	135	0101 1101
^ (CIRCUMFLEX)	94	5E	136	0101 1110
_ (UNDERSCORE)	95	5F	137	0101 1111
` (BACK SINGLE QUOTATION MARK)	96	60	140	0110 0000
a	97	61	141	0110 0001
b	98	62	142	0110 0010
c	99	63	143	0110 0011
d	100	64	144	0110 0100
e	101	65	145	0110 0101
f	102	66	146	0110 0110
g	103	67	147	0110 0111
h	104	68	150	0110 1000
i	105	69	151	0110 1001

Character/Key	Decimal	Hex	Octal	Binary
j	106	6A	152	0110 1010
k	107	6B	153	0110 1011
l	108	6C	154	0110 1100
m	109	6D	155	0110 1101
n	110	6E	156	0110 1110
o	111	6F	157	0110 1111
p	112	70	160	0111 0000
q	113	71	161	0111 0001
r	114	72	162	0111 0010
s	115	73	163	0111 0011
t	116	74	164	0111 0100
u	117	75	165	0111 0101
v	118	76	166	0111 0110
w	119	77	167	0111 0111
x	120	78	170	0111 1000
y	121	79	171	0111 1001
z	122	7A	172	0111 1010
{ (LEFT BRACE BRACKET)	123	7B	173	0111 1011
| (VERTICAL LINE)	124	7C	174	0111 1100
} (RIGHT BRACE BRACKET)	125	7D	175	0111 1101
~ (TILDE)	126	7E	176	0111 1110
DEL (DELETE KEY)	127	7F	177	0111 1111

Reference Books

The following is the list of books for your further reading toward becoming UNIX guru! And, I am grateful and in debt to these authors for learning UNIX, preparing my class lectures and writing this book.

A Practical Guide to the Unix System V, second edition, by Mark G. Sobell (The Benjamin/Cummings Publishing Company, Inc., ISBN 0-8053-7560-0).

UNIX for Programmers and Users: A Complete Guide by Graham Glass (Prentice-Hall, Inc., ISBN 0-13-480880-0).

LIFE WITH UNIX: A Guide For Everyone by Done Libes and Sandy Ressler (Prentice-Hall, Inc., ISBN 0-13-536657-7).

UNIX POWER TOOLS by Jerry Peek, Tim O'Reilly, and Mike Loukides (O'Reilly & Associates, Inc., ISBN 0-553-35402-7).

UNIX System V Bible: Commands and Utilities by The Waite Group's Stephen Prata and Donald Martin (SAMS, ISBN 0-672-22562-X).

UNIX System Architecture by Prabhat K. Andleigh (Prentice-Hall, Inc., ISBN 0-13-949843-5).

UNIX Shell Programming, revised edition, by Stephen G. Kochan and Patrick H. Wood (Hayden Books, 06-672-48448-X).

UNIX Application Programming: Mastering the Shell by Ray Swart (SAMS, ISBN 0-672-22715-0).

Index